SPEAK WITH CONFIDENCE:
A PRACTICAL GUIDE

Eighth Edition

ALBERT J. VASILE
Bunker Hill Community College

HAROLD K. MINTZ

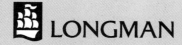

LONGMAN

An imprint of Addison Wesley Longman, Inc.

New York • Reading, Massachusetts • Menlo Park, California • Harlow, England
Don Mills, Ontario • Sydney • Mexico City • Madrid • Amsterdam

Editor-in-Chief: Priscilla McGeehon
Acquisitions Editor: Michael Greer
Development Manager: Lisa Pinto
Development Editor: Nancy Crochiere
Marketing Manager: Megan Galvin
Supplements Editor: Mark Toews
Project Coordination and Text Design: York Production Services
Cover Design Manager: Nancy Danahy
Cover Designer: Kay Petronio
Cover Illustration: José Ortega/SIS
Cartoonist: Steve Miles
Full Service Production Manager: Joseph Vella
Photo Researcher: Mira Schachne
Senior Print Buyer: Hugh Crawford
Electronic Page Makeup: York Production Services
Printer and Binder: Quebecor Fairfield
Cover Printer: Coral Graphic Services, Inc.

For permission to use copyrighted material, grateful acknowledgment is made to the copyright holders on p. 440, which are hereby made part of this copyright page.

Library of Congress Cataloging-in-Publication Data

Vasile, Albert J.
    Speak with confidence : a practical guide / Albert J. Vasile,
Harold K. Mintz. — 8th ed.
        p.   cm.
    Includes index.
    ISBN 0-321-04427-4 (alk. paper)
    1. Oral communication.   2. Interpersonal communication.   3. Public
speaking.   I. Mintz, Harold K.   II. Title.
PN4121.V35   2000
808.5′1—dc21   99-20046
                                                                CIP

Please visit our Website at http://awlonline.com

ISBN 0-321-04427-4

12345678910—ARF—02010099

■

To my superbly talented wife, Evelyn,
and to each member of my young
and wonderful family who make me
so eager to anticipate "tomorrow" . . .
and to my special and dear friend
Charlie Flagg, 1931–1996
I miss him very much.
Albert J. Vasile

■

CONTENTS

11 BE PERSUASIVE   234

12 FIRST AID ON USING AUDIOVISUAL AIDS   271

16 LET'S GO TO WORK   364

Appendix A: Speeches to Study   396

Appendix B: Suggested Speech Topics   419

Appendix C: Common Sexist Words and Phrases and Suggested Nonsexist Alternatives   425

Appendix D: Some Commonly Mispronounced Words   431

Glossary   433

Credits   440

Index   441

PREFACE

A MESSAGE TO YOU, THE PROFESSOR, AND THE STUDENT

Almost 25 years ago, *Speak with Confidence* pioneered a new philosophy and writing style for a basic one-semester speech book. It has evolved, developed, and matured into this eighth edition, which incorporates the best of previous editions and also countless new improvements. Yet, the basic principles of our philosophy remain the same:

- Practical information, usable immediately.
- Anecdotes, cartoons, and historical references that teach valuable speech lessons.
- Easy-to-understand language.
- A conversational style that speaks *to* students, not *at* them.
- Concern for the student by way of encouragement, praise, and support.
- Photographs of prominent people and students speaking/communicating.

For almost 25 years, *Speak with Confidence* has been adopted by community colleges, business colleges, and four-year colleges and universities all across America, and has even visited several countries in Europe and Asia. Its acceptance is, indeed, heart-warming.

SOME MAJOR IMPROVEMENTS AND ADDITIONS TO THE EIGHTH EDITION

In every chapter of this eighth edition, the language, style, and content have been sharpened in terms of clarity, conciseness, and relevance to student needs. Responding to the ever-increasing number of students from other countries and cultures, including those whose primary language is not English, who take speech courses, the feature, "In Other Words" (which first appeared in the seventh edition) has been greatly expanded. This vocabulary aid, which appears in the margins of many pages throughout the book, includes the meanings of commonly used American idioms, phrases, and expressions.

In further response to the shrinking nature of our global community, this edition expands coverage of intercultural/multicultural communication; I really believe that this topic will be of significant interest and benefit to all students.

New photographs of outstanding communicators are included, and many of the cartoons have been updated or replaced with new ones. As one of our trademarks, every chapter contains the most current events that our deadline will allow, as well as many classic examples. This new edition contains three new memorable speeches for study and analysis: President Reagan's eulogy following the explosion of the space shuttle *Challenger*; Elizabeth Dole's speech at the 1996 Republican National Convention; and President Clinton's contrition speech to the nation in 1998. You will also find new suggested topics, not only in applicable chapters but also in Appendix B, reflecting some of the concerns as we enter the new millennium.

Without question, this eighth edition represents the most ambitious revision effort ever undertaken in the life of this book. I hope you find it not only educationally enjoyable, but also fun to read.

Specifically, here are some of the major new additions and improvements, by chapter:

Chapter 1   Me Study Speech? You've Got to Be Kidding

- The Importance and Application of Ethics.
- The Ethical Responsibilities of the Speaker.
- The Ethical Responsibilities of the Listener.
- The Meaning of Plagiarism and How to Avoid It. (Current and recent examples of the preceding).
- Expanded list of *Things to Discuss in Class* (At end of chapter).
- Expanded "In Other Words" feature.
- Expanded intercultural references.

Chapter 2   Your First Talk: Getting to Know You

- Expanded list of Eponymns in the *Vitalize Your Vocabulary* section at the end of the chapter.
- Expanded section on Nervousness.
- Expanded section on Question-and-Answers.
- Expanded "In Other Words" feature.
- Expanded intercultural references.

Chapter 3   You Don't Have to Say It to Convey It

- Expanded section on "What Is Nonverbal Communication?"

Chapter 4   You Can Overhear, but You Can't Overlisten

- Expanded section on "Communication Activities."
- Expanded "In Other Words" feature.
- Expanded intercultural references.

Chapter 5   Make It Clear, Concise, Correct, . . . & Cohesive

- New additional reading containing all the sounds in the English language.
- New *Vitalize Your Vocabulary* listing of words of Spanish origin.
- Expanded "In Other Words" feature.

Chapter 6   Know Your Listeners and Speak Their Language

- Significantly expanded section on "Age" in the section on "Audience Analysis."
- More current events and statistics including the CNN/*Time* magazine debacle and the resignation of a top government official for using a poor choice of words.
- New examples of concrete and abstract words.
- Significantly expanded section on "gobbledygook" and double talk, including many new and interesting examples.
- New section on nonsexist language, including many examples.
- Expanded section on "Putting Words into Sentences," including many historical examples.
- Expanded "In Other Words" feature.

Chapter 7   Selecting a Speech Topic and Doing Research

- Updated material on current cable TV networks.
- Newly rewritten section on "Learn to Use the Library," which includes the latest information on the use of computers, software, databases, the Internet, web sites, and online facilities to assist in doing research. PowerPoint is also included with other applications and the latest illustrations and graphics.
- New information on "Taking Notes" and more text on plagiarism, with actual examples.
- Expanded and updated "Vitalize Your Vocabulary" section consisting of basic computer terms.
- Expanded "In Other Words" feature.

Chapter 8   Putting It All Together

- New extensive material on the subject of "Purpose and Thesis Statement," with many examples.
- New extensive material on "Outlining," with more examples.
- Expanded information regarding the arrangement of main points of a speech in section "According to Time."
- Expanded "In Other Words" feature.

Chapter 9   Delivering Your Speech

- Expanded cross-cultural references.
- Expanded section on "Speaking with Enthusiasm" and "Speaking with Empathy."

- New specific physical exercises to help relieve tension before speaking.
- Expanded "In Other Words" feature.

Chapter 10   Be Informative

- Expanded and updated section on "Knowledge Is Power," emphasizing the new electronic-computer generation.
- More poignant examples under the heading "Comparisons."
- New section on "Audiovisual Aids."
- New updated list of "Suggested Topics for Informative Talks."

Chapter 11   Be Persuasive

- Updated situations emphasizing "The Importance of Persuasive Speaking."
- New section on "How to Select a Topic."
- New material and examples on the subject of "Fact and Opinion."
- New, more comprehensive, material on "Analogic Reasoning."
- Elizabeth Dole's electrifying speech at the 1996 Republican National Convention, complete with analysis and sentence and topic outlines.
- New updated list of "Suggested Topics for Persuasive Talks."
- Expanded "In Other Words" feature.

Chapter 12   First Aid on Using Audiovisual Aids

- New section on "How Visuals Can Aid You," with special emphasis on students from other countries/cultures.
- Further discussion on use of electronic/computer equipment.
- Current illustration of "Murphy's Law" in action involving Microsoft Chairman Bill Gates.
- New graphic on PowerPoint.
- New information and more hints on using an easel.
- New extensive section on "Consider Using Laptop or Personal Computers, LCD Panels, and Presentation Software."
- Expanded "In Other Words" feature.

Chapter 13   Saying a Few Words . . . Very Few!

- New section on "The Eulogy or Special Tribute Speech" contains the eulogy by former President Ronald Reagan following the explosion of the space shuttle *Challenger*.

Chapter 14   Let's Meet and Discuss It

- Expanded section on "The Meeting."
- New information on "Parliamentary Procedure" at meetings.
- Expanded "In Other Words" feature.

Chapter 15   What Do You Say After You Say "Hello"?

■ Expanded section on "Your Eyes" when communicating.
■ Expanded "In Other Words" feature.

Chapter 16   Let's Go to Work

■ Updated and expanded section on "What Employers Look For."
■ New text regarding companies using computers to scan resumés and what the job seeker can do about it.
■ More information on resumé preparation, including the use of computers, software, and CD-ROMs.
■ More information regarding the subject of wages.
■ New "Vitalize Your Vocabulary" listing of Economic and Financial terms.
■ Expanded "In Other Words" feature.

Appendix A   Speeches to Study

■ Newly added speeches by Barbara Bush and President Clinton.

Appendix B   Suggested Speech Topics

■ Newly added and updated topics.

Appendix C   Common Sexist Words and Phrase and Suggested Nonsexist Alternatives

■ Newly added—A list of over 200 common sexist words and phrases with suggested nonsexist alternatives. Perhaps the most complete such list ever published in a public-speaking textbook.

Appendix D   Some Commonly Mispronounced Words

■ Newly added—A list of the 100 most commonly mispronounced words.

Glossary

■ Updated and expanded.

SUPPLEMENTARY MATERIALS

The ancillary package for the eighth edition of *Speak with Confidence* includes the following instructional resources:

Resources for Instructors

Instructor's Manual/Test Bank
The Instructor's Manual includes chapter objectives, chapter outlines, a wealth of thought-provoking classroom activities, and suggestions for

further study. The Test Bank contains hundreds of challenging and thoroughly revised multiple-choice, true-false, and short answer questions along with an answer key. The questions closely follow the text chapters and are cross-referenced with corresponding page numbers.

TestGen-EQ 2.0 CD-ROM

The printed Test Bank is also available electronically through our computerized testing system, TestGen-EQ 2.0. This fully networkable test-generating software is not available on a cross-platform CD-ROM. TestGen-EQ's friendly graphical interface enables instructors to view, edit, and add questions, transfer questions to tests, and print tests in a variety of fonts and forms. Search and sort features allow instructors to locate questions quickly and arrange them in a preferred order. Six question formats are available, including short-answer, true-false, multiple-choice, essay, matching, and bimodal.

Teaching Public Speaking

This introduction to teaching the public speaking course offers suggestions for everything from lecturing to designing classroom assignments to incorporating cultural diversity into lesson plans. Essential for graduated teaching assistants and first-time instructors, it may also provide new insight to the more experience professor. An extensive bibliography and a listing of media resources is also included.

Great Ideas for Teaching Speech (GIFTS)

This unique supplement offers instructors a myriad of creative ideas for enlivening their public speaking course. All of the assignments found in *GIFTS* have been successfully employed by experienced public speaking instructors in their classrooms.

ESL Guide for Public Speaking

The ESL Guide for Public Speaking provides strategies and resources for instructors teaching in a bilingual or multilingual classroom. It also includes suggestions for further reading and a listing of related web sites.

Longman's Public Speaking Video Library

Longman's video collection for public speaking includes a wide variety of films on topics such as preparation for public speaking, critiquing student speeches, speaker apprehension, and audience assessment. We also offer a variety of accompanying, printed video guides. Please contact your local sales representative for more information on titles and availability.

Resources for Students

The Speech Writer's Workshop CD-ROM

A virtual handbook for public speaking, this exciting public speaking software is now available on CD-ROM. The software includes four separate features: (1) a *speech handbook* with tips for researching and preparing speeches plus information about grammar, usage, and syntax; (2) a *speech workshop*, which guides students through the speech writing process while displaying a series of questions at each stage; (3) a *topics dictionary*, which gives students hundreds of ideas for speechesóall divided into subcategories to help students with outlining and organization, and (4) a *citation database* that formats bibliographic entries in MLA or APA style.

Student Guide to PowerPoint

Designed to introduce students to PowerPoint, this student guide explains how to sue the program as a tool for planning, organizing, and delivering oral presentations. The supplement covers all of the requisite skills for mastering PowerPoint including outlining, designing, and modifying slides; using graphics and animations; and presenting a slide show.

Studying Communication

This booklet introduces students to the field of communication and to the way in which research in the discipline is conducted. The booklet also offers students a variety of practical suggestions for how to get he most out of their study of communication including how to read a textbook, how to take a test, and how to write a paper for a communication course.

THANK YOU

No one book—or any worthwhile project, for that matter—can be completed, let alone be successful without the help of many talented individuals. This eighth edition of *Speak with Confidence* is no exception. Many people contributed mightily with their ideas, suggestions, recommendations, and wise counselling to bring this eighth edition home.

I am very pleased with the final product and would like to thank the following persons for sharing their unique talents and efforts, resulting in this, the finest and most comprehensive edition yet—number eight—of *Speak with Confidence*.

Let me begin my expressions of thanks by saying that the publisher is, indeed, quite fortunate to have the services of such a high caliber and efficient person as Editor-in-Chief Priscilla McGeehon. Thank you, Priscilla for your strong leadership. Special thanks go to my Development Editor, Nancy Crochiere; for the second time, I have come to rely upon her greatly. As in the seventh edition Nancy not only offered her professionalism and talent but also her guidance, which I appreciated. And what can I say about Steve Miles, whose great cartoons have adorned the pages of *Speak with Confidence* since the first edition. . . . Another great job, Steve.

Sincere thanks also go to Donna Erickson, Acquisitions Editor; Laura Barthule, Assistant Editor; and to Kristinn Leonhart who so very capably took over from Laura. It has been a real pleasure working with such professionals as Elsa van Bergen, Production Coordinator; Mira Schachne, Photo Editor; and Debbie Stone, Copyeditor—what a perfectly smooth trio.

Three of my colleagues at Bunker Hill Community College deserve high praise: Roger Richards for his exceptional contributions in such areas as outlining, note taking, and speech annotation; and Librarian Linda Weinstein and Public Service Library Diane Smith, for the excellent work on library research and the use of computers.

I would also like to thank Kristina Worcester, Library Information Services Director at Regis College, for the countless times I happened to stop by for a "little" help while doing research.

Responsible reviewers are extremely important to new development and revisions. For their critical analysis and significant contributions, I would like to express my gratitude to:

Brent E. Adrian, Professor at Central Community College
Beth C. Taylor, Professor at Marian College
Robert Pucci, Professor at Hostos Community College
Beverly Van Citters, Professor at Citrus College
Darrell W. Spencer, Professor at Marion College

As usual, I've had the great privilege of constantly calling upon two of my closest friends and advisors, attorney Andrew Aloisi and Bob Callaway for their expertise in law/politics and business/industry, respectively. Thank you very much.

And, once again, I share my pleasure and celebrity with the one person who has done so much to make my life so much easier as I completed this edition: my wife Evelyn. Her roles as trusted advisor, critic, and researcher cannot be expressed in mere words.

And, finally, very very special thanks go to our 6-year-old grandson, Brian Walter—commander-in-chief of countless legions of military troops, equipment, and aircraft, which he has strategically deployed in and around my study during the eighth edition revision. The presence of his many hours on "active duty" in my study provided me with the much needed breaks, many chuckles, a multitude of questions, and, always, inspiration. Many of his forces remain "on duty" in, around, over, under, and inside my desk as well as on bookshelves, around the fax machine, computer, and printer. He has supplied me with a tremendous amount of joy and love. Brian, I thank you and I salute you.

Albert J. Vasile

ME STUDY SPEECH? YOU'VE GOT TO BE KIDDING

More men have talked their way up the ladder of success than have climbed it in any other way.

Bruce Barton, best-selling author,
advertising pioneer, and lecturer

After reading and understanding this chapter you should know:

- The importance of this course in enriching your personal life and your career.

- The benefits you will get from working at this course.

- Ways to conquer shyness, if you're shy.

- The importance of making business and social contacts.

- The importance and application of ethics.

- The ethical responsibilities of the speaker and listener.

- The meaning of plagiarism and how to avoid it.

CHAPTER PREVIEW

Assuming that you do the assigned work, you will gain substantial benefits from this course: more self-confidence; an increased ability to communicate one to one within a group, and to a group; help in conquering shyness; understanding the importance of ethics from the standpoint of the speaker and listener and the seriousness of plagiarism; a keen sense of personal accomplishment; and a heightened ability to listen. These benefits can help you attain your full potential in the career and lifestyle you seek. In other words, as many former students have said, this course may well turn out to be the most important one of your college years.

Appearing in this (and every) chapter is a feature called "In Other Words," which will greatly benefit foreign and ESL students. To aid in their understanding of common American idioms and phrases these expressions will be defined in the margin of the page on which they are introduced.

SOUNDING OFF

It is difficult to recall any era in our history more saturated with controversial issues than today—issues such as crime and violence in our neighborhoods; our multitrillion (with a T) dollar national debt; the ever-increasing numbers of teenage pregnancies, abused children, and battered women; the demise of the family; the continuing AIDS problem; test-tube conception; abortion; and animal and human cloning, to cite a few. Such areas of concern have motivated thousands of otherwise inactive Americans to become activated, from writing to their local newspapers to joining and, in some cases, organizing groups and movements to express their views and exert their influence.

In recent elections, voters in several states publicly shouted their anger at government by adopting "initiative petitions": citizen-sponsored petitions that, if approved by the voters, become law. The petitions sought to limit the number of terms an elected official can serve; roll back taxes, fees, and fines; and restructure state and local government.

More and more citizens are calling radio talk programs nationwide to express their opinions and, in many cases, their anger about some of the continued major concerns as we enter a new millennium: a sex scandal in the White House, the number of politicians and government officials who either were forced to leave office, resigned, were indicted or convicted and even went to prison for unethical, questionable, or criminal behavior. In 1995 alone, 825 politicians and government officials were indicted as opposed to 45 in 1970.[1] Other concerns persist—such as the poor quality of public education and parents' demands for vouchers; elimination of bilingual education; the growing power and influence of insurance companies over doctors, hospitals, and patients; young children shooting and killing their schoolmates and teachers; and more and more teenagers drinking, driving, and smashing their cars, killing themselves and other teens. Some other concerns include the questionable state of our Social Security system and lack of job security due to the large number of mega mergers by large corporations, causing many layoffs. More and more Americans are taking to the airwaves as their forum for sounding off.

Talk radio is so popular throughout America that many politicians tune in regularly or direct members of their staff to do so to monitor the frustrations and concerns of their constituents. And, quite frequently, a legislator may personally call a talk program to respond to a particular issue.

If you feel that you need more self-confidence and assertiveness to express yourself—by calling a radio talk show, speaking before a group, or just conversing one on one—then taking this course is a positive beginning.

---

[1]Ronald Brownstein, "Life in the Time of Scandal." *U.S. News,* 27 April 1998, 13.

In Other Words:

Let's face it, you're taking this basic course in speech for one of two reasons:

1. You *want* to.
2. You *have* to.

If you *want* to take the course, you have nothing to worry about. Apparently, you appreciate the importance of oral communication and the boost that this course can contribute to the career and lifestyle you want. If you simply exert the effort, you will develop into a more self-confident communicator whom people will listen to and respect.

If you've been "drafted" into the speech course, this is a ***different ballgame.*** To most Americans, the idea of compulsion is self-defeating, destructive, and, in many instances, antilearning. Yet, during college or after college, we sometimes have to do things that we don't want to do.

different ball-game—different situation

For example, if we decided to obey traffic lights and speed limits only at our own convenience, what would happen? If pilots decided not to abide by their preestablished flight patterns and procedures from takeoff to landing, what would happen?

If this course is required and you're not really ecstatic about taking it, try to control your enthusiasm by accepting this experience with an ***open mind.*** Who knows, you may enjoy the course. You may find yourself warming up to the challenge and even thriving on the zestful ***give-and-take*** of verbal jousting in class. ***Take the plunge*** on a positive note. Remember, you'll never know what you're capable of doing until you try.

open mind—not prejudiced

give-and-take—good-natured exchange

take the plunge—exert effort, make the attempt with enthusiasm

How Important Is This Course to You?

Every day you communicate orally without giving it a thought. You greet people. You express opinions and desires. You ask questions, and you answer them. You agree with people, and you disagree. Sometimes you try to influence them.

Have you ever envied someone else's ability to express thoughts and opinions authoritatively? Have you ever experienced a situation in which you wished you had had the confidence and ability to communicate ideas and opinions? Do you have problems meeting people and making new friends? Have you ever wished you were a better conversationalist? If you answered "yes" to all or some of these questions, then get set for one of the most important courses of your life.

Talking, listening, writing, and reading are acts of communication that you perform throughout your life. Of these four acts, there's no question that talking and listening predominate in business, social, personal, and political relationships. For every word you write, you may speak thousands of words to carry you through a typical day. Consider the following circumstances in which effective oral communication may be crucial to you:

- Voicing your opinions at home, in classes, in politics, at the office, and at weekend orientations.
- Evaluating and selecting courses with your faculty adviser. In order to receive maximum benefit from the consultation, you must be able to express your course selections in the light of your long- or short-range goals.
- Interviewing for a job or seeking a raise or promotion. Unless you express yourself knowledgeably and confidently, what would your chances be?
- Disagreeing with your boss or immediate supervisor without being disagreeable.
- Wanting some time off from your job without having to call in sick.
- Handling a delicate situation such as sexual harassment on the job (male or female).
- Expressing your views at a school committee meeting on the subject of sex education being taught at your child's school.
- Testifying as a witness in court or at a hearing.
- Participating in community, business, or political action groups. PTAs and consumer, taxpayer, environmental, and labor organizations, for example, need people who have ideas and the ability to communicate them as well as to execute them. How many of us shy away because we lack confidence in our ability to champion our beliefs?

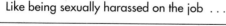
Like being sexually harassed on the job . . .

An ability to communicate orally will be crucial in your chosen career, whether you're interacting with a doctor or patient as a nurse, explaining a design or decision in engineering, asking for specific instructions in electronics or accounting, preparing and giving a report to your superiors or peers in the business world, or explaining a process in computer technology. No matter what your vocation—sales, education, marketing, advertising, administration—being able to SPEAK WITH CONFIDENCE will be an invaluable asset to your personal development.

Since these experiences will confront you throughout life, you should prepare yourself to cope with them to your advantage. No matter who you are, the keys to achieving your lifetime goals are your competence on the job and your ability to communicate effectively with your fellow humans.

Some of the specific skills that you can learn from taking this course include analyzing an audience; selecting an appropriate topic; researching and organizing your material; outlining your talk; methods of delivering your talk; expanding your vocabulary; understanding the importance of nonverbal communication; using audiovisual aids; and giving informative and persuasive talks.

We thought that you might be interested in the opinions of some of your peers who have completed this course. Here are some representative quotations:

- "I liked the course very much, even though I was going to drop it because I didn't have confidence in myself to get up in front of people. I have that confidence now and I think it's great."
- "My initial reaction to this course, at the beginning, was utter panic. Needless to say, however, by the end of the semester this course turned out to be the best I ever had."
- "The course was terrific. I received confidence, warmth, and a real feeling of belonging."
- "This course has helped me tremendously, not only to be able to better communicate in my other classes but also on the job when communicating with my peers and superiors. Thank you."
- "Not only has this course taught me a great deal about myself, but I learned a lot from and about my classmates."
- "Because of the number of foreign students in the class, I've developed a much better understanding not only of their culture, which was tremendously interesting, but also of their personal concerns regarding their country."
- "This course gave me the courage and confidence that I needed to be able to stand and give a talk in front of an audience. The book helped me to learn and understand the proper ways to address a group of people. I never thought that a textbook could be so much fun to read."

Although this course can do much for you, you should understand that it is a basic course, only a beginning. One semester won't transform you into a scintillating and dynamic speaker/communicator, but it certainly can help. The speaking skills that you learn will develop and improve through practice over a period of time.

OVERCOMING SHYNESS

There's nothing wrong with being shy—if that is what you want. Please read the preceding sentence again, especially the last six words. These words—"if that is what you want"—say it all. If you're shy and you feel comfortable with your shyness, it's because you *choose* to be that way, but you don't *have* to be. Although you weren't born shy, there may be a multitude of reasons, especially during your adolescent years, for your development in that direction. One valid reason might be that you were never encouraged to participate in conversation or in other activities involving social exchanges. Another reason might be that you allowed people to make you feel inferior or inadequate.

I think that it's interesting to note that according to Stanford University psychologist Philip Zimbardo, Ph.D., a shyness authority and author of *The Shy Child*, more than 80 percent of all Americans have reported feeling shy at some time in their lives. Many women suffer from shyness because they were brought up to equate being bashful with being feminine. This is particularly prevalent in some Asian, Middle-Eastern, and Latin American cultures, but it also occurs in American culture.

Whatever the reason for your shyness, the vital point is that if you don't want to be shy, you don't have to be. You must decide, and it could be one of the most crucial decisions you'll make during your lifetime. Overcoming shyness will allow you to:

- greet and meet people comfortably
- participate in conversations
- express (instead of repress) your opinions
- socialize more
- cultivate new friendships and renew old ones
- become more assertive (say "no" or disagree without being aggressive or feeling guilty)

We strongly believe that your shyness is not due to your physical appearance or to a lack of talent, but rather to your own low estimation of yourself. You must constantly strive to think about yourself in a positive manner. You can reinforce this principle by first deciding that you're going to change, and then by repeating to yourself dozens of times daily such positive thoughts as:

"I am going to be more outgoing."

"I am an attractive person."

"I am going to be more friendly to people."

"I'm no longer going to be shy. . . . I'm no longer going to be shy. . . . I'm no longer . . . ."

"People are going to like me."

"I can contribute to a conversation as well as any of my friends can."

"I am a good person and I have a lot to offer."

By reiterating such statements, you will help raise your levels of self-esteem and self-confidence. Author Diane Baroni, in her article on self-esteem, put it rather nicely when she stated that "In truth, this precious gift [self-esteem] can be had once you learn to parent *yourself*. Be lavish with love, praise, respect, and you'll feel a soaring sense of worth!"[2] At the same time, your degree of shyness should gradually diminish. You should already start to feel positive about yourself because you've made an important decision—independently. You must constantly remind yourself that you're no longer going to accept your shyness, and you must constantly visualize yourself as being more gregarious. It's a very important beginning.

This course will present you with many opportunities to develop ways to overcome your diffidence, and your class environment will provide you with the necessary encouragement. Your most important men-

---

[2]Diane Baroni, "Esteem—why is it so hard to get?", *Cosmopolitan*, September, 1996, 238.

tor at this stage will be your speech instructor who will, most likely, be supportive, understanding, and sympathetic. Make an appointment to see your instructor as soon as possible and explain your decision and goal. As your speech course progresses, listen carefully to your classmates and ask questions after their talks.

In addition, before and after class, make an effort to talk to a classmate, even if you start with a simple greeting such as "Good morning," "Hi, *how are you doing?*" or "I enjoyed your talk today. You know what I'd like to ask you?" Every day, try to start a conversation with a different classmate, and always try to remember names. It will be difficult at first, but will become easier as the days pass.

When you begin to feel more self-confident and relaxed, expand this new approach to people in your other classes, at home, at work, and at social gatherings. If you notice someone at a social occasion whom you would like to meet or who appears alone, *go out of your way* to *strike up* a conversation. Take a deep breath, smile, and confidently approach that person. Extend your hand and introduce yourself. Often you'll be pleasantly surprised with the results. That person may be grateful to meet and talk with someone who is friendly.

Remember, being friendly and outgoing could open new vistas for a more meaningful, interesting, and exciting personal, as well as professional, life for you. It's your *choice.* Good luck!

how are you doing?—how are you? (a cordial greeting)

go out of your way—make an effort

strike up—to start or begin

People listen to and respect a self-confident talker.

MAKING BUSINESS AND SOCIAL CONTACTS

Almost everyone would agree that making contacts and knowing the *"right people"* are invaluable aids in moving ahead. Making contacts can help you move ahead in your career and in many other ways. Perhaps you are looking for summer or part-time work; perhaps you want a favor from a politician—a letter of recommendation or introduction, perhaps you are seeking college admission or membership in a prestigious organization. Your chances of achieving these goals will be immensely improved if you know people in a position to help you.

"right people"—people who can help you; people with authority

You should realize that it's no shame to ask for a favor. What is a shame is to need something and not get it because you don't know anyone who could possibly *open some doors* for you. (This topic is discussed further in Chapters 15 and 16.)

open some doors—do you a favor; help you acquire something

Since knowing the right people may make a significant impact on your life, you should strive to meet and interact with as many people as possible. You never know when they may be able to *"come through"* for you. *By the same token,* you should be helpful to others whenever you can, because helping is *a two-way street.*

"come through"—do what is needed

Your sincere desire and ability to meet people should become an integral part of your daily life. The way to include them in your life is to communicate orally—speak, listen, question, answer, and get involved.

by the same token—in the same way

WHAT THIS COURSE CAN DO FOR YOU

a two-way street—something that goes both ways; for example, helping others, because you never know when they can help you

Provided that you expend the effort—and it is vital that you do—this course will help you to:

- develop more self-confidence when interacting with people, one to one, within a group, and to a group
- be more **assertive**
- improve your ability to listen
- learn how to present your ideas more clearly, logically, and forcefully
- acquire a sense of accomplishment
- learn the secrets of meeting and being accepted by people
- be more convincing
- develop a more positive self-image
- *Sell yourself* to an employer, a group, or friends

sell yourself—convince others of your positive qualities

You can start to develop these abilities and reap the advantages by exerting yourself in the following ways:

1. By giving many talks on various topics. In this way, you'll communicate your views, experiences, and feelings to your colleagues.
2. By responding to questions from the audience after your talk. The key to performing well in a question-and-answer period is to

know your subject thoroughly. If you've done your homework, you will, like most people, be exhilarated by your effort. The adrenaline racing through your veins could produce *a new "high"* for you. As a result, you will speak more forcefully and fluently than ever before.

a new "high"—
new excitement

3. By asking questions after others have spoken. Listening intently and having some knowledge of the subject under discussion will enable you to ask interesting and penetrating questions. Perhaps you will disagree with the speaker or perhaps you can shed light on a questionable point; in that case, think first and then speak your mind. Your self-confidence will grow once you notice that others listen to you. Remember, the more often you speak, the more self-confident you'll become.

4. By talking or debating with fellow students. The question-and-answer session after a talk often triggers discussion among class members, sometimes without involving the original speaker. Someone may ask a question or present an opinion that incites others to reply. This exchange may result in a sizzling, crackling demonstration of the power of the spoken word to move people.

"And then I shoulda said . . . ."

5. By meeting, greeting, and conversing with students from other cultures and countries. Not only will they appreciate your friendliness, but this experience could prove to be interesting and culturally rewarding to you.

6. If English is not your first language, take this great opportunity to listen intently to the English-speaking students in your class and your instructor so that you can become more proficient in the English language. And please *keep in mind,* if a speaker or your professor is talking too fast, raise your hand and ask her or him to please slow down.

keep in mind—to remember

After each talk, you'll feel a sense of accomplishment, and rightfully so. Even after your first effort, you'll admit not only to great relief (which you've earned) but, far more important, to a feeling of tremendous satisfaction. With each talk you give, you can only become more confident, and that glow of achievement will intensify.

Keep in mind that this course will not only teach you how to research, prepare, and deliver an effective speech in public or private, but also help you develop your self-confidence whether you are interacting one to one, participating in a small group, or speaking before a large gathering. Remember, once you achieve self-confidence, you will be able to do almost anything you want, provided, of course, that you prepare properly.

Building self-confidence will enable you to stand up for yourself when someone treats you condescendingly or discriminates against you. Teresa Fischette, a Continental Airlines ticket agent, did just that when she was fired in May 1991 for not wearing make-up. Some weeks earlier the company had issued a new appearance code for customer-contact personnel, and the code required women to use cosmetics.

Teresa, who had always disliked make-up, refused to comply and was discharged. "Make-up should be a personal choice," she said. "It's not fair to ask women to adorn themselves with make-up when it's not part of the job. . . . I think this is a women's-choice issue."[3]

Not one to be pushed around, Teresa fought back with attorneys and rallied public support when she appeared on 20 radio talk shows, the *CBS Nightly News,* and the *Oprah Winfrey Show.* Because Teresa stood up for her rights and used her speaking skills and because the negative publicity tarnished the reputation of Continental Airlines, its chairman apologized to her face-to-face. He even restored her job, with back pay.

Now you see that one person can make a difference, especially if that person can SPEAK WITH CONFIDENCE. And that's what this book is all about.

---

[3] *Boston Globe,* 11 May 1991, 1.

WHAT'S THIS ABOUT ETHICS?

Among the sincerest qualities that you, a speaker, can enjoy is credibility and trust (further discussed in Chapter 3)—that is, the degree of believ-ability that your audience has in you and your message. Another trait equally as significant and one that enhances your credibility is the hall-mark—**ethics.**

As a competent public speaker you should always strive for excel-lence, which includes high ethical standards. (As a matter of fact, you should always strive for excellence in everything you do every day of your life.) But, *getting back* to the subject of ethics, it is one that has been discussed, debated, and dissected for ages by such philosophers as Aristotle, Plato, and Quintilian and is currently discussed on campuses throughout most parts of the world.

getting back—to return

"... and as I have said many times ... ask not what your country can do for you ...
ask what you can do for your country!"

Instead of becoming involved in an ambitious, multisided, verbose, and pedantic discussion on the subject of ethics, let's simply state that being ethical is being honest, truthful, fair, decent, and considerate and having high morals. To be sure, our early developing years were inundated with lectures, admonitions, and discussions about right and wrong. It is hoped that these lessons, whether at home or at school, were not only well learned but are still inculcated and should certainly apply when communicating to an audience.

Therefore, in an effort to minimize the theoretical and maximize the pragmatic, let's focus on the following three facets of ethical behavior with which you'll mostly be concerned:

- ethical responsibilities of the speaker
- ethical responsibilities of the listener, and
- plagiarism and how to avoid it

Ethical Responsibilities of the Speaker

As an ethical speaker, you should:

1. Fully understand the objectives and ramifications that your message may have on your audience. If your topic is controversial or even explosive you want to be sure not to direct your comments to specific individuals or groups. You can get your points across without getting personal.

2. Be very much aware of the audience's *make-up*. Are different age groups, political groups, or ethnic groups represented? (See Chapter 6.)

3. Be fully prepared. While researching your topic, gather the most current and complete documented data and sources (see Chapter 7) and transform them into easily understandable language (see Chapter 5) for *all* members of your audience. If nonnative speakers are present, it would be considerate and surely appreciated to slow your delivery.

4. Avoid excluding information, even though it may be contrary to your primary message. Presenting both sides is not only fair, but emphasizing and defending your position can earn you respect and credibility.

5. Know the difference between fact and opinion (see Chapter 11) and be sure that your listeners are aware when you are employing them. When using facts, state the source. When stating your opinion or editorializing simply state, "In my opinion . . ." or simply, "I feel . . . ." Audiences resent being manipulated, and so would you.

6. Always credit and cite your sources. Taking someone else's ideas, or words as if they were your own is wrong. It is plagiarism. Plagiarism is not only unethical, it is *out-and-out* stealing and

make-up—age, sex, ethnicity, educational and economic level, etc. of your audience

out and out—actually, definitely

could result in some serious consequences. I'll have more to say on this subject a little later in this chapter.

7. Try to answer every question during your question-and-answer period (if there is one) as honestly and *straightforwardly* as possible. If you don't know an answer to a question, say so. Simply stating, "I don't know the answer but I can *look it up* and have it for you at the next class or meeting," would be satisfying and appreciated.

straightforward —clearly, easy to understand

look it up—find

Ethical Responsibilities of the Listener

Just as a speaker has ethical responsibilities to his or her audience, you as a listener have ethical responsibilities to the speaker. Remember, a completed oral communication cycle includes a speaker who has something to say and a listener to assimilate that message and provide vital feedback to the speaker. (Further discussed in Chapters 3 and 4.)

As an ethical listener, you should:

1. Prepare yourself thoroughly for a learning experience. If possible, try to find out something about the speaker and her topic. What's her background? Is she a recognized authority in her field? Has she authored any articles or books on the subject? What is the

speaker's motivation for her viewpoints? The more you can ascertain beforehand, the better you'll be able to evaluate the message and the messenger.

2. Keep an open mind. (Further discussed in Chapter 4.) Even if you think what the speaker has to say may, even in part, be contrary to your viewpoint, you have a responsibility and an obligation to yourself and the speaker to absorb the complete message. Possibly your original views may be strengthened; but there's also the chance that the speech may be so compelling and persuasive as to soften or even change your opinion completely. Whatever happens, you should, at least, come away a better-informed person. And no matter how much you may disagree with the message, the speaker is entitled to his "Freedom of Speech" as much as you are.

3. Concentrate on the message. As further discussed in Chapter 4, your mind is capable of assimilating many more words per minute than any speaker can deliver, leaving a significant gap to entertain distractions. Discipline yourself to concentrate totally on the message. One effective way to do this is to take notes during the speech. Another would be to write down questions that you may ask during the question-and-answer period. Don't permit your *mind to wander.* Don't think about things to be done at home, problems at work, what you did last weekend or what you plan to do next weekend. Don't be distracted by people coughing, chairs moving, or students coming in late. Always *think* the message and the messenger—what is being said and how it's being said.

mind to wander—to be distracted

4. Provide feedback. As a responsible speaker, you are making constant eye contact with your audience—you are looking for feedback. As a responsible listener your eyes should be riveted on the speaker so that you can provide that critical feedback. If your eyes are wandering around the room, looking at your watch, sneaking a peek at your homework, or if you are yawning or whispering to a classmate, you're communicating negative messages to the speaker. But, if you're sitting upright in your chair, looking alert, looking at the speaker and his or her every move, smiling and occasionally nodding approval, you're telling the speaker that you not only understand what is being said, but you're interested in it.

5. Compensate for speaker flaws. (Further discussed in Chapter 4.) Some speakers may display certain characteristics that detract from their message. Perhaps the speaker has a nervous cough, constantly pauses, has a monotonous delivery, or speaks too fast. Maybe she remains rigid in one position, doesn't move or gesture, or appears fidgety and is constantly moving. The speaker's clothes may not coordinate, jewelry may fly about with every gesture, or long hair may be stubbornly falling over one eye. Such flaws can,

at times, provide more fascination than the speaker's message. Try to overlook such distractions and immerse yourself in the message.

Plagiarism and How to Avoid It

Without becoming excessively didactic, **plagiarism** is not ethical, is not right, and is not being honest. It is stealing. Whenever you take someone else's ideas and or words and *pass them off* as though they are your own, you are plagiarizing, which can lead to serious consequences. Presidential candidate Senator Joseph R. Biden, Jr., was forced to withdraw from the 1988 campaign after members of the press discovered that two of his speeches were the works of others. A dean of communication at a large university lost his prestigious position when it was discovered that a speech he had given was written by someone else and was delivered practically verbatim. Students found guilty of plagiarism either receive failing grades, are suspended or expelled, or put their academic degrees in jeopardy. There is no excuse for plagiarism because it is so easy to avoid—JUST GIVE CREDIT WHERE CREDIT IS DUE. Simple statements such as:

pass them off— pretend

> "From an article I recently read in [name the publication, date, and author] it clearly states . . . ."

> "The solutions that I just presented come, in part, from a three-part series written by [name author, publication, and date]"

> Or a simple, "According to [name author and publication]. . . ."

Remember, when you're quoting, summarizing, or paraphrasing someone else's work, just *cite the source* and avoid some unpleasant situations.

To Avoid Plagiarizing

1. Be sure to research a variety of sources; don't restrict yourself to only one.
2. During your research, keep an accurate listing or bibliography of all your sources and save them.
3. List all of your sources on 3-by-5 cards for convenience and accessibility. Write on one side only and be sure to number them.
4. Study and critically analyze all the information so that you'll be able to form your own conclusions. This should enable you to present your thoughts in your own words and in your own style of speaking.
5. When you're preparing your speech, be sure to include the sources. Don't wait until you've finished your preparation.
6. In your final draft, check to be sure that all the sources are properly cited.
7. And finally, it might not be a bad idea to have your sources prepared as a handout for those who request one.

Again, I would like to emphasize that developing all the skills explained in this book to a high level of proficiency is not a realistic goal to accomplish in one or two semesters. But this course can be a terrific beginning.

Nothing is more frustrating than having something to contribute to a discussion at school, at home, at work, or at a social affair—but not doing so for lack of self-confidence. "To sin by silence," said Abraham Lincoln, "when they should protest makes cowards of men." This course will help you make your contribution.

THINGS TO DISCUSS IN CLASS

1. List a few topics that you can talk about for at least three minutes.
2. How would speech training help you in your current career or in one that you plan to enter?
3. Name a few benefits that you hope to gain from this course.
4. Which public figure do you consider an excellent speaker? Why?
5. Which public figure do you consider a poor speaker? Why?
6. Can you recall any times when you wanted to express your viewpoints and didn't? Why?
7. Do you ever envy friends because they express themselves better than you do?
8. Have you ever started to express yourself, then suddenly stopped for some reason?
9. Do you feel more confident when speaking to one person than when speaking to a group?
10. Do you have more (less) difficulty speaking to people of the opposite sex?
11. Bring to class three or four political ads from the newspaper and discuss their contents relative to what you've just learned about ethics.
12. You decide to base your next speech on a paper that your friend submitted in another class last semester. Is this ethical or not? Explain.

2

YOUR FIRST TALK: GETTING TO KNOW YOU

The first time I attempted to make a public talk . . . I was in a state of misery . . . my tongue clove to the roof of my mouth, and, at first, I could hardly get out a word.

David Lloyd George, prime minister of England from 1916 to 1922 and one of the most eloquent speakers of this century

After reading and understanding this chapter, you should be able to:

- **Appreciate the importance of knowing your subject well.**

- **Prepare a short, interesting talk about yourself.**

- **Deliver the talk about yourself.**

- **Grasp the importance of eye contact and gestures.**

- **Realize the importance of good posture, some movement, and the limited use of notes.**

- **Understand that nervousness strikes everybody.**

CHAPTER PREVIEW

This chapter will introduce you to some of the ways of giving a good, stimulating talk. Since it's easier to talk with people you know, the sooner you get to know each other, the better. That's why your first talk will probably be an autobiographical sketch from four to six minutes long.

Thorough knowledge of a subject gives speakers more self-confidence than does anything else. Since you know yourself best, you should be able to talk for at least four to six minutes about yourself.

All of us like attention and respect. When you're "front and center," you're the focus of attention. If you follow the suggestions in this chapter and those in later chapters, you will earn the respect of your peers and other listeners.

Everybody, including professional speakers and actors, gets nervous before a performance. It's a normal reaction that usually diminishes soon after you get involved in your message. Since it's almost impossible to eliminate all **nervousness,** you should strive to control it. Suggestions are offered for that purpose.

Eye contact with your listeners is vital, so look them right in the eye. This arouses them initially and gives you the momentum to keep them interested. Eye contact also provides you with feedback on how you're doing.

Gestures support and dramatize your ideas. As long as your gestures are spontaneous and vigorous, use them. In addition, they're an excellent outlet for your nervous energy. Other nonverbal elements touched on briefly are movement, posture, facial expression, and appearance.

If using note cards will give you confidence, use them; professional speakers often do. Just don't read so much from the cards that you disrupt eye contact with your listeners.

This first talk will probably be the toughest one of all. Remember that giving good talks requires that you do your homework beforehand. Homework includes rehearsing, preferably with at least one listener.

Appearing in this (and every) chapter is the feature "In Other Words," which will greatly benefit foreign and ESL students. To aid in their understanding of common American idioms and phrases, these expressions will be defined in the margin of the page on which they are introduced.

In the Spotlight

If you've never addressed a group before, this will be an exciting and memorable experience. Although your talk will probably be short, it could provide you with enough challenge and motivation to exert a positive influence on your life. Your instructor may ask you either to talk about yourself or to interview a classmate and then give a talk about him or her. No matter which talk you give, this chapter will guide you in how to plan and present it.

Since most of you are more relaxed when communicating with people you know, your instructor may feel that it's a good idea for everyone to give a brief autobiographical sketch. In this way you'll learn to know each other sooner and *"get the feel"* of giving a prepared talk before a group.

get the feel—to experience or learn the way something feels

This short autobiographical talk will afford you an opportunity to listen to all members of the class introduce themselves. What an excellent chance to find out which classmates have the same interests as yours! Perhaps, while listening to someone interesting, you'll look forward to the class break or a chance to meet at the cafeteria to develop a more personal relationship on a one-to-one basis.

What an excellent opportunity to listen to other students from different countries and cultures describe their homeland experiences and way of life; their family responsibilities, schooling, and traditional celebrations; their reactions to coming to America. Listen to what their impressions are now and of their hopes for the future.

So prepare yourself to absorb what your classmates have to say and listen carefully for possible clues of mutual interest or concern. This talk is an important first step in developing new friends. In addition, this will be your introduction to a critical aspect of speech communication—audience analysis. (See Chapters 6 and 11.)

The distance from your seat to the speaker's stand may be only 15 feet, but it may seem like a mile to you when it's your turn to speak. This is understandable because of your anxiety about what's to come. Many things will **zip through** your mind, such as "I wonder if I'll be able to move when I'm called. I'll just play dead—on second thought, who'll be playing?" or "What am I doing here?" Believe it or not, you're here to give your first talk.

zip through—rapidly go through

You shouldn't let this talk upset you because, in all probability, you won't be graded or critiqued. Your professor may wish only to introduce you to how it feels to stand up and speak before a group—and to convince you that there's nothing mysterious or life threatening about doing so.

Know Your Subject

There seems to be some disagreement among speech professors as to the relative importance of knowing your topic versus your delivery when it

"What am I doing here?"

comes to presenting an effective talk. Some say *knowing your subject* counts for about 75 percent and *your delivery* about 25 percent. Others believe that it's about equal, fifty-fifty. But the one thing that is indisputable is the fact that the more you know about your subject, the better your chances of being an effective communicator. No one knows you better than you do, and no other topic should interest you more or provide you with more material, so your own life is an excellent topic for your first talk.

Preparing your first talk should be a simple exercise. With paper and pencil in hand, conduct a self-inventory and make notes. Think about your childhood, parents, and relatives. Where were you born and raised? Which schools did you attend? What made you decide to go to college? Why this one? Has any one person had a strong influence on you? Why did you select your major area of study?

Were you in the service? If so, what branch and what rank did you hold? How was basic training and where did you take it? What type of work did you do in the military and where were you stationed? Did you have any spine-tingling encounters?

Maybe you're working. Do you like your job—why or why not? How long have you worked there?

Do you ever travel? Where have you been and with whom? How long were you there? Would you like to return—why or why not?

Don't overlook your hobbies or other interests. Do you play a musical instrument? Perhaps you play for a group. If so, where and how often? Maybe you're *into* karate, automobile repair, ceramics, exercising, or gourmet cooking. Share your experiences.

into—interested in

Are you married or single? Do you have children? If so, how old are they? Maybe you're a grandparent. What made you decide to return to school? How much of a challenge is it? Are you a full-time or part-time student? What are your plans when you graduate?

Have you met any unusually interesting people or celebrities? Tell us about them. When and where did you meet them and under what circumstances? What were your impressions of them? If you've never met a celebrity but want to, who would it be and why?

You should now have some ideas on how to prepare for your first talk. Go over the preceding questions again and use them as a guide. I'm sure you can expand on them.

If your first talk in class doesn't appear serious—that is, if you're smiling, laughing and joking, making faces during your speech—you could very well damage your credibility in any future talks that may be of a serious nature. That's not to say that you can't give an effective persuasive talk later in the semester and it's not to say that you can't be a little humorous in your first talk. But remember, if the first impression you give your listeners is that you're a comedian and you're not taking this assignment seriously, you just may find it very difficult, and frustrating, to transform your image from a *lightweight* to a *serious contender*.

lightweight—someone not to be taken seriously

serious contender—someone to be taken seriously

If you're new to our country/culture, you can *count on* the fact that what you have to say may be of great interest to your classmates and your professor. Where do you come from? Your family, your education, the decision to come to America, and your hopes and dreams are only a few observations that you could weave into a very interesting talk. You can also anticipate many questions during your question-and-answer session following your talk as your listeners look forward to learning more about you and your country/culture.

count on—to be sure of

Remember, you can be an interesting person. You have something to say: You do things; you have likes and dislikes; you have opinions, dreams, and ambitions. Here is your chance to express them. Good luck.

Before we present a sample introductory talk, here are a format and outline that you may want to consider.

My name is _____.

My friends call me _____.

I live at _____

and my family consists of _____.

I attended the following schools: _____.
My favorite subject(s) were _____.
My extracurricular activities consisted of _____.

I am presently employed at _____
and my responsibilities are _____.
The days and hours I work are _____.
What I like best about my job is _____.
What I don't like about my job is _____.

I've decided to come to this college because _____.
My major is _____.
My plans after I graduate are _____.
I participate in the following college activities: _____.
I am a full-time/part-time student and I'm taking courses in _____.
My biggest obstacle in coming to college is _____.
As far as what my family thinks about my coming to college, _____.
I decided to return to college because _____.
My major is _____.

I enjoy traveling and have visited _____.
Of all the places I visited, I enjoyed _____
the most because _____.

I was a member of the Armed Forces (mention branch, length of service, duty stations, and occupational specialty): _____.

My short-term goal is _____.
My long-term goal is _____.

Some of the things I enjoy doing are _____.
Some of the things I don't enjoy are _____.
My biggest gripe is _____.
The one thing that gives me great pleasure is _____.
I think the biggest problem facing our society is _____.

How you complete these statements should give your classmates *a handle* on who you are and where you come from and could lead to some stimulating relationships.

a handle—some idea

Your instructor may ask for an **outline** before you speak (see Chapter 8). If so, the outline for your talk may look something like this:

Title: Autobiographical talk

I. Personal information
  A. Name, age, hometown
  B. Family members
      1. Parents
      2. Brother(s)/sister(s)
      3. Spouse and children
      4. Pet(s)
II. Schools attended
  A. Middle school
  B. High school
      1. Type of program enrolled in
      2. Favorite course(s)
      3. Most memorable teacher/coach
      4. Extracurricular activities
III. Post–high school education
  A. Schools attended prior to this one
  B. Why I selected this school
  C. What I am majoring in
  D. Long-term and short-term goals
  E. Extracurricular activities
IV. Occupational experience
  A. Past job(s)
      1. Description and duties
      2. Description and duties
  B. Present job(s)
      1. Description and duties
      2. Likes and dislikes
V. Military service
  A. Branch and location of basic training
  B. Military schools attended
  C. Rank and job description
  D. Duty station(s)
  E. Other travel opportunities
VI. Hobbies/Interests
  A. Outdoor activities
  B. Indoor activities
  C. Collections
VII. Future career goals

Here's a sample introductory talk.

Sam Adams

1   Hi. My name is Sam Adams and my friends call me Sam. I live in Quincy with my mother, father, and two younger sisters; Kaitlyn who's 18, and Christine who's 16. I'm 21 years old. As a matter of fact, I turned 21 last month and, yes, I am now legally able to enjoy that famous, refreshing beverage that bears my name.

2   My family has lived in Quincy for over fifty years and I attended public schools in the city. Quincy is known as the City of Presidents because it's the birthplace of John Adams, the second president of the United States and his son, John Quincy Adams, who was our sixth president. They are both buried here in Quincy Center in the Church of the Presidents . . . because they're dead . . . and that's our history lesson for today.

3   I'm a graduate of Quincy High and did fairly well there. My average for the four years was a B⁻ and, actually, I think I could have done better but I enjoyed playing sports a little more than studying. I played basketball and soccer. In fact, for the past two years I've been coaching soccer for a youth soccer league. It's fun working with the younger kids and teaching them the game.

4   My favorite subjects in high school were math and computers. English and history didn't rank very high on my list of favorite courses. Along with playing basketball and soccer, I also belonged to the computer club, which I enjoyed very much because not only did we have the chance to listen to guest speakers from the computer industry but, on occasion, we visited various companies in the area.

5   When I graduated from high school, I took a job with a small computer company in Cambridge right near Harvard. The work was very interesting, at first, and the money was real good. After a couple of years with the company I realized that I could go only so far with just a high school diploma and, frankly, I was getting bored with what I was doing.

6   Working in a small company, I got to know people in other departments, which gave me a good chance of looking at the bigger picture of the computer industry. I decided to return to school. In fact one of the girls, with whom I became friendly, very friendly, suggested I give some thought about going to Harvard. Right. Harvard. To go to Harvard my mother and father would have to mortgage the house then I would have to mortgage my mother and father.

7   Anyway, when I went to give my notice, my supervisor asked me if I would be interested working part-time, if he could arrange

it, while I returned to school. To make a long story short, I was offered a part-time position and I took it. It's working out very well because not only am I able to pay my tuition, but I'm also able to save some money.

8   I selected this two-year college because it has a great computer program and the tuition is reasonable. I will be graduating this year with an Associate in Arts degree with my concentration in Computer Information Systems. My average, so far, is a 3.8 and I am a member of the Honor Society. In the fall, I hope to attend Boston College, where I plan to continue my studies in the computer field.

9   I've enjoyed my two years here at Boston Community College very much . . . especially because of the professors, who seem to be interested and communicate well with the students. If you want to sit and talk with them, or if you need extra help, they're there. For the past three semesters I volunteered to serve as a tutor in the Computer Lab. I really enjoy helping other students and wish I had more time to do it.

10   As far as what my family thinks about my coming to college, they were very pleased. I think that they would have been more pleased if I had come to college right after high school, but I wanted to go to work and make some money. But to get anywhere in the business world, especially in computers, you have to have a four-year college degree. I know it's early yet, but there's a pretty good chance that I'll go on to graduate school.

11   Traveling? I enjoy traveling and have been to England, Ireland, and Disney World in Florida with my family. During the summers, a group of us rent a cottage on Cape Cod, where on weekends we party, sail, party, golf, party, and, sometimes, swim. The one standard rule that we have is that anyone who comes to our parties must hand over the car keys, which are locked up until the next day. No one is allowed to drive once they enter the cottage and start partying. We've had many parties, lots of fun, but never a problem.

12   My biggest gripe is something that I think most of us with cars can relate to . . . and that's the ridiculously high cost of automobile insurance if you're under 25. My automobile insurance costs almost as much as my car is worth. That really *bugs* me.

bugs—annoys

13   I think the biggest problem facing our society today is the violence in the public schools, especially by kids carrying guns and other weapons. This is not a local problem but one that is nationwide . . . and very little, if anything, seems to be done about it. I just don't understand why troublemakers are permitted to stay in school; even if they're expelled, they're eventually reinstated.

14   The one thing that gives me great pleasure is . . . weekends; when I can really relax.

15   In conclusion, I would like to say that I enjoyed giving this "first" talk. But, if I said that, I would be lying. No, I'm only kidding. It really wasn't so bad, but I'm glad it's over. Are there any questions?

After you've finished your talk, you might answer questions from the class. This question-and-answer session (further discussed at the end of this chapter), more than any other exercise, will help you develop self-confidence because you'll have completed your formal talk, and you should be able to relax and answer questions on a subject that you thoroughly know—you.

Question-and-answer sessions have uncovered some unusual experiences, including the following:

- A young woman in the class appeared on TV programs several times a week and communicated to deaf viewers in sign language.
- A mother and her son and daughter attended this school at the same time. Each was enrolled in a separate section of speech classes.
- A young man enrolled in the course because he wanted to enter politics. He did, and won his campaign.
- A student told the class she signed up for this course to meet a prospective husband. You guessed it—a year later she was married.
- During semester breaks and summer vacations, a student works at Walt Disney World in Florida.
- A student told the class of her two hobbies—sky diving and hang gliding.
- A mother of two children worked one summer driving a cab. She was robbed twice and shot at once. She no longer drives a cab.

Here are some topics you might consider if your professor chooses not to assign an autobiographical talk. Remember, your first talk, if you have a choice, should be on a topic that you know very well.

out of sight—very expensive

1. Why I decided to come (return) to college
2. Tuitions are going right *out of sight*
3. Trying to juggle a job and classes
4. My most memorable teacher
5. The need for a longer school year
6. Daycare centers on campus
7. Being a single parent
8. How to select a reliable baby-sitter
9. Parent(s) should be more selective about what television programs their children watch
10. Some problems of being a parent today
11. Latch-key kids
12. Living at home vs. living on your own
13. Searching for your first apartment
14. What is safe sex?

15. How to prevent date rape
16. My most embarrassing experience
17. An unforgettable vacation
18. How to buy a good used car
19. Why I own a foreign car
20. A person who has greatly influenced me
21. My biggest gripe
22. Saving money by using food coupons

Of course, the kind of topic that you know well depends on your background. In recent years, there's been a significant increase in the number of foreign students enrolled in my speech classes. Here are some titles of talks that they shared with us:

1. Some Basic Differences of Buddhism, Shintoism, and Islam
2. The KGB
3. The After-Effects of Chernobyl
4. Comparing the Cities of Moscow and Stalingrad
5. How I Escaped from a North Vietnamese Prison Camp with My Young Family
6. The Chinese Calendar and the Celebration of Holidays
7. I Was a Prisoner in a Nazi Concentration Camp
8. I Was a Participant at Tiananmen Square[1]
9. Trying to Leave Russia
10. Why My Family Left Cuba
11. Living in Haiti
12. The Woman's Role in Japan
13. American Statehood for Puerto Rico
14. Life as a Palestinian
15. Living at a Kibbutz

ICE CUBES IN THE STOMACH

Suddenly the professor calls your name—it's your turn to address the class. Your heart pounds with such force that you think it can be heard across the room, your forehead breaks out with beads of perspiration, your mouth goes dry, and your stomach quivers.

You're experiencing an attack of nerves—**stage fright**—that is not unique to you. Most people get it, whether they admit it or not. This sensation, in varying degrees, occurs thousands of times daily: on an individual's first day on a new job, on a first date, and on a student's first day at a new school. It happens to actors and actresses just before the curtain

---

[1] A prodemocracy demonstration attended mostly by students, many of whom were massacred at Tiananmen Square in Beijing, China, in 1989.

goes up or the camera starts to roll, to students in other speech classes throughout the country ready to give their first talks, and to your own classmates who have spoken before you and to those who will follow you. Even instructors aren't immune.

rattles—makes one nervous

For example, the week before each semester begins, the thought of facing four classes, each of approximately thirty strangers, *rattles* me. The thought of walking alone into each classroom, with students staring and trying to assess their "prof," and knowing that this first encounter is crucial in establishing respect and rapport for the entire semester, leads to many anxious moments. But once I start two-way communication and *break the ice,* the problems melt away. Then, when the first class ends, I enjoy a tremendous feeling of relief and accomplishment.

break the ice—begin conversing; get something started

on your toes—alert

Nervousness can be a form of positive energy that will keep you *on your toes.* If you accept it as normal, which it is, it will help you do your best. In a new environment, there is no stigma to feeling nervous or even frightened before speaking. It is a normal reaction, and its intensity will lessen the more you speak.

Even the great and the powerful suffer from nervous attacks. In a talk before London journalists years ago, a famous British cartoonist, David Low, said that every time he had to make a speech he felt as if he had a block of ice, nine inches by nine inches, in the pit of his stomach. Later he was approached by a member of the audience, Winston Churchill, one of the greatest speakers of this century. "Mr. Low," asked Churchill, "how large did you say that block of ice is?"

"Nine inches by nine inches," replied Low.

"What an amazing coincidence," said Churchill, "exactly the same size as mine."

uptight—tense

There's no cure for nervousness, but to help control it, you should admit that you're nervous, a bit *uptight,* queasy, even petrified; some textbooks call it **speaking apprehension** or **speech tension.** You should be greatly relieved to learn how many of your peers share your feelings, and things don't seem quite that bad if you're able to talk freely about them. Discuss them at home, at school, at work, with other members of your class, and certainly with your instructor.

Even royalty suffers from pangs of nervousness. At her royal wedding in July 1981, the bride, Lady Diana Spencer, called the groom "Philip Charles Arthur George" instead of Charles Philip Arthur George. He, in turn, omitted (or forgot?) the word "worldly" in pledging to share all his worldly goods with her.[2] In retrospect, perhaps it was a bad omen, as they divorced some years later.

Here are two more examples of stage fright sufferers—this time of two mega-superstars of show business. Since 1976 when Barbra Streisand was stricken with stage fright she refused to perform before a live audi-

---

[2]*New York Times,* 30 July 1981, 1.

ence. And it wasn't until New Year's Eve 1994, over twenty years later, that she struggled with the decision and agreed to perform live in Las Vegas. You might be interested to know that for her two sell-out shows she earned more than $20 million.[3] Who says it doesn't pay to have confidence? In the other incident, the late Frank Sinatra confessed to a national TV interviewer that after decades of performing, he still trembled with stage fright. He continued, ". . . the first four or five seconds I tremble every time I take a step and walk out of the wing onto the stage."[4]

Robert L. Montgomery put it quite nicely when he said, "The human voice is an amazing thing; it starts working the moment you're born and doesn't stop until you stand up to speak in public."

While there's no simple antidote for nervousness, you can take steps to help control this unwanted, involuntary behavior. Here are some suggestions:

1. Be totally prepared.
   a. Plan your presentation.
   b. Research and outline your topic.
   c. Cite your sources, if applicable.
2. Practice your talk several times out loud.
3. Take deep breaths before you're called to speak.
4. Don't hesitate to admit and discuss your apprehension with classmates and your instructor before the speech.
5. While waiting to be called, think only positive thoughts.
6. Realize that everyone in the audience is pulling for you, they want you to succeed just as much as they want to succeed when it's their turn.
7. Constantly remind yourself that there is no other person anywhere in the world like you and that your audience is looking forward to getting to know you.

No single action is more important in helping you develop self-confidence and in allaying that uptight feeling than *knowing your subject cold.* Chapter 9 contains further suggestions on what you can do, both before and during your talk, to help relieve tension and to diminish your nervousness.

knowing your subject cold—being very familiar with your subject

And speaking of nervousness, you might enjoy the speech in Appendix A given by Mark Twain entitled, "Mark Twain's First Appearance," in which he discusses his experience with "stage fright."

FRONT AND CENTER

When the initial shock of hearing your name has subsided, slowly draw a few deep breaths. This should help ease that uptight feeling. Walk to the

---

[3] *Parade Magazine,* 30 January 1994, 2, Walter Scott's "Personality Parade."
[4] *Boston Herald,* 16 May 1988, 11, "Celebrity."

Keep your cool.

front of the classroom with purpose and confidence. Don't shuffle your feet, don't look at the floor, and don't make any remarks to class members. Once you begin your talk, all their attention will be riveted on you.

Before starting to speak, you may find it reassuring to look around the classroom. You may sense encouragement from familiar faces. You may also observe a look of genuine understanding from those who appreciate your feelings because it will soon be their turn. You now realize that you're not alone. The preceding speakers sweated through the same experience, and the following speakers will do the same. The more quickly you appreciate this, the more relaxed you'll become.

As soon as you get wrapped up in what you're saying, perhaps 20 to 30 seconds into your talk, your nervousness should diminish. This is why we emphasize knowing your subject thoroughly. (In this regard, it may be helpful to memorize the first few sentences, and perhaps even the closing one, to avoid the hesitant, awkward, "Well, I guess that's just about it.")

SAY IT WITHOUT WORDS

First impressions are crucial to communicators, and all of you are communicators. Every day you see people, you greet people, and you meet people—at work, at school, and at social or business functions. Before you even say a word, you transmit impressions, favorable or not, through **nonverbal communication,** the conscious or subconscious transmission and reception of unspoken messages. (You are being introduced to this topic because it will be an integral part of your autobiographical talk. Chapter 3 is devoted entirely to this subject.) Some features of nonverbal communication include:

- **Your walk:** Is it slow, fast, listless, jerky, confident, or hesitant? Do you march, saunter, strut, shuffle, or stalk?
- **Your posture:** Are you straight as a drill sergeant? Do you slump, shift from one leg to the other, droop, or lean on the **lectern** (speaker's stand)?
- **Your facial expressions:** Do you smile, frown, or smirk? Do you look condescending, absorbed, disappointed, or troubled?
- **Your eyes:** Are they expressive, twinkling, shifty, piercing, friendly, cold, or penetrating?
- **Your dress:** Are you neat or sloppy? Is your hair combed? Are your colors coordinated or clashing?
- **Your cosmetics:** What amount of aftershave lotion, cologne, perfume, hairspray, or antiperspirant did you apply? Too much or not enough? Is your make-up caked on? Do you look like someone from Mars?
- **Your gestures:** What do you do with your hands, head, and shoulders? Are you constantly touching your face, ears, hair, or jewelry? Are your hands clasped in front of or behind you? Are they in your pockets? Are your head and shoulders constantly moving or immobile?

All the above nonverbal characteristics transmit messages that can have an important effect on the success of your oral presentation.

First impressions are usually long lasting. How many times have you prejudged a person by any of the above criteria, only to change your assessment after you've become better acquainted? How many times have you reached a negative opinion of a person before he or she has had the opportunity to communicate orally?

Indeed, nonverbal communication can often influence your opinions more forcefully than the spoken word. The old aphorism that actions speak louder than words is more than mere rhetoric.

In all communication, you don't always have to say it to convey it, and in nonverbal communication you may often transmit messages entirely different from what you think you're transmitting. Call it what you like—**body language, silent language, soundless speech,** or nonverbal communication—it is an eloquent form of message transmission and reception. (For more on nonverbal communication, refer to Chapter 3.)

Importance of Eye Contact

Perhaps you know the feeling of approaching several of your friends who are involved in a discussion. When you join the group, you notice that the speaker doesn't look at you but continues looking at the others. Your presence isn't acknowledged, and you feel left out.

Eye contact with your audience is extremely important. Without it you will have immense difficulty conveying interest and sincerity. What is your reaction when you listen to someone who doesn't look you in the eye, at least occasionally? The speaker's believability is seriously impaired. When you appear before a group, you should remember that the people are not only listening *to* you, they are also looking *at* you.

As tempting as it is, don't gaze out windows, at notes, or at the floor or walls. Some speakers, by looking at people in the last row of a large audience, can give the impression that they're looking at everyone in front of them. In a smaller group, however, look at the students to your left, then to your right, then in between. Make eye contact. Don't make the mistake of some beginning speakers who focus their eyes solely on the professor. Just remember, people like to be talked to and looked at simultaneously.

Making eye contact means that you, the sender, are making a connection with your audience, the receiver. You're transmitting a message, and without eye contact the transmission is broken and communication is disrupted.

Eye contact with your audience is extremely important.

By maintaining eye contact with your audience you can receive visual feedback. Your listeners' eyes can tell you if they're getting your message. Do they look confused, bored, doubting, satisfied, or interested? Do they seem to enjoy and understand what you're saying? Do they look drowsy? As long as you're aware of *telltale* signals from your audience, the communication cycle can be complete. You have a message to communicate with your mind, your voice, your body, and your eyes—you maintain eye contact with your audience and you receive messages in response to your spoken thoughts. If you fail to look at your audience, you can't receive any reaction from them. (For more on eye contact, see Chapter 3.)

telltale—obvious

What about Gestures?

Many people **gesture** as naturally as they breathe. Perhaps you know people who would be speechless if their hands were tied behind their backs. If you find it natural to move your hands and arms while communicating, continue to do so. If, however, you tend to be carried away by gestures, don't be too concerned about them now because you'll learn to control them as the course progresses.

Your instructor will make suggestions as to the degree and effectiveness of your gestures. One practical exercise is to speak before a mirror and watch your body movements. Being videotaped is the best way to see yourself exactly as you appear to others.

Try to become more aware of how people gesture (nonverbal communication is also discussed in Chapters 3, 5, and 16) when they talk—for example, groups of students, your teacher, friends, family members, your boss, and performers on TV. Are their gestures meaningful and expressive, or do they look awkward and meaningless?

Hands always seem to be a problem for inexperienced speakers, but they don't have to be. We've already mentioned gesturing. You may use one or both hands simultaneously, but not constantly. On occasion you may clasp your hands behind your back. If there's no **lectern,** which is a speaker's stand resting on a table or desk to hold papers and notes (not to be confused with **podium,** an elevated platform or stage), you may hold notes in your hands. Be sure to keep your hands away from your face, hair, neck, ears, and nose. Also, if you wear necklaces, pendants, earrings, or bracelets, leave them alone. Fiddling with them distracts people.

Moving Around

As far as movement is concerned, many speakers feel that they must stay in one place and remain completely motionless. Not so. You should feel free to move around. Taking a few steps in either direction from the stand is desirable as long as you move smoothly, not jerkily, like a puppet.

However, avoid perpetual motion, for example, swaying back and forth or from side to side, crossing and uncrossing your feet, or fidgeting

Many people gesture as naturally as they breathe.

with your hands and fingers. Movement can be effective when done in moderation, with purpose and naturalness. It helps you develop poise and confidence, and it constructively channels your nervous energy.

Standing Tall

Good posture—standing straight and squarely on both feet—conveys an impression of confidence and alertness. Your posture communicates attitude, just as your face and voice do. Don't slouch, lean against a table, or drape yourself over the speaker's stand. These actions detract from your overall appearance and create a negative effect on your audience.

Perhaps the best way to improve your posture is to observe yourself on videotape or in a full-length mirror. There you can see if you're standing tall or hunched over, if your head is held high or drooping, and if your weight is equally distributed on both feet.

There's no question about it—erect posture helps you look sharper, feel more alert, and is a sign of good health.

TAKE NOTE

Using notes is recommended because they can give you a feeling of confidence and security. In fact, many professional speakers use them. Just

It's okay to relax, but . . . .

be careful not to rely on them to the point that you read the entire talk without looking at your audience.

If there is no lectern, 3-by-5 cards can fit comfortably in the palm of your hand without annoying the audience. If your classroom is equipped with a lectern, 4-by-6 cards (or even standard-sized 8½-by-11 inch paper) may rest on it without being noticed. Try to keep your cards lying flat so they won't distract your audience, and, as you finish with one, simply slide it to the side unobtrusively. If you have more than two cards, number them in case you drop or misplace them (these things do happen).

QUESTION-AND-ANSWER SESSION

As you conclude your talk, don't lower your voice so that it becomes almost inaudible. Keep it strong and confident until you finally ask, "Are there any questions?" Some of your classmates and even your professor may have a few. If they do, you should feel complimented and, by this time, relaxed enough to answer them easily and naturally.

While you're answering questions, try not to focus your attention solely on the questioner. If the answer is long, you may glance around the class, but when you're concluding your reply, look again at the questioner. Pause a second or two as if to ask, "Did I answer you satisfactorily?" Then *field* the next inquiry.

field—ask for

During the question-and-answer session if you feel that a questioner's voice is too low or soft for everyone in the class to hear then repeat the question. Nothing is more aggravating than sitting in the middle or near the rear during a lecture and hearing answers to inaudible or partly audible questions. If you don't understand a question, there's a pretty good chance others don't either. In this case, ask that the question be repeated. Then, repeat it yourself so that the questioner will know that you understand it and so will your audience.

handled—answered, dealt with

When you've *handled* all the questions, breathe deeply and return to your seat confidently. Don't rush. Don't crumple your notes and stuff them into your pocket, and don't collapse into your chair. Just sit down quietly.

Knowing your subject and responding knowledgeably during the **question-and-answer period** will do more than anything else to bolster your self-confidence.

After a talk, many students feel that their nervousness was vividly displayed when, in most cases, just the opposite is true. In reality—and we wouldn't kid you—you don't look even half as nervous as you feel inside. Just ask your classmates.

Congratulations! You've given your first talk. Was it as difficult as you thought it would be? Was it as traumatic an experience as you envisioned? It probably was. But you did it, and this was the most difficult talk you'll ever make—your toughest obstacle course. Your other talks should be easier and more enjoyable.

THINGS TO DISCUSS IN CLASS

1. Be aware of eye contact among your friends, colleagues, speakers, and TV performers. When you are personally involved, observe the importance and effect of eye contact among your associates.

2. Using the format presented in this chapter as an aid, prepare and rehearse a four- to five-minute autobiographical talk.

3. Notice how people gesture when they speak. Do the gestures of anyone in particular impress you? Why or why not?

4. Watch speakers on TV, especially religious personalities, and observe their physical movements while speaking. Do they move at all? Do their

movements coincide with their message? Are their movements distracting? Prepare to discuss your answers in class.

5. When you meet an individual for the first time, what determines your first impression of that person?

6. What are your personal feelings about judging an individual solely on the basis of physical appearance?

7. Do you have friends who never look directly at you when they talk with you? How do you feel about this behavior?

What Do You Remember from This Chapter?

1. What two elements in speaking do more than anything else to help you acquire self-confidence?

2. Is getting nervous before speaking uncommon? Explain.

3. Why is eye contact so vitally important?

4. When you speak before a group, why is it important to look around constantly at individuals in the audience rather than to focus on a limited area?

5. Do gestures enhance your ability to communicate? Why?

6. What must you be aware of when you use notes?

7. What are two things you can do to help control nervousness?

8. Explain why good posture is important to a public speaker.

Vitalize Your Vocabulary

You can have a clear, musical voice, an attractive appearance, good eye contact, and a solid knowledge of your subject; but if your vocabulary is weak and vague, your presentation will also be weak and vague. Whether you're communicating with one or two people or a group of 30, an extensive vocabulary is a major asset. That is why, starting now and continuing with each succeeding chapter, we include a list of words (and their most basic meanings) that educated people should not only understand, but be able to use.

The lists of words vary considerably. Some lists contain families of words that relate to the same subject, for example, government and politics, health care and phobias, business and finance, computers and data processing. Other lists consist of synonyms and antonyms, words based on Latin and Greek roots, words from native Americans, and words from Japan that have entered our language. In response to requests from students and professors who have used this book, the number of words has been expanded.

We hope that these brief glimpses into the intriguing world of words will galvanize you into exploring more deeply into that world.

English words derive from countless languages, principally from Latin and Greek, and from other sources such as literature, art, and science. Among the most fascinating words are "eponyms"—words based on the names of real or mythical people who have accomplished something unusual.

Eponyms

blanket (n.) A large covering of wool or synthetic cloth material on a bed to provide warmth. The credit goes to Thomas Blanket, an Englishman, who around 1380 first made these bed coverings.

bogus (adj.) Something that is counterfeit or fake, not genuine. Attributed to a Mr. Borghese who, in the 1830s, did a fantastic business in flooding the American West with counterfeit bank notes.

booze (n.) An alcoholic drink. Attributed to Mr. E. Booze who was a distiller in Kentucky around 1840. He sold his booze using his own name in bottles shaped like log cabins.

boycott (v.) To join together in refusing to buy, sell, use, or deal with; (n.) the act of boycotting. Derived from Captain Charles C. Boycott (1832–1897), a landlord's agent, whose job was to collect high rents from impoverished Irish tenant farmers.

Braille (n.) A system of printing and writing, using-raised dots, to enable blind people to communicate. Devised by the French teacher Louis Braille (1809–1852).

cardigan (n.) A sweater or jacket that opens full length down the front, usually long-sleeved and collarless. Named after the seventh Earl of Cardigan (1799–1868), an English general.

casanova (n.) A man who has a reputation for being a promiscuous lover, with many female conquests. After Giovanni Casanova, an Italian adventurer and writer of the eighteenth century.

chauvinist (n.) An extremist in any cause, often militaristic or patriotic. Derived from Nicolas Chauvin, one of Napoleon's most fanatical followers.

Chesterfield (n.) A man's overcoat with concealed buttons and a velvet collar. Named after an Earl in Chesterfield in the nineteenth century after he gave explicit instructions to his tailor on how he wanted it made.

condom (n.) A sheath made of rubber or latex and used by men during sexual relations to avoid pregnancy or sexually transmitted disease. First introduced in England around 1700 by a Dr. Condom.

crapper (n.) A flush toilet which was invented by Thomas Crapper (1837–1910), a Victorian English engineer.

derrick (n].) A large crane for lifting and moving heavy objects, especially during construction projects. Named after Thomas Derrick, a well-known hangman during the reigns of Elizabeth and James I around 1600.

dunce (n.) A stupid or lazy student. Named after John Duns Scotus (1265–1309), a Scottish philosopher and theologian.

Ferris wheel (n.) A large upright wheel with seats hanging from the frame. Very popular at fairs and expositions, this amusement attraction was named after its inventor George W.G. Ferris in 1895–1896.

gerrymander (v.) To rearrange a voting district so as to favor the party in power. After Massachusetts Governor Elbridge Gerry, who in 1812 carved out a district whose shape resembled a salamander.

hooker (n.) A prostitute. During the Civil War, General Joseph Hooker's troops were encamped for a time in Washington. Prostitutes who "serviced" them became known as "Hooker's Division." After the troops moved out the women were then called "hookers."

Jacuzzi (n.) Underwater jets of water in a tub that massage the body is named after its creator, Italian-born Candido Jacuzzi (1903–1986).

leotard (n.) A one-piece, tight-fitting garment that covers the torso and is now worn by dancers and acrobats. Named for Jules Leotard, a nineteenth-century French trapeze artist.

Levi's® (trademark) Blue jeans. Named after Levi Strauss, a Texas merchant who popularized them in the 1800s.

Listerine® (trademark) The popular antiseptic mouthwash. From Joseph Lister, 1st Baron of Lyme Regis (1827–1912) the founder of antiseptic surgery.

machiavellian (adj.) Deceitful, unscrupulous, crafty. In accordance with the political ideas explained in "The Prince," a classic book written by Niccolo Machiavelli (1469–1527), Italian statesman, political philosopher, and author.

masochist (n.) A person who receives sexual pleasure from being physically abused. Named after the Austrian novelist Leopold von Sacher-Masoch (1836–1895) whose writings and bizarre lifestyle reflected this obsession.

maverick (n.) An independent-minded person who usually goes against popular opinion. Named after the American pioneer Samuel A. Maverick (1803–1870) who was known for shady business practices as a rancher.

mentor (n.) A wise and trusted advisor. In Greek mythology, Mentor was the loyal friend and advisor of Odysseus (and instructor of his son Telemachus), from Homer's "Odyssey."

mesmerize (v.) To hypnotize or be held spellbound. Derives from the name of the Austrian physician and hypnotist Franz Anton Mesmer (1734–1815), who was known for hypnotizing his patients.

nicotine (n.) A poisonous substance that is the chief active ingredient in tobacco. From Jean Nicot, a seventeenth-century French diplomat who introduced Turkish tobacco into France.

pasteurize (v.) To destroy disease-producing bacteria and to stop fermentation in milk, beer, cider, and wine by heating the liquid to high temperatures. From Louis Pasteur (1822–1895), French chemist and bacteriologist.

sadist (n.) A person who enjoys inflicting pain on another. Named after the Marquis de Sade (1740–1814), French soldier and novelist who conducted experiments on pain and wrote about them.

sandwich (n.) Two or more slices of bread with a filling of cheese, meat, jam, or fish between them; (v.) to squeeze between two persons, places, things, etc. After John Montague (1718–1792), the fourth Earl of Sandwich, who ate this way so as not to leave the gambling table for meals.

saxophone (n.) A woodwind instrument with a curved metal body. Invented by Antoine Sax (1814–1894), a Belgian maker of musical instruments.

stonewall (v.) To refuse to answer in the face of questioning. This behavior, very common in recent times, is attributed to the great American General Thomas J. "Stonewall" Jackson who fought for the South in the Civil War. He earned this title when he and his troops "stood like a stone wall" against the enemy during the famous Battle of Bull Run.

vandal (n.) Someone who deliberately destroys or damages another's property. The word derives from the Vandals, a Germanic people, who traveled southward from Scandinavia in the first four centuries A.D., causing tremendous devastation on Gaul, Spain, and North Africa.

3

You Don't Have to Say It to Convey It

He that has eyes to see and ears to hear may convince himself that no mortal can keep a secret. If his lips are silent, he chatters with his fingertips; betrayal oozes out of him at every pore.

Sigmund Freud (1856–1939), founder of psychoanalysis

After reading and understanding this chapter, you should be able to:

- **Define nonverbal communication.**

- **Explain the vital role that nonverbal communication performs in the messages we transmit and receive daily.**

- **Observe and explain the various personal modes that communicate nonverbal messages.**

- **Explain the roles of nonpersonal factors such as time, space, clothes, and objects in nonverbal communication.**

- **Understand more fully how some other cultures communicate nonverbal messages through eye contact, gestures, time, and space.**

CHAPTER PREVIEW

This chapter deals with nonverbal language—the "language without words" that we use, consciously or subconsciously, to convey and receive messages. This language is often termed body language, face language, silent language, and silent messages. You may, in fact, depend more on this wordless language than you do on words.

Some personal elements of nonverbal language include posture, eye contact, facial expressions, tone of voice, body movement and gestures, clothes, smell, taste, and touch. Some impersonal elements are objects (artifacts), space, and time.

Also discussed is intercultural/multicultural communication, and how various cultures throughout the world communicate certain nonverbal messages.

Your appearance creates powerful first impressions, even before you utter a word. How often have you misjudged someone initially because he wore a beard or she exuded a perfume that you couldn't stomach? On the job and in your social life, your appearance can help you or hurt you—tremendously.

Impersonal aspects of nonverbal communication also create impressions about you. Time, and how you use it in relation to others, tells something about you. If you're a high-ranking manager, for instance, you can keep your employees waiting. Space, or "turf" as it is sometimes called, is another impersonal element that denotes your status and authority. As a manager, you probably have an office with a large desk, windows, a rug, extra furniture, air conditioning, recessed lighting, plants, and paintings on the walls. All these artifacts represent power, prestige, and prosperity.

Our personal lives are influenced by our use of nonverbal language. Depending on how we control it, career decisions may be positively or negatively affected.

Appearing in this (and every) chapter is the feature "In Other Words," which will greatly benefit foreign and ESL students. To aid in their understanding of common American idioms and phrases, these expressions will be defined in the margin of the page on which they are introduced.

WHAT IS NONVERBAL COMMUNICATION?

We have all heard any number of sayings and phrases that clearly demonstrate the importance and messages of **nonverbal communication,** such as:

"Actions speak louder than words." Perhaps you can recall, as a child, the number of times you were told (verbal) not to do something, but you persisted to the point that the only "language" you really understood was a slap (nonverbal) on the hand or rear.

"It wasn't so much *what* he said, but *how* he said it." Try to recall a number of situations to which this statement applies to.

"She had a look that could kill." If your mate discovers you where you shouldn't be, with someone you shouldn't be with, and doing something you shouldn't be doing, you'll understand this remark.

I'm sure that you'll have no difficulty understanding the implications contained in the following colorful sentences:

Following the police exam, Erik was feeling rather blue, really down in the dumps.

When Michelina found out that her roommate was going out with her former boyfriend, she saw red.

The nonverbal elements of communication are extremely important, in some instances more so than the spoken words. In fact, when a person's actions and words appear contradictory, the actions often communicate the true feelings. Indeed, it is estimated that when communicating one-on-one, as much as 90 percent of the message is communicated nonverbally.[1]

As you learned in Chapter 2, nonverbal communication is the conscious or subconscious transmission and reception of unspoken messages. While authorities differ about the exact impact, they all agree that the meaning of nonverbal messages is much more significant than verbal messages.

Nonverbal communication is often referred to by other terms, such as the **silent language, body language,** *face language, silent messages,* and *"beyond words."* No matter what it is called, it means the conscious or subconscious transmission and reception of messages other than spoken words.

Nonverbal communication is a vast and ever-growing field of study and research. Some of its elements include facial expressions, eye contact, gestures, other body movements, and **paralanguage**—laughing,

---

[1] Albert Mehrabian, *Silent Messages* (Belmont, CA: Wadsworth, 1981), 76.

coughing, throat clearing, **vocal pitch,** and **pauses.** Other elements include space, time, sight, taste, smell, touch, clothes, color, sound, environment, weather, lighting, and objects. This is just a partial list of nonverbal elements. We will discuss only those over which you may have some control and which you may find important and common in your daily life.

How We Communicate Without Words

We cannot NOT communicate. We communicate simply by being alive. Messages are transmitted to others via our sex; body frame; scars, birthmarks, and other visible features; hair color and style; skin and eye color, as well as the quality of our complexions. How many of us have made initial judgments of people from a superficial first glance—and been wrong?

Our **self-image** is crucial not only to us personally, but to how others perceive us. More and more people, regardless of age or sex, are spending thousands of dollars for cosmetic surgery simply to look and feel more appealing or to change their image. Vive la sex appeal!

Our very presence or absence "says something." If, for example, you had registered for a certain course and then cut several classes, what messages might your absence transmit to the instructor? He might think you were ill, or that you were still vacationing, or that you had changed your mind and signed up for another course. In fact, maybe you had changed jobs and your new hours prevented you from going to that first class, or perhaps you had to stay home with an ill child. The instructor, though, might interpret your absence as apathy.

If you sign up for a course and attend from day one, your presence alone would transmit some of the following messages to your instructor: He would know your sex, approximate height and weight, and probably your taste in clothes or make-up. He may even know your socioeconomic background and your general health or, from the way you dress, whether you're conservative or liberal. Your facial expressions may announce that you're happy, sad, nervous, friendly, shy, frightened, or restless. Where you sit in class (front row, back row, near the door) and how you sit (straight up, slouched, feet resting on the chair in front of you) are other nonverbal signs that communicate messages to your instructor. Such messages are transmitted by your presence—even before you speak a word.

We communicate nonverbally by who we are; our appearance; the way we walk and stand; our facial expressions and eye contact; the way we move, gesture, and touch; and our **vocalics,** or paralanguage.

Our Appearance

Before we even open our mouths, we make an impression, favorable or unfavorable. The clothes we wear often communicate our status in life and our degree of self-confidence. Just from observing a person's apparel, you may have said that the person "has class" or "has no class." Author Alison Lurie, in her book *The Language of Clothes*, mentions that even before she's close enough to talk to a person, she knows that individual's sex, approximate age, and social status and has a fairly good idea of that person's occupation, ethnic origin, personality, opinions, tastes, sexual desires, and current mood.

What you wear to work can be as important as your job performance. According to a survey of over one hundred top executives of major corporations:

- 96 percent said that their employees had a better chance of getting ahead if they knew how to dress.
- 72 percent said they would stall the promotion of a person who didn't dress properly.
- 84 percent turned down people who dressed improperly for job interviews.[2]

An authority on apparel writes, "When you step into a room, even though no one in that room knows you or has seen you before, they will make ten decisions about you based solely on your appearance." He further states: "To be successful in almost any endeavor, you must be sure that these decisions about you are favorable, because in that first impression you make—*you are what you wear.*"[3]

For example, what impression would you make if you appeared before a group impeccably dressed but with messy hair and dirty fingernails? Your perfume, cosmetics, aftershave lotion, and deodorant (or lack of it) convey messages. Is your breath always fresh and your body clean? If not, it will be no secret.

Posture often reflects your attitude, pride, confidence, and general health. If your instructor observes—and she's adept at this—that you're sitting erect and looking at her, she'll probably conclude that you're alert and interested in her lecture. If, on the other hand, you're drooping in your chair, she'll conclude that you're tired, bored, or daydreaming.

A classic example of how posture can reflect your image took place in our nation's capitol. A slouched-over and shuffling secretary of defense was accompanied to a very important press conference by the ramrod-straight presence of the chairman of the Joint Chiefs of Staff. This

---

[2]John T. Molloy, *Dress for Success* (New York: Warner Books, 1975), 36.
[3]William Thourlby, *You Are What You Wear* (New York: New American Library, 1978), 1.

A dental appointment? Root canal, perhaps?

prompted another high-ranking officer to complain of the secretary, "Why can't he stand up straight?"[4]

At the next chance, notice the way people walk. You can almost tell their mission by their posture and stride: Are they fast-paced, slow-paced, skipping, ambling, hunched over, or walking tall? Is one in a hurry? Perhaps he's late for a date. Is another slouching along? Maybe she's dreading a dental appointment. Good posture projects a positive image.

Our Facial Expressions

No nonverbal code, perhaps, can be so easily misread as facial expressions because so many people control them so well. Controlling these expressions can camouflage true feelings. We are better prepared to lie with our face than with any other nonverbal cue. Perhaps you can recall a situation when you were eating something you really didn't like, but, so as not to offend the cook, you said it was "delicious," and your remark was reinforced by your feigned smile and nod. You've heard the saying, "She lied through her teeth." When you consider that facial muscles can create thousands of different expressions, this saying makes sense.

---

[4]*U.S. News & World Report,* 12 July 1993, 32.

To ensure **credibility** when speaking, we should strive to have our facial expression and verbal message coincide. Imagine the reaction if you smiled while talking about a tragedy such as the homeless or babies born with AIDS, or if you flashed an expression of indifference while congratulating someone on a happy occasion. Conversely, crying at a wedding is acceptable because, presumably, these are tears of joy.

Research tells us that facial expressions can communicate the following meanings: surprise, fear, happiness, contempt, disgust, anger, interest, determination, and sadness.[5] The following quote from Ralph Waldo Emerson is appropriate: "A man finds room in the few square inches of his face for the traits of all his ancestors, for the expression of all his history, and his wants."[6]

Our Eyes

Eye contact is necessary to establish and maintain a beam of communication between you and your listeners. If you're listening to a lecture and suddenly the speaker starts reading a long passage verbatim, the chances are that this strong line of communication has been disrupted and your attention may wander.

Eye contact also makes it possible for you to receive that all-important **feedback** from your listeners which, in turn, permits you to respond to their behavior and reactions. If you're speaking too fast or too softly, if your listeners appear perplexed or bored, or if they seem to be pleased or sympathetic to your message, you should be able to "read" these nonverbal messages by looking directly at the members of your audience. Constant eye contact greatly enhances your credibility and makes your message more personal.

Along with your facial muscles, eyes can convey approval or disapproval; they can include or exclude a person during a conversation; they transmit happiness, sadness, confusion, and even terror. Eyes tell us if someone is interested or not. Eyes can communicate at a glance. If you've ever visited a singles bar, you've probably experienced the dynamics of communication via glances, winks, and stares.

Our culture teaches us that it's impolite to stare. The next time you're on a bus or a train, single out a person and stare at him or her. See how long it takes before the situation becomes awkward. When children are being scolded, they try to avoid eye contact but are ordered to "Look at me when I talk to you."

The next time you're in an elevator, notice how little eye contact takes place because of the occupants' proximity to each other. They will

---

[5]Paul Ekman, W. V. Friesen, and P. Ellsworth, *Emotion in the Human Face* (New York: Pergamon Press, 1972), 57–65.
[6]Ralph Waldo Emerson, "Behavior," *The Conduct of Life* (1860).

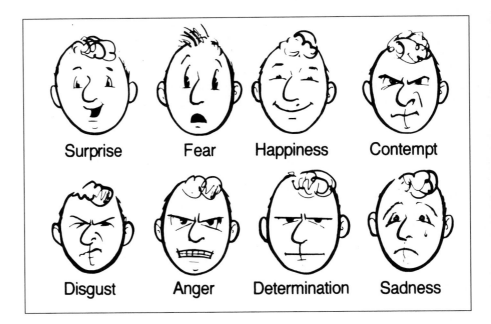

stare at the flashing floor numbers, the floor, or the ceiling, but seldom at each other unless, of course, they're seeking contact. Most people tend to increase eye contact with those from whom they seek approval or recognition. Eye contact greatly enhances your verbal message because you're looking directly at the people you wish to inform, persuade, inspire, or actuate.

Over the years, I've found that some of my foreign students—particularly many Japanese, Vietnamese, Chinese, Russian, and some Middle Eastern students—resist maintaining eye contact with their audience. Instead, they'll look at notes, the lectern, the floor, ceiling, and walls. In part, this is due to their culture: many of them have been raised to find prolonged eye contact embarrassing, or taught that it's rude or a sign of disrespect. (Yet, although they shy away from looking at and around the class, some of these students will look almost exclusively at their professor because, as many have said, "It gives me a sense of security.") While many American students also have difficulty making eye contact, this is less from cultural teachings and more often just a bad habit.

Our Body Movement

To appreciate the almost total power of nonverbal communication, watch a professional pantomimist perform—it is sheer artistry. Some of the classic characterizations in show business belong to such superstars as Jerry Lewis, the team of Penn and Teller, and the late Jackie Gleason, Lucille Ball, Charlie Chaplin, Red Skelton, and, of course, the unforgettable pauses and expressions of Jack Benny. (Fortunately, and thanks to the multitude of cable channels many of these memorable stars can still be seen and appreciated on "reruns." It would be worthwhile to seek out some of these classics.) Their artful use of apparel, movement, eye contact, gestures, and facial expressions brings laughter and tears to millions of all ages. The ways in which they move their arms, hands and fingers, head and eyes and the ways they sway, stoop, and bend are sheer genius. Even when they don't utter a word, their messages are always understood.

Kinesics is the study and application of body movement. Your kinesic behavior can significantly reinforce your verbal message. Such movement adds variety to your overall delivery, as opposed to standing rigidly in one spot.

When speaking before a group, occasionally move back...then come forward. Move your upper body slightly to the left to address the left side of your audience, then slightly (you guessed it) to the right to give equal time to those on the right. Get real bold, take a full step or two to the right and then to the left of the lectern. I suppose we could call this speech or oral choreography. Want to get more personal with your listeners? Good. You can do that simply by moving closer to them, and if you wish to make emphatic points, take a step for each point, perhaps speaking in a lower voice for emphasis. Movement can also help you relax by releasing excess energy.

Move—but don't overdo it!

In Other Words: Remember, remaining motionless while you speak is like speaking in a monotone. It's not only boring but it will surely lose your audience's interest in your message.

Our Gestures

Gestures play a large role in our daily communication and are usually most effective when performed spontaneously. There's no question that effective gestures enhance and supplement verbal messages. A hitch-hiker pointing his thumb, an umpire calling a player out at home plate, and an officer directing traffic at a busy intersection are examples of communicating explicitly without words, as is the sign language of the hearing impaired.

However, if you constantly use the same hand or arm when making a point or if your gesturing becomes mechanical, then this activity can quickly become repetitious and boring. Strive for variety and spontaneity.

When giving directions, many people find it easier to accompany spoken words with hand movements—straight, to the right or left, up or down. We've probably all been shown, by the extension of the arms, the size of "the fish that got away." A scholar of nonverbal communication has aptly stated, ". . . we respond to gestures with an extreme alertness and, one might also say, in accordance with an elaborate and secret code that is written nowhere, known by none, and understood by all."[7]

You must be especially wary when communicating with people from another culture. Don't be naive like the Florida beauty queen who was "invited to participate in a parade in Port-au-Prince. She accepted graciously—but then spent the whole time atop her float, waving innocently to the crowd, unaware that in the language of Haitian gestures she was proclaiming 'Screw you! Screw you!'"[8]

As the world gets smaller and smaller, and the number of foreign students attending colleges and universities in the United States gets larger and larger, it's crucial to try to understand how nonverbal messages are perceived by students from other cultures. For example, according to Roger Axtell, author of *Gestures: The Dos and Taboos of Body Language Around the World*, the closed thumb and forefinger "OK" sign can represent an obscenity to a German, and to a Middle Easterner it could mean you're putting a curse on someone. Russians and Brazilians also take the OK sign as an insult. To the Japanese, it represents money and to the French, it means zero, zip.

top notch job—a performance of the highest quality

In our culture the gesture of "thumbs up" means you did a *top notch job,* but to Nigerians and Australians, however, this gesture has vulgar connotations. To Germans, it means number one, and to the Japanese,

---

[7]Edward Sapir, *Human Message Systems* (New York: Harper & Row, 1976), 82.
[8]"The Language of Gestures Can Give You Away," *Elle*, May 1991, 198.

. . . in any language.

number five. Interestingly enough, shaking our heads (no) and nodding our heads (yes) means just the opposite to Bulgarians.

In his book, Roger E. Axtell tells us that Queen Elizabeth II has developed certain body motions and gestures to transmit messages to her entourage. According to Raymond Fillager, a writer and lecturer about the royal family, Her Majesty uses her purse to convey some twenty different signals to her attending staff. For example, when she shifts her handbag from her right arm to her left, it's a signal to "Come and rescue me from this situation!"

When students from other countries/cultures get up to speak, observe their nonverbal communication and don't hesitate to ask questions. You may be spared from embarrassing someone or being embarrassed.

Our Touch

Haptics is the study of communication through touch. Perhaps the most personal mode of communicating without words is **touch.** It can signal both positive (handshake) and negative (slap in the face) attitudes, depending on the individual being touched and his or her cultural patterns.

For example, one study shows that students in the United States reported being touched twice as much as did students in Japan. It is unacceptable in Japan to be touched by strangers, and, as a result, the Japanese make it a point to maintain their distance. In contrast, Middle Easterners, Latin Americans, and southern Europeans commonly engage in same-sex touching while speaking, whereas such actions are not common in Asia and northern Europe.[9]

Touching is a crucial aspect of most human relationships. It can communicate disapproval and punishment, tenderness and passion, approval and encouragement. Everybody—rich or poor, young or old, famous or unknown—is affected by touching. For instance, in his autobiography, former President Ronald Reagan recalls the moments right after he was shot in 1981 by a would-be assassin. "I was lying on the stretcher only half-conscious when I realized that someone was holding my hand It was a soft, feminine hand. I felt it touch mine and then hold on tight to it. It gave me a wonderful feeling. Even now I find it difficult to explain how reassuring, how wonderful it felt."[10]

Touching starts at birth when babies are introduced to the "outside world" and continues when parents take charge with feeding, holding, cuddling, rocking, stroking, burping, bathing, and changing. Studies show the staggering importance of touch: Orphaned babies placed in institutions have died because they were never cuddled or held.

Touching symbolizes different things to different people, depending on the specific situation, environment, time of day, and anticipated intent. Some individuals enjoy, and even crave, touching and being touched. Touching can be an expression of friendliness and affection and may signal sexual desires. Other people regard being touched as disrespectful and even offensive.

Our culture teaches us that it's improper for an individual of lower status to touch one of higher status unless encouraged to do so. For example, it may be acceptable for a professor to put an arm around a student, but not for a student to embrace a professor. A manager may touch someone from the mailroom but not vice versa.

Our culture frowns on a male hugging, embracing, or kissing another male. If you saw two women dancing or holding hands, you probably wouldn't think too much about it, but if you saw two men dancing or holding hands, you might interpret this as an act of femininity or homosexuality. However, in sports, a player who scores a winning touchdown, goal, or basket may be spontaneously hugged by his fellow players to show their joy.

Although our culture has established certain taboos regarding male-to-male touching, there are times, for example at a funeral, when no

---

[9]Joseph A. DeVito, *Human Communication* (New York: HarperCollins, 1991), 176.
[10]*An American Life, the Autobiography of Ronald Reagan* (New York: Simon and Schuster, 1990), 260.

other action could equal a warm embrace for manifesting affection, love, or sympathy.

How we touch, what part of the body we touch, and the duration of the touch are all important factors in interpreting a message. Notice people shaking hands, hugging, kissing, or pinching. Can you "read" them and their intentions? Touching, according to the messages communicated, can range from the very impersonal to the very personal.[11]

Our Vocalics

Vocalics is "how we say it" as opposed to what we say. Some elements of vocalics are voice quality, pitch, inflection, emphasis, rate of delivery, pauses, and tone of voice. For example, let's assume that your instructor had a female colleague from New England tape record the following message: "All of you are lucky to be in this speech course." After listening to this tape, the class would probably agree that the speaker had a message, it was conveyed in English, and everyone in the class understood it. But beyond this, the class would probably be able to say other things about the voice on the tape machine. They would be able to identify the voice as a white American female, probably from the Northeast because of her regional accent. They probably would agree that her voice sounded professional. Her diction was articulate and pleasant, she pronounced her words correctly, and she had no problem breathing. The class could probably tell if she were young, middle-aged, or older.

They might have received other messages as well, such as that her voice was soothing, she sounded alive and happy, and she would probably be fun to be with. Whatever it was that enabled the class to infer these messages—other than the actual spoken words—is paralanguage, or vocalics.

The quality of your voice—its pitch, rate of delivery, **inflection,** emphasis, and even **pauses**—plays an important role in helping you to effectively deliver your message. Take the simple question "Where have you been?" Say it aloud four times, but put emphasis first on the word "Where," then on the word "have," then on the word "you" and finally on the word "been."

Where have you been?

Where have you been?

Where *have* you been?

Where have *you* been?

---

[11]R. Heslin, "Steps Toward a Taxonomy of Touching," paper presented to the Midwestern Psychological Association, Chicago, May 1974.

"Where have you been?" "Where *have* you been?" "Where have *you* been?" "Where have you *been?"*

Where have you *been?*

You should have no difficulty interpreting the various messages received from the same sentence.

When preparing and practicing a speech, especially a talk designed to persuade, it is very important to go over your main points carefully to be sure that they're not only clearly identified, but also that the words are correctly emphasized. Emphasizing a wrong key word may significantly change the meaning of a sentence or even an idea, just as the tone of your voice can easily convey the direct opposite of what you intend to say.

Remember, *how* you say things can often be more important than *what* you say.

OTHER CODES

There are other **codes** or elements equally significant in nonverbal communication, such as time, space, and artifacts (objects).

Time

Chronemics is the study of communication through the use of time. Most of us are very time conscious, and time plays a vital role in the messages we convey. Many people consider time more valuable than money, and, indeed, most of our lives are influenced by a time schedule.

How important is time? To many people, time represents status and power. For example: A boss can keep a worker waiting, and can also be late for a meeting, without consequence. A doctor can keep a patient waiting. A college president can keep a dean waiting, who in turn can keep a division chairperson waiting, who can keep a department chairperson waiting, who can keep a professor waiting, who in turn can keep a student waiting. The more influential your position, the more command you have over your time and over other people's time.

Time should play an important role in the classroom. Be sure to be present on the assigned day of your talk and stay within the time limit of your talk. Always be on time for your class. Never enter the classroom while a classmate is delivering a speech, and always remain attentive to the speaker, even though class time may be running out. Don't start to collect your books or to reach for your jacket until your colleague is finished speaking. This is only common courtesy, which you should expect to receive under similar circumstances.

Being late or even last to arrive may be interpreted as a symbol of status, depending on a person's importance or popularity. I remember one time in college when my speech professor arrived late for class. As he approached the lectern, I foolishly told him he was late. Without hesitation, he slammed his books down on the lectern, glared at me, and bellowed, "As long as you're in my class, don't you ever forget this—instructors are

"I wonder if she forgot me?"

never late. Only students can be late and that I will not tolerate. Do you understand?" Did I understand? *Did* I understand? Did *I* understand? Did I *understand?* You bet I did and I'll never forget it!

It's common knowledge that, on occasion, airline flights have been delayed for the arrival of a VIP. At a candidate's fundraiser, the candidate is usually the last to arrive. At a nightclub or concert, the star is usually the last to perform. At the theater, the leading performers are most likely to be the last to respond to curtain calls.

It's now time to turn our attention to how this element is perceived in other cultures. As in America, most Germans consider being "on time" important—it is a sign of respect. Punctuality is also an accepted way of life for Indians, Chinese, Japanese, and in most countries of Northern Europe. **On the other hand,** Indonesians, Saudi Arabians, and Nigerians enjoy the philosophy that what can't be done today can be done tomorrow. This *laid-back* philosophy regarding time is also enjoyed by people in Southern Europe, Latin America, and the Middle East[12] where *closing up shop* and taking an afternoon siesta is a daily way of life. (I'm all for that.)

What's interesting to note is that while the French are very time conscious, just across the channel, the Irish enjoy spending their time much more casually . . . which is clearly articulated in their famous quote, "When God made time, He made plenty of it."

Before we run out of time, you might find the following facts interesting and possibly useful for one of your talks. The average person squanders a total of 13 years in meaningless activity. Five months of our lives are spent waiting for traffic lights to change, eight months opening junk mail, one year looking for things we've misplaced, two years trying to return phone calls, four years performing basic housework, and five years just waiting in lines.[13]

And far from being a meaningless activity, the average American spends six years eating. Personally speaking, I must confess that I probably expend considerably more time than that on such a pleasurable activity.

Remember . . . you can "use time." You can "waste time." You can "kill time." You can "save time." You can "do time." You can "sell time." But you can't "buy time."

Space

How you use **space,** while speaking, can contribute to the overall effectiveness of your talk. Remaining behind the lectern while speaking can create a barrier between you and the audience. The lectern is a symbol of

on the other hand—to mention the opposite

laid-back—very relaxed

close up shop—to temporarily close; to close for a few hours

---

[12]Donald W. Klopf. *International Encounters, The Fundamentals of Intercultural Communication* (Englewood, CO: Morton Publishing, 1991), 220.
[13]Letty Cottin Pogrebin, "It's About Time," *Family Circle,* 27 November 1990, 34.

"Excuse me, sir, can you tell us what time it is?"

authority and is impersonal in nature. If you wish to become informal and more intimate during certain parts of your talk, then escape from the lectern and move closer to your audience. The usual nonverbal response of your classmates as you approach them should be more attentiveness.

Anthropologist Edward T. Hall coined the word **proxemics** to describe the study of space as a communicative mode. "Every living thing has a physical boundary that separates it from its external environment."[14] He explains in his book, *The Silent Language,* that each of us has a personal area of space surrounding us, clearly established by an invisible boundary. This personal area, which he refers to as a "bubble," establishes distances at which we feel the most comfortable when interacting with people, and any attempt by another person to enter this area constitutes an intrusion. Notice how uneasy people become in crowded situations such as in an elevator, in a bus, or at the theater, when a stranger sits uncomfortably close. If you would like to experiment, the next time you're talking to a person, slowly inch a little closer, then a little closer—and observe that person's physical reaction.

And if you really want to have some fun, *strike up* a conversation with someone whose back is almost to the wall and start to advance

strike up—to start

---

[14]Edward T. Hall, *The Silent Language* (New York: Anchor Books, 1973), 163.

Table 3.1 **Space Distances Involved in Communication**

	Intimate Distance (0–18 inches)
Close	(0–6 inches) Touching distance, whispering, confidential
Distant	(6–18 inches) Audible whisper, comfortable
	Personal Distance (18–48 inches)
Close	(18–30 inches) Within touching distance, friendly
Distant	(30–48 inches) Beyond touching range, courteous
	Social Distance (4–12 feet)
Close	(4–7 feet) Formal range, nonpersonal or occupational
Distant	(7–12 feet) More formal, barriers can appear
	Public Distance (12 feet and beyond)
Close	(12–20 feet) Across a room, strong voice required
Distant	(beyond 20 feet) Public speaking, shouting

slowly while you're talking. Then prepare to witness an interesting situation when he or she discovers that no further retreat is possible. The chances are that the individual will slowly retreat. Hall's categories of interaction distance are listed in Table 3.1.

We take our space very seriously. We see signs declaring "No Trespassing," "Police Take Notice," "Keep Out," or "Private Property." These signs indicate private ownership, and intruders enter at their own risk. Throughout history, millions of people have been killed in wars over infringement on someone else's space. Territorial waters and air space are usually respected by all governments.

Territorial behavior is often evidenced in our daily lives. In a home, it's not unusual for each family member to sit in the same chair at every meal. When we walk down the street at night, it may bother us to sense a stranger approaching us from behind. While eating in a crowded cafeteria, some people resent a stranger asking permission to sit at the same table. How would you feel if you were waiting in line at a restaurant or theater and someone stepped in front of you?

Space may also indicate a person's status and authority. Many wealthy people live in very large homes and estates where the servants' quarters are removed from the rest of the house. At one time, a two-car garage symbolized status—now it's a three-car garage. Position and influence at work can usually be determined by the size of a person's office, its view, and the assignment of a private parking space.

And now, to take up a little more space, let's look at how some other cultures perceive space. We find that Latin Americans, Italians, and Puerto Ricans will stand noticeably closer to each other when communicating than Americans, Germans, Japanese, and Chinese. The latter

"In case you haven't noticed—you're in my space!!"

prefer more distance between them when interacting. African Americans tend to stand closer to each other than do Caucasian Americans.[15]

And, according to author-researcher Mark L. Knapp in his book *Essentials of Nonverbal Communication,* cultures in which people do interact more closely by touching each other more often, prolonging eye contact, and even speaking louder, include many Arab, Latin American, and Southern European cultures. The opposite is true with most Asians, Indians, Pakistanis, Northern Europeans and North Americans.

Our Artifacts

The **artifacts,** or objects, in our possession transmit clear messages about us that can enhance or hinder a speaker's oral performance. When General Norman Schwarzkopf, the victorious commander in chief of Operation Desert Storm in the Persian Gulf, spoke to the Corps of Cadets at West Point in May 1991, he appeared before the student body

---

[15]See note 12.

dressed in his combat field outfit, rather than his full-dress uniform, for maximum effect. And he achieved it.

A firefighter or a police officer speaking before a group of local citizens would be more credible dressed in official uniform. But how persuasive would a public official be talking to a group of senior citizens about the government's plan to reduce the budget of low-cost housing units while wearing a $600 suit and a Rolex watch and sporting a two-carat diamond ring after having arrived by chauffeured limousine?

Our clothes, furniture, paintings, cars, home, and jewelry are explicit indicators of our behavior and status. A wedding band says we're married. A ring on the right hand may say we're available. A police officer's badge shouts authority, and a uniform may announce a person's occupation.

Some people, on entering one room, feel comfortable and warm, whereas in another room they feel nervous. Is there any question that furnishings, including rugs, lamps, mirrors, and wall covering, contribute to the room's personality? People communicate more easily in comfortable surroundings than in uncomfortable ones.

A person driving a Mercedes 450 SL and one driving a dune buggy will communicate vastly different messages. And so will the individual who skippers a 45-foot yacht, as opposed to one who owns a 12-foot Boston Whaler.

Many people derive a sense of pride and self-worth from their collections. The wealthy may collect paintings, jewelry, diamonds, and gold worth a fortune. Other popular collector's items are cars, stamps, coins, dolls, trains, Waterford crystal, guns, butterflies, and fine wines. Many people enjoy their collections, but some also look on them as symbols of power, status, challenge, and accomplishment.

WE CANNOT NOT COMMUNICATE

As we mentioned earlier, certain nonverbal cues can be faked and may contain different messages from what's actually being transmitted. It is easy to misinterpret parts of nonverbal language. Remember, nonverbal cues are not absolute. We must consider them in the total context of the situation in which they are produced.

Some revealing observations on nonverbal communication are contained in a published interview with a prominent Boston trial lawyer. He talks about the extreme importance of nonverbal communication in relation to selecting a jury. What does he look for and why? He prefers women jurors "because they're more attentive and sensitive" and jurors who smile because "[a] happy jury is a good jury."[16]

---

[16]*Quincy Patriot Ledger*, Quincy, MA, 31 May 1983, 1.

Table 3.2 Attitudes Communicated Nonverbally

Defensiveness Arms crossed on chest Legs crossed Fistlike gestures Pointed index finger	**Openness** Open hands Unbuttoned coat
Evaluation Hand-to-face gestures Head tilted Stroking chin Peering over glasses Pipe smoker gestures Putting hand to bridge of nose	**Confidence** Hands in "steeple" position Hands behind back Back stiffened Hands in coat pockets Hands on coat lapels
Suspicion Arms crossed Sideways glance Touching, rubbing nose/eyes Buttoning coat Drawing away	**Nervousness** Clearing throat Whew sound Whistling Fidgeting in chair Hand covering mouth while speaking Not looking at other person Jingling money in pockets Tugging at ear Perspiration Wringing hands
Insecurity Pinching flesh Chewing pen, pencil Rubbing thumb over fingers Biting fingernails Hands in pockets	
Cooperation Upper body in sprinter's position Open hands Sitting on edge of chair Hand-to-face gestures Tilted head Unbuttoned coat	**Frustration** Short breaths Tsk sound Tightly clenched hands Wringing hands Fistlike gestures Pointing index finger Rubbing hand through hair Rubbing back of neck

Gerard Nierenburg and Henry Calero, *How to Read a Person Like a Book* (New York: Pocket Books, 1973).

During jury selection, he observes how people walk to the jury box and how they are dressed. Is the walk positive and aggressive or slow and passive? Is the head held high or at half-mast? Are the shoulders slumped or is the posture erect? The attorney is looking for nonverbal clues to the potential juror's attitude and outlook on life. Knowing if a person is the nervous or calm type can be quite significant. From the individual's apparel and personal grooming, he may try to judge occupation, origin, living habits, and economic and social status.

This trial lawyer knows more than just the law. He is keenly observant and proficient in understanding and interpreting people's nonverbal messages. They can be crucial not only in dictating how the lawyer will present his case to the jurors, but also in trying to anticipate how the jurors will react and make decisions.

Most of us tend to express certain behavioral attitudes with various nonverbal actions. Table 3.2 lists some common ways that we communicate such attitudes nonverbally.

THINGS TO DISCUSS IN CLASS

1. Listen to a voice on the radio and jot down as much information as possible based on the speaker's vocalics. Discuss your findings in class.

2. While traveling to or from work or class, pay attention to the nonverbal messages around you. Then make a list of the messages you perceive. Discuss them in class.

3. The next time you're talking with a friend, slowly move closer and closer. Tell the class your friend's reaction.

4. Select someone in your neighborhood with whom you've never spoken. Tell the class as much as you can about that individual based on that person's nonverbal codes.

5. Explain to the class what nonverbal messages you think you transmit to others. The class may wish to respond with interpretations of your messages.

6. Discuss the verbal and nonverbal cues that your instructor employs in teaching this class.

7. If your class has access to a video camera and videocassette recorder (VCR), you may wish to record some of the following exercises as a learning experience in nonverbal communication. Play back the videotape to see how many members of the class received the nonverbal messages that you feel you actually transmitted. The exercises should not run more than a few minutes.

   a. Through facial expressions and with your eyes, try to convey different moods, for example, anger, fear, happiness, sadness, and surprise.

   b. Pretend that you're at a marketplace in a foreign country. The vendor, who doesn't understand English, shows you something. You admire it and try it on but feel it's too expensive. You want it. Nonverbally, communicate this to the vendor and bargain for a lower price.

   c. Again, you're in a foreign country where a language barrier exists. You're at a restaurant, and, when the waiter arrives, you attempt to order a full-course breakfast nonverbally.

   d. You're in a pet shop. Without words, convey to the class where you are and what you see. You look at various pets and then pick up the one you intend to purchase.

e. In silent language, demonstrate a line of work performed by a member of your family. First, you must identify the individual and then that person's occupation.

f. Using body language only, describe a vacation spot you would like to visit and the mode of transportation to get there.

g. Visually describe your favorite hobby.

h. If you have a full- or part-time job, describe it without saying a word.

i. Communicate, nonverbally, your major and your short- and long-term educational goals.

WHAT DO YOU REMEMBER FROM THIS CHAPTER?

1. Define nonverbal communication and give several examples.
2. Explain the statement. "We cannot NOT communicate."
3. What can posture tell us about a person?
4. List five gestures that convey explicit meanings.
5. Explain vocalics and give five examples.
6. Give an example of time being interpreted as a symbol of status.
7. What is proxemics?
8. List the four categories of interaction distance.
9. What is kinesics and its relevance to nonverbal communication?
10. List five phrases or sayings that demonstrate the importance of nonverbal communication.
11. Which nonverbal code can easily be misread? Explain.
12. List five types of messages that a person's eyes and facial expression can transmit.
13. List three synonyms for nonverbal communication.
14. Explain chronemics and haptics.
15. How is punctuality observed by the German and Japanese cultures as opposed to the Saudi Arabian and Irish cultures?
16. When the Irish proudly declare that, "When God made time, He made plenty of it," what does this convey?

VITALIZE YOUR VOCABULARY

A solid knowledge of synonyms (words that have the same basic meaning but may differ in tone and appropriateness) will impart vigor and variety to your speech. An excellent and proven source of synonyms and antonyms (words that mean the opposite) is *Roget's Thesaurus* of Words and Phrases. It does not, however, explain differences in meaning; for those shades of meaning you should consult a modern, authoritative dictionary.

Consider the basic meanings of the adjectives "slim" and "slender;" synonyms are "trim" and "svelte." These four adjectives are complimentary. On the other hand, synonyms like "bony," "gaunt," and "skinny" are anything but complimentary and may even be insulting. The word "thin" falls somewhere between the first four adjectives and the last three. This example proves the vital importance of understanding different shades of meanings.

Each group of words in Table 3.3 is a set of synonyms; however, each group in Column 2 represents antonyms for those in Column 1.

Table 3.3 Synonyms and Antonyms

Column 1	**Column 2**
	Antonyms of Words in Column 1
big, huge, large, immense, vast, kingsize, enormous, tremendous, colossal, mammoth, jumbo, gigantic, gargantuan, ample, abundant	small, little, tiny, petite, peewee, puny, miniature, diminutive, pocket-sized, minute, microscopic
brave, courageous, fearless, bold, valiant, heroic, game, valorous, gallant, lion-hearted, spunky, plucky, dauntless, gutsy, audacious, adventurous, nervy, intrepid	afraid, cowardly, fearful, timid, yellow, faint-hearted, lily-livered, weak-kneed, chicken-hearted, dastardly, pusillanimous
pleased, delighted, charmed, elated, intrigued, gratified, tickled pink, satisfied, sold on, carried away	complain, gripe, bitch, grouse, whine, beef, weep, bellyache, wail, crab, squawk, lament, mutter, fuss, moan and groan, grumble
genuine, authentic, valid, real, true, actual, bona fide, legitimate	fake, phony, artificial, counterfeit, mock, spurious, adulterated, make-believe, bogus, substitute, ersatz, pseudo-
pliable, flexible, tractable, yielding, bending, receptive, malleable, pliant, responsive, relenting	stubborn, obstinate, inflexible, rigid, immovable, bull-headed, adamant, unbending, unyielding, uncompromising, intransigent, resolute
slim, slender, lean, slight, frail, delicate, spare, underweight, gaunt, bony, skinny, scrawny	fat, stout, corpulent, obese, fleshy, beefy, plump, paunchy, full, rotund, tubby, roly-poly, pudgy, chubby, heavy-set, portly, well-fed, thick-bodied, rich, swollen

Roget's International Thesaurus, 3rd edition (Harper & Row, 1977).

4

YOU CAN OVERHEAR, BUT YOU CAN'T OVERLISTEN

Nobody has ever listened himself out of a job.

Calvin Coolidge, thirtieth president of the
United States, 1923–1929

After reading and understanding this chapter, you should know:

- **The difference between hearing and listening.**

- **The importance of listening well.**

- **Some major reasons why we listen.**

- **Some ways to become a more efficient listener.**

- **The different types of listening.**

- **The vital correlation between vocabulary development and efficient listening.**

The act of listening comprises a significant portion of our daily activities. It is the other half of the communication process since, without listeners, we cannot communicate orally. Yet, few of us pay attention to improving our ability to listen.

Hearing is a passive biological function, whereas listening is, or should be, an active intellectual function that involves your mind, eyes, ears, and memory. As a listener, you influence speakers by your reactions. If you show interest through your facial expression or body language, you will see speakers perk up. If you show boredom or confusion through inattention or lack of eye contact, you will see that speakers tend to change their approach to avoid risking failure.

We listen for several reasons: to become informed, to understand, to evaluate, and to enjoy. Any intellectual activity that can affect your life to such an extent deserves to be done well. Suggestions for sharpening your listening skills are offered, but they will benefit you only if you make a commitment to improve yourself.

Appearing in this (and every) chapter is the feature "In Other Words," which will greatly benefit foreign and ESL students. To aid in their understanding of common American idioms and phrases, these expressions will be defined in the margin of the page on which they are introduced.

When you were a child, how often did your parents criticize you for not **listening**? As a parent, how frequently do you direct your children to listen? At one time or another all of us are guilty of not really listening to what's being said. Our inattention can lead to embarrassment, to argument, and, at times, to even more serious consequences.

All too often in interpersonal communication (between two or more people), we absorb only what we want to, at home, school, or play. Many times we choose not to pay attention to certain people because they are boring or *long-winded.* We have that arbitrary ability to *"tune out"* certain people, and let's face it, sometimes it can be beneficial. Nevertheless, it's safe to say that the rewards of effective listening are greater than those of "tuning out."

In Other Words:

long-winded— speaks too long

*tune out—*ignore

COMMUNICATION ACTIVITIES

A study conducted by researchers at a leading university found that adults spend about 70 percent of their waking hours engaged in communication activities. It concluded that the average adult devotes 9 percent of this time to writing, 16 percent to reading, 30 percent to speaking, and 45 percent to listening.[1]

Moreover, studies declare that after a ten-minute oral presentation, the average listener (and a large percentage of students rank below average!) hears, receives, comprehends, and retains only about 50 percent of the message. After forty-eight hours most listeners remember only about 25 percent of what they heard.[2]

College students spend almost 90 percent of their school time listening. And here's something interesting: Research indicates that students who listen effectively earn better grades and achieve beyond what their intelligence levels might have predicted.[3] Another study found that we listen half again as much as we speak; we speak almost twice as much as we read; and we read almost twice as much as we write.

We wake up in the morning to the sounds of an alarm clock, a radio, or someone's voice. We may have conversation at breakfast, at work, at school, on public conveyances, or in a car pool. We might attend a business meeting, a lecture, or a luncheon. We might hear someone speak in person or on the radio, TV, or telephone. We might attend a concert, a movie, or a social or civic function. Think of all the times in one day, for example, that we listen. How much of that listening experience will we be able to recall? Are we actually *listening* and *understanding*, or are we just *hearing* things? There's a world of difference.

---

[1]James J. Floyd, *Listening: A Practical Approach* (Glenview, IL: Scott, Foresman, 1985), 2.
[2]Lyman K. Steil, Larry L. Barker, and Kittie W. Watson, *Effective Listening* (Reading, MA: Addison-Wesley, 1983), 88.
[3]Walter Pauk, *How to Study in College* (Boston: Houghton Mifflin, 1989), 121–33.

That arbitrary ability to "tune out" certain people

Despite these statistics, listening, the communication activity we engage in most of our waking hours (a third of our lives), is the one that our educational system ignores the most. In most colleges today, courses in basic writing are mandatory for all freshmen. Because of increasing alarm over our low national reading scores, reading courses are offered and, at some colleges, they're required. Courses in public speaking and oral communication are offered on most college campuses and, in some instances, taking at least one is a requirement for a degree. But how many institutions require a student to take a course in listening?

In your precollege education, your school's curricula probably emphasized writing skills over reading, reading over speaking, and speaking over listening. Perhaps because we spend so much time listening, we feel that we can do it efficiently. What a false conclusion this is!

The fact is that the business and educational communities complain that workers and students don't know how to listen. In the business world, where listening could mean making or losing money, employees spend about 60 percent of their workday listening, and executives spend approximately 57 percent of their business day listening.[4] One of the first

---

[4]Andrew D. Wolvin and Carolyn Gwynn Coakley, "A Survey of the Status of Listening Training in Some Fortune 500 Corporations." *Communication Education* 40, April 1991, 153.

companies to address this problem was a Fortune 500 international corporation, which took two steps.[5]

- It set up special listening programs worldwide for all its employees who want to attend.
- It invested hundreds of thousands of dollars in a two-page color advertising campaign in several national magazines, which ran for months. The theme was "We understand how important it is to listen."

The importance of this activity is effectively expressed in the following excerpt from their ad:

> The fact is, listening, like marriage, is a partnership, a shared responsibility between the person speaking and the person listening. And if the listener doesn't show genuine interest and sensitivity to what's being said, the speaker will stop talking. And the communication will fail.[6]

This program was a resounding success, as the company witnessed an increase in productivity and a decrease in employee accidents. Is it any wonder that many other corporations both gargantuan and small now offer similar "more-effective listening" training programs for their employees?

LISTENING AS AN INTELLECTUAL ACTIVITY

You can listen more effectively and improve your comprehension markedly if you work at it. Listening is just as important to interpersonal communication as is speaking; in fact, "listening is the other half of talking. If people stop listening, it is useless to talk—a point not always appreciated by talkers . . . ."[7]

While hearing is a biological activity, listening is an intellectual one because it requires more than just ears. In fact, it has been said that you hear with your ears, but you listen with your brain. Effective listening is a holistic activity that should include the following active efforts of your mind, eyes, ears, and memory:

- *Your mind.* You should summon your logical reasoning capacity to grasp the intended meaning of the speaker's message. Understand the differences between fact (something that is documented and known to be true), opinion (a personal view, not necessarily factual), and inference (drawing your own conclusions from or about something you

[5]Sperry Corporation, *Newsweek*, 20 October 1980, 89.
[6]Ibid.
[7]Stuart Chase, "Are You Listening?" *Reader's Digest*, December 1962.

Listening is an intellectual activity.

have heard, read, or seen). We'll discuss logical reasoning in more detail in Chapter 11.

- *Your eyes.* You should observe the speaker's posture, gestures, facial expressions, mannerisms, and movements. All these combine to communicate vital messages.

- *Your ears.* Listen carefully to the speaker's voice. Is it pleasant, harsh, reassuring, authoritative, or weak? How about inflection, rate of speaking, pauses, loudness, and animation? Are they in "sync" with the message? In other words, is the speaker's nonverbal message enhanced or contradicted by the oral one?

- *Your memory.* Try to recall as much as you can about the topic at hand. Are you hearing new or contradictory information? Did the speaker omit anything? If so, what and why? By recalling as much as possible about the speaker's message, you should have a solid basis on which to compare or contrast the message with your own knowledge of the subject.

As a listener, you can help the speaker by communicating through your facial and body actions. When you're looking at the speaker, show interest: lean forward occasionally and appear to *catch every word;* even *jot down* a few notes or a question you may wish to bring up later. These

catch every word—to listen attentively and understand

jot down—write, make note of

positive responses tell the speaker that the message is *getting across* to you. If you slouch in your chair, whisper to your neighbor, read a book, or look just plain bored, the speaker will be well aware that he or she has problems.

getting across—
being understood

REASONS FOR LISTENING

Following are some of the major reasons why we listen:

- to enjoy
- to become informed
- to understand
- to express sympathy
- to evaluate

To Enjoy

Listening for enjoyment is light listening, for example, engaging in a pleasant conversation, listening to music, or watching a movie or TV show for relaxation. This type of listening should not involve any strain but should be casual and relaxed. The change of pace should be enjoyable and pleasant.

To Become Informed

In the second type of listening, you seek new information. You listen to the radio for the weather report or school-closing announcement, you attend a class lecture or a business, social, or civic meeting. You establish in your mind the motive for listening, and then you direct complete interest in, attention to, and concentration on the speaker. If your instructor announces that there'll be a quiz following a short lecture, you're motivated to listen. "Know how to listen and you can learn even from those who speak badly," said Plutarch, Greek essayist and biographer, about 2000 years ago.

To Understand

How often have you formed opinions of speakers and subjects before they have even begun or finished talking?

Many people find listening to understand most difficult because it requires restraint, fair-mindedness, and objective thinking. As a consequence, many of the world's problems have resulted from selfishness, disregard of other people's opinions, and failure to attempt honestly to understand another's viewpoint. Listening to understand doesn't mean that you must agree or disagree but that you must approach the subject with an unbiased, open mind. You must also listen totally to the message, striving to understand what is being expressed and why. Allow yourself to grasp the entire message before you react.

Owen D. Young, lawyer and corporation executive, put it quite nicely when he said, "The man who could put himself in place of the other man, who can understand the workings of other minds, need never worry about what the future has in store for him."

To Express Sympathy

"sympathetic ear"—willing to listen to someone else's problems

"sound off"—to strongly express your views

breaking loose—strongly express yourself

attentive ear—someone who'll listen

If you're that rare person with a *"sympathetic ear,"* then probably every day you listen to someone *"sound off"*—a relative, friend, classmate, co-worker, stranger, or perhaps even your boss. To share or just listen to someone's pent-up feelings *breaking loose* can have a therapeutic effect on the talker and will distinguish you as a person who cares. This type of listening can be personally rewarding because practically everyone, sooner or later, needs an *attentive ear.* For example:

- Your good friend feels that his boss is exploiting his abilities while skimping on salary.
- A classmate is distraught because all sections of a course she wanted were closed.
- A family member didn't get the promotion he felt he deserved.
- On the way to work someone slammed into your boss's brand new car and she wants to vent her emotions.
- Your neighbor just found out that his three children need dental braces.

To Evaluate

Of all of the types of listening, evaluative listening is the most difficult and the most important because it requires the most effort. There are a number of questions to bear in mind when listening to evaluate:

- What is the main purpose of the talk?
- Is the talk informative, entertaining, persuasive, or inspirational? Is it meant to activate?
- Is the speaker making logical and valid points?
- Are the arguments convincing? Are they based on fact or on opinion?
- Is the speaker an authority on the subject or does he or she just *have an axe to grind?*

have an axe to grind—have something to complain about

- To what needs of the audience is the speaker appealing?
- Can you clearly understand the speaker's message?
- Do the nonverbal elements of the talk coincide or conflict with the verbal message?

These are only some of the countless questions you should consider when listening to evaluate. You now have some idea of the complexity and depth of **evaluative listening.**

last word—absolute truth

Do you usually take statements uttered by well-known people as the *last word,* or do you make an effort to seek out the other side before formulating an opinion? If you're in a position to disagree with or question

Everyone needs a sympathetic ear.

people, do you? Remember that you may disagree without being disagreeable. Whether the issues are international, national, local, business, educational, political, or social—evaluative listening is especially crucial.

A catastrophic breakdown in evaluative listening occurred not too long ago at the airport in the Canary Islands, near Spain. The pilot of a KLM jumbo jet either didn't hear or heard incorrectly the order to "stand by for takeoff." At the very same moment, the pilot of a Boeing 747 also didn't get the message. He taxied beyond the runway exit, placing his aircraft in the path of the KLM jet taking off without permission. Poor listening by both pilots caused the most tragic disaster in the history of aviation—581 people killed.

A similar catastrophe occurred in 1996 over Charkhi Dadri, India. New Delhi air controllers told a Kazakh cargo plane that it was flying straight at a Saudi Boeing 747 passenger jet. The pilot's acknowledgment was the last word the air controllers heard from either aircraft before they collided—death toll: 349 people. Transcripts indicated that the pilots were misled by their instruments or misunderstood the tower's directions.

It pays to listen to someone who *knows the score*—and then to evaluate correctly. As Oliver Wendell Holmes once proclaimed, "It is the province of knowledge to speak and it is the privilege of wisdom to listen."

knows the score—knows what he or she is talking about

How to Be a Better Listener

Diogenes, a Greek philosopher who lived 2300 years ago, demonstrated wisdom when he said, "We have two ears and only one tongue in order that we may hear more and speak less."

To be a better listener you must first *want* to be one. You must realize the many benefits of improved listening, and you must be prepared to exert the required effort. When you come to class, you know that you'll hear people talk, so prepare to listen. Develop a positive attitude toward the speakers. Tell yourself that you'll hear some exhilarating topics and that, in all probability, you'll learn something new. Motivation can spell the difference between just hearing something and listening and understanding it.

If you're planning to attend a lecture or to listen to a speech outside class, you can get ready for it by learning what you can about the speaker. Who is she? What's her background? Is she an authority on the subject? What's her motive for speaking? What could you anticipate getting from the lecture? By increasing your interest in the speaker and her subject before the event, you can't help but listen more effectively. (This would be a good time to review some of the responsibilities of an ethical listener in Chapter 1.)

The following are some suggestions for honing your ability to listen:

- Develop your vocabulary.
- Concentrate on the message.
- Keep an open and objective mind.
- "Read" the speaker.
- Put yourself in the speaker's place.
- Take notes.
- Compensate for a speaker's flawed delivery.
- Get ready for the wrap-up.

Develop Your Vocabulary

Once you commit yourself to improving your listening efficiency, the best step you can take is to expand your vocabulary. Vocabulary development is so vital to effective listening that we have included a "Vitalize Your Vocabulary" section in fifteen of the chapters in this book.

Fully understanding the meanings and inferences of words is crucial to your total comprehension of a speaker's intended message. Being able to put the speaker's language and message in proper perspective is a significant first step in developing your listening efficiency.

Concentrate on the Message

Interpersonal communication should be on a constant beam from the speaker to the listener and back to the speaker. Don't interrupt this beam by daydreaming or succumbing to other kinds of distractions. Try not to think about last night, this morning, or tonight. If your thoughts begin to wander, take charge and direct them back to the speaker and his or her message. If the speaker is boring, challenge yourself to make the effort.

Another obstacle to total concentration is the fact that we think much faster than we speak. A comfortable speaking rate lies between 130 and 160 words per minute. The brain, however, can deal with approximately 500 words per minute. So you can see that, while we're listening, we have quite a bit of spare time. We must guard against becoming distracted during this spare time.

From the moment the speaker approaches the stand, rivet your eyes on him. Remember that eye contact is as important to the speaker as it is to the listener. Look interested and you will be interested. Watch his facial expressions and gestures while he's speaking. You can receive many clues to his meanings by observing his mannerisms. As discussed in Chapter 3, gestures can be eloquent.

Beware of distractions. Little things can *throw you off:* books dropping, people talking and coughing, fire sirens wailing. The speaker himself can be distracting. His outfit may be as loud as the fire siren, his gestures may be uncontrolled, or he may be constantly swaying. If these or any other distractions occur, then you must intensify your concentration on the message because nothing inspires a speaker more than an interested audience.

throw you off— distract you

If the speaker is a student who's not completely at ease with the English language, you may want to double your concentration to ensure you understand the message—especially if the as-yet not-so-confident student chooses, for the most part, to read her or his speech verbatim.

Keep an Open and Objective Mind

Don't have the attitude "I know what she's going to say and she's *all wet.*" Preconceived opinions limit your ability to benefit from a true communicative experience. Be objective. *Hear the speaker out.* Then, if you disagree, ask her to clarify certain points. Give the speaker every courtesy that you would want if you were speaking.

*all wet—*mistaken

*hear the speaker out—*listen before forming an opinion

Keeping an *open mind* is one of the more difficult techniques to master for effective listening because many people may be opinionated and make hasty judgments. They establish personal views even before the speaker opens her mouth. As mentioned in Chapter 3, a person's grooming, posture, walk, and eye contact, or lack of it, can nonverbally transmit positive or negative messages.

*open mind—*not prejudiced; giving it a fair chance

"Read" the Speaker

If the speaker gives his speech a title, grasp it. Closely follow the introduction and main points. In the introduction he should state what will be covered. Take note of the subject and anticipate the main points. How do they relate to the other points mentioned? Is he accomplishing what he set out to do? What about the soundness of his ideas? Are they valid? Are they logical? Does he have supporting material, and how does he use it? These are some thoughts to consider while you're listening.

Put Yourself in the Speaker's Place

You may be better able to understand and absorb a talk if you try to put yourself in the speaker's place (empathic listening). This means you must strive to feel, think, act, and react like the speaker. What motivated her to select this topic? What is her educational and professional background? What are her qualifications to speak on this subject? What action or reaction is she seeking from the audience and why?

place yourself in the speaker's shoes—put yourself in the speaker's situation; see it from his or her standpoint

If you can successfully *place yourself in the speaker's shoes*, not only will you understand her message better, but you will take a giant step toward becoming a more effective and responsive listener.

Take Notes

jot down—write down

Taking notes can enhance your listening ability because it engages you in two activities—listening and writing. The secret to taking notes is to *jot down* only the main points. Whatever format of note taking works for you is the one you should use—complete sentences, phrases, or key words. Writing down key points as you hear them helps you grasp and remember them. As we mentioned in Chapter 1, taking notes is one way to provide the speaker with that all important feedback.

to come up with—to produce

To enhance your note-taking proficiency, I recommend and encourage students to record the lecture on a small tape recorder. Then, at your first opportunity play the tape back and along with your written notes, you'll be able *to come up with* a more comprehensive documentation of the lecture for future review. How does that sound?

Compensate for a Speaker's Flawed Delivery

Not all speakers have read this book (what a shame!), thereby denying themselves some of our practical principles that might help alleviate bad delivery habits. Poor speech habits can detract from the message the speaker is trying to convey. He may talk in a monotone or pause often with *uh's*, *er's*, and *you know's*. Playing with notecards, eyeglasses, or a watch may discourage the audience from listening efficiently.

In this case, what you must do—and it isn't easy—is to separate the speaker from the speech. Just remember, many speakers have significant things to say but, unfortunately, erect obstacles that impede listeners. If you can discipline yourself to ignore the speaker's deficiencies, you may be rewarded with some valuable viewpoints and insights.

Get Ready for the *Wrap-Up*

wrap up—the conclusion

Be ready for the conclusion of the talk. It will be the speaker's final chance to imprint her message in the minds of the listeners. At this time, she may repeat some important points that you may have missed during the talk. Listen for them and ask yourself the following crucial questions: Did I get the message? Do I agree, or do certain points need clarification? What were the strongest and weakest arguments?

Since some students—especially those whose first language is not English—may hesitate to ask questions, I would like to emphasize its importance for two reasons. First, asking questions will enable you to better understand the subject, and second, it will give you valuable experience in speaking. And if you're a beginner in our language, the more you speak it, the sooner you will master it. Remember, we are all friends and we all want each other to succeed in this course.

So, for all concerned, never be too embarrassed to ask questions. There is no more important process in education than asking questions.

THINGS TO DISCUSS IN CLASS

1. Describe a job environment, school environment, or social environment that you consider ideal for listening.

2. Do you agree that attentive listeners help a speaker communicate better? Explain.

3. What distractions hamper your listening in this class? What can you do about them?

4. What have you observed to be the most common listening deficiencies? Prepare to discuss them.

5. Honestly evaluate your own listening habits. Can you improve them? How?

6. After another student has given a short talk, prepare a brief summary of the main ideas presented. You may do this on your own, or your instructor may call on members of the class at random for a response.

7. Find a very quiet spot at home and for several minutes relax, close your eyes, and try to listen to every sound. Attempt to identify the sounds, their sources, and the directions from which they come.

WHAT DO YOU REMEMBER FROM THIS CHAPTER?

1. Approximately what percentage of your waking hours is involved in listening?

2. How can a listener aid a speaker?

3. Name some types of listening.
4. List some hints for better listening.
5. What is the difference between hearing and listening?
6. How can vocabulary enhance your listening efficiency?
7. How can taking notes enhance your listening efficiency?
8. Give two reasons why it's beneficial to ask questions.
9. Name three speaker flaws that could detract from his or her message.
10. Explain "Getting Ready for the Wrap-up."

VITALIZE YOUR VOCABULARY

Words from Japan

With the globalization of the world's economy and culture, many words from foreign countries have entered our language. In recent decades, as Japan has emerged as a world power and a leader in technological expertise and industrial productivity, many Japanese words have become part of American English.

Here is a sprinkling of Japanese words that you should know, together with their symbols:

banzai 万歳
Literally meaning a million, "banzai" is a carryover from the Chinese language, where it means something like "long live the king." Now, it means "three cheers" or "hip-hip hooray." It is said when celebrating something (usually three times in succession) and is accompanied by raising both arms.

bonsai 盆
A type of miniature tree.

futon 布団
A mattress placed on the floor.

geisha 芸者
A female entertainer who serves at a private party.

geta 下駄
Wooden sandals.

harakiri 腹切
Suicide by disembowelment.

hibachi 火鉢
A charcoal grill.

honcho 班長
Boss; literally, squad leader.

judo 柔道
Japanese art of self defense. The fundamental principle of judo is to utilize the opponent's strength to one's own advantage.

kamikaze 神風
A suicide pilot. A divine wind, specifically the typhoon that wrecked the Mongol invasion of Japan in the thirteenth century.

karate 唐手
The Loochoo (Ryukyu) art of self-defense, of hitting or jabbing opponents with one's fist or kicking them. It was introduced from China and gradually became a unique art of combat that uses no weapons.

kimono 着物
A traditional Japanese robe.

nisei 二世
Americans of Japanese descent.

rickshaw 力車
A man-pulled cart.

sake 酒
Wine made from rice.

sayonara さよなら
Good-bye.

sushi 寿司
Uncooked fish.

teriyaki 照り焼き
A type of marinade.

tsunami 津波
A tidal wave.

yen 円
Monetary currency.

MAKE IT CLEAR, CONCISE, CORRECT . . . & COHESIVE

5

First learn the meaning of what you say, and then speak.

Epictetus, *Discourses* (2nd c.), 3.23,
tr. Thomas W. Higgingson

After reading and understanding this chapter, you should know:

- **The skills that contribute greatly to effective delivery.**

- **Ways to sharpen these skills.**

- **The differences between articulation and pronunciation.**

- **The importance of listening to yourself when you speak.**

- **Ways to be more expressive in your speech.**

- **The three major accents, or "dialects."**

- **The importance of pauses.**

- **The importance of pacing.**

CHAPTER PREVIEW

This chapter zeroes in on various aspects of delivering a talk: voice, pronunciation, articulation, rate of speaking pauses, and expression. Emphasis is placed on voice and pronunciation.

Your voice influences your speech and also your daily interpersonal communication. A pleasant, expressive voice is an asset in school, on the job, and in your social life. Such a voice is capable of inflection, the ability to go up and down comfortably in order to express different feelings, emotions, and ideas.

Almost all voices can be improved. Listening to your own voice on a tape recorder may spur you to act to improve it. Some practical suggestions on pitch, volume, and proper breathing are offered.

Your pronunciation and articulation immediately mark you as either an educated or an uneducated person. Sloppy speech and rigid lips result in omitted sounds, slurred syllables and the addition of incorrect sounds. Ideas are presented to upgrade pronunciation and articulation to the standards recommended by authoritative dictionaries.

Other topics discussed in the chapter are the rate of speaking, the use of pauses, and the importance of expressing inner feelings and emotions.

Appearing in this (and every) chapter is the feature "In Other Words," which will greatly benefit foreign and ESL students. To aid in their understanding of common American idioms and phrases, these expressions will be defined in the margin of the page on which they are introduced.

Every spring, college campuses throughout the nation are visited by representatives from industry and government to recruit potential employees. Recruiters at several large state universities were asked to explain why they had rejected certain students. In almost 70 percent of the cases, the primary reason was that the rejected students did not "talk effectively during the interview."

My speech consulting practice affords me a rewarding opportunity to train men and women both in groups and individually, at all levels (from entry to top executive) in both the public and private sectors. Over the years, I have asked many executives, who have authority to approve an employee's promotion to a supervisory level, what qualities they considered paramount in making their final decision. The overwhelming response was the ability to communicate orally in clear and understandable language.

In Other Words:

CLEAR AND UNDERSTANDABLE LANGUAGE

How many times have you called a company, spoken to a salesperson, heard a lecture at school, or talked to someone on the telephone only to recoil in shock over the gibberish which left you exclaiming, "I don't believe this!" You've found it almost impossible to understand the individual. Perhaps the person mumbled, ran words together, didn't articulate, talked in a monotone, took a breath midword or midphrase, or spoke too quickly or too slowly. It's amazing the number of people who communicate daily with the public and don't realize their speech shortcomings or who fail to improve their oral communication skills, especially many elected officials.

Through months and years of study, discipline, practice, trial and error, perseverance, and even failure, people can develop their speaking abilities. You should understand that Luciano Pavarotti was not *born* a great singer, Gabriela Sabatini was not *born* a great tennis player, Albert Einstein was not *born* a great physicist, and Katharine Hepburn was not *born* a great actress.

The art of speaking to communicate knowledge, ideas, and feelings is no exception. All the theoretical knowledge of public speaking will not make you outstanding in the art, and it will not improve your ability, unless you're willing to commit yourself totally. It will take work, perhaps even a *bit of needling* from your family and friends, but if you have the will and motivation to sharpen your speaking effectiveness, nothing can deter you and it will be immensely worthwhile.

bit of needling— small amount of kidding

In my childhood, I wanted to become a radio announcer. I practiced reading, pronunciation, **enunciation,** interpretation, projection, and—the most difficult challenge of all—eliminating my Boston accent. I practiced in the bathroom, in the cellar, even in my brother's car. I took my share of ribbing, but even today I enjoy these reminiscences every time I appear before a microphone or TV camera. And you, too, can be success-ful . . . if you want to. It will, however, take determination and persever-ance. As Ted Engstrom said, "The rewards for those who persevere far ex-ceed the pain that must precede the victory." Rereading this quote several times will increase its meaning. If you want to do something, make up your mind to do it; then go at it *with gusto.*

with gusto—with enthusiasm

Certain elements contribute to effective and lively delivery: your voice, breathing, pronunciation, articulation, rate of speaking, pauses, pacing, expression, and oral visualization.

YOUR VOICE

There is no more versatile instrument in the world than your voice. Yet, as with any instrument, its effectiveness depends solely on the way you use it.

Listen to Yourself

The immediate reaction of most people when they hear their voices played back on a tape recorder is usually shocked disbelief. You may re-call such statements as "That sounds horrible," "Good God, that's not *me!*" or "You mean I sound like *that*?" In almost all instances, the sad fact is that you *do* sound like that. If you're serious about speech devel-opment, you should use a good tape recorder to hear yourself as others hear you. It is an invaluable aid.

Speech skill doesn't remain on a plateau; either it improves or it re-gresses. You must always work to improve it because that's the only way to banish poor speaking habits. Your tape recorder will "tell." The sound of your voice may play as great a role in getting your message across as do the words themselves.

The most effective way to improve your speech habits is to hear what you're doing wrong as you speak. This will not be easy. When you've reached the stage of recognizing your speech faults, then you'll be able to correct yourself. Listen very seriously whenever your speech pro-fessor offers suggestions on how to improve your speech.

Listening to yourself occasionally on a tape recorder is excellent—but you must discipline yourself to listen critically to every word and sound. Now let's briefly discuss some important characteristics of voice quality and delivery.

Here Comes the Pitch

Every voice has a **pitch.** Pitch refers to the highness or lowness of your tone, or sound. A person whose pitch is too high, too low, or monotonous (continuously on the same level) not only may transmit a negative im-pression but may risk losing listeners completely.

"I sound like that???"

The Pitch Is Too High   Your voice may sometimes be pitched too high because of nervousness (remember your first talk?), fright, or over-anxiousness to respond. If you suffer no physical problems that affect your voice, the more often you speak, the more relaxed your throat muscles will become, resulting in more pleasant vocal sounds. A good exercise to lower a high pitch is to read aloud solemn passages very slowly.

The Pitch Is Too Low   You may know some people who speak with a very low, bass sound. Usually they speak slowly. Reading aloud happy, lively material—children's stories, for example—at a fast pace is a good exercise that may help to raise a low pitch slightly.

The Voice Is Monotonous   The person who speaks in a **monotone** is like *Johnny-one-note* on the piano. After a short while, the sound is boring, dull, and lifeless. The voice lacks inflection, that is, the raising and lowering of pitch.

Johnny-one-note—playing only one note

To avoid or eliminate a monotone, you must find your normal range. This is the vocal area that is most comfortable for you to carry on a normal conversation and from which you may easily raise or lower your pitch. One way to find your normal range is to match your vocal tones with the tones of a piano. Most women can usually start around middle C on the keyboard, and men an octave lower (if you're not familiar with the keyboard, ask someone who is). Your normal pitch range should be the notes in the scale that feel comfortable for you as you sound them, and from which you may comfortably go up and down. An acceptable range for a normal, healthy voice is about one octave, for example, C to C, or thirteen half-notes inclusive. (If you lack access to a piano, see your instructor about assisting you with this exercise, using a piano at your college.)

Once you establish your normal pitch range, use it. Listen to how it sounds and feels so that speaking in your full range becomes as natural as breathing. The up-and-down inflection of your pitch adds variety and vividness to your delivery. A good example of someone who speaks in a monotone is a hypnotist, someone who places a person under hypnosis (puts an individual into a deep sleep or a trance). If you have a monotonic delivery, you'll probably render the same effect on your listeners.

CAUTION
Your voice box is such a delicate, complex mechanism that abuse of it can lead to irreparable damage. Never force yourself to lower or raise your pitch drastically. Be sure to consult with your instructor before attempting to change your pitch.

The Rate of Speech Is Monotonous   A person who speaks each syllable, word, phrase, and sentence at the same rate of speed suffers from what speech authorities call **monorate.** The delivery, just like the monotonous voice, is boring, dull, and lifeless. It lacks variety and vividness. In other words, this type of delivery lacks pacing; this is discussed later in this chapter.

Volume

Some people have naturally loud or soft voices. If you speak too loudly or too softly, your audience will communicate this message to you nonverbally. For example, when you start to speak, do your listeners all move back in their chairs as if blown there by a gust of wind? Or do they move up to the edge of their seats, turning their ears in your direction?

The size of the room and the audience should determine your **vocal volume.** If you have a soft voice, start by asking the audience, "Can you hear me in back?" Speaking too loudly or too softly is not only annoying, it leads to a breakdown in speaker–listener communication.

Besides speaking too loudly or too softly, a speaker must be aware of a third aspect of volume—variety. When your loudness or softness does not vary, your voice becomes boring.

BREATHING

Proper breathing is vital to speech communication because the outgoing breath provides the power for producing sound. Perhaps you know people who take several breaths in midphrase or midsentence. You feel that any minute they will require a tank of oxygen.

Learn to breathe deeply; practice filling your lungs with as much air as possible as quickly as possible. This healthful exercise will enable you to communicate a message-idea without interruption. Take a deep breath—mainly through your mouth—read something aloud, and stop when you have to breathe. Time yourself to see how long you can read.

Lung capacity varies widely among people. Some professional singers can hold a note comfortably from 20 to 30 seconds, and some seasoned speakers can complete a marathon sentence in one breath. The ability to speak from 15 to 20 seconds on a single breath is attainable through deep breathing and should allow you to surmount any difficulty in finishing a sentence without gasping for air. As an added benefit, breathing deeply helps dispel nervousness by feeding your body with more oxygen.

PRONUNCIATION

Nothing stands out more negatively in a speaker than mispronunciation. (If you have a question about the correct pronunciation of any word, consult a dictionary.) Pronunciation, **articulation,** rate of speaking, vocal volume, and proper breathing all contribute to the effectiveness of your communication. Defects in any of these areas can, unfortunately, impair your communication style.

Your environment—family, friends, city or section of the country where you live—has a tremendous influence on your pronunciation and speech habits. Regional accents, or "dialects," abound in our country. The three major accents are:

- General American—spoken by the largest segment of our population—includes the Midwest, the West, and parts of the Southwest. This dialect is most often heard on radio and TV and in movies.
- Northeast—includes the New England and Middle Atlantic states.
- Southern—includes the areas south of the Mason-Dixon line.

Each of these three major accents, or American dialects, has a beauty and style all its own, and none is superior to the others. They are all acceptable and totally correct. Even within these geographical areas, local and regional dialects exist. Bostonians can easily be identified because they tend to overlook the letter *r* in the middle or at the end of words. For example, they say, "Pahk yah cah in the Hahvahd yahd." They also

"You can pahk ova theya—just gimme the kah keez."

tend to sound an *r* when one doesn't appear, as in *Cuber* for *Cuba*, *Americer* for *America*, *delter* for *delta*, and *tuner* for *tuna*.

Here's an example of how a Boston accent caused not only bewilderment, but embarrassment, as well. A very good friend of mine, a senior executive of a large global computer company, was addressing about six hundred employees at his plant in Germany. During his speech he observed that each time he mentioned the Saturn missile, a sea of blank looks stared at him from the audience. Himself puzzled from the strange feedback, he was greatly relieved when he finally concluded his presentation. His German host wasted no time bombarding him with many questions to learn more of the innovative and obviously revolutionary development of this so called "satin or cloth missile." It was only then that my American friend realized that by not pronouncing the *r* sound in the word *Saturn*, *it came out* satin.

it came out—it sounded like

An accepted standard dictionary can be a great aid in improving your pronunciation. Even though recognized dictionaries are accepted throughout the country, some of their recommended pronunciations are ignored in certain locales. Generally, it is wise to use the pronunciation typical of the region you're in, even though it may not be "correct," rather than to allow yourself to sound eccentric. Be flexible enough to bend a little to avoid embarrassment.

Another way to improve your pronunciation is to pay close attention to professional speakers and actors and then try to emulate them. A tape recorder will verify your progress. Learning to sound words correctly and clearly will require time and effort, but once you achieve this goal it will pay you lifelong dividends at work and socially.

ARTICULATION, OR DICTION

Articulation, diction, and **enunciation** have the same basic meaning. They refer to clarity, intelligibility, and distinctness of your speech—in other words, the way you produce **vowel** and **consonant** sounds: all the parts of words and nothing else.

Incorrect articulation usually results in leaving off parts of words, adding parts to words, or slurring words together. It is possible, then, to articulate clearly a mispronounced word. Misarticulation is quite different from mispronunciation. Pronunciation pertains to standards of acceptability either of a particular region or of a dictionary; articulation concerns only the distinctness or clarity of the words.

It's important to articulate sounds clearly. Voice each syllable carefully so that the entire word sounds crisp and understandable. **Sloppy speech** results from not taking the time to pronounce all the sounds in a word and from running words together. For example:

Whatimas zit?	for	What time is it?
What'sitdoin outside?	for	What's it doing outside?
How'ya doin?	for	How are you doing?
Ahdunno.	for	I don't know.
Whaja say ya name is?	for	What did you say your name is?
Howzitgowen?	for	How is it going?
Whatchadowen?	for	What are you doing?
Whujasay?	for	What did you say?
Whutsamatta?	for	What's the matter?

Here are some examples of slurred words:

kinda	for	kind of
becausa	for	because of
sorta	for	sort of
wanna	for	want to
needa	for	need to
hafta	for	have to
mindta	for	mind to
shoulda	for	should have
woulda	for	would have
coulda	for	could have
shouldna	for	should not have

Not opening the mouth enough is a major cause of poor diction, especially among neophyte speakers. Because the mouth is not opened sufficiently to allow all the sounds to evolve into clearly spoken words, the sounds seem to be struggling somewhere down in the throat. A beneficial exercise is to repeat vowel sounds aloud slowly, holding the sound of each vowel a full breath (AAAAAAAAAA—EEEEEEEEEE—IIIIIIIIII—and so on). Practice until you produce a full, forceful sound and can feel the

"Jweetjet?" "No . . . Dijoo?"

muscles in your lips and mouth working. Don't hesitate to overexagger-
ate your lip and mouth movements. Do this every time you speak until
the feeling becomes *second nature.*

second nature—
natural

Nothing in our spoken language is more beautiful than fully stressed
vowel sounds. When you sound them within a word, voice them a little
longer. This is called an increase in **duration,** or length, of the sound.
Notice the different durations of the *aw* sounds in the words "draw"
"fog," and "sock." An increase in duration of vowel sounds adds color
(variety and vividness) to your speech delivery.

Notice how professional singers, actors, and speakers treat these
sounds within words of a song or speech—it's sheer artistry. Listen closely
to the delivery of such public figures as Jay Leno, Barbara Mandrell, Paul
Simon, Bonnie Raitt, James Earl Jones, and Candice Bergen.

Although we have five vowels in English, there are more than five
vowel *sounds.* For example, note the different sounds produced by the
letter *a* in the following words: aggravate, fat, hall, and bah; or the letter
e in: be, been, sex, feet, and term; or in the letter *i* in: bin, high, kill, field,
and evil; or the letter *o* in: hot, go, out, order, and oil; or the letter *u* in:
cup, union, pure, fur, and guitar. **Prolongation** of these sounds adds interest and color to speech.

You can learn to produce more colorful vowel sounds, which can
lead you to a more captivating delivery. However, it will take commitment, time, and effort. Practice the following vowel sounds aloud and
listen to them carefully:

A (ay)	betrayed	be-traayed
	delayed	de-laayed
	conveyed	convaayed
E (ee)	received	re-ceeved
	believe	be-leeve
	reprieve	re-preeve
I (eye)	divide	di-viide
	revise	re-viise
	coincide	coin-ciide
O (oh)	behold	be-hoold
	resold	re-soold
	foretold	fore-toold
U (you)	preview	pre-vyuu
	review	re-vyuu
	through	thruu

Another cogent reason to stress vowel sounds is that they impart carrying power to your voice. Relax your neck, throat, mouth, and lips; breathe deeply; open your mouth wide; and let these sounds roll out full and strong. As a result, your listeners will hear and understand you better, and appreciate you more.

The following are common pronunciation and articulation problems to be aware of:

Not Pronouncing All Vowels and Consonants

Bar*br*a	for	Bar<u>ba</u>ra
bat*tr*y	for	bat<u>te</u>ry
boun*dr*y	for	boun<u>da</u>ry
can*i*date	for	can<u>di</u>date
cho*cl*it	for	cho<u>co</u>late
di*m*ond	for	d<u>ia</u>mond
fe*bu*ary	for	Fe<u>bru</u>ary
go*v*ament	for	gove<u>rn</u>ment
gran*it*	for	grant<u>ed</u>
jew*ler*y	for	jew<u>elry</u>
li*br*y, Li*bar*y	for	li<u>bra</u>ry
la*br*atory	for	la<u>bo</u>ratory
p*lee*ce	for	<u>po</u>lice
r*a*member	for	<u>re</u>member

Running the Last Consonant of a Word into the First Vowel of the Next Word

your rown	for	your/own
her rauto	for	her/auto
your rinterview	for	your/interview
as zif	for	as/if
for rus	for	for/us
this sevening	for	this/evening

Near Reast	for	Near/East
the yumpire	for	the/umpire
her rage	for	her/age
his sage	for	his/age
her rapple	for	her/apple
his zonner	for	his/honor

Producing Incorrect Sounds of Letters

axe	for	ask
dem	for	them
dis	for	this
exscape	for	escape
git	for	get
jist or jest	for	just
nucular	for	nuclear
pitchah	for	picture
wid	for	with
winduh	for	window
yestiday	for	yesterday
tuday	for	today
tunight	for	tonight
tumorrah	for	tomorrow

Eliminating Word Endings, Especially -ing in Verbs

walkin	for	walking
talkin	for	talking
coughin	for	coughing
slep	for	slept
crep	for	crept
fine	for	find
ben	for	bent
sen	for	send
reveren	for	reverend
fence	for	fenced

Adding or Reversing Vowels and Consonants

athaletic	for	athletic
athalete	for	athlete
alumnium	for	aluminum
acrost	for	across
calvery	for	cavalry
evuning	for	evening
interduction	for	introduction
laundary	for	laundry
mischievious	for	mischievous
often	for	often (silent t)
perduce	for	produce

per*vent*	for	prevent
wun*st*	for	on*ce*
skoo*wull*	for	sch*ool*
skejoo*wull*	for	sche*dule*

It's important, however, not to go completely *overboard* and o-v-e-r-e-n-u-n-c-i-a-t-e, which will result in stilted and phony-sounding speech.

overboard—to the extreme

RATE OF SPEAKING

For most people, a comfortable **rate of speaking** lies between 130 and 160 words per minute. Speaking too fast can cause poor diction—running words together, slurring words, and dropping word endings—which could result in listeners' complaining, "What did he say?" A machine-gun delivery can easily lose your listeners.

On the other hand, talking too slowly may irritate your listeners even more than talking too fast. When speakers take what seems like five minutes to draaaaag out a phrase or sentence, they are setting up their listeners to yawn or lose interest. A sluggish speaker can easily convey an impression of shyness and lack of confidence or interest.

From this moment on, you should be conscious of your delivery rate. Listen to yourself on a tape recorder.

PAUSES

Some reasons for pausing are to provide emphasis and variety in your delivery, *pull your thoughts together,* allow time for your audience to absorb an important point, and make transitions before stressing a major point or introducing new material.

pull your thoughts together—gather your ideas

Pausing is an art that every professional performer strives to master in order to achieve maximum effectiveness. Listen closely to how performers such as Tony Randall and Barbra Streisand pause in dialogues and songs. Notice how comic pros like Steve Wright, Joan Rivers, Arsenio Hall, and the late Jack Benny (on TV reruns) use pauses to get laughs. Certainly a master of this art is radio and television news commentator Paul Harvey.

Although pauses are the punctuation marks of speech, you must be careful not to pause excessively, which can lead to a staccato delivery. This can be abrasive to the ear and can *short-circuit* communication. With practice, determination, and the right number of pauses sprinkled at the right times, you can give your delivery more variety, excitement, and interest.

short-circuit—to interrupt

On the other hand, far too many speakers can't endure a moment of silence. Either from nervousness, habit, or both, they fill pauses with

Pausing is an art.

sounds or words such as *like, er, ah, um, OK, right, you know,* and *or something.* Very often they're not even aware that they're making these sounds called **vocalized pauses.**

If you tend to sputter during pauses, don't despair. Become conscious of it, concentrate on conquering it, and try to keep your mouth closed during pauses. Here again, perseverance pays off.

PACING

If you were on a long drive and kept your speed at exactly 55 miles per hour, chances are you would soon become bored and later, perhaps, drowsy. Wise drivers thus slow down, speed up for a while, then return to average speed. These drivers repeat this tactic until they reach their destinations.

World-class runners practice the same basic procedure. They may start out with a burst of speed, slow down a bit, pick up speed, continue at a *comfortable clip,* and then, when approaching the final stretch, exert a surge of energy and speed to propel them to victory.

comfortable clip—a comfortable pace

Both drivers and runners perform a very important function of delivery—they pace themselves. It would be wrong to say that you should never talk quickly or slowly. It's only when you do either of these constantly that you sabotage communication.

To use **pacing** effectively means to speak at an interesting rate of delivery, with enough variety to hold your listeners' interest. To describe an exciting event, you would speed up your delivery. When quoting statistics or emphasizing several points, you would slow your pace. Speaking at a constant rate, either fast or slow, can only lead to monotony and the loss of your audience's attention.

EXPRESSION

When you speak, you communicate through facial expressions and body actions as well as by the words you choose and how you say them. Do your words convey exactly what you intend them to? Are you saying them with conviction and feeling, or are you just mouthing them? There is a difference between a person who bids you "good morning" with a warm smile and one who mutters it like a robot.

After you've prepared a speech, go over it carefully, noting the important points you wish to make. Review the title, opening remarks, main body, supporting statements, and transitional phrases. What points do you want to *drive home* in the conclusion? What is your appeal and to whom?

drive home— make clearly understood

Understand what you want to say and practice saying it. Pause to attract attention, show your fingers to enumerate steps, raise an eyebrow to ask a question, frown to show disbelief, or lean toward the audience to make a personal point or to let it in on a secret. Don't hesitate to repeat a point several times if necessary.

What you are doing is making your talk come alive, and this effort will entice your audience to be more interested and motivated by your message. *Strive to convey emotions and feelings in your words and delivery.*

ORAL VISUALIZATION

A highly effective way to express yourself with animation is to recall first as many experiences as possible. Then select what you need for your talk and visualize it when you're communicating.

When was the last time you were frightened, lonely, depressed, or disappointed? Have you ever been hungry, cold, in pain, or grief-stricken? Can you remember experiencing moments of extreme joy, happiness, or pleasure? Do you remember any of your failures and successes? Hopefully, the latter outnumber the former.

Think about these and other experiences you may have had, if they relate to the topic about which you're planning to speak, until you're practically able to relive them.

If you're trying to convey some of these emotions and experiences, recall them again and again and try to visualize them as you communicate with your audience. Look at your listeners and, as you speak, feel and live your words.

By mastering **oral visualization,** you'll not only communicate deeper meaning to your audience, but you'll also generate "electricity" from your message to your listeners, who will reflect it back to you through their expressions. You will have completed the full cycle of successful interpersonal communication. "Eloquence lies as much in the tone of voice, in the eyes, and in the speaker's manner, as in his choice of words."[1]

THINGS TO DISCUSS IN CLASS

As previously mentioned, no instrument is more useful in voice development than the tape recorder. Most speech classes have access to one—so use it, whenever possible, to record some of the following exercises. There's no better learning experience for personal and instructor evaluation than listening to your own voice.

1. Record about a minute of your voice on tape. The material may be preselected or impromptu. The purpose of this exercise is for you to hear your voice and delivery as others do. As you listen to the playback, be alert to your pitch, inflection, pronunciation, rate of speaking, breathing, and expression.

2. When you breathe, you should inhale as much air as possible to avoid taking a breath in the middle of a word, phrase, or sentence. Try reading each of the following sentences on a single breath:
   a. The future belongs to those who are willing to prepare for it.
   b. They say money isn't everything, but you must admit it sure beats poverty.
   c. Breathing is a basic biological process that continues as long as life is maintained.
   d. More people could enjoy much happier lives, if they could only learn to be more assertive.
   e. "Nature has herself appointed that nothing great is to be accomplished quickly and has ordained that difficulty should precede every work of excellence."—Quintilian

3. Here are some words that are often mispronounced and misarticulated; usually one sound is substituted for another. Use a dictionary, if neces-

---

[1]La Rochefoucauld, *Maxims* (1665).

sary, to write the correct pronunciation beside each word before you record your voice.

anesthetist _____

chasm _____

chiropodist _____

diary _____

et cetera _____

handkerchief _____

hearth _____

indict _____

jewelry _____

masochist _____

nuclear _____

picture _____

pronunciation _____

robot _____

4. Here are some words that are often mispronounced and misarticulated; usually one or more sounds are omitted. Follow the same instructions as in exercise 3.

accessory _____

arctic _____

asphyxiate _____

casualty _____

correct _____

environment _____

February _____

figure _____

length _____

picture _____

probably _____

recognize_____

regular _____

twenty_____

5. Here are some words that are often mispronounced and misarticulated; usually one or more sounds are added to the word. Follow the same instructions as in exercise 3.

accompanist _____

across_____

chimney _____

disastrous_____

escape _____

film _____

laundry_____

athlete _____

athletics _____

monstrous _____

often _____

positively _____

statistics _____

6. Here are some words that are often mispronounced and misarticulated; usually the accent is placed on the wrong syllable. Follow the same instructions as in exercise 3.

admirable _____

amicable _____

autopsy _____

barbarous _____

comparable _____

guitar _____

impotence _____

incomparable _____

irreparable _____

magnanimous _____

mischievous _____

police _____

preferable _____

theater _____

7. Here are some words that are often mispronounced and misarticulated; usually two or more sounds are reversed. Follow the same instructions as in exercise 3.

asterisk _____

cavalry _____

hundred _____

introduction _____

irrelevant _____

perspiration _____

prescription _____

prevent _____

professor _____

solemnity _____

voluminous _____

For further practice in pronunciation, especially for students whose primary language is not English, see the list of commonly mispronounced words in Appendix D.

8. As you read the following sentences aloud, prolong the vowel sounds to produce full, rich tones.

    a. The most beautiful sounds in our language are produced when we open our mouths and prolong the vowel sounds within words.

    b. Be nice to people on your way up the ladder, because you'll meet the same people on the way down.

    c. The friendly, round-faced native traded corn and coffee for a large amount of cinnamon-flavored honey.

    d. Noreene maintained that Gregory Wayne should not be blamed for the injury, which became inflamed.

    e. Running into debt isn't so bad; it's running into your creditors that could produce problems.

    f. Round and round went the wheel and when it came to a stop, it landed on my lucky number—13.

    g. The orange was large, perfectly round, seedless, firm, deliciously juicy, and sweet.

9. Read the following sentences aloud with feeling and expression. Try to visualize the words and thought-ideas as you read.

    a. The battalion of tall, determined waves slowly, but steadily, approached the unsuspecting, jagged shore like military columns. When they arrived, their fury was unleashed as they exploded against the rocks and ledges.

    b. The raindrops happily tiptoed across the barn's metal roof almost in unison. Then, as if playing a game, they decided to slide off onto the soft, soggy ground.

    c. "We shall fight on the beaches. We shall fight on the landing grounds. We shall fight in the fields and in the streets. We shall fight in the hills. We shall never surrender."—Winston Churchill

    d. "If a free society cannot help the many who are poor, it cannot save the few who are rich."—John F. Kennedy

    e. He rose, shivering, chilled, infected, bending beneath this dying man, whom he was dragging on, all dripping with slime. He walked with desperation, without raising his head, almost without breathing.

10. You may find the following two readings interesting because they contain all of the sounds of the English language.

> It is usually rather easy to reach the Virginia Theatre. Board car number 56 somewhere along Churchill Street and ride to the highway. Transfer there to the Mississippi bus. When you arrive at Judge Avenue, begin walking toward the business zone. You will pass a gift shop displaying little children's playthings that often look so clever you will wish yourself young again: such things as books and toys and, behind the counter, a playroom with an elegant red rug and smooth, shining mirrors. Beyond this shop are the National Bank and the Globe Garage. Turn south at the next corner; the theater is to your left.

> We have all heard the saying: "Laugh and the world laughs with you. Weep and you weep alone." Laughing is the sensation of feeling

good all over, and showing it mostly in one spot. Nothing shows a man's character more than what he laughs at. To laugh means to love mischief, but with a good conscience. Man is the only animal who laughs and weeps, for he is the only animal who is struck with the difference between what things are and what they might have been. If animals suddenly got the gift of laughter, they would begin by laughing themselves sick about man, that most ridiculous, most absurd, most foolish of all animals. Life is not any use at all unless we find a laugh here and there.

WHAT DO YOU REMEMBER FROM THIS CHAPTER?

1. Name three elements that contribute to effective delivery.
2. How can you find your normal pitch range?
3. What is a good exercise that will help eliminate a monotonous delivery?
4. Why is proper breathing important to oral communication?
5. Explain the following terms: "oral visualization," "pacing," "duration," and "articulation."
6. Comment on the statement "She was a born singer."
7. Is it a good idea to listen to yourself when you speak? If so, why?
8. Name the three major accents found in the United States.
9. When speaking before an audience, how can you tell if you're speaking too loudly or too softly?

VITALIZE YOUR VOCABULARY

Words of Spanish Origin

Because of the continued growth of the Spanish population and influence within our culture, many Spanish words or words of Spanish origin have been introduced to our vocabulary.

Here are some with which you may already be familiar:

adios (interj.) Goodbye
adobe (n.) Sun-dried bricks made of clay and straw and used to construct homes.
aficionado (n.) A great enthusiast or fan
barrio (n.) A section of a city or town mainly inhabited by Spanish-speaking population
bonanza (n.) Sudden prosperity
canyon (n.) A deep valley with very high sides
corral (n.) A fenced enclosure to restrict animals

embargo (n.) A government order prohibiting certain ships from entering or departing certain ports

desperado (n.) A notorious bandit

fiesta (n.) A festival or celebration

guerrilla (n.) A member of a small band of soldiers engaged in warfare

hacienda (n.) A large estate

junta (n.) A small group ruling a country or territory

hoosegow (n.) A jail

hurricane (n.) A violent storm with very high winds

lasso or **lariat** (n.) A long rope with a noose at one end to capture a horse or other animal

mantilla (n.) Lace or silk head covering

mosquito (n.) Those nasty little insects

patio (n.) A paved area beside a house used for outdoor entertaining

piñata (n.) A papier-mâché figure filled with candy or toys that children break open on special occasions

plaza (n.) A very large public place or open square

ranch (n.) A large area maintained to raise livestock or a single crop

renegade (n.) An outlaw or deserter

rodeo (n.) A public display of cowboy skills

siesta (n.) An afternoon nap (a favorite of your author)

sombrero (n.) A tall-crowned wide-brimmed hat made of either straw or felt

vigilante (n.) A person who takes the law into his or her own hands

KNOW YOUR LISTENERS AND SPEAK THEIR LANGUAGE

You will be successful only to the extent that you cast your thought in accordance with the make-up of your forum.

Cicero, *Paradoxa Stoicorum* (46 B.C.)

After reading and understanding this chapter, you should know:

- **The importance of audience analysis.**

- **Some ways to research your audience.**

- **Some differences between oral and written communication.**

- **The difference between concrete and abstract words.**

- **Some examples of loaded words, clichés, slang, and vocalized pauses.**

- **How to use words that motivate people.**

CHAPTER PREVIEW

The words and sentences that flesh out your thoughts, feelings, and opinions critically influence your total impact on your audience. For that reason, audience analysis should rate top priority in preparing for any talk. Several ideas are given to help you with that analysis.

Your career can be helped or hindered by the way you use words in speech. Some examples of the power of words are sprinkled throughout the chapter. Many different kinds of words are discussed—specific and abstract words, short and pretentious words, loaded words, clichés, and slang.

Next, oral communication and written communication are compared. They share traits, such as clarity, accuracy, and appropriateness, but you should always be aware of differences between the two methods of communication.

As for sentences, some suggestions are advanced regarding their length, structure and human warmth. Again, real-life examples spice up the text.

The chapter closes with several steps for developing your use of language to its full potential, including how to avoid sexist language.

Appearing in this (and every) chapter is the feature "In Other Words," which will greatly benefit foreign and ESL students. To aid in their understanding of common American idioms and phrases, these expressions will be defined in the margin of the page on which they are introduced.

AUDIENCE ANALYSIS

Before you speak to any audience, you should learn as much about its members as possible. Only in that way can you best adapt the level of your language and the content of your talk to your listeners.

Where are you likely to speak? Certainly, in this class you'll give several talks, and since you know most, if not all, of the students, you should face no major problems in adapting your approach to them. Another speaking possibility exists in your workplace. For example, your department manager may ask you to explain and demonstrate a procedure to some fellow employees. Or you may be chosen to address your department on behalf of the local blood donor drive. In both speech situations—in class and on the job—you're familiar with your audience; you speak their language; you have things in common with them.

A third speaking possibility exists in any organization (social, cultural, athletic, and so on) that you belong to. You may be asked to speak at the next meeting or at the annual banquet. Here again, you know the people involved, their backgrounds, their education level, and their attitudes, and that's a tremendous advantage for you.

Since we're upbeat and positive in this course, we'll assume that you've given successful talks under all three circumstances, and with this course under your belt, you can do it again, only better. Since good speakers are hard to find and word about them travels fast, suppose that one day you get an invitation to speak to an organization in which you don't know a soul. What do you do now? If you feel able to *handle the topic* you're asked to speak on, accept this rare challenge. Here's where **audience analysis** *comes into play.* Be sure to ask the person who invited you for information about the members, information that encompasses a broad spectrum, such as in the following areas.

handle the topic—know enough of

comes into play—becomes important

Age

Are the audience members recent college graduates, golden agers, or business executives in mid-career? Just remember, age exerts a powerful impact on people's attitudes, values, and motivations. Yes, they all speak English, but with differences based on occupation, education, and so on. Yes, they're Americans, but with different needs and interests. For example, back in the 1930s your grandparents, as young people, may have been ecstatic over President Franklin D. Roosevelt and his New Deal; as senior citizens in the 1990s, they may have switched to republicanism. Back in the 1930s they probably romanced to music of the big bands, but chances are that you prefer another type of music. Age does make a difference.

A look around your classroom may instantly reveal classmates representing a wide range of ages—from high school graduates to golden age citizens (the new term for senior citizens). Studies show that the average

Know your audience and speak their language.

college student is getting older. Each member of your audience comes from an era or generation representing different cultures, values, and acceptable behavior, whether they're from Generation-X, the twenty-some-things, baby boomers, post–baby boomers, or the golden agers. If your audience is comprised of mixed groups (different ages), then it's all the more essential to consider not only what you select to *talk* about but how you decide to *say* it.

Different ages can reflect attitudinal differences. Let's go back to mid-1998 and the biggest sex scandal in the history of the United States. The scandal took place within the White House and involved a sitting president, Bill Clinton; a young female intern, later an employee at the White House, Monica Lewinsky; and Federal Independent Prosecutor Kenneth Starr. Starr served the president a subpoena to give sworn testimony before a grand jury investigating whether he had sex with Miss Lewinsky. Despite months of appearances before a Washington grand jury by White House aides, friends and associates, and others who may have personal information concerning this scandal and the growing talk of possible impeachment, the president's popularity ratings remained surprisingly high. Why?

Monday, August 17, 1998, saw another unprecedented event take place in the White House. For the first time in American history a sitting president testified, under oath, via closed circuit television, before a federal grand jury eight blocks away.

Later that same evening, in a relatively short address (a little more than four minutes) to the nation, he admitted, "Indeed, I did have a relationship with Ms. Lewinsky that was not appropriate. It constituted a

"I'll tell you my average age if you'll tell me yours."

critical lapse in judgment and a personal failure on my part for which I am solely and completely responsible."

President Clinton also told Americans that, "I know that my public comments and my silence about this matter gave a false impression. I misled people, including even my wife. I deeply regret that." (The entire speech can be found in Appendix A.)

Even though throughout his address he failed to mention that he had lied or that he was sorry, and offered no apology to anyone, immediately following his speech his popularity ratings rose even higher. Why?

I think that you'll find the answers rather interesting. How about a little research project? (You may want to take a peek at the next chapter dealing with research.) During your research, you may want to be on the lookout for such information as: What was the average age of the poll participants? How many national polls were taken? How did the men respond as opposed to the women? Were the respondents married or single? How many were disinterested in the scandal regardless of the president's innocence or guilt? How many felt he was guilty but should suffer no further punishment other than his public humiliation? Did the current state of the national economy play any role in the polls? How many thought the whole incident too embarrassing to the country or simply too trivial to warrant further attention? Your research should prove not only interesting but eye opening. Look particularly carefully at how various age groups responded. Your effort could make for an interesting speech.

On October 8, 1998, the U.S. House of Representatives overwhelmingly voted to authorize its Judiciary Committee to "investigate fully and completely whether sufficient grounds exist for the House of Representatives to exercise its constitutional power to impeach William Jefferson Clinton, president of the United States of America." And, on December, 19, 1998, the U.S. House of Representatives voted in favor of two of four articles of impeachment against President Clinton. The first alleging that he committed perjury in his August, 17, 1998 grand jury testimony and the second that he obstructed justice. Bill Clinton became only the second president—and the first in 130 years—to face a legal trial in the U.S. Senate, which began January 11, 1999. On Friday, February 12,1999, The U.S. Senate voted to aquit President Clinton on the articles of impeachment permitting the President to complete his second term of office.

Sex

If you're invited to speak to a women's or men's organization, you know the answer to this question at once. Quite often, however, audiences are mixed fairly evenly, although at times one sex may predominate. Let's say that you're to speak to a group of women.

In today's world, as opposed to 20 or 30 years ago, women do just about everything that men do. They occupy high positions in business, government, education, and politics. They attend the same colleges, including the service academies, and they participate in just about all sports. Yet, there are differences between men and women that you, as speaker, should make allowances for in your preparation. You would not, for example, use the same anecdotes at a meeting of Women in Management as you would with a contingent of professional football players. The use of nonsexist language is discussed later in this chapter.

Interest in Topic

Are the members of the organization interested in the topic or are they required to attend, regardless of their interest? If the latter is true, what types of material will most likely pique their curiosity?

Attitude Toward Topic

Do they have prejudices that will interfere with their listening or understanding? Are they sympathetic? If so, you should prepare material that will capitalize on that positive attitude.

Knowledge of Topic

The level of understanding possessed by the audience will largely determine the intellectual level of your talk. If the listeners know little, you should start with basics. If they know the basics, you should try to carry them at least a few steps beyond their current status.

Education

As you prepare your talk, keep three depressing facts in mind:

- The average adult in America has but slightly more than a high school education.
- The national illiteracy rate is higher than ever.
- A recent study released by the U.S. Department of Education finds that almost half, or nearly 90 million, American adults lack the literacy to cope with modern life.[1] *(How does that grab you?)* Would you like more alarming statistics? One-third of high school seniors couldn't identify Abraham Lincoln or the countries the United States fought during World War II. Only 6 percent could correctly answer the following math question: "Christine borrows $850.00 for one year and pays a simple interest rate of 12 percent. What will be the total amount of money she repays?" A major insurance company reports that 44 percent of its applicants couldn't read at the ninth-grade level. Some 80 percent of a major manufacturer's applicants flunked its fifth-grade math and seventh-grade English tests.[2]

How does that grab you?—What do you think of that?

Generally, a talk on tax shelter investments to assembly-line auto workers should be geared at a different level than the same talk given to computer analysts. Both groups probably know little about such investments, but the computer analysts are, on average, more educated and used to dealing with complex or technical information on a daily basis.

Cultural Interests

Do members of your prospective audience spend evenings watching TV movies and drinking beer at a local tavern, or do they read the Harvard Classics and attend concerts of Beethoven and Mozart? Do they play bingo and 21, or do they pursue the intriguing intricacies of contract bridge and chess? Answers to questions such as these can help you choose the most appropriate material and language for your audience. Your choices can be crucial in determining the success or failure of your presentation.

---

[1] *Time,* 20 September 1993, 75.
[2] Walter E. Williams," Let's Fire Education Experts." *Boston Herald,* 12 May 1997, 19.

Occupation

If, for instance, many members of your audience work in a particular field, say electronics, you'd be wise to include some references to that specialty. More often, however, audiences tend to represent a variety of occupations, and that fact *rings a warning bell to you* to make allowance for many differences among people. White-collar workers often differ in attitude and interests from blue-collar workers. Business employees and business owners have different values on many issues. Civil servants may well react differently from military personnel. A line of reasoning may succeed with one occupational group and fail with another. All these differences represent a challenge to you.

rings a warning bell to you— alerts you

Economic Status

People's feelings and attitudes toward government policies, political parties, labor unions, and current happenings are deeply colored by their economic status. Individuals with high incomes are usually interested in stock market activities and tax legislation. People with low income, on the other hand, are more concerned about having enough to live on and a roof over their heads. You would approach people at these two economic levels in different ways.

Religious Affiliation

If you're not familiar with the religious beliefs held by members of the audience, you may say something that could offend some of them. Do most of them belong to the same religion? Don't forget that Protestants, Catholics, Jews, Mormons, and Muslims are likely to have different attitudes toward such issues as divorce, abortion, and the Middle East.

Race and Ethnicity

There are many racial and ethnic groups in the United States, the largest ones being: blacks, about 11 percent of the population; Latinos (which include Cubans, Mexicans, and Puerto Ricans), about 9 percent; Asian Americans, about 2.9 percent; and Native Americans, .8 percent.[3] As an indication of the rapidly changing demographics, it's estimated that by the year 2005, Latinos will surpass blacks as the nation's largest minority group.[4] In addition, many ethnic groups define themselves through their common ancestry, for example, Italian or Irish Americans.

---

[3]U.S. Bureau of the Census.
[4]*U.S. News & World Report,* 20 October 1997, 64.

If you're invited to speak to audience members from a particular ethnic group, you should try to get acquainted with its history, values, motivations, and achievements. You should also inquire about their command of English. If they've been in the United States only a few years, you should use simple English and avoid slang and idioms (regional expressions). Your audience will appreciate your efforts and you will be more understandable.

As we suggested at the outset of this discussion on audience analysis, you should be able to get most of the needed information from the person who invited you, from officers of the organization concerned, or from people who have spoken to the group in the past. What would really *be "cool"* is to get yourself invited to one of the group's meetings to observe *firsthand* your future audience.

be "cool"—be good or be great

firsthand—personally, or in person

LANGUAGE AND YOUR FUTURE

You can have a powerful delivery, an expressive voice, an attractive appearance, and thorough knowledge of your subject, but if your words are poorly chosen, your speech will fail to communicate.

With the right words, you can communicate your thoughts, your feelings, and your emotions. With the right words, you can teach people, give them understanding, entertain them, persuade them to change attitudes, and even persuade them to do your bidding. But before you can do any of that, you should learn as much as possible about words.

Words are double-edged tools of communication that can both help you and hurt you. They can make you happy or miserable; they can inspire you or depress you; they can propel you toward a full, useful life; or they can hinder your progress. Whoever said "Sticks and stones may break my bones, but words will never hurt me" lived in a world of fantasy, not in the real world of men and women, of love and hate, of success and failure, of hope and despair, of honesty and crookedness.

In the 1976 Democratic presidential primaries, Governor Jimmy Carter said, "I see nothing wrong with ethnic purity being maintained" (in the suburbs). The expression "ethnic purity" outraged millions of black and liberal voters, and it shook up his smoothly functioning campaign. Carter later apologized for that blunder.

Eight years earlier, a similar incident occurred in the Republican presidential primaries. This time, however, it ended in a shambles for George Romney, governor of Michigan and a powerful candidate. Powerful, that is, until he said that the White House had "brainwashed" him regarding the Vietnam War. That one word torpedoed Romney's campaign for the nomination, because anyone who could be brainwashed is not shrewd enough or strong enough to be president of the United States.

The way you use words will leave an indelible impression on people's minds. From your words, people will form opinions of your education, intelligence, and character, as well as your economic and social status. You may be highly intelligent, but if you trample on the English language, most bright, educated listeners will write you off as someone who's not going anywhere, someone who's a loser.

Mangling the language will place you in a predicament similar to that faced by Commodore Cornelius Vanderbilt, a nineteenth-century American shipping and railroad tycoon. Because he had little formal education, he was embarrassed when he had to deal with "all them British lords. I know I am smarter than they are," he said, "but they sound smarter." Tape-record yourself sometime, and evaluate how your language sounds.

Before discussing words and their ways, let's first compare oral and written words, because some words are better suited to speaking and others are better suited for writing.

"Sorry, we don't need no grammar books."

COMPARISON BETWEEN ORAL AND WRITTEN COMMUNICATION

There are many differences between communicating in written and spoken words—one to one or one to many. Because speaking is face to face and personal, it is much more direct than writing. Hand and body gestures, facial expressions, and vocal variety help greatly to support face-to-face communication. It is also reinforced by instant feedback from listeners in the form of smiles, frowns, applause, catcalls, clenched fists, and so on. An alert speaker who is sensitive to feedback can *"shift gears"* and adapt to changing circumstances.

"shift gears"—be prepared to change to a different direction

Writing, however, depends solely on words and punctuation to deliver the message. Writing has no gestures and no voice, and if there is any feedback, it takes time to reach the writer.

Good talking is wordy, repetitive, and far less structured than efficient writing. (Perhaps that's why so many more people find talking well much easier than writing well.) A good speech, reproduced word for word on paper, usually does not read well because it rambles and repeats words and thoughts. It is not nearly as disciplined and organized as good writing.

Effective talking is aimed at people's minds and hearts through their ears, and ears prefer short, direct, conversational sentences. Long, involved sentences are acceptable in writing for two reasons: (1) The eye can absorb many more words in an instant than the ear can hear. (2) If readers stumble on a marathon sentence, they can read it again. Not so with spoken words—once uttered they're gone, especially in a speech. If listeners miss a sentence, both they and the speaker have lost part of the message, there is no going back, except perhaps during the question-and-answer period. In a conversation, of course, a listener can ask the speaker to repeat. Table 6.1 (see p. 116) summarizes and offers insight into the differences between speaking and writing.

Now let's focus on three standards that apply equally to talking and writing—*clarity, accuracy,* and *precise wording.*

Clarity

If the audience doesn't understand the message instantly, then the speaker has, to some extent, failed. Thus, every possible measure must be taken to ensure that all your words and thoughts are perfectly clear to the audience.

Throughout your talk, words are your prime means for helping your audience understand your message. And to harness the profound power of words, you should develop a lifelong habit of using a dictionary and a thesaurus. If you do not exploit these resources, you will fail to achieve your full potential as a listener, speaker, and conversationalist.

Table 6.1 Linguistic Differences Between Speaking and Writing

Speaking	Writing
Wordy, repetitive	Concise, seldom repetitive
Tends to wander around topic	Better organized, sticks to topic, more relevant
Short sentences—roughly 5 to 20 words	Sentences usually longer
Simple sentence structure—usually S-V-O (subject-verb-object) sequence	More compound, complex, and compound, complex sentences
Informal style may be spiced with slang, contractions, sentence fragments	More formal style—very little slang, if any; few contractions and sentence fragments, if any
Depends heavily on personal pronouns—"we, us, you, they, them, I, me"	Depends less on personal pronouns
Is reinforced with facial and vocal expressions and hand, arm, body gestures	Depends on words and punctuation to get message across; format or layout may help
Feedback is usually instantaneous	Feedback may take days, weeks, or longer
Verbal transitions are same as in writing; pauses and change in body position can signify a new topic coming up	Verbal transitions are same as speaking
Can be marred with **vocalized pauses**—"er, ah, like, ya know"	No equivalent distractions
Planned strategic pauses can produce a powerful effect	No verbal equivalent
Uses more concrete words and shorter words	Tends to be more abstract and polysyllabic

Another device that will help you achieve clarity in your talk is a summary. If your talk consists of three well-researched major points, list those points in your introduction so your audience will know at once what ground you will cover. Discuss them in depth in the body, then summarize them at the end of your talk, and emphasize any conclusions that they lead to; an example of such an ending is given in Chapter 8.

Another aid to clarity is the use of transitions—words that indicate the connections between ideas—which show whether you are continuing *in the same vein* or are about to shift to another topic. (Transitions are covered in more detail in Chapter 8, and many are tabulated there.)

A common speaking fault is failing to define technical terms, or jargon. For example, one student gave what could have been an interesting talk on his profitable hobby. He is a disc jockey and conducts dances for

in the same vein—on the same topic

colleges and various organizations, and often performs at weddings. During his presentation, he frequently used esoteric terminology such as *pots, cans, fade, segue, equalizer, dBs, mixer,* and *control board.* As a result, very few students understood what he was talking about.

Most hobbies, professions, trades, and sports have their own language, vernacular, shop talk, or jargon. Whether your subject is plumbing, carpentry, auto mechanics, sports, journalism, cooking, ceramics, or law, you must realize that the audience may not be familiar with your subject. You should, therefore, be prepared to explain uncommon terms and to ask if they understand your language. Confucius, the Chinese philosopher, said it all 2400 years ago: "In language, clearness is everything."

Checking Accuracy of Research Material

As a conscientious speaker, you must see to it that your information is as current and as accurate as research can make it. The surest way for you to damage your credibility is to spew forth misinformation or outdated information.

How many times have you seen a story, a name, an important fact, or a charge against someone retracted in newspapers? Unfortunately, the damage was done when the misinformation first appeared in print. Such unwarranted embarrassment and mental anguish could have been avoided if someone had taken the time to recheck the information. If your talk is on a current or crucial topic, ***do your homework*** and ***arm yourself*** with quotations and sources to fortify your facts.

do your home-work—be well prepared

arm yourself—have at your disposal; gather together

Here's a monumental example of consequences incurred when two respected media members failed to check and recheck their sources for accuracy. CNN (Cable News Network) and *Time* magazine reported an explosive story saying that the U.S. military had dropped lethal nerve gas in Laos in 1970 during the Vietnam War to kill American defectors. A short time later CNN retracted the story when an independent investigator concluded that the story "could not be sustained." Result: two of the show's producers were fired, the senior executive producer resigned, and correspondent Peter Arnett was reprimanded. *Time* magazine retracted a print version of the same story, which it ran in conjunction with the news network.[5]

Remember, there is no substitute for accuracy . . . only damage to your credibility for the lack of it.

Precise Wording

Your language should be suitable to the subject, audience, and occasion. For example, a speaker who's addressing a Parent-Teacher Association

---

[5]*U.S. News & World Report,* 13 July 1998, 22.

by the same to-
ken—in the same
way

should avoid the statistical and psychological jargon of advanced educational researchers. ***By the same token,*** he should not indulge in teenage slang. All good speakers analyze their audience first and adapt their language accordingly. (See Chapter 11 and the introduction to this chapter.)

Are you ready now for a historical anecdote relevant to the precise use of words? When Thomas Jefferson, author of the Declaration of Independence, presented his credentials, at age 36, as the U.S. minister (now called ambassador) to France, the French premier said, "I see that you have come to replace Benjamin Franklin."

"I have come to succeed him," corrected Jefferson. "No one can replace him."[6]

Later in his career, Jefferson was elected governor of Virginia and third president of the United States. However, even if you utilize words the way he did, I can't guarantee that you'll become governor of your state or president. But, then again, who knows?

Here's a more contemporary example in which a poor choice of wording led to the resignation of a high government official. While attending an academic conference, Assistant Secretary of the Army Sara Lister referred to the U.S. Marines as "extremists." "Whenever you have extremists," she said, "you've got some risks of total disconnections with society, and that's a bit dangerous." Several hours after reactions of indignation and outrage from the commandant of the Marine Corps and conservative leaders on Capitol Hill, she submitted her resignation.[7]

COMMAND OF THE LANGUAGE

We are concerned here with two goals—to capture and condense some insights and practices of the best oral communicators. From them we can learn a great deal about using words to get results. What follows is not the Ten Commandments on using language, but simply guidelines or suggestions on how to generate maximum power in your command of the language.

Concrete, Specific Words Versus Abstract Words

For informative as well as persuasive speaking, there's no question that **concrete,** specific words carry a message most effectively. Concrete words pertain to tangible things—objects that we can perceive through our senses. The meanings of such words should be easily understood and

---

[6]*Bits & Pieces,* March 1985, 2.
[7]Gregory L. Vistica and Evan Thomas, "At War in the Pentagon." *Newsweek,* 8 December 1997, 44.

leave little room for personal interpretation. Obviously, the more concrete words you use, the better your chances will be that the listener will comprehend your intended message exactly.

If **parallel construction** can be built into a sentence of such words, the emotional impact can be intensified. Here are two statements composed of concrete, specific, vivid words strengthened and immortalized with parallel construction. In 1933, President Franklin D. Roosevelt said to the Depression-battered American people:

> I see one-third of a nation ill-housed, ill-clad, ill-nourished.

Early in World War II, Prime Minister Winston Churchill declared to the English people, staggering under military setbacks and facing conquest by Hitler's Germany:

> . . . we shall fight on the beaches, we shall fight on the landing grounds, we shall fight in the fields and on the streets, we shall fight in the hills; we shall never surrender.

Note the striking force of the parallel construction in that sentence. Note that the words are short and specific and that they permit instant understanding. Not even one abstract, nebulous word emasculates those sentences.

Here are some basic examples of concrete, specific words:

college campus	paycheck	man
syllabus	flood	woman
airplane	desk	gun
traffic jam	chair	mansion
day-care center	bus	book

You cannot, of course, avoid **abstract words** in public speaking. Sometimes they're necessary and serve a worthwhile purpose, but remember that they're subject to various interpretations and arguments depending on people's backgrounds, religion, education, nationality, and so on. When using abstract words, be sure to define and explain them to avoid any misunderstanding or misinterpretation of your message.

Abstract words pertain to intangible things, such as ideas, concepts, beliefs, attitudes, and values that cannot be seen. Here are some examples:

punishment	fear	education
socialism	justice	integrity
human rights	ideology	democracy
liberty	freedom	philosophy
ethics	morality	justice

Short, Simple Words Versus Long, Pretentious Words

For the purpose of informing or inspiring your listeners, simple, one- or two-syllable words are usually better suited. A classic example of using such words is Lincoln's Gettysburg Address. He delivered it not to inform people, but to inspire them. Of its 266 words, 195 consist of one syllable.

Here's another example, one of Shakespeare's more popular sonnets, which begins with "Shall I compare thee to a summer's day?," contains 114 words, and 92 of them contain one syllable. If Lincoln and Shakespeare can do it, so can you. (These two masterpieces of literature appear later in the chapter.)

Yet, some audiences expect longer, more elegant words. The more you know about your audience, the better you can judge what kinds of words to use. Table 6.2 provides a sample listing of what some people refer to as pompous and pretentious words, together with their simple, direct equivalents.

A glaring example of pompous, inappropriate language was given by the former U.S. ambassador to Great Britain, Walter H. Annenberg, when he was presented to Queen Elizabeth. She asked him a simple question

Table 6.2 Comparison of Words with Similar Basic Meanings

Showy, polysyllable words	Short, direct equivalents
ablution	washing
ameliorate	improve
assimilate	absorb, digest
cognizant of	aware of
conflagration	fire
consolidate	unite, combine
contiguous with	touching
delineate	describe
designation	name
effectuate	carry out
enumerate	count, list
facilitate	make easy, simplify
expedite	speed up
incombustible	fireproof
initiate, institute	begin, start
innocuous	harmless
modification	change
optimum	best
progenitor	forerunner
subsequent to	later, next
termination	end

"Before we did anything, we had to extinguish the conflagration."

about his housing arrangements and he replied: "We are in the ambassadorial residence subject, of course, to some of the discomfiture as a result of the need for elements of refurbishing and rehabilitation." He might have said, "We're redecorating now so the house is a bit messy."[8]

Equally verbose and pedantic is the following letter from a Houston, Texas, high school principal to a student's father:

> Our school's cross-graded, multi-ethnic, individualized learning program is designed to enhance the concept of an open-ended learning program with emphasis on a continuum of multi-ethnic, academically enriched learning using the identified intellectually gifted child as the agent or director of his own learning.
>
> Major emphasis is on cross-graded, multi-ethnic learning with the main objective being to learn respect for the uniqueness of a person.

The parent wrote the principal:

[8]Barbara Walters, *How to Talk with Practically Anybody About Practically Anything* (Garden City, NY: Doubleday, 1970), 136.

I have a college degree, speak two foreign languages and four Indian dialects, have been to a number of county fairs and three goat ropings, but I haven't the faintest idea as to what the hell you are talking about. Do you?[9]

The kind of language the ambassador and the principal used has been called **"gobbledygook."** It's been around a long time. Believe it or not, one of its major opponents has been the U.S. government. The Bureau of Land Management of the Department of the Interior many years ago issued a book entitled *Gobbledygook Has Gotta Go.*[10] It's full of examples of inflated prose and deflated revisions. For example, it cites the following passage written in the early years of our country to oppose efforts to limit voting rights to people who owned property:

> It cannot be adhered to with any reasonable degree of intellectual or moral certainty that the inalienable right man possesses to exercise his political preferences by employing his vote in referendums is rooted in anything other than man's own nature, and is, therefore, properly called a natural right. To hold, for instance, that this natural right can be limited externally by making its exercise dependent on a prior condition of ownership of property is to wrongly suppose that man's natural right to vote is somehow more inherent in and more dependent on the property of man than it is on the nature of man. It is obvious that such belief is unreasonable, for it reverses the order of rights intended by nature.

The government manual cites Benjamin Franklin's version of the same argument as being much more effective:

> To require property of voters leads us to this dilemma: I own a jackass; I can vote. The jackass dies; I cannot vote. Therefore, the vote represents not me but the jackass.

This type of language—ostentatiously comprised of pompous, superfluous, multisyllabic loquaciousness—abounds even more so today. Much of it is designed to confuse, confound, *stretch the truth,* alter the real meaning—and is really basically nonsense. Here are some words of wisdom by a top spokesman at the Justice Department referring to the explosive issue of forced busing. The Acting Civil Rights Chief wrote (and *keep in mind* we must assume that he was serious) "Forced busing is a misnomer. School districts do not force children to ride a bus, but only to arrive on time at their assigned school."[11] (Hell-O?) Other synonymous terms to denote convoluted speech include *political correctness, doublespeak,* and *doubletalk.*

Here are a few more examples from a column written by John Leo:

stretch the truth—to lie

keep in mind—be aware

---

[9]*Boston Sunday Herald American,* 6 February 1977, 23.
[10]*Gobbledygook Has Gotta Go.* Washington: Bureau of Land Management. U.S. Department of the Interior, 45–46.
[11]John Leo, "Language in the Dumps." *U.S. News & World Report,* 27 July 1998, 16.

- When requested for updated illegitimacy rates, a federal agency replied that it preferred

  > less judgmental terms such as nonmarital child-bearing or alternative mode of parenting.

- The athletic department of a major university expels players who steal not for "theft" but for "violating team rules regarding personal property."
- Students no longer "flunk" tests in many schools, but have actually "achieved a deficiency."[12]
- And you "gotta love" this quote from an unidentified U.S. Army major explaining to a reporter the decision to bomb and shell a certain village in Vietnam.

  > It became necessary to destroy the town to save it.[13]

Although some of you may think the following bit of prose humorous, it's a pretty good example of what you can do with those wonderful things we call words.

> I used to think I was poor. Then they told me I wasn't poor, I was *needy*. Then they told me it was self-defeating to think of myself as needy, I was *deprived*. Then they told me deprived was a bad image. I was *underprivileged*. Then they told me underprivileged was overused. I was *disadvantaged*.
>
> I still don't have a dime. But I have a great vocabulary.[14]

Loaded Words

Some words that concern race, religion, and politics can provoke heated and sometimes overpowering reactions. **Loaded words** can either infuriate or humiliate people, and they can induce people to commit irrational acts. Loaded words are like a loaded gun; they can cause devastating damage. Here are examples of words that spell potential *danger* to you and to others:

Regarding race and religion: Whitey, Honky, Racist, Nigger, Wasp, Hebe, and Kike

Regarding nationality: Gringo, Spic, Harp, Wop, Dago, Polack, Chink, Jap, and Slant-eyes

Regarding political philosophy: Radical, Anarchist, Skin-head, Reactionary, Nazi, Communist, Right wing, and Left wing

---

[12]Ibid.

[13]Gorton Carruth and Eugene Ehrlich, *American Quotations.* (Avenel, NJ: Wings Books, 1988), 569.

[14]Jules Feiffer, *Jules Feiffer's America from Eisenhower to Reagan,* ed. Steven Heller. Copyright 1965 by Random House, Inc., and Alfred A. Knopf, Inc.

"Homeless? No, just under-domiciled."

Terms such as "Flag burner," "Baby killer," and "Do-gooder" could also prove to be incendiary.

Whereas loaded words are extreme in their potential for trouble, there are other words and their synonyms that can either be complimentary or belittling. Here are some examples:

Complimentary	Belittling or Disparaging
slender	skinny
inexpensive	cheap
imported	foreign
prudent	stingy
pre-owned	used
cocktail lounge	bar
discriminating	finicky
deliberate	indecisive
courageous	reckless
thrifty	tightwad

make or break you—contribute to your success or failure

In some situations your choice of words can either *make or break you.* Think before you speak.

We use approximately 2000 words in our daily conversation. And of those 2000 words, the 500 that we use most often have more than 14,000 different dictionary definitions.[15] How about that? Then, is it any wonder that we should be most vigilant when we search for the words we choose to use?

Clichés

Clichés are expressions that have been used so often that they have become meaningless. Since they reflect a sparse vocabulary and a pallid imagination, avoid them "at all costs." Below are a few examples:

clean as a whistle	easy come, easy go
good as gold	hard as a rock
light as a feather	ugly as sin
tough as nails	goes without saying
last but not least	in the final analysis
lean over backward	slept like a log

And, of course, the really stale and overused, "I wouldn't touch that with a 10-foot pole."

Slang

The use of **slang** depends largely on the occasion of your talk and on the relationship between you and the audience. At a formal or even semiformal affair, slang would violate good taste even if you know most of the guests.

Slang terms can be generational such as *hippie* from the 1960s and *yuppie* from the 1990s. (Can't wait to see what the new millennium will bring.) Other examples of slang would include words like "neat," "cool," "awesome," and "wicked." And how about the use of the verbs "go" and "like" to mean "says" as in "He goes: 'Yeah, I was really lucky to get into Professor Vasile's speech class.'" or "She's like: 'Oh! That's cool, I had him last sememster and he's really an awesome teacher.'" *In any case*, it's important to resist the temptation to overuse slang; too much of it can degrade any talk.

In any case—no matter what happens

USE NONSEXIST LANGUAGE

Sexism refers to attitudes and behavior that are based on traditional stereotypes of sexual roles and usually result in the discrimination and degrading of one sex—most often, women. Sexist language is insulting and demeaning.

---

[15]Kathleen T. McWhorter, *Academic Reading,* 2nd ed. (New York: HarperCollins, 1994), 94.

Nonsexist language is also called gender-neutral or gender-free language. An excellent set of guidelines to help you avoid sexist language not only when speaking but writing, as well, was published by the National Council of Teachers of English.[16] The following is based, in part, on that guide.

Whenever possible, use the word *man* exclusively to mean "male person," thereby avoiding the more inclusive meaning of "all of humanity." For example,

Instead of Using	Try Using
mankind	humanity, human beings, people
manmade	handmade, synthetic, manufactured
the best man for the job	the best person for the job
the common man	the average person

Try to use the same titles for both men and women when the jobs could be held by each of them. For example,

businessman/businesswoman	business executives or manager
chairman/chairwoman	chairperson, chair, moderator
policeman/policewoman	police officer

Try to avoid sex-role stereotyping. That is, avoid words that conjure up a specific gender. For example,

Stereotyped Male Words	Stereotyped Female Words
doctor	nurse
professor	secretary
pilot	elementary school teacher
engineer	domestic help
mechanic	stitcher
barber	model
detective	librarian
heavy equipment operator	coed

Because of our environment, bad habit, prejudice, or just plain laziness, it's easy to communicate in language that is sexist. Some people are completely unaware of doing so. But, with effort and conscious awareness, you should have very little difficulty speaking in a manner that can earn you more respect and credibility.

(For an alphabetical partial listing of common sexist words and phrases and their suggested nonsexist alternatives, see Appendix C.)

---

[16]Guidelines for Nonsexist Use of Language published by the National Council of Teachers of English, 1111 Kenyon Road, Urbana, IL 61801

PUTTING WORDS INTO SENTENCES

What else needs be said about spoken sentences? By all means, they should be of different lengths, mostly short, say from 5 to 20 words. These figures are merely estimates that stress the vital importance of short, conversational sentences.

Varied structure is another vital aspect. Try to avoid composing all your sentences in the same form. More than half of your sentences can follow the conventional *subject-verb-object* pattern, but if *all* of them are structured like that, you may lull your listeners to sleep.

In his immortal Gettysburg Address, Abraham Lincoln pointed up a third valuable lesson, that of the personal, human approach. Even though the occasion was most solemn, the dedication of a national cemetery, he touched his listeners with noble ideas clothed in personal pronouns and nouns in every sentence: "... our fathers ... we ... us ... they ... the brave men, living and dead, who struggled here ... of the people, by the people, for the people ...." Such words breathe life and humanity into communication; use them. Here is the entire address. Read it from time to time to savor its beautiful thoughts expressed in majestic language.

Lincoln's "Gettysburg Address"

FOURSCORE and seven years ago our fathers brought forth on this continent a new nation, conceived in liberty and dedicated to the proposition that all men are created equal. Now we are engaged in a great civil war, testing whether that nation, or any nation so conceived and so dedicated, can long endure. We are met on a great battlefield of that war. We have come to dedicate a portion of that field as a final resting place for those who here gave their lives that that nation might live. It is altogether fitting and proper that we should do this. But, in a larger sense, we cannot dedicate—we cannot consecrate—we cannot hallow—this ground. The brave men, living and dead, who struggled here have consecrated it far above our poor power to add or to detract. The world will little note nor long remember what we say here, but it can never forget what they did here. It is for us, the living, rather to be dedicated here to the unfinished work which they who fought here have thus far so nobly advanced. It is rather for us to be here dedicated to the great task remaining before us—that from these honored dead we take increased devotion to that cause for which they gave the last full measure of devotion; that we here highly resolve that these dead shall not have died in vain; that this nation, under God, shall have a new birth of freedom; and that government of the people, by the people, for the people, shall not perish from the earth.

William Shakespeare's Eighteenth Sonnet

1 Shall I compare thee to a summer's day?
2 Thou art more lovely and more temperate.
3 Rough winds do shake the darling buds of May,
4 And summer's lease hath all too short a date.
5 Sometime too hot the eye of heaven shines,
6 And often is his gold complexion dimmed,
7 And every fair from fair sometime declines,
8 By chance or nature's changing course, untrimmed;
9 But thy eternal summer shall not fade,
10 Nor lose possession of that fair thou ow'st,
11 Nor shall Death brag thou wand'rest in his shade,

12   When in eternal lines to time thou grow'st.
13   So long as men can breathe or eyes can see,
14   So long lives this, and this gives life to thee.

Your thoughts and the way you phrase them are often influenced by context—by surrounding circumstances—and by events preceding your talk. A relevant example is the attention-getting introduction often used by Jimmy Carter in the 1976 Democratic presidential primary campaign. In 1976, Watergate, one of the worst political scandals in U.S. history, dominated American newscasts and newspapers, and the principal perpetrators of that shame were mainly lawyers based in Washington, D.C. Here are the opening remarks of many of Carter's campaign speeches:

> Hi, I'm Jimmy Carter and I'm running for president. I am not a lawyer. And I am not from Washington, D.C.

Also, in his vote-winning speeches Carter said something that struck a responsive chord among Americans wearied and angered by deceit in high office:

> I will not lie to you.

He communicated—and the voters sent him to the White House. Short, personal sentences can be very convincing.

One more outstanding introduction comes to mind: the one used occasionally by President Harry S Truman in the nip-and-tuck presidential campaign of 1948. The pollsters tabbed him as a loser to Republican nominee Thomas E. Dewey, governor of New York. Here is Truman's no-nonsense, no-doubletalk introduction:

> My name is Truman, I'm president of the United States, and I'm trying to keep my job.

He communicated—and the voters sent him back to the White House.

A third example of a blockbusting statement was President Reagan's answer regarding the very sensitive issue of age. During the second TV debate with his opponent Walter Mondale, in response to a question referring to his ability to keep up with the demanding schedule of his office (an obvious attempt to introduce the age question), President Reagan confidently declared:

> And I want you to know that I will not make age an issue of this campaign. I am not going to exploit for political purposes my opponent's youth and inexperience.[17]

What a *comeback.* He communicated—and the voters sent him back to White House.

comeback—an excellent reply

---

[17]*Newsweek,* November/December 1984, special issue, 109.

To further illustrate the power of using carefully chosen short, simple words, here's a handful of famous quotes that enjoy a comfortable niche on the bookshelf of American history. They were uttered by some of our country's "word masters." Although the quotes are identified, you might enjoy, as a learning experience, doing some research to discover *when* these words were articulated and under what circumstances. Who knows, perhaps you may find one that could be developed into an informative, interesting speech.

1. "The eagle has landed."—Neil Armstrong
2. "My fellow Americans: ask not what your country can do for you—ask what you can do for your country."—John F. Kennedy
3. ". . . Of the people, By the people, and For the People."—Abraham Lincoln
4. "Nuts!"—General Anthony McAuliffe
5. "I know not what course others may take; but as for me, give me liberty or give me death."—Patrick Henry
6. Here are two big ones from Harry: "The Buck Stops Here." and, "If you can't stand the heat, get out of the kitchen."—Harry S Truman
7. "The only thing we have to fear is fear itself."—Franklin D. Roosevelt
8. "I shall return."—General Douglas McArthur
9. "I have a dream."—Martin Luther King, Jr.
10. "I feel your pain."—Bill Clinton
11. "Read my lips."—George Bush

Notice the number of words with only one syllable.

Speaking of words, let me leave you with some written by Anna Hempstead Branch:

God wove a web of loveliness, of clouds and stars and birds, but made not anything at all so beautiful as words.

THINGS TO DISCUSS IN CLASS

over the heads of—hard to understand

talked down to—overly simplified, to the point of being insulting

1. Tell the class about a recent experience in which you felt that the speaker either talked *over the heads of* or *talked down to* the audience.
2. Give an example of the power of words and how it affected people's lives.
3. Relate to the class an experience in which a speaker received negative treatment from the audience because of insufficient audience analysis prior to the presentation.
4. Identify a speaker (a professional on TV or radio, a professor, and so on) whose ability to communicate successfully with an audience you greatly admire and explain how that person communicates effectively.

5. Try to think of someone in public life who is an excellent communicator. Prepare to discuss that person in class.

6. Try to think of a speaker who is successful as a communicator who uses a large number of concrete words. Prepare to discuss that person in class and list several examples of concrete language.

WHAT DO YOU REMEMBER FROM THIS CHAPTER?

1. Explain the importance of researching and analyzing an audience.
2. Explain two differences between oral and written communication.
3. What types of words carry the message most effectively in informative speaking?
4. What is a danger in using abstract words in communication?
5. Explain two ways to research an audience effectively.
6. List two ingredients critical to achieving clarity in your talk.
7. Give two examples each of abstract and concrete words.
8. What historic speech contains 266 words, 195 of which consist of one syllable?
9. Explain the term "gobbledygook."
10. What is sexist language. Give five examples.
11. List five stereotypical male words and five stereotypical female words.

VITALIZE YOUR VOCABULARY

Words of Native American Origin

Many words have entered the English language from dozens of Native American dialects. Here are some of the more common ones:

barbecue	papoose	squaw
canoe	pecan	tepee
cougar	potato	tobacco
hickory	pow-wow	toboggan
hominy	raccoon	tomahawk
moccasin	skunk	wampum
moose	squash	wigwam

Some less well-known Native American words are:

calumet (n.) A pipe smoked as a token of peace.
caribou (n.) Deer found in the arctic regions of North America.

caucus (n.) A closed meeting of members of a political party to decide on policy and to select candidates for office.

chautauqua (n.) An annual summer recreational and educational program.

mackinaw (n.) A short double-breasted coat of heavy woolen material, often plaid.

maize (n.) Corn.

peyote (n.) A drug derived from cactus.

sachem (n.) The chief of a tribe or the head of an organization.

sequoia (n.) Giant redwood trees of California.

There are hundreds, possibly thousands of Native American names of places in the United States—for example:

Allegheny	Erie	Nantucket	Seneca
Appomattox	Kalamazoo	Narragansett	Spokane
Biloxi	Kennebec	Nauset	Susquehanna
Buffalo	Malibu	Niagara	Tallahasee
Catskill	Manhattan	Oneida	Texarkana
Cayuga	Mashpee	Penobscot	Tuskegee
Chesapeake	Miami	Pensacola	Waco
Cheyenne	Milwaukee	Peoria	Walla Walla
Chicago	Mobile	Potomac	Wichita
Conestoga	Mohegan	Saratoga	Winnebago
Cucamonga	Mohave	Scituate	Yakima
Dakota	Muskogee	Seattle	Yuma

To show that the United States had been "the land of the Indians,"[18] the early settlers recorded the names of 27 of the 50 states that are derived from Native American words. Here they are with their general meaning:

Alabama—"clearers of the thicket"

Alaska—"great land"

Arizona—"place of little springs"

Arkansas—"the people who live downstream"

Colorado—"red river"

Connecticut—"at the long tidal river"

Idaho—"the sun is coming up"

Illinois—"superior men"

Iowa—"sleepy ones"

---

[18]"Naming the Hunting Grounds," *U.S. News & World Report,* 8 July 1991.

Communicate with confidence.

Kansas—"people of the south wind"

Kentucky—"meadowland"

Massachusetts—"people near the great hill"

Michigan—"big lake"

Minnesota—"sky-tinted water"

Mississippi—"big river"

Missouri—"people with the dugout canoes"

Nebraska—"flat water"

New Mexico—from the Aztec "Mexica," followers of the war god Mexitli.

North Dakota—"friends"

South Dakota—"friends"

Ohio—"beautiful river"

Oklahoma—"red people"

Tennessee—"area of traveling waters"

Texas—"ally"

Utah—"land of the sun"

Wisconsin—"gathering of the waters"

Wyoming—"upon the great plain"

Finally, consider the name of the largest recreational lake in Massachusetts:

Chargoggagoggmanchauggauggagoggchaubunagungamaugg

The Nipmuck Indians gave this lake the longest name of any waterway in the world.[19] The name means: "You fish on your side of the lake and I'll fish on my side, and nobody fishes in the middle."

---

[19]*The Boston Herald,* 19 January 1988, 7.

7

SELECTING A SPEECH TOPIC AND DOING RESEARCH

Nature has herself appointed that nothing great is to be accomplished quickly, and has ordained that difficulty should precede every work of excellence.

Quintilian, eminent Roman teacher
of speech (A.D. 30?–96?)

CHAPTER OBJECTIVES

After reading and understanding this chapter you should know:

- How to go about selecting a topic.

- Several ways to conduct research.

- How to use library facilities.

- How to take research notes.

- How to summarize, paraphrase, and select apt quotations.

- How to compile a bibliography.

CHAPTER PREVIEW

If you're asked to select your own speech topic, choose one that interests you, one that you can handle, and one that suits your audience. Your next step usually involves paring down the topic to a manageable size that you can cover in a short talk. When the topic is focused clearly in your mind, its time to seek solid information—very often the only basis of effective interpersonal communication in business and professional careers.

There are several ways to find information, and you should feel free to use the ways that will suit your needs best: dredge up your own experiences, opinions, and observations; contact various organizations and agencies, both public and private; consult nonprint media (television, radio, documentary films, and recordings); interview specialists from all walks of life, and utilize libraries.

You'll probably find the bulk of your information in print—newspapers, journals, magazines, and books. It's vital that you read and take notes with a critical eye. Question constantly. The fact that a statement is published does not guarantee its accuracy.

Appearing in this (and every) chapter is the feature "In Other Words," which will greatly benefit foreign and ESL students. To aid in their understanding of common American idioms and phrases, these expressions will be defined in the margin of the page on which they are introduced.

CRITERIA FOR SELECTING A TOPIC

Before you can give a brief, stimulating talk, you need a topic and information on it. Your instructor may assign a topic and ask you to research it. At other times the assignment may specify a general area—for example, taxes, welfare, spouse abuse, or illegal aliens—and call on you to select a particular facet of it. Some students prefer to have a specific topic selected for them because it's easier than having to choose one themselves.

If the instructor tells you to choose your own topic, your first reaction will probably be, "What will I talk about?" Without question this is the most common response by students. With a little thought and with the suggestions in this chapter, you may find that selecting a topic is not as difficult as you first imagined. In any event, you should weigh the following guidelines in searching for a topic:

- Your interest in it.
- Your ability to handle it.
- Its appropriateness to the audience.

The Topic Should Be Interesting to You

If you're not interested in the topic, chances are that nobody else will be, and your talk will probably fizzle. Interest, enthusiasm, or zeal—call it what you will—is reflected in your voice and by your nonverbal communication. Audiences sense enthusiasm, or the lack of it, in a speaker, and they respond accordingly. Remember Ralph Waldo Emerson's statement "Nothing great was ever achieved without enthusiasm!"

What you talk about should depend on what interests you. Perhaps you're engaged in one of the following hobbies:

- video/computer activity
- aerobics/bodybuilding
- repairing and reconditioning antique cars
- collecting coins or stamps
- collecting comic books
- collecting sports cards
- collecting international dolls/figurines
- listening to music at home and at concerts
- partying
- cycling
- jamming (dancing)

If you're interested in politics and government, you may consider one of the following:

- Don't say, "What's the use of voting?"
- Judges should be elected instead of appointed

Audiences sense enthusiasm, or the lack of it.

- What we need is a woman as president
- The vice president should be elected by the people and not selected by the presidential candidate
- The president should be elected by popular vote rather than by the Electoral College
- The federal government is too large
- How does a bill get through the legislature?

How about choosing one of the following topics if you enjoy sports?

- The adventure of scuba diving
- Getting high by sky diving
- The case against expansion teams
- Is jogging healthful or harmful?
- Pro athletes are overpaid
- Sports complexes should not be subsidized by the taxpayers
- Our Olympic sports teams should be federally subsidized

If you have strong feelings on education, how about one of these?

- Politics has a role in education
- Speech should be a required subject

- Students should be permitted to evaluate their teachers and the results should be available to students
- Attendance in class should be required
- Earning a college degree should take three years instead of four
- Students should be able to attend their state colleges free of charge

In Other Words:

Do you still want more topics for talks? Then you and your classmates might venture into a **brainstorming** session, a technique used occasionally in the business world to dredge up solutions to problems (see Chapter 14). In brainstorming, the cardinal rule is complete freedom to suggest any topic without being criticized: No matter how zany or *cockeyed* an idea seems, *nobody should ridicule it.* Following these wide-open, nonthreatening rules, a cooperative group can often create answers to a problem—in this case, producing more topics for your talks. All the suggestions should be recorded on the chalkboard and on your notepad and evaluated at the next class session, when everybody has simmered down. The worthwhile ideas can be used and the poor ones discarded.

cockeyed—foolish

If you're deeply interested in a particular topic, chances are your audience will be, too. Your enthusiasm can't help but be transmitted to your listeners because it's contagious. If you can get totally *wrapped up* in your subject, the end result could be electrifying.

wrapped up—become totally involved

John Wesley, founder of the Methodist church in the eighteenth century, was once asked how he attracted such large audiences and held them spellbound. "I set myself on fire," he replied, "and they come to watch me burn."

The Topic Should Be Within Your Capability

In other words, can you *handle the topic* on the basis of your personal experiences, book learning, firsthand knowledge, family background, personal convictions, and acquaintances in specific fields? If some or all of these factors are in your favor, then the odds are that you'll be able to prepare for and speak intelligently on your selected subject.

handle (the topic)—to know enough about (the topic)

For example, let's assume that you're planning a talk on the operation and safety of a nuclear power plant. Nuclear safety has been a vital concern since the Three Mile Island accident in Pennsylvania in 1979; our concern has been further intensified by the Chernobyl disaster in the Ukraine in the former Soviet Union in 1986. To handle this kind of topic, you need a strong technical background, several visits to a nuclear plant, and interviews with engineers and administrators. Then, you face the challenge of compiling all this scientific information and translating it into a level of English that your audience can understand.

Suppose, however, that you want to address the question "Should the use of marijuana be legalized?" You could easily find yourself knee deep in facts, opinions, half-truths, and myths. Consider the sources of information available to you; for example, acquaintances who smoke pot and swear by it, law enforcement officials who think otherwise, doctors involved in the treatment of drug addiction, and legislators determined to control the problem. Remember to check out as many sources of information as possible, because almost all controversial issues are complicated and seldom lend themselves to simplistic solutions.

The Topic Should Be Suitable to the Audience

Knowing the make-up of your listeners will help you shape a more effective person-to-person communication. To know your listeners, you should try to answer several questions about them: What are their average ages, ethnic background, occupation, financial status, sex, and educational level; and what other elements may affect your performance?

Consider a speaker at a meeting of the National Organization for Women. If he or she explains innovative tactics that would help qualified women break into public school administration, higher echelons of civil service, or corporate executive suites—the three areas in which women have traditionally been shut out—the audience may respond with a standing ovation.

In other words, try to assess the problem from the standpoint of the audience. Put yourself in the role of an active listener and ask yourself these questions: What do I expect from this speaker? Will the message be interesting, informative, and understandable? Will I want to hear more? (Audience analysis is discussed in depth in Chapters 6 and 11.)

SELECTING MATERIAL AND NARROWING THE TOPIC

A common tendency among beginning speakers is to select a subject that is so general it cannot be covered thoroughly in a short presentation. Suppose you find a subject that arouses your curiosity, for example, how to cope with violence in a permissive society. Should you use this subject for a talk? Definitely not, because it's so vast and complex that you couldn't even dent it in a half-hour. You must restrict the subject so that you can discuss it in the allotted time, usually four to six minutes.

What you need now is a statement that focuses your talk into one clear, concise sentence (a **thesis statement**)—for instance:

> To reduce the amount of violence in American society, our judicial system must begin to impose much stiffer prison sentences.

sink your teeth into—develop

Now you have a vital, current statement that you can *sink your teeth into* in a short speech. Not only that, but this statement will save you much library time because it will help restrict your research to relevant information. From a speaker's viewpoint, a talk without solid, current

"I'd like to talk a minute about intergalactic exploration . . . ."

information isn't worth giving, and from an audience's viewpoint, it isn't worth listening to. Your next step is a quest for knowledge, in other words, research.

DOING RESEARCH

The difference between a speech stocked with the latest accurate information and a speech lacking it can be the difference between acceptance and rejection by the audience. We say "acceptance" because most audiences listen to and respect a knowledgeable speaker. This hard-won knowledge will give you an injection of self-confidence, and, together with your listeners' respect, *you're off and running.* The following ideas will help you ferret out information on any topic.

you're off and running—you're prepared to proceed

Probe Your Own Knowledge, Experience, and Observations

If you stop to think, you'll probably discover opinions, ideas, and knowledge that you didn't know you had. *Jot them down*—they may form the

jot them down—write them down

basis of your research. And don't forget to question friends and acquaintances, because some of them may know a good deal about your topic.

Try to recall as many experiences as possible—lectures that you've heard, both in and out of school, as well as impressions and comments about those lectures. What do you remember about their question-and-answer sessions? Jot them down. How about your workplace? Are any of your associates from another country or culture? Have they ever expressed opinions? Jot them down. Have you ever been in the military service—perhaps stationed overseas? What do you remember about your assignment, the people, and their culture? Jot these memories down. Probing your own mind, you'll be amazed at what you'll be able to *come up with.*

come up with—
discover

Write to Government Agencies and Private Organizations

Some federal agencies such as the Departments of Health and Human Services, Housing and Urban Development, Transportation, and Labor Statistics publish many reports on special topics. If you phone them (ask for the public information office) or write them, be very specific in your request. The only *drawback* is that you may have to wait a long time for an answer. Some state agencies will also provide you with information.

*drawback—*dis-
advantage

Examples of other authoritative sources are:

- organizations such as the Carnegie, Rockefeller, Ford, and Sloan Foundations
- "think tanks"—Center for the Study of Democracy, American Enterprise Institute, and Brookings Institution
- special-interest groups—Sierra Club and Greenpeace (environment), Common Cause and League of Women Voters (politics), Better Business Bureau and Chamber of Commerce (business)
- professional and trade associations—American Bar Association, American Medical Association, National Automobile Dealers Association, and International Brotherhood of Electrical Workers

Research the Visual Media

Check out TV and radio documentaries and talk shows, audio and video tapes, films, film clips, and cassettes. These nonprint media have been assuming more and more importance as carriers and recorders of vital information.

Suppose that you're curious about the solemn occasion and exact wording of President Franklin D. Roosevelt's declaration of war against Japan on December 8, 1941. You could, of course, turn to the Congressional Record, biographies of FDR, or history books to find the answer. But another approach will allow you to capture the real-life gravity of that momentous day: Ask your audiovisual department to get a video presentation of the declaration so that you can appreciate President Roosevelt's unique voice and speaking style.

Your library probably has a collection of audio and video tapes on all kinds of subjects. Check with a librarian to see if any tapes deal with the topic of your talk. If you're lucky, a television channel (especially cable) may show a documentary on your topic. If you can watch it or even tape it with a **videocassette recorder (VCR),** you're that much ahead in your quest for knowledge and understanding.

Speaking of cable TV, it offers a multitude of excellent educational research resources. For example, when you get a chance, tune into The History Channel, The Animal Channel, The Discovery Channel, C-Span, and, of course, the award-winning series "Biography" on the A&E Channel, to mention a few. Do some research to locate others.

Talk to People

Authorities on various subjects are everywhere, and many of them are willing to share their expertise. Be sure to have a list of questions ready so that you won't waste experts' time. After they have answered your questions, thank them and leave immediately.

A tape recorder can be used in a face-to-face information quest because it is a time saver, but first request permission from the interviewee to use the recorder. Some people are "allergic" to being taped and tend to *clam up.*

clam up—not respond

Don't feel that you must always seek out authorities sitting on top of the organizational pyramid. Some of them tend to be "long" on administrative plans, policies, and procedures but "short" on *street smarts.* On the other hand, many people in everyday positions essential to the functioning of society can brief you on problems in specialized areas, and they may do so if you ask. You'll be astonished at what you can get simply by asking.

street smarts—everyday knowledge

Do you want to know about muggings, rapes, and armed robberies? Talk to police officers, judges, prison officials, and victims. Do you want to learn about financial hardships plaguing homeless people and welfare families? By all means, talk with sociology professors, but don't forget to talk with welfare mothers, social workers, and members of legislative committees on human services. This many-sided approach to gathering information allows you to "see" an issue as it is *in the real world,* and not just as it appears in print and nonprint media.

in the real world—as it exists in everyday life

Read

The most dependable and extensive of all information sources, reading opens endless horizons to you. Just about "everything you ever wanted to know about anything but were afraid to ask" can be found in books,

Talk to the "woman in the street."

magazines, journals, newspapers, government reports, almanacs, encyclopedias, dictionaries, diaries, and so on.

Reading is like having a passport to anywhere in the world and an invitation to conversations by the finest men and women of past centuries.

How much information should you garner? Far more than you need. Learn from the best filmmakers. They normally shoot at least five times more film than they'll use; then they select the best footage and splice it into a unified package. *By the same token,* the best speakers usually gather and master two or three times more material than they'll use. This extra knowledge *pays dividends* in the confidence and fluency with which they deliver their talks and answer audience questions.

by the same token—in the same way

pays dividends—is beneficial

Learn to Use the Library

To extract the maximum benefit from the printed word, you must know how to use a library. So, let's touch on the highlights of exploiting your library's resources.

Some libraries still have **card catalogs** that list their holdings, but most now use electronic **databases** (large collections of data organized in a computer so that the data can be expanded, updated, or retrieved in seconds) to store library records. If you can find library material using a terminal or personal computer, then using a card catalog will seem simple. So let's first discuss this new development and then return to the card catalog.

Card catalogs are now being replaced by computerized databases. Some libraries subscribe to dozens of databases that provide information on countless numbers of specific areas and subjects. This information is accessible to you through computer terminals in your college library. Many libraries now make information available on the **Internet,** which means you can tap into your college library resources from off campus. You can usually get instructions on how to access the various databases by pressing certain "help" commands on the keyboard. The instructions will appear on the terminal screen.

Databases can save you hours of arduous manual research because they'll search through thousands of information resources in seconds. The computer will display on screen the titles of all articles and books related to your search and will provide you with all the reference information needed to locate the source material. Computer reference retrievals can usually be printed using a nearby printer or downloaded (transferred) onto a computer floppy disk (a small flexible disk for storing data).

Database searches can scan for titles, authors, subjects, and, occasionally, keywords or phrases. However, when you request a database search using keywords, you must use very precise keywords (descriptors) relevant to your topic to narrow the number of retrieved references. If you run into a roadblock—and most students do at times—don't hesitate to ask the librarian for guidance. Some typical database titles are: Academic Indexes, Business Index, Governmental Publications Index, Health Index, Investext, Legaltrac, and National Newspaper Index. Some other popular databases include ERIC, DIALOG, LEXIS/NEXIS, and INFOTRAC. Commonly available are programs on **CD-ROM** (Compact Disk-Read Only Memory). The list of available programs in the CD-ROM Directory continues to grow steadily.

Entire volumes of multimedia encyclopedias are now available on CD-ROMs for research at home or in your dorm room. Two popular ones are *Encarta* and *Compton*. Encarta, for example, features a 29-volume encyclopedia, over 1000 articles, 8 hours of sound, samples of 60 languages, 100 animations and video clips, 7800 photos and illustrations, and more.

And for those of you just starting to explore cyberspace, you've probably already discovered some of the major **ISP** (Internet Service Provider) companies such as America On-Line, CompuServe, and Prodigy. Internet access can bring more information than you need to your desktop in seconds. Since no one controls what moves from one computer to another

Megahours of spellbinding sight and sound entertainment.

across the Internet, the challenges to the information seeker are greater than ever. The Internet is an incredible communication tool that brings to the world of information things like **e-mail** and the **World Wide Web.** These have a profound effect on the way data is stored, organized, and retrieved. Quite frankly, *between you and me,* the multimedia accessories available on many computers make research a fun and entertaining activity while improving the quality of what can be accomplished. But more about that later.

between you and me—secretively, between only us

Let's get back to the basics of finding a book in the library using the online catalog. Begin by looking at how books in libraries are located using an **online** library catalog. Remember, periodicals are also routinely accessed using electronic means. Learning how to use the book database will help you when you expand your library search to locate magazines, journals, and newspapers.

Library holdings information is held in computerized databases. The three major ways to find materials in a library haven't changed since the days of the card catalog. Things are still organized by title, author, and subject. The electronic databases, however, make it possible to search by keywords (descriptors) as well. Keyword searches require precision but with a little practice you'll discover how to retrieve efficiently an increased number of references per search.

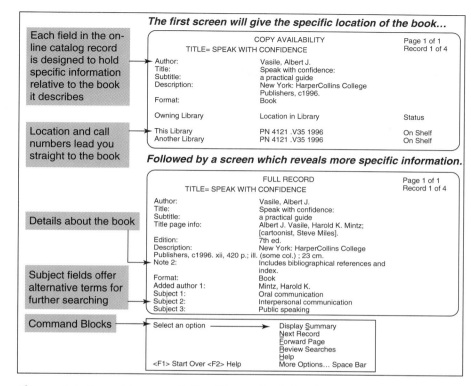

Figure 7.1 Record from an Online Library Book Catalog

Figure 7.1 shows a typical library holding record from an online public access library catalog. Each record contains a call number that indicates the book's location in the library. The note **field** of a record will usually provide some details about the physical description of the book and the subject field will provide alternate headings under which you might find books on the same or closely related subjects.

Once you find the book on the library shelf, you can save time by skimming the table of contents and index for the particular phrases of a topic that you plan to discuss.

Check Out Periodicals (Magazines, Journals, and Newspapers)   In the periodical section, you'll find the latest authoritative information on countless specialized fields. Timeliness is the tremendous advantage that periodicals offer—information that may be only weeks or days old, in contrast to books that require several months to a year to publish.

To find articles in periodicals relevant to your topic, turn to the indexes, especially *Readers' Guide to Periodical Literature*. This guide lists, by subject, the contents of more than 175 popular American publications. Without question, it is the best source of general information on current topics and is an excellent aid in getting your research off the ground. The *Guide* is published bimonthly in green paperback and annually in green hard cover. Here's a sample listing of magazines indexed in the *Guide: Atlantic, Business Week, Down Beat, Ebony, Esquire, Forbes, Glamour, Harper's, Ladies' Home Journal, Money, Nation's Business, Popular Science, Reader's Digest, Sports Illustrated, Time, U.S. News & World Report, Vital Speeches of the Day,* and *Writer.*

Check Out Indexes   If you're searching for material on business, industry, education, or public affairs, consult some of the following indexes:

Bibliography Index
Business Periodicals Index
Christian Science Monitor Index
Dun & Bradstreet
Education Index
Humanities Index
New York Times Index
Psychological Abstracts
Public Affairs Information Service
Social Services Index
Ulrich's Periodical Directory
United Nations Documents Index
Wall Street Journal Index

For science and technology, use the following:

Applied Science & Technology Index
Aviation and Space Technology

For statistical data, you might dig into various government publications as well as the following:

Information Please Almanac
United Nations Statistical Yearbook
U.S. Statistical Abstracts
World Almanac

To learn about people, consult the following:

Current Biography
Dictionary of American Biography
International Who's Who
Leaders in Education
Who's Who in America

Who's Who in Finance and Industry

Who's Who in Law

Use Quotations from Authorities and Use Anecdotes   If you're searching for appropriate quotations and anecdotes relevant to your talk, consult the following excellent sources:

Bartlett's Familiar Quotations

Little, Brown Book of Anecdotes

Oxford Dictionary of Quotations

Seldes' The Great Quotations

Stevenson's Home Book of Quotations

The International Thesaurus of Quotations

Treasury of Women's Quotations

Look at Encyclopedias   For general information and for an overall view of thousands of subjects, you can't beat the following standard encyclopedias:

Collier's Encyclopedia

Encyclopedia Americana

Encyclopedia Britannica

Use a Dictionary and Thesaurus   To attain a versatile and descriptive vocabulary—a deeply envied asset—you should use various types of wordbooks throughout your life. The following are among the best:

Funk & Wagnall's New Standard Dictionary

Random House Dictionary of the English Language

Roget's International Thesaurus

Webster's Dictionary of Synonyms

Webster's Third New International Dictionary

Read Newspapers and Magazines   Daily and weekly newspapers are the most common sources of supporting material. Many papers have earned national and international reputations as authoritative sources of information on current and past topics and issues. You'll strengthen your talk considerably if you can quote from such highly respected newspapers as the *New York Times, Washington Post, St. Louis Post-Dispatch, Atlanta Constitution,* and *Wall Street Journal.* They give superb coverage of political, social, and business topics in the United States and around the world. The *New York Times* even has an index that dates back to 1913.

If your talk concerns local or state issues, you should examine local, daily, and weekly papers. Some of these papers publish columns on various issues by nationally prominent journalists.

Other excellent sources for supporting information are weekly national news magazines such as *U.S. News & World Report, Newsweek,* and *Time.* Many other magazines and publications (some general and others specialized) are also available at your college or local library and offer endless possibilities for conducting research.

Your Best Bet May Be the Internet   The Internet links one computer to another to another, bringing together information sources from around the globe. The **World Wide Web** is a **hypertext** information system that organizes information in a format that's easy to deliver and access. Integration of text with graphics, audio, and video, which you may navigate through using inexpensive **browsers,** is revolutionizing the world of facts and information. It's also making your job more challenging in that it's more important than ever for you to know how to critically assess and evaluate information in efficient and effective ways.

You should take the time to learn about the new tools available to researchers. Whether you're looking for information to bring credibility and dimension to your talk or you're looking for examples of how great orators deliver their material, the World Wide Web is a good place to go for information. You can listen to Martin Luther King, Jr.'s, "I Have A Dream" speech online or tap into U.S. government statistics from the most recent census if you know what you're doing.

Becoming computer literate is intertwined with being information literate. This will not all come together with one or two trips to the library or the computer lab. If you intend to use the Internet for research, save yourself some time and aggravation by learning the basics. Before you begin using online resources, it helps to know and gain experience with:

- the difference between using a terminal and a personal computer
- how to use keyboard and a mouse to issue computer commands
- how to use a graphical browser like Netscape to navigate the World Wide Web
- how to use web-based **e-mail** to store and sort information
- how to use a **search engine** such as Alta Vista
- how to use an online index such as Yahoo
- how to print and **download** files to a disk
- how to **cite** information from an electronic source

A lot of the information found on the web is the same information found in books on the library shelves. So why use the Internet if it's no different from going to some of the more traditional resources we've already discussed in this chapter? Good question. First, there's already more information on the World Wide Web than what could be stored in the largest of libraries and it's increasing every day. Secondly, an electronic medium has the ability to sort and search far beyond human limits. Therefore, it's important to realize that the search for information is not a choice between paper and electronic resources. The Internet hasn't made hardbound books and paper versions of magazines extinct.

The Internet brings us more information, faster, in a format that makes information more manageable than ever before; but by itself it can't do it all, at least not yet. Looking for information is as much an art as it is a skill. Using only one tool to access and sort information limits the scope and quality of your research. The Internet and the World Wide Web outperforms other tools for speed and quantity but there's still a long way to go before electronic sources can guarantee the accuracy and security that quality information delivery requires. Don't limit yourself by relying on one tool any more than you would rely on one set of encyclopedias for information.

Here's one final hint for exploiting your library. Get acquainted with reference librarians. No matter *how sharp you are,* research is a time-consuming process that librarians can speed up by guiding you to the right reference aids. However, don't expect them to do your research; that's your task.

how sharp you are—how intelligent or alert you are

MAKING A BIBLIOGRAPHY

At this point you're primed to dip into reference works in order to locate sources of information. Magazines, journals, newspapers, books, and Internet sources are all fair game in the hunt. Whether you plan to refer to a few sources or to a dozen, you should number and list them on notepaper or 5-by-7-inch **note cards.** This list (Figure 7.2) is your preliminary **bibliography;** the list of sources that you actually use in your talk is your final bibliography.

If you decide to use the Internet for research, it is particularly important to keep an accurate record of what you find, including when and where you found it. Unlike a paper source, electronic sources may change overnight, making it difficult, sometimes impossible, to retrieve the information again. To avoid wasting time and relying on sources that cannot be verified later on, you should use the most current guidelines published by the American Language Association for creating a bibliography so that your list of sources is a useful and valid one.

Evaluating Your Sources

Before studying your sources, you might save time by evaluating them and *weeding out* the poor ones. Some yardsticks for judging the worth of a magazine or newspaper article, a book chapter, or information on a website are:

weeding out—eliminating

AFFIRMATIVE ACTION IN EDUCATION

Back to square one: [minority admissions at the University of Texas and University of California, Berkeley]. A. Cohen. il *Time* v151 no15 p30–1 Ap 20 '98

Don't get hysterical [minority education at University of California after end of affirmative action] J. Leo. il *U.S. News & World Report* v124 no16 p12 Ap 27 '98

Exam question [affirmative action via government test prep aid to minority students] C. Lane *The New Republic* v215 no15 p6 Ap 13 '98

How to even the score: test prep [minority access to LSAT tutors] R. Ratnesar. il *Time* v151 no15 p31 Ap 20 '98

In defense of preference [cover story] N. Glazer. il *The New Republic* v218 no14 p18–21+ Ap 6 '98

Lies, damn lies and racial statistics [University of California overplays drop in minority admissions] C. Krauthammer. il *Time* v151 no15 p32 Ap 20 '98

Testing Texas [impact of Hopwood v. University of Texas Law School decision] J. Traub. *The New Republic* v218 no14 p20–1 Ap 6 '98

Figure 7.2 Preliminary Bibliography

- date of publication (This is not always a reliable measure.)
- reputation of the author (Is he or she a recognized authority in the field?)
- reputation of the publisher (What is the firm's **track record**?)

track record—proof of performance

clout—prestige

For example, an article dealing with international news in the *New York Times* or *Los Angeles Times* carries far more *clout* than a similar article in a small-town newspaper. Admittedly, one or both of the last two yardsticks may be difficult to apply, but they do help in comparing one work against another and in deciding which would make a better source.

in control—acts as an evaluator, approving and disapproving material before it is made available to the general public

Evaluating what you find using the Internet is not as easy as it seems since, as we considered earlier, no one is *in control* of the Internet. E-mail headings aren't always accurate representations of where the information originated from since aliases can be used and points of origin distorted electronically. Graphics are easily tampered with using image-editing software, and text is easily manipulated using word-processing programs and text editors. (Talk about ethics!)

Although there are no foolproof methods for considering the credibility of a website, there are some elements common to most reliable sites. Figure 7.3 shows a typical World Wide Web page. As with paper sources, you are considering the origin of the page. For example, if the American Psychological Association provides material on mental health, your source is much more credible than an e-mail message from a listserv where a group is discussing various forms of neurotic eating disorders. Other things to use as measures of reliability include (but are not limited to):

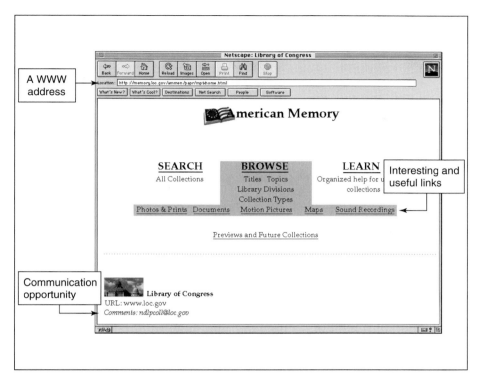

Figure 7.3 A World Wide Web Page

- date—When was the page last updated?
- feedback—Is there an e-mail address or other indication that the originator is interested in improving quality through suggestions and requests from users?
- delivery quality—spelling, continuity of thought, organization, etc.
- content review—clear, informative, original, objective, accurate, verifiable
- author—biography or other description of writer and/or editor of content
- advertising—clearly distinguishable from other site content
- functionality—are the **links** to useful, quality sources, and do they work?
- purpose—statement of intent or reason for presenting information

TAKING NOTES

The purpose of taking notes is to record accurately information and ideas that you believe will be useful in developing your speech. Since using someone else's words without giving proper credit, known as *plagiarism* (see Chapter 1), is considered a major form of cheating/stealing, you need to be careful to record information, not words, whenever possible. There are times, of course, when a writer's words are so striking that you will want to use them. Quoting occasionally from your sources is permissible, provided that you indicate that you are quoting. In writing, quotation marks serve this purpose. In speech we usually say "quote" and "unquote" to signal the beginning and end of a quotation: "The professor described the student's paper as quote, dramatic but unconvincing, unquote."

Whenever you write down the exact terminology of a writer, be sure that you place the borrowed words in quotation marks in your notes. If you fail to do so, you can find yourself plagiarizing without knowing that you are doing it. Well-publicized cases of plagiarism by politicians and professional writers have focused attention on plagiarism in recent years. Two columnists of the *Boston Globe*, among others, have recently lost their jobs because of accusations of plagiarism. In the classroom, the consequences of plagiarism can be a failing grade or even suspension.

Figure 7.4 presents an original passage and Figure 7.5 shows notes taken from that passage.

Take a few notes.

[Source: Charles N. Barnard, "Blimps: Big, Beautiful, & Everywhere You Look." *Smithsonian*, June 1998, pp. 32–33.]

Visionaries have always seen a future for airships that goes far beyond advertising, however. In South Africa, the Hamilton Airship Company has formulated plans for a luxury dirigible of near-*Hindenburg* proportions. It would carry 30 passengers across the Atlantic from Johannesburg to New York in 10 days at speeds of up to 100 miles per hour. In New York City, Donald Trump recently conceived a plan to ferry 160 high rollers a day to his casino in Atlantic City aboard a luxury airship. The exorbitant cost, not any lack of engineering feasibility, caused him to shelve the idea.

A company called Airship Management Services (AMS) is working with a company in Saudi Arabia to provide a blimp for surveillance during the hajj, the annual gathering of millions of Muslims in Mecca and Medina. AMS blimps have already helped with crowd management at the Los Angeles, Seoul and Atlanta Olympics—examples of what many believe will be a growing airship market: police work and border patrols.

A German company, CargoLiftr AG, is planning to build a gigantic cargo-carrying airship capable of flying 80 mph. When fully inflated, it will be longer than the Washington Monument is tall. It's aimed at the $9-billion-a-year market for transporting freight to places where planes can't land and for carrying cargo—turbines and power-generating equipment, for example—that is too bulky and heavy (up to 150 tons) for airplanes.

Figure 7.4 Original Passage from *Blimps: Big, Beautiful, & Everywhere You Look.*

Here's a time-tested tip on using research note cards. Indicate the following on each card: a brief heading, information from one source and on

Figure 7.5 Notes on Original Passage in Figure 7.4

Several ideas have been advanced for the use of blimps:

1. Transatlantic passenger flights from Johannesburg to New York. Speeds up to 100 mph.

2. "Ferry 160 high rollers" from New York to Atlantic City. Plan by Donald Trump abandoned because of cost.

3. Surveillance during the hajj, the annual gathering of millions of Muslims in Mecca and Medina.

4. Crowd control at the Olympics—already done at Los Angeles, Seoul, and Atlanta.

5. "Growing airship market: police work and border patrols."

6. Transporting cargo to places where planes can't be used.

one topic, and the source (for example, magazine name, author, title of article, volume number, date, and page number).

As a modern researcher, you enjoy a tremendous advantage over historical information seekers such as Thomas Jefferson, Charles Darwin, and Winston Churchill. Say, for example, that you run across a few pages full of meaty, relevant information in a book, magazine, or encyclopedia that can't be borrowed. You could easily waste an hour or so copying the pages in longhand. Since almost all libraries have photocopy equipment, use it to save time. Reading important information into a cassette tape recorder can also save time. (Be sure to document the source.) And, of course, the biggest time-saver at the library is the computer, where you come, you search, you find, and with a press of a key or mouse—*voilà*—you have a printout. Isn't modern technology marvelous?

voilà—there it is, to express success or satisfaction

CAUTION
When you quote, summarize or paraphrase an individual or published source without giving due credit, you are guilty of plagiarism, a very serious offense, especially since passage of the copyright law in 1978. An update to the U.S. Code enacted in 1997 provides greater protection in the area of intellectual property by addressing criminal infringement of copyright.

No question about it, conducting research can be a prolonged, difficult, and sometimes discouraging activity, but the overall results will be most rewarding.

THINGS TO DISCUSS IN CLASS

1. List two subjects that interest you but that, because of your lack of knowledge, would require research if you were planning to talk about them.

2. Would you prefer to select your own topics or to have them selected for you? Why?

3. List a speech topic that would apply only to one specific audience. Explain your reasons for choosing it.

4. Select a topic that would interest the class and list some possible sources of information on it.

5. Research one significant event that took place on the day you were born.

6. List two topics that you think would make interesting talks. Make sure that you narrow each topic so that it can easily be covered in a four- to six-minute speech.

7. Discuss the types of information you can find in the *Readers' Guide to Periodical Literature*.

8. Select what you feel is an interesting topic, then go to the library and prepare a bibliography on it.

What Do You Remember from This Chapter?

1. After you've decided on a topic for a talk, what should the next steps be?
2. List several ways to find information.
3. Name some guidelines to be used in searching for a topic.
4. What role does the audience play in your selection of a topic?
5. Name two sources that provide statistical data.
6. Name two publications that specialize in word usage.
7. What type of information can you find in a library's card catalog file?
8. Explain the difference between a summary and a paraphrase.
9. List two sources of information on business, industry, public affairs, or
   education.
10. Name two sources that would supply information on people.
11. When using the Internet for research, why is it so important to keep an ac-
    curate record of what you find, including when and where you found it?
12. Explain how the Internet practically revolutionized the activity of research-
    ing information.

Vitalize Your Vocabulary

Basic Computer Terms

back up (v.) To make a copy of important data to be used if your current file
   is destroyed.

boot (v.) To start the computer.

byte (n.) The amount of computer memory needed to store one character of a
   specified size, usually 8 for a microcomputer and 16 for a larger one.

CD-ROM (Compact Disk-Read Only Memory) (n.) Term applied to a variety
   of storage formats by which audio, text, and graphics are retrieved from
   the disk by laser beam.

cursor (n.) The movable symbol on the computer monitor (screen) that indicates the place where the operator is working.

database (n.) A large collection of information stored in a well-organized
   format that can be retrieved by specific software.

debug (v.) To eliminate a mistake within a computer program or its electrical system.

DOS (Disk Operating System) (n.) Used on IBM-compatible PCs.

download (v.) To transmit data from a central to a remote computer, from a file server to a workstation, or from a computer to a floppy disk.

e-mail (n.) Electronic mail. Tool for sending messages over the Internet.

field (n.) One of many sections that come together to constitute an electronic record.

file (n.) A collection of data considered a single unit.

floppy disk (n.) A small, inexpensive removable disk used to record and store information.

font (n.) A set of type characters used for printing information.

format (n.) The arrangement by which data are stored or displayed.

hard copy (n.) Printed computer output.

hard disk (n.) A metal disk covered with a magnetic recording surface usually installed inside PCs for added storage capacity.

hardware (n.) Equipment that makes up a computer such as chips, boards, wires, and transformers. Term also applies to other computer-related pieces of equipment such as printer, modem, keyboard, and monitor.

hypertext (n.) A section of web-page text that responds to a user command by establishing a connection to a file of information.

interface (n.) Interaction between hardware, software, and operator.

Internet (n.) An electronic network linking computers together, originally called ARPANET, the Advanced Research Projects Agency of the U.S. Department of Defense.

ISP (n.) Internet Service Provider. Establishes connections between computers and the Internet.

keyboard (n.) A set of keys (like a typewriter) used to type data into a computer.

links (n.) A hypertext screen section, usually underlined words or a framed graphic, that responds to a user's command to move from one file of information to another on a web page or to another website.

load (v.) To put information or data into the computer.

megabyte (n.) A unit of measure for the information stored in either the computer's hard drive or floppy disk; 1 megabyte equals 1 million characters (bytes) of data.

memory (n.) The computer's storage capacity.

menu (n.) Programs, functions, etc. displayed on the monitor for user selection.

modem (n.) A device used to transfer computer information over phone lines.

mouse (n.) A palm-sized device with one or more buttons that when rolled across a flat surface points at and selects items on a computer screen for input.

network (n.) Terminals and computers linked together for the purpose of interacting with each other.

online (adj.) Connected to the Internet.

operating system (n.) The main control program that runs the computer, such as Macintosh, DOS, OS/2.

PC (n.) Personal computer.

power surger (n.) An electrical device into which the computer is plugged to prevent loss of data or information due to a sudden jolt or loss of electric power; a surge protector.

printer (n.) A device that prints data and graphics from the computer.

RAM (n.) Random Access Memory.

ROM (n.) Read-Only Memory.

screen (CRT, monitor) (n.) A screen for viewing what's being displayed by computer.

search engine (n.) A World Wide Web tool designed to look for and display information in response to a user's query.

software (n.) Programs for directing the operation of a computer.

terminal (n.) A keyboard or video display unit used for entering information into or receiving information from a computer.

URL (n.) Uniform Resource Locator, another name for a website address.

user friendly (adj.) Not intimidating; easy to use.

virus (bug) (n.) A destructive program that is secretly attached to an existing program that can alter or delete data and can cause other computer malfunctions.

window (n.) A separate viewing area on a display screen.

word processor (n.) A program to allow an operator to write, edit, and correct text or documents on the computer.

work station (terminal) (n.) A PC that serves a single user.

WWW (n.) World Wide Web. An international collection of information searchable using text or graphic browsers.

PUTTING
IT ALL
TOGETHER

Order and simplification are the first steps toward mastery of a subject. . . .

Thomas Mann, *The Magic Mountain* (1924)

After reading and understanding this chapter, you should know:

- The two principal types of outlines.

- The six parts of an outline.

- How to prepare an outline.

- The four parts of a talk and how to bond them together.

- How to come up with a title for your talk.

- How to prepare an introduction to your talk.

- How to prepare a conclusion to your talk.

- What transitions are and how to use them.

CHAPTER PREVIEW

At this stage you've done your research and you know your subject. Now you must plan, or outline, your talk. In the long run, a good outline will save you far more time than you will devote to preparing it. The two most common types of outlines, the topic outline and the sentence outline, are explained and illustrated.

When you construct your talk, you may work on the body first and then the introduction or conclusion. A well-thought-out introduction will usually win audience goodwill and interest. Numerous suggestions for effective introductions are given, and all of them appear in introductions quoted from actual speeches. In addition, some ideas for forming conclusions are listed, and excellent examples are included.

Since every talk should have a title, actual titles of many speeches are listed, along with pointers on their distinguishing characteristics.

In every talk you give, the introduction, body, and conclusion should be linked smoothly to each other by means of transitions. Examples of transitions, together with the conditions that call for their use, appear in a table at the end of the chapter.

Appearing in this (and every) chapter is the feature "In Other Words," which will greatly benefit foreign and ESL students. To aid in their understanding of common American idioms and phrases, these expressions will be defined in the margin of the page on which they are introduced.

In Other Words:

NOTE
The way you organize your talk can "make or break" your overall performance. For that reason, this chapter deserves a great deal of your time and effort.

PREPARING AN OUTLINE

turned over in your mind—thoroughly review

You've done your research, you've uncovered more than enough material (always a wise policy), you've *turned the material over in your mind,* and you understand it *inside out.* Where do you go from here?

inside out—thoroughly, completely

What you need now is a plan to organize all the information you've gathered. In a sense, you're in the same position as an architect about to design a building, an airline pilot about to fly the Atlantic, or a motorist about to drive from New York to San Francisco. To accomplish these objectives, the architect needs blueprints, the pilot needs a flight plan, and the motorist needs road maps.

by the same token—in the same way

By the same token, you need a plan, or **outline,** of your talk. Before grimacing at the thought of preparing an outline, weigh the advantages of doing so:

■ It helps you decide what information to use, how to sequence it, and what information to omit.

■ It helps you classify information and separate main ideas from subordinate ones.

■ It helps you see the relationships between main ideas and their supporting materials and helps you determine whether those relationships are logical.

■ It saves you time by revealing possible gaps or redundancies in your body of information.

■ It helps you organize your talk and therefore makes your message more easily understood. And, after all, isn't that the point? Of course it is.

An outline, whether it's for a five- to seven-minute talk (quite likely in this course) or a twenty-minute talk, should consist of six parts: a **title;** a **purpose** (what you want your audience to get from your speech); a **thesis statement** (the main idea of your talk); an **introduction** designed to win the attention of your audience; a **body,** or discussion; and a **conclusion,** which is comparable to the punch line of a joke. You'll recall that there are only four parts of a talk as opposed to six parts of an outline. The purpose and thesis, by themselves, are not part of the talk but should be woven into the introduction. They are included in the outline to help you keep in focus the response you seek from your audience and the message that you wish to communicate.

The body of your outline should encompass three to five main points, each supported by data. Strive to use various types of data, such

"This is just the outline—wait'll you see the speech!"

as statistics, quotations, definitions, anecdotes, contrasts, comparisons, and examples. Keep in mind, however, that everything you include must be relevant to the *topic at hand.*

Before we *dip our toes* into the sea of outlining, let's spend a little time on the important aspects of the purpose and thesis statement.

topic at hand— the topic being discussed

*dip our toes—*to begin

Purpose and Thesis Statement

The **purpose** of a talk is the speaker's objective; that is, what the speaker hopes to achieve by giving the talk. The purpose may be informative, persuasive, or entertaining. The statement of purpose should be developed around a strong verb and should be stated as an infinitive: to convince, to demonstrate, to urge, to defend, to clarify. You should never attempt to give a talk without a clear understanding of what your purpose is. The purpose is the glue that holds the various parts of a talk together. If any element does not contribute to achieving the purpose, it doesn't belong in the talk. If you're trying to convince your audience that your team is going to win the championship this year, you shouldn't get involved in describing the stadium. If you're explaining the nutritional value of vegetables, don't waste time talking about the cholesterol content of eggs.

The **thesis statement** is a sentence that summarizes the content of the speech. It must agree with the purpose. If the two do not match, they should be revised; chances are that you haven't thought enough about what you're going to say. If you forget the thesis statement and try to jump from your topic to your introduction, you're heading for trouble.

The importance of the purpose and thesis statement, as well as the difference between them, can be observed in the following examples. Let's assume that you've decided to give a talk on the subject of going to college. That's a good first step. What you need next is a purpose and a thesis statement. Here are some possibilities:

Purpose: To encourage the listener to attend college.

Thesis statement: There are many reasons why you should seek a college education.

Purpose: To explain the benefits of a college education.

Thesis statement: A college education provides a number of important benefits to the student.

Purpose: To weigh the pros and cons of going to college.

Thesis statement: There are both advantages and disadvantages involved in going to college.

Purpose: To show that not everyone should go to college.

Thesis statement: It is a myth that everyone should go to college; there are a number of reasons why any given individual should not go.

Purpose: To outline the costs of going to college.

Thesis statement: Going to college requires a substantial financial investment.

Purpose: To suggest ways to reduce the costs of going to college.

Thesis statement: There are many sources of financial support available to help the college student reduce costs.

Each of the above examples, and many others that you might come up with, represents a very different speech. As you can see, it isn't enough simply to know that you're going to give a talk about going to college.

Once you have settled on your purpose and thesis statement, you're ready to develop an appropriate outline. At this point, you may find it helpful to expand the thesis statement to include your major points: There are many sources of financial support available to help the college student reduce costs—scholarships, loans, part-time jobs, attending a publicly supported college, commuting. OK, let's now wade into the very exciting and stimulating topic of outlining.

Principles of Outlining

Applying the following principles of outlining will help you achieve the benefits discussed above:

- Use a standard numbering system for main points and supporting points. A popular system uses Roman numerals (I, II, III, etc.) for main points, capital letters (A, B, C, etc.) for first-level supporting points, and Arabic numerals (1, 2, 3, etc.) for second-level supporting points.
- Use one symbol for each point.
- Be sure that topics numbered at the same level are equal in importance.
- Keep your outline fairly simple. If it becomes complicated, you know that your speech will be too involved.

The outline below illustrates these principles:

I. Main point
    A. First-level supporting point
        1. Second-level supporting point
        2. Second-level supporting point
    B. First-level supporting point
II. Main point

This numbering system and its indentions clearly highlight relationships among items in an outline. For example, main points I and II above are equal (sometimes called coordinate) in importance or value. Likewise, first-level supporting points I.A. and I.B. are also equal to each other but are subordinate to main point I. In turn, second-level supporting points I.A.1. and I.A.2. are equal to each other but are subordinate to first-level supporting point I.A.

If your outline sticks to the principles of equality and subordination explained here, you're on your way to a logically organized outline.

It's absolutely vital that topics numbered at the same level be equal in importance. The following example, inserted here as a caution to you, violates this cardinal rule:

I. Use of telephones is increasing worldwide (the world).
    A. It is increasing in South America (a continent).
    B. It is increasing in North America (a continent).
    C. It is increasing in the United States (a country).
    D. It is increasing in Asia (a continent).

Just as first-level supporting point I.A. (South America) is subordinate to main point I. (the world), so first-level supporting point I.C. (a country) is subordinate to a continent (North America). Therefore, I.C. doesn't belong here; it belongs at the next lower level—I.B.1.—and should be indented further. The outline should look like this:

I. Use of telephones is increasing worldwide (the world).
    A. It is increasing in South America (a continent).
    B. It is increasing in North America (a continent).
        1. It is increasing in the United States (a country).
    C. It is increasing in Asia (a continent).

Your English professor may have told you that in a formal outline you should not have a single subpoint because subpoints represent divisions of the points they are supporting and you can't divide something into one part. An outline for a short talk, however, can be a bit more informal.

Let's assume you've decided to give a talk encouraging your listeners to consider a career in real estate. As you brainstorm the topic, you *jot down* the following outline:

jot down—write

You should consider real estate as a career for the following reasons:

tied to—confined to

I. It can be very rewarding financially.
II. You're not *tied to* a desk all day.
III. You have to have a car.
IV. There will always be a demand for your services.
V. It's a great job.
VI. You have to pass a state examination to get a license.
VII. You meet a lot of interesting people.
VIII. The commissions are substantial.
IX. You have the chance to help people.

As you go back over the outline, you see that you've developed a list of points related to a real estate career, but not all of them are advantages. First of all, you realize that point III, although true, isn't an advantage of a real estate career. (Being able to deduct car expenses on your tax return may be an advantage, but not the need to have a car.) You strike that line from the outline.

Continuing down your list, you see that point V isn't a supporting point for your argument either. Rather, it is a restatement of your main point. So you remove it from the outline.

Next you realize that having to pass an exam is not an advantage but rather a requirement. You drop that from your outline too. You're left with the following:

I. It can be very rewarding financially.
II. You're not tied to a desk all day.
III. There will always be a demand for your services.
IV. You meet a lot of interesting people.
V. The commissions are substantial.
VI. You have the chance to help people.

On closer scrutiny you see a lot of overlapping among your points. Lines III and V support point I. Lines IV and VI both relate to working with people and should be combined under an appropriate heading. You think of additional supporting points and hopefully end up with this:

I. It can be very rewarding financially.
   A. There will always be a demand for your services.
   B. The commissions are substantial.
      1. Though salesmen share commissions with brokers, they do quite well.

II. You're not tied to a desk all day.
   1. You spend a lot of time in your car.
   2. You can do much of your phone work at home.
III. You have the chance to work with people.
   A. You get to meet a lot of interesting people.
   B. You have the chance to help them.

Types of Outlines and Sample Outlines

Speakers most commonly use sentence and topic outlines. You will want to use both. You should use the sentence outline in planning your talk because it will force you to think through the point you want to make about each of the topics you plan to discuss. But when you present your talk, you will be much better off with a topic outline. Having a sentence outline in front of you while you're speaking will tempt you to read it. And you don't want to do that if you want to give an effective speech. Listeners want to be spoken to, not read to. Moreover, a paper on which you have written a sentence outline will be too cluttered to permit you to find your place readily.

Coming up now is a subject for a sentence outline. Let's say that a year ago you went on a health kick that has drastically changed your lifestyle, especially concerning diet. You've read up on these topics because you want to be healthy, and now you're eager to tell the class about a diet that pays off in better health and appearance. The following outline is suitable for a five- to seven-minute talk, and its title is even spiced with a touch of slang:

Title

If You Want to Be Healthy, You Gotta Eat Smart

Purpose

To explain why a sound diet is important to one's health and what makes up a healthful diet

Thesis Statement

To get the nutrients you need for good health, you should eat daily, in varying amounts, from the four basic food groups.

Introduction

I. Sensible nutrition, based on eating from the four food groups, is vital to achieving good health and keeping it.
II. An essential nutrient is any food in the diet necessary to maintain life, to carry on normal functions, and to promote growth and repair of the body.

III. The Japanese diet is the exact opposite of ours. The Japanese people live longer than we do and have fewer cases of cancer and heart disease than we do.

Body

I. According to the U.S. Department of Agriculture,[1] you should base your daily diet on the following food groups:
  A. Pastas, rice, cereals, whole-grain bread—6 to 11 servings
  B. Vegetables—3 to 5 servings; fruits—2 to 4 servings
  C. Milk, yogurt, cheese—2 to 3 servings; meat, poultry, fish, dry beans, eggs, nuts—2 to 3 servings
  D. Sweets, oils, fats—use sparingly

Conclusion

Because of this diet, I feel much better and look much better. It can do the same for you. Start today.

The following partial sentence outline carries the numbering system one step further and, at the same time, illustrates another pitfall for you to beware of. Assume that a speaker is to argue that Los Angeles—or any large metropolitan area, for that matter—is facing a crisis in traffic congestion and desperately needs more public transportation. Let's say that the outline looks like this:

I. Traffic congestion is on the brink of strangling the entire city.
  A. Every 24 hours more than 1.3 million autos enter, leave, or pass through Los Angeles.
    1. Most autos carry only one person; the average is 1.3 persons.
    2. Most rush-hour traffic is inbound between 7 and 9 A.M. and outbound between 4 and 6 P.M.
    3. Autos cause air pollution.
  B. Public and private parking facilities are inadequate.

tossed out—omitted

Notice that item I.A.3., air pollution, has nothing at all to do with traffic congestion and should be ***tossed out.***

Earlier we mentioned two types of outlines: sentence and topic. The topic outline, except for the thesis statement (main idea), consists only of key words or phrases. As an example of a topic outline, let's convert the above sentence outline on big-city traffic to a topic outline:

I. Los Angeles on verge of collapse from traffic
  A. 1.3 million autos in and out daily

---

[1]*Newsweek*, 27 May 1991, 48.

      1. One person in most autos; average 1.3
      2. Rush hour traffic: 7–9 A.M., 4–6 P.M.
   B. Parking areas inadequate

Observe above how each indention represents a narrowing down of information. All outlines should adhere to this principle; that is, they should move from general information to more and more specific information.

So far we've emphasized the benefits of sentence outlines because, by their very nature, they contain more detailed information than topic outlines. However, to show you *the other side of the coin,* here's a complete topic outline that could serve as the basis of a four- to six-minute talk.

the other side of the coin—another way of doing the same thing

Title

The Many Costs of Buying a Car

Purpose

To explain the many expenses involved in buying a car

Thesis Statement

If you are thinking about buying a new car, be sure to consider all of the many expenses involved.

Introduction

   I. Alternatives to consider before buying a new car.
     A. Public transportation
     B. Borrowing or leasing a car when you need it
     C. Taking cabs
     D. Sharing a car
     E. Buying a used car

Body

   II. Don't overlook any of the following expenses:
     A. Initial costs
       1. Down payment
       2. Sales taxes
       3. First-year insurance premium
       4. Registration
     B. Ongoing expenses
       1. Monthly payments
         a. Principal
         b. Interest

    2. Upkeep
      a. Gas and oil
      b. Periodic routine maintenance
      c. Unexpected major repairs
    3. Insurance beyond the first year
    4. Annual taxes and fees
  C. Hidden expenses
    1. Depreciation
    2. Denial of other things the money could buy
    3. Loss of opportunity to invest

Conclusion

If you decide that you can afford all the expenses I have outlined, shop wisely—and happy driving!

Because of the great importance of having the knowledge of and being able to prepare an effective outline, here's another topic outline. This one covers the topics of this chapter and you can use it to study.

Putting It All Together

   I. Prepare an Outline
     A. Types of Outlines and Sample Outlines
  II. The Body of Your Talk
     A. From Simple to Complex
     B. From Cause to Effect
     C. From Effect to Cause
     D. From Problem to Solution
     E. According to Space or Location
     F. According to Time
 III. The Introduction of Your Talk
     A. A Startling Statement
     B. Reference to the Occasion and Sponsor
     C. Reference to the Audience
     D. Reference to the Speaker
     E. Reference to Literature
     F. Questions to the Audience
     G. An Anecdote
     H. Quotation from an Authority
     I. Statistics
     J. A Look to the Future
 IV. The Conclusion of Your Talk
     A. A Summary of Key Ideas
     B. A Prediction
     C. A Quotation—Emotional or Factual
     D. A Quotation from an Authority

Topic outlines are also well-suited to help you deliver your talks. Simply convert your sentence outline into a topic outline, type it double-spaced onto one or two 5-by-7-inch cards, and lay them on the lectern. Glancing occasionally at the card for a second or two should *trigger* your knowledge and memory of the subject so that you can keep on talking and still maintain eye contact with your audience.

trigger—stimulate

THE BODY OF YOUR TALK

Since every talk should have four parts—a title, an introduction, a body, and a conclusion—your outline must reflect that arrangement of elements. In preparing your talk, however, outline the body first and then the introduction or conclusion. The reason for this sequence is that you need to know your message before you can introduce it.

As mentioned before, the main points and subpoints that support your thesis statement comprise the body, or main discussion, of your presentation. For short talks, such as you'll probably give in this basic course, three or four main points should be enough.

Clearly, it's impossible to know in advance how many points and subpoints you'll end up with or, for that matter, how many paragraphs each point will require for adequate coverage. You'll find the answers when you translate all the bits and pieces that form your outline into sentences and paragraphs. You can arrange your main points in any one of the following sequences:

- from simple to complex—a much-used strategy in teaching
- from cause to effect
- from effect to cause
- from problem to solution
- according to space or location
- according to time

From Simple to Complex

If, for example, you're explaining and demonstrating various tennis strokes to your class, you'd logically start with the basic forehand and

Be sure to start with elementary concepts.

backhand. You'd then cover more advanced strokes such as the serve, smash, and volley. If you were to begin with the smash and the volley, you would confuse and discourage most novice players; they'd lose interest. In other words, when discussing something technical or new to an audience, be sure to start with elementary concepts and then move to the more difficult.

From Cause to Effect

Reasoning from cause to effect involves a situation, event, or condition (an effect) that will happen in the future. For example, in a speech on energy conservation, you might reason that if you insulate your house or apartment (install storm windows and doors, caulk them, lower the thermostat, use an economical shower head, and so on), your heating bill will decrease substantially. All these causes, but especially insulation, will result in an effect—a lowered heating bill.

Here a caution is in order. An effect is usually produced by more than one cause. For example, to win most of its games, a football team needs a sharp, hard-driving coach, talented players who are willing *to go all the way,* some "cooperative" opponents, and a smidgen of luck.

to go all the way—to exert maximum effort

From Effect to Cause

"Effect to cause" reasoning involves finding a cause for an event that has happened. Suppose you witness an auto accident and notice that one of the two drivers moves unsteadily, slurs his or her words, and has slightly glazed eyes. You may conclude that the accident was caused by a driver under the influence of alcohol.

For another example, suppose that the number of burglaries in your city has doubled in the past two years, and in the same period your police force was cut 40 percent. In a speech, you might assert that the increase in crime (effect) was caused, at least partially, by the cutback in police protection.

These simple cases illustrate the kinds of thinking that we do throughout life. Some cases, however, are not so clear-cut; because they combine many causes and effects, they will require hard, straight thinking.

From Problem to Solution

Pollution of air and water is a critical problem in today's industrialized societies. Some of the steps being taken to solve the problem are: improving the internal combustion engine, controlling the exhaust of industrial smokestacks, and restricting the dumping of waste into bodies of water. In your speech, first state a problem, then suggest possible solutions.

According to Space or Location

Let's say that you want to discuss the mountain ranges in the United States. A logical approach would be to start with the White Mountains in New Hampshire and move westward to the Sierra Nevada in California. Or you could go the other way around. But you would surely not go from New Hampshire to California and then back to the Rockies in Colorado.

According to Time

Suppose you decide to give a talk on how our economy has historically evolved. You would go back to the eighteenth century to discuss our trailways and waterways; next you would move to the nineteenth century with the advent and proliferation of our railroads; you would then *point out* how the twentieth century gave us not only superhighways but larger, faster, and more efficient aircraft; and finally, you would prophesy (with considerable confidence) that our new millennium (the twenty-first century) will see an explosion of electronic and other technological innovations to develop informational and communication services further.

point out—mention

THE INTRODUCTION OF YOUR TALK

Now that you know what the substance of your talk will be, you're in a much better position to forge a strong introduction. Such an introduction is vital to the success of your talk because it can win over your audience immediately. Since the first few sentences are crucial, you should consider memorizing them. Rehearse them until you can speak smoothly and confidently.

Your introduction should serve three major functions:

- to divulge the purpose of your talk
- to gain audience goodwill
- to arouse audience interest

To achieve those aims, your introduction may include any one or a combination of the following:

- a startling statement
- reference to the occasion and sponsor
- reference to the audience
- reference to the speaker
- reference to literature
- questions to the audience
- an anecdote
- quotation from an authority
- statistics
- a look to the future

All these suggestions are illustrated in the following examples from actual speeches.

A Startling Statement

Suppose you're to speak about a few very wealthy and generous people who believe in helping poor youngsters get an education, and you begin like this:

> In the largest gift of its kind in Massachusetts, a Connecticut couple has pledged $2.5 million to put 67 East Cambridge second graders through college.
> The gift to the entire second-grade class of the Harrington School will provide motivational counseling, tutoring, mentoring and a summer school program through the next 10 years as well as free tuition for four years of college or vocational school.[2]

This introduction should grab your audience's interest immediately.

---

[2]*The Boston Globe*, 15 June 1991, 1, 20.

Reference to the Occasion and Sponsor

Good afternoon. It's a pleasure to be here today. And it's especially appropriate that the YWCA should be sponsoring this seminar on civic responsibility and the corporate woman. Few organizations have put themselves on the line quite the way the "Y" has in its concern to provide equal opportunities for growth and development to everyone.

Looking back through history, whenever there's been an important women's issue, or relevant needs to be addressed, the "Y" has been there. This includes being in the forefront in initiating programs for women returning to the labor market after absences of many years; offering career-oriented workshops for teenagers; and using "Y" buildings, which were formerly dormitories, as shelters for battered women or as senior citizen centers.[3]

Reference to the Audience

Madam Chairman, Distinguished Guests, Ladies and Gentlemen. Thank you for that kind introduction. It is indeed an honor for me to have been invited to address the Empire Club of Canada. Before I begin my prepared text, I'd like to ask all war veterans in the audience to please stand up at their places, and remain standing.

Now, would everyone who has ever taken a Red Cross First Aid or Water Safety course please stand.

Would those who have ever volunteered for the Red Cross, are Red Cross employees or have ever made a donation to a Red Cross international appeal, a local Red Cross or United Way campaign please join those already standing.

And finally, of those still seated, if you have ever donated blood or received a blood transfusion, would you also please stand?

Ladies and Gentlemen, it gives me great pleasure as Secretary General to dedicate my presentation to the constituents of the Red Cross. Please be seated.[4]

Reference to the Speaker

I did not want to come to Los Angeles to give this lecture for many reasons. I am neither a philosopher nor a political activist. However, because of the heated debate between biomedical scientists and antivivisectionists, I felt an obligation to speak on behalf of the right of the incurably ill to hope for cures or relief from suffering through research using animals. I am crippled—by paraplegia—which today is incurable. Those of us who have an incurable disease or have permanently crippling injuries can only hope for a cure through research. Much of this

---

[3]Mary M. Gates, "The Changing Role of Women in Voluntarism: Individual Growth and Worth," speech delivered to the YWCA, Seattle, Washington, 27 February 1981.
[4]George B. Webber, "The Red Cross—Our Path into the 21st Century," speech delivered to the Empire Club of Canada, Toronto, Ontario, Canada, 19 February 1987.

"I rise so you can see me—speak so you can hear me—
and sit down so you can like me."

experimental work will require the use of animals, and accordingly, we must find some compromise that defends both human rights and animal welfare. In the determination of a compromise between the reduction of human suffering and the violation of animals' welfare, which at times includes causing pain or discomfort; I unequivocally choose to reduce human suffering.[5]

Reference to Literature

Thank you for this chance to keynote Kent State's honors week events. We gather this week to recognize academic achievement. Oddly, the theme of these proceedings is the approach of 1984, the year George Orwell made a metaphor for totalitarianism. I say "oddly" because the central feature of Orwell's *1984* was the mass mind—whole populations thinking in state-imposed uniformity. Such uniformity strikes me as the antithesis of the individual intellectual excellence that we gather to

[5]Dennis M. Feeney, "Human Rights and Animal Welfare," *American Psychologist* (June 1987), 593–94.

honor this week, the excellence that René Descartes celebrated in saying, "I think, therefore I am."[6]

Questions to the Audience

Many of you—maybe most—have seen poverty at close range, have had contact with people who are homeless, hungry, ill, who subsist on low wages or insufficient welfare grants, who live in miserable surroundings that are shocking and repulsive. . . .

You have asked yourself: what is wrong, why isn't something done about it? Are those appalling conditions to be blamed on an evil economic system, on a heartless society, on an unconcerned government, on powerful, malevolent forces? If our social-economic system is so bad, how did it make the great majority of our people better off than most of the rest of mankind? Evidently, it does produce the greatest good for the greatest number. Why do millions of people, especially the needy from all over the world, envy us Americans and would like to come here if they could? Why, as we found out in the past few months, do so many people in overseas countries view the United States with admiration, why do they try to find a way to adopt or copy our political-economic system, so they might be able to live as well as most of us do? Our living standards are drastically higher than those in most of Africa, Asia, South America and even ahead of much or most of Europe.

Should we then conclude that we Americans, smug in our comfort, neglect the less fortunate in our midst—that we just do not care about people who income-wise are the lowest 10 percent or 20 percent of our population?[7]

An Anecdote

They've asked me to give you some advice this morning on *service.* I am always a little reluctant to give this speech because I remember the grade school student who wrote,

"Socrates was a Greek philosopher who went around giving people good advice. They poisoned him."

Last week I heard of a discussion that actually occurred between a banker and his customer in Texas. The farmer came in and told the banker he had some good news and some bad news. The banker said, "Well, let's hear the bad news first." The farmer said, "You know the crop loan I've taken out from you every year the last ten years?" The banker said, "Yes." "Well, this year I can't pay it back. And you know the mortgage I have on my land?" "Yes." "I can't pay it back either. And the couple of hundred thousand I still have outstanding on my

[6]Alton W. Whitehouse, Jr., "The Misinformation Society: Renewing Our Commitment to the Power of Education," speech delivered at Kent State University Honors Week, Kent, Ohio, 20 April 1981.
[7]Roger A. Freeman, "Does America Neglect Its Poor," speech delivered to the Stanford Alumni Association, San Francisco, California, 14 March 1990.

tractor and the other equipment?" "Yes." "They're all yours." There was a moment of silence. And then the banker said, "Well, what's the good news?" The farmer smiled: "I want you to know that I'M GOING TO KEEP ON BANKING WITH YOU!"

Well, the good news from here is that I'm going to keep talking![8]

Quotation from an Authority

With the publication of his book, *The Making of the President—1960,* the late Theodore White achieved instant recognition as one of America's foremost political writers. The success of his book was so great that it insured the favorable reception of his subsequent books that followed each presidential election through 1980.

One of the things that Teddy White did so well was to paint a verbal picture of the United States, a picture based on his personal observations along the campaign trail combined with the then available statistical data.

His last book was written after the 1980 election and contained a dramatic sentence that I have never forgotten. This is what White wrote:

"At the end, with all the attention and programs, big cities were on their way to tragedy: they had become warehouses for the very poor or enclaves of the very rich, while common civility had become a memory."

The significance of White's description of the big city is that it is painted in terms of rich and poor with no reference to the middle class which has historically been the foundation of the city.[9]

Statistics

Mr. President, Mr. Speaker, fellow delegates, colleagues and friends: I stand before you today not only as your president-elect, but also as a dean and as a professor. As a professor, I am programmed, once started, to speak for fifty-five minutes. However, I have been reminded that the story of the creation of the world is told in Genesis in 400 words, that the world's greatest moral code, the Ten Commandments, contains only 297 words, that Lincoln's immortal Gettysburg Address is but 266 words in length and that the Declaration of Independence required but 1,321 words to set up for the world a new concept of freedom. I think I get the point."[10]

A Look to the Future

Today the Soviet Union is disaggregating and the U.S.A. has shed her imperial role, abandoned her economic dominance and is turning inwards.

---

[8]Robert Williams, "The Do's and Don'ts of Service," speech delivered to the American Banker Conferences, New York, New York, 19 June 1990, and Los Angeles, California, 28 June 1990.
[9]James C. Gardner, "The Changing American City," speech delivered to Premier Mortgage "Breakfast Brigade," Shreveport, Louisiana, 16 October 1990.
[10]C. John Tupper, "A New American Revolution: Do Your Own Thing vs. Guaranteeism," speech delivered to the California Medical Association, 12 March 1979.

At one and the same time, we are losing both our great enemy and our great friend. Locked in struggle, they have remained locked in decline.

What is more, America has chosen a different path. As *Time*, that very American magazine, recently wrote, and I quote,

> by 2020, a date no further into the future than John F. Kennedy's election is in the past, the number of U.S. residents who are Hispanic or non-white will have more than doubled to nearly 115 million.

> Only a short time later, the population of European descent will be a minority. To quote *Time* again, "the 'average' U.S. resident, as defined by Census statistics, will trace his or her descent to Africa, Asia, the Hispanic world, the Pacific islands, Arabia—almost anywhere but white Europe . . . ."[11]

THE CONCLUSION OF YOUR TALK

With your main discussion and introduction ready to go, you should be all set to work out a conclusion. Two cautions are in order: (1) A conclusion should not drag on and on, and (2) it should not contain any new material.

Here are some ideas to incorporate in your conclusion:

- a summary of key ideas
- a prediction
- a quotation, either emotional or factual
- a quotation from an authority
- an anecdote or question, or both
- a challenge to the audience
- a call to action
- a historical reference

All these suggestions are illustrated in the following conclusions from actual speeches.

A Summary of Key Ideas

> In conclusion, I feel sure that these programs of communication are proving of great benefit to both managers and employees. Even if they were expensive, *which they are not*, it would still be worth it. *The cost of economic ignorance would be much, much greater.* After all, better communication reaps the following benefits for a corporation:
>
> - Employees know decisions and the reasons for them.
> - Less misunderstandings occur.

---

[11]James Goldsmith, "Europe—Why and How," speech delivered at The Institute of Directors Annual Lecture, London, England, 12 June 1990.

- The possibility of cooperation with change is greatly increased.
- The damaging effects of rumor are lessened.
- The role of management is reinforced.

Managers, union leaders and rank-and-file employees readily understand the need for these improvements in their relationships. And, as the Japanese have proved, whether working with their own nationals, or American or Australian workers, employee understanding and involvement works for everybody's benefit. Certainly we are experiencing these benefits in some corporations in Australia.

Enterprise Australia is proud to have contributed toward these advancements in employee communication.[12]

A Prediction

In reality, I believe, we will evolve along a more conventional and prosaic trajectory. Barring some cataclysmic developments on the energy front, the automobile is likely to remain the preferred means of transportation of most Americans well into the next century—although, as we have noted, it will be a vehicle vastly different in design and performance. At the same time, public transportation—or, I should say, collective transportation—will assume a much more significant role in our daily lives. Transit of tomorrow will have more varied forms and utilize a wider range of vehicles, service modes, and operating arrangements, as it tries to serve a broader, more differentiated market.

While public transportation will tend to become more flexible and personalized, the automobile will. . . .

Rail transit of the surface variety may. . . .

Finally, pedestrians will have regained some of the territory they lost to the automobile during the last fifty years, as cities and suburbs impose more stringent requirements on the use of cars in congested centers and residential neighborhoods.

And—oh yes—we will still have rush-hour traffic and potholes. They will be there to remind us of the good old days back in the late 1980s, when gasoline was still only one dollar a gallon, when parking in government buildings was still free, and when one could still afford the luxury of driving to work in one's own automobile.[13]

A Quotation, Either Emotional or Factual

In conclusion, we need to be reminded of the famous words of the Protestant minister who recounted the prevailing attitude during the Holocaust:

---

[12]J. T. Keavney, "Australia: Turning Away from Socialism," speech delivered to the Board of Trustees of the American Economic Foundation, New York, New York, 19 January 1981.
[13]C. Kenneth Ovski, "Urban Transportation: A Profile of the Future," speech delivered at the NASA Colloquium on Profiles of the Future, Washington, DC, 11 September 1979.

You might conclude with a prediction for the future.

. . . They came first for the Communists, and I didn't speak up because I wasn't a Communist.

Then they came for the Jews, and I didn't speak up because I wasn't a Jew.

Then they came for the trade unionists, and I didn't speak up because I wasn't a trade unionist.

Then they came for the Catholics, and I didn't speak up because I was a Protestant.

Then they came for me, and by that time no one was left to speak.

Thank you.[14]

---

[14]R. Y. Woodhouse, "Equality Faces a Dangerous Decade: Defend Our Beliefs and Speak Out," speech delivered at the Naval Supply Systems Command Human Resource Management Conference, Seattle, Washington, 18 November 1980.

A Quotation from an Authority

I want to conclude my talk by quoting in its entirety a brief but, I think, superb exposition of what I've been trying to say. The author is Leo Rosten, and, believe it or not, I once worked with him too. He called his little essay *The Power of Words*, and it goes like this:

> They sing. They hurt. They teach. They sanctify. They were man's first immeasurable feat of magic. They liberated us from ignorance and our barbarous past. For without these marvelous scribbles which build letters into words, words into sentences, sentences into systems and sciences and creeds, man would be forever confined to the self-isolated prison of the scuttlefish or the chimpanzee. 'A picture is worth 10,000 words,' goes the timeworn Chinese maxim. 'But,' one writer tartly said, 'it takes words to say that.' We live by words: Love, Truth, God. We fight for words: Freedom, Country, Fame. We die for words: Liberty, Glory, Honor. They bestow the priceless gift of articulateness on our minds and hearts—from 'Mama' to 'infinity.' And the men who truly shape our destiny, the giants who teach us, inspire us, lead us to deeds of immortality, are those who use words with clarity, grandeur and passion. Socrates, Jesus, Luther, Lincoln, Churchill.
>
> The power of words . . . .[15]

An Anecdote or Question, or Both

And I'll close with a true story to illustrate how we *are* set apart and what our values really are. During the days of the Soviet triumph with their first Sputnik, a grade school class in Russia was discussing that remarkable feat—eclipsing the whole world in scientific genius. The teacher asked the class if they were thrilled with the prospect of a Russian satellite probing space and perhaps some day landing a Russian on the moon.

The class smiled with pride and agreed it would be a great achievement to go to the moon. But one thoughtful student broke the silence and spoke a different kind of response.

"Yes, it would be wonderful to go to the moon," he said. "But I would like to know—when may we go to Vienna?"[16]

A Challenge to the Audience

So, one of the challenges in the 1990s is to structure ourselves to deal with this "interdependent independence" that will be necessary for twenty-first century existence.

---

[15]Melvin J. Grayson, "The Last Best Hope: Words," speech delivered to the Society of Consumer Affairs Professionals in Business, New York, New York, 3 April 1981.
[16]Harvey C. Jacobs, "Finding Your Way Through the Woods: It's a Lifelong Challenge," speech delivered at the Defense Information School, Fort Benjamin Harrison, Indianapolis, Indiana, 24 January 1981.

The technologies of communications and third-generation computers provide us the opportunity to pursue individuality to a degree not possible before. At the same time, they allow us to share and access the experience and knowledge of others. Most important, they provide the only analytical resource capable of dealing with the incredible environmental, economic and other structural interdependencies of the world.

Again, the transition to a fully integrated third generation has more profound implications than all computer history to date. It will be a challenging, exciting, potentially rewarding new era.

Henry Ford said, and I quote: "A generation ago there were a thousand men to every opportunity, while today there are a thousand opportunities to every man." Ford made that statement in 1927. I don't really know about then. But I do know about now. The Third Computer Generation will open up more opportunities than ever before. Not to every man and woman, perhaps, but without question, to those who are prepared. Whether you are or not is up to you.[17]

A Call to Action Now

It's time for action for *all of us.*

Here's what *you* can do.

First, we can all follow Lyn Banke's admonition and take this opportunity to raise the level of concern among our legislators.

Write to them. Let them *know* what the need is. Let them *know* how child care will benefit our society and our economy.

And second, start an active effort in your own organization or company to identify and address child care needs.

And while we're at it, we need to focus on what we can do, *not* just complain about what we *can't.*

It's clear to me, and I hope to you that the child care that's provided in this decade—and into the next century will be no better than we make it.

Thank you.[18]

A Historical Reference

Mr. Lincoln would not offer government as the *first* alternative for dealing with problems. He would focus government action where it could be used best: to break down barriers to freedom and opportunity: to enable every man and woman to fulfill their potential, develop their God-given talent, and pursue their inalienable right to human happiness.

After all, isn't that what the terrible battle fought here was really about—the noblest effort any people ever made to dismantle the cruelest barrier to human freedom?

---

[17]Robert M. Price, "Computers in the '90s," speech delivered at the Minnesota Executive Speaker Series, University of Minnesota, Minneapolis, Minnesota, 13 February 1990.
[18]Stephen E. Ewing, "Nourish Thy Children," speech delivered to the Child Care Coordinating Council, Livonia, Michigan, 30 March 1990.

One hundred and twenty-seven years after Gettysburg, Lincoln's belief that all human beings are created equal and endowed with inalienable rights—the faith upon which liberal democracy is based—is beginning to prevail around the world.

Because of democracy's long march from Independence Hall through Gettysburg to the very streets of Moscow, the *world* knows the simple yet profound truth: the yearning for freedom cannot be extinguished, the struggle for inalienable rights will never end short of victory; nothing can deny the transcendence of democracy.

As Americans, we cannot rest until the blessings we enjoy are shared by all. Let us fulfill our Nation's destiny by making Mr. Lincoln's great proposition of democracy—set forth on this battlefield—into a self-evident truth for every man, woman, and child on this earth.[19]

THE TITLE OF YOUR TALK

Just as every book has a title and every newspaper story a headline, so every talk should have a title. Your title is an ad, a billboard for your speech. And audiences generally appreciate knowing immediately what they are about to hear rather than waiting to find out your message. They usually learn the title of your talk either from a printed program, the chairperson, or the **MC** (Master of Ceremonies). In class, your instructor may have you write your title on the chalkboard. If you try to imagine a movie without a title, you can appreciate the importance of a title for your talk.

Usually, the most propitious time to consider a title is after you've developed the main ideas of your speech. It's possible, however, that during the process of building the introduction, body, and conclusion of your talk, a striking title may suddenly appear, seemingly out of nowhere. If it does, you're lucky. If it doesn't, try to create one that meets these criteria:

1. It should be provocative enough to pique your listeners' interest.
2. It should be short and simple; say, from three to ten words.
3. It should indicate the purpose and content of your talk.

Table 8.1 lists some titles taken from speeches published in the journal *Vital Speeches of the Day*, along with their outstanding traits.

TRANSITIONS, OR CONNECTING LINKS

Just as a brick wall needs cement to keep it intact, a speech needs something to hold it together. That "something" is **transitions**—statements,

---

[19]Jack Kemp, "Lincoln's Vision of Democracy," speech delivered to the Lincoln Fellowship of Pennsylvania, Gettysburg, Pennsylvania, 19 November 1990.

Table 8.1 Types of Speech Titles

Traits	Titles
Questions	"How Can We Control Teen-age Crime? "Where Is This Black Progress?"
Alliteration	"Inventors, Invention, and Innovation" "Private Property and Perestroika"
A complete sentence	"Nothing Much Happens Without a Dream"
A famous title	"The Ten Commandments of a Quality Community"
Similar last syllables	"Foundations, Traditions, and Directions in U.S. Health Care"
Imagination	"I Touch the Future—I Teach"
Fairy tale opener	"Once upon a Time"
Startling statement	"Raising Corn and Beans and Hell"
Brevity	"Welcome Home"
Words that rhyme	"Town and Gown" "TV's Jiggle and Wiggle"
A play on words	"Today's Dollar Doesn't Make Much Sense" "If You Don't Think Dieting Is Serious Business What Do Its First Three Letters Spell?"

questions, or phrases that allow you to smoothly connect one idea to the next—moving from the introduction to the body, from the various major points within the body to their supporting details right into the conclusion. Transitions also show the relationships between ideas.

You see transitions in daily communication, but when you speak to a group, you may forget them. Don't. They help your listeners follow your train of thought and, thus, make your communication task easier.

Table 8.2 lists some simple transitional words and phrases that can be used to connect sentences and the conditions that call for their use.

The most important type of transition in an effective speech is the smooth movement from one section of the speech to the next. Since inevitably the attention of listeners will wander, if you want to be understood easily, you will need to provide reminders of where they've been and where they're going as your speech unfolds.

To help your listeners follow you, you should adopt the habit of the country preacher who was asked how he managed to come up with a first-rate sermon every Sunday. He said, "It's really quite simple. You have to do just three things for the congregation: First, tell them what you're going to tell them; then tell them; then tell them what you told them." Adhering to the preacher's formula will supply much of the help your listeners will need to follow you. Reinforcing the structure with phrases and sentences that guide your audience from one of your points to the next will provide the rest. The following excerpts from a speech

Table 8.2 Transitional Words and Their Uses

To indicate	Use these transitions
Place	adjacent to, on the opposite side, diagonally across, diametrically opposite
Time	after a few hours, meanwhile, in the meantime, afterward, immediately, earlier, later, then
Purpose	for this reason, to this end, with this goal
Concession	of course, to be sure, naturally
Comparison and contrast	on the other hand, nevertheless, on the contrary, in contrast, in the same way, conversely, however, in like manner, similarly, whereas
Summary or repetition	in other words, to review briefly, in short, on the whole, to sum up, as previously noted, here again, in summary, in brief, if I may repeat
Explanation	for example, in particular, more specifically
Addition	furthermore, in the second place, besides, moreover, again, in addition, equally important, finally, also
Cause or result	on that account, therefore, as a result, thereupon, for this reason, consequently, accordingly, under these condition, hence
Conditions	although, because, even though, since, if, unless, under these circumstances, nevertheless, otherwise, this being so

demonstrate how the preacher might have handled a recommendation of his favorite restaurant:

1. *Tell them what you're going to tell them:*
   At the end of your introduction preview your main points.

   I recommend the Culinary House because [main point #1] the food is outstanding, [main point #2] the atmosphere is charming, and [main point #3] the prices are right.

2. *Tell them:*

   [transition] First, [main point #1] let me tell you about the Culinary House's awesome food. [Descriptions of the speaker's favorite dishes follow.]

   [transition] But you expect more than good food from a first-class restaurant. You also want to enjoy it in [main point #2] a quiet, home-like atmosphere. [Details about the atmosphere follow.]
   [transition] So far I've talked about the good food and the pleasant atmosphere. For the college student on a restricted budget, however, the greatest attraction of the Culinary House may well be [main point #3] its reasonable prices. [Examples of reasonable prices follow.]

3. *Tell them what you told them (conclusion):*
   After the discussion of prices, recapitulate your main points.

   [transition] In summary, the next time you are looking for a restaurant where [main point #1] you will find delicious food [main point #2] served in a cozy atmosphere [main point #3] at prices that won't even make you use your credit card, pay a visit to the Culinary House. You'll be glad you did!

After you've selected and narrowed your topic, performed your research and apply what you've learned from this chapter, you should feel quite confident about putting together an interesting and effective talk. Good luck.

THINGS TO DISCUSS IN CLASS

1. Give the class an example of a sentence outline and a topic outline. Explain why you prefer one over the other.
2. Find two speech titles you consider outstanding. Explain why you think so.
3. Write an outline for a short talk on any subject you could give in class. Don't forget the title.
4. Consult the journal *Vital Speeches of the Day* for an outstanding introduction and/or conclusion. Bring either one to class for discussion.
5. In your library, investigate several sources, such as *Vital Speeches of the Day,* and bring to class a few examples of the various ways that speakers arranged their main points during their talks.
6. Bring to class a short speech and point out its transitions.
7. Select two general topics that you feel would make an interesting talk, and suggest two titles for each topic.

WHAT DO YOU REMEMBER FROM THIS CHAPTER?

1. Why should you outline your talk?
2. Describe the two principal types of outlines.
3. List a few characteristics of a good title.
4. What are the chief purposes of an introduction?
5. Explain the main parts of a speech.
6. Mention a few ways to prove your main points.
7. What elements should be present in a conclusion?
8. What are transitions and why should you use them?
9. What two cautions should you keep in mind regarding the conclusion of your talk?
10. Explain the difference between a main point and a subpoint.

VITALIZE YOUR VOCABULARY

Because thousands of English words are derived from Latin words, there's no question that the study of Latin would strengthen your English vocabulary. But you don't have to study that ancient language in order to benefit from it. To increase your word power, we suggest that you learn the meanings of some Latin prefixes and roots. By doing this, you'll improve your command of the English language in speaking, writing, reading, and listening.

To get you moving, below are a few Latin prefixes and roots, along with their meanings, and some sample English words that use them:

Prefixes	Meanings	Sample Words
ambi	both	ambidextrous, ambiguous
anti	against, opposite	antifreeze, antibiotic
circum	around, on all sides	circumference, circumlocution
equi	equal	equidistant, equilibrium
intra, intro	within	intramural, intrastate, introvert
sub	under, beneath	subcontract, subhuman, submarine
super, supra	above, over	superhighway, supersonic, supernatural

Now let's do the same with some Latin roots:

Roots	Meanings	Sample Words
aqu	water	aquarium, aquatic, aqueduct
aud, audit	hear	audio, audience, auditorium
ben, bene	good, well	benefactor, benefit
cid, cis	cut, kill	homicide, incision, suicide
cred	belief, trust	credible, credit, creed
flu, fluct	flow	fluctuate, influence
leg	law	legal, legislate, legitimate
medi	middle	medieval, mediocre, medium
nov	new	innovate, novelty, renovate
tors, tort	twist	contortion, distort, torque
viv	life, lively	vivacious, vivid

If some of these sample words are not clear to you, then poke your nose into that dust-covered dictionary.

DELIVERING YOUR SPEECH

9

All the great speakers were bad speakers at first.

Ralph Waldo Emerson, "Power,"
The Conduct of Life (1860)

After reading and understanding this chapter, you should know:

- **The various methods of delivering a talk.**

- **The advantages and disadvantages of each method.**

- **The difference between an extemporaneous and an impromptu talk.**

- **How to deliver a talk that you have prepared.**

- **The importance of speaking with enthusiasm.**

- **The importance of practicing your talk.**

- **How to cope with nerves before you speak and while you're speaking.**

- **How to develop your style and confidence as a speaker.**

There are four methods of delivering a speech, speaking extemporaneously, reading from a manuscript, speaking from memory, and speaking impromptu. For most people, an extemporaneous talk is the most effective. It requires you to know your subject in depth and allows you to use note cards. You can also look at your listeners and speak in the language most appropriate to them and to you.

Those who have significant statements to make to the public or to a special audience often read from a manuscript. Beginning speakers who need 110 percent security also tend to read. The disadvantages of reading are that usually, the talk sounds "read," eye contact is lost and the speaker may become addicted to reading all the time. If, however, you must read your talk, try to follow the suggestions given in this chapter.

Speaking from memory invites trouble. What do you do if you forget a word? In addition, this method of delivery can sound cold and mechanical. Memorizing, however, can

help you in your introduction and conclusion. Memorizing is also recommended for very short talks, such as introducing a speaker or presenting or accepting an award. (See Chapter 13.)

However there is another way of speaking. If you are called on to say a few words—without prior notice—you are speaking impromptu. The best advice on speaking impromptu is to have some remarks prepared if there is any likelihood you might be called on without warning.

Other topics discussed in this chapter are the importance of practicing your talk, ways to relieve tension before and while speaking and developing style and confidence as a speaker.

Appearing in this (and every) chapter is the feature "In Other Words," which will greatly benefit foreign and ESL students. To aid in their understanding of common American idioms and phrases, these expressions will be defined in the margin of the page on which they are introduced.

SPEAKING EXTEMPORANEOUSLY

In Other Words:

The most successful speakers in business, politics, religion, and education speak extemporaneously. After analyzing the audience in advance, they perform the following regimen:

- Select a topic and limit it to the time available.
- State the purpose of the talk.
- Decide on three or four main points and a few subpoints under each.
- Research the topic and prepare a bibliography.
- Gather supporting material.
- Prepare an outline.
- Put it all together.
- Prepare an introduction and conclusion, sometimes memorizing them.
- Prepare note cards.
- Practice the speech aloud two or three times, with or without note cards, and, preferably, to a few critical listeners.

By doing these tasks, successful speakers smooth their **delivery** and bolster their self-confidence. If you follow this method of preparing your talk, you should be so immersed in your topic that you need refer only occasionally to your note cards or outline.

An **extemporaneous** talk enables you to speak in your own style, even to the extent of choosing some words on the *spur of the moment.* Thus, your presentation will not sound memorized, or "canned." Since note cards reinforce your memory and give you confidence, you'll be able to maintain that all-important eye contact and, at the same time, convey sincerity and spontaneity. You can even move away from the lectern because you're not chained to a written manuscript. With these advantages, you can talk in your own conversational style and, thus, establish a rapport with most audiences.

spur of the moment—immediately, without preparation

As you can see, extemporaneous delivery offers you a great deal of latitude. If you wish to quote someone, you can read the quotation verbatim or recite it from memory. Be sure to cite the source. If you give the talk more than once, chances are that you will not use the same wording each time. The talk will be conversational and spontaneous—the reward for advance preparation.

On the other hand, there are pitfalls to be aware of: looking at note cards too often or playing with them can distract an audience; and a weak, limited vocabulary will not result in a spontaneous, vivid, and attention-getting speech.

All things considered, extemporaneous speaking is the most effective method of delivery and the one that you should try to master.

The talk will be conversational and spontaneous.

Using Note Cards in Extemporaneous Speaking

After you've studied your topic and know it well, it's time to prepare note cards if you need them. Suitable notes consist of key words and phrases that will remind you of your main points and subpoints. Keep your notes as concise as possible and print them, on one side only, in large capitals so you can skim them in a flash and resume eye contact with your listeners.

For a five-minute talk, your notes should fit on a 3-by-5-inch note card. If you have quotations and statistics, put them on other cards. Whenever you use two or more cards, be sure to number them just in case you drop or misplace them. (We discussed using notes at the end of Chapter 2.)

Speaking with Enthusiasm

One of the most significant elements of oral delivery is speaker **enthusiasm.** If you're genuinely excited and stimulated by your topic, then the chances are excellent that you can conduct this "electricity" to your audience.

Having enthusiasm for your topic means speaking with sincerity about your topic and speaking with **empathy** for your listeners. It means talking with excitement—elevating your voice here, then lowering it a bit there. (Remember our discussion on inflection in Chapter 3?) It means talking quickly on occasion, and slowly at other times. (Pacing is covered in Chapter 5.) It means emphasizing action and descriptive words and phrases. (Oral visualization is covered in Chapter 5.) It means pausing just before making an important point or two, or after making important points, to allow the audience time to let the message **sink in**. (You will find more on pausing also in Chapter 5.) And it certainly means looking directly at members of your audience to make your listeners active participants in the speaking event.

sink in—be understood

Enthusiasm comes from believing in yourself and what you have to say. Enthusiasm means being excited about being able to share your message with your audience. Your enthusiasm should be clearly revealed through your eyes, your facial expression, your movement, your body gestures, your voice and, yes, your carefully chosen words. You should be able to almost feel this remarkable sensation tingling from your fingertips.

OTHER METHODS OF DELIVERY

The other three methods of delivering a speech—reading from a manuscript, speaking from memory, and speaking impromptu—do not approach the extemporaneous method in overall effectiveness; however,

You can conduct "electricity" to your audience.

they are useful in certain speaking situations. We now turn to a discussion of these three methods.

Reading from a Manuscript

We strongly urge beginning speakers to refrain from reading their entire talks. There are, however, circumstances in which very limited reading may be helpful, such as when you're presenting statistics or a quotation.

When accuracy is extremely important, speakers will often read from a **manuscript.** For example, officials who must make policy statements don't want to risk omitting points or being misunderstood or misquoted. Reading from a manuscript also allows them to use precise, polished language and helps comply with time limits. For example:

■ the president of the United States addressing the Congress and the nation on budget cuts or the need to increase taxes
■ a judge announcing a very important, perhaps a landmark, decision
■ a corporate spokesperson explaining to stockholders why he or she recommends a merger
■ a school committee spokesperson announcing the reason for the massive layoffs of teachers and administrative personnel

These speakers are fully justified in reading their statements; they can't afford a wrong word. For you, as a nonprofessional, however, reading your entire speech word for word could create one or more of the following problems:

■ Your speech may sound read and, therefore, lack spontaneity and enthusiasm. It could sound dull.
■ Your delivery could become staccato instead of flowing smoothly.
■ You may, occasionally, hesitate, creating annoying and meaningless pauses. (This definitely will diminish your credibility.)
■ You may make mistakes, such as mispronouncing, skipping, or repeating words.
■ You may read too fast, making it difficult for your audience to understand you.
■ You may become so engrossed in your manuscript that you forfeit rapport with your audience by not looking at them.
■ You may be so "glued" to the manuscript that you can't move about and gesture.
■ You may communicate only isolated words instead of whole ideas.
■ You may become so dependent on reading your talks that you will not develop skill in other methods of delivery.

If, however, you feel compelled to read your speech verbatim, then consider the following tips:

1. Don't use words you don't normally use, because you'll *run the risk* of mispronouncing them or hesitating when you approach them.

2. Be sure that your sentences are short and understandable. A listener has only one chance to hear what you're saying (unless, of course, you repeat very important points). Keep this in mind when you write your speech. Remember that you're writing for the ear—which likes short, conversational sentences—and not for the eye, which can go over material several times.

3. Type your speech in all caps, either double-spaced or triple-spaced. Number each page and type only on one side of the paper. For ease of reading and quickly finding your place again after looking at the audience, use the large ORATOR style type which is available for electric typewriters with interchangeable elements, or use a word processor. When you finish a page, turn it or slide it aside quietly.

4. Practice reading your speech aloud over and over until you know it so well that you can look at your audience more than at your manuscript and so that your speech will sound conversational. This will take a great deal of practice, but it'll be worth the effort.

run the risk—take the chance

Rehearsing is imperative. Once I listened to a speaker who read his entire speech and had not practiced sufficiently. The last line at the bottom of one page was repeated as the first line of the next, and he read both! It hardly sounded as though the speaker was in command.

Speaking from Memory

The riskiest method of delivering a talk is to memorize it and to speak completely from memory. This method often lacks warmth, feeling, and enthusiasm because the memorized words usually pour forth very mechanically. The chilling risk is that forgetting a word or key phrase could throw you into a state of panic.

Very few people can deliver memorized speeches effectively. Those who can are very likely professionals who have been speaking this way for years because they have trained and developed their memory.

Many years ago, as a college student in a speech class, I was assigned a short memorized talk. I chose to speak on memory development, since I was interested in improving this ability. I started by explaining how important memory can be in everyday living, how it is a God-given talent to some but one that can be developed with perseverance and application by others. I stated, "Basically there are three important factors involved in the development of memory. One is association." On the blackboard I wrote the words "One—Association." "Two," I continued, "is repetition." Again, approaching the blackboard, I wrote "Two—Repetition." Then, facing the class, I announced, "And three!" . . . dead air, silence. I drew a blank. The silent seconds seemed like horrendous hours and, for the life of me, I couldn't remember the third point.

Suppose you forget a word.

getting (oneself) together—regaining composure

The class thought my performance was humorous, as I stood motionless with a look of desperation. After *getting myself together,* I embarked on an impromptu talk on the fallacy of attempting memorized speeches.

Memorizing can help you with introductions and conclusions, the two most crucial parts of a talk. Memorizing your opening and concluding remarks allows you to begin and end confidently and enables you to look at your audience directly instead of glancing at notes. *By the same*

by the same token—in the same way

token, it may be wise to memorize a short talk (a minute or so), for example, introducing a speaker or presenting or accepting an award (discussed in Chapter 13).

If you happen to be gifted with a highly retentive memory, speaking entirely from memory does offer a few other advantages: You're free to move around the platform and use gestures; you can more accurately meet time limits; and you can phrase your opinions, ideas, and facts in precise, polished language. We must add, however, that very few people can deliver a memorized talk spontaneously and enthusiastically.

Speaking Impromptu

An **impromptu talk** is one for which you've had no previous notice, so you're denied the advantage of preparation. Yet, if you analyze your daily conversation, you'll find that most of it, by far, is impromptu: in class, over coffee, at home, on the phone, with a date (or somebody else's date), on the job, and during interviews. In all these cases, except interviews, you may be conversing with one or a half-dozen people. You talk, they listen; they talk, you listen.

Because of your experience or degree of involvement in a group or organization, you should have a pretty good idea whether you may be called on "to say a few words" at a formal meeting. Before going to a meeting, banquet, or any other gathering, ask yourself, "If I were called on to speak, what would I say?"

An impromptu situation doesn't require a fifteen-minute talk. Driving home one sharp point in a few minutes of a carefully prepared *"off-the-cuff"* talk can make you look like a pro. If there's any possibility, no matter how remote, that you may be asked to say a few words, prepare some comments. It's better to be prepared and not be called on than to be called on and not be prepared.

"off the cuff"— impromptu, without preparation

Although you may be ready to say a few words, you must focus your thoughts on a specific topic. Here are some ideas that may help:

- Refer to what previous speakers have said and add your own opinion.
- Comment on some of the topical views expressed by people at your table. They could be a fertile source of ideas.
- Compare the past and present, with possibly a word on the future.
- Compare certain advantages and disadvantages.
- State the problem and a possible solution. (Perhaps you may wish to recommend that a special committee be named to investigate the matter further and then file a report at the next meeting.)
- State the importance of the problem and its effect on your daily lives.
- Consider the topic from the viewpoints of childhood, adulthood, and old age.
- Consider the topic from political, economic, or social aspects.
- Consider the topic geographically—by city, state, country, or the world.

One or more of these approaches should work for you, because your obligation is to speak only two or three minutes. But you have to think fast; make no mistake about that. And under no circumstances should you start by apologizing for your lack of preparation.

If you're completely unprepared to speak about a particular topic and don't wish to address the group, bow out as gracefully as possible (again, prepare a short statement ahead of time). Something like the following will do: "Thank you very much for asking me to speak, but quite frankly, I'm not prepared at this time and will have to pass. However, I'll be pre-

An "off-the-cuff" talk can make you look like a pro.

pared at the next meeting and, if you so desire, will be more than happy to speak then."

We have discussed four methods of delivery—speaking extemporaneously, reading from a manuscript, speaking from memory, and speaking impromptu. Since the most effective speech delivery may contain a combination of all of these, experiment with them to establish the style most comfortable for you.

"PRACTICE IS NINE-TENTHS"

You've just studied the major methods of delivering a talk, but one crucial step still remains before you face your audience—rehearsal.

Facing an audience is not theory. It's your *moment of truth,* and there's no better way to prepare for that moment than to practice aloud beforehand. Many beginning speakers skip this exercise and then regret

moment of truth—that time when you must accept reality of the situation; when one's courage and skill is about to be tested it. Ralph Waldo Emerson, the "Sage of Concord," *struck the bull's-eye* when he said, "Practice is nine-tenths."[1] He knew the truth of that aphorism because he made outstanding speeches in public for 50 years.

struck the bull's eye—made an excellent point

Unique proof of Emerson's words was the acceptance speech delivered by President Gerald Ford at the Republican National Convention in August 1976. It was "the best speech of my life," he said later. It electrified the delegates and gave them hope of victory. It changed Ford's lifelong image as a bumbling, stolid, lackluster speaker to a powerful, dynamic, fighting-mad speaker who could inspire an audience.

How did he do it?

First of all, the speech was planned for many weeks. President Ford spent more time rewording and polishing it than any other speech he had given in his 37-year political career. For two weeks, with the aid of a speech coach, he practiced delivering it. In addition, he went through two complete videotaped rehearsals, always concentrating on delivery. As a result of all this work, he was able to maintain almost constant eye contact with his audience and to use powerful, spontaneous gestures at the right moments. The main ingredients that made the speech a smashing success were Ford's efforts—the importance he placed on it and his emotions of the moment. No wonder he was interrupted with cheers more than 65 times.

Great speakers are made, not born. If Gerald Ford could do it at age 62 you can do it at 22, 32, or whatever.

Preparation and practice are the keys to successful speaking. The purpose of practice is to ensure, as much as possible, that your talk in front of the audience will flow smoothly. Try to practice your talk before at least one person who will offer a suggestion or two. If you can't find a volunteer, use a tape recorder (a videotape recorder is even better because you see and hear yourself as an audience does), and then listen to the playback. It's a sobering and educational experience. Another idea is to speak before a mirror; you'll benefit from this once you get over feeling self-conscious about doing it.

You have three choices for practice: a live audience, a tape recorder (audio or video), or a mirror. In fact, why not use all three? Whichever method you choose, PRACTICE before you face your audience.

And don't forget to devote attention to seemingly minor details. In 1962 President John F. Kennedy made a historic speech in Berlin (see Appendix A). The following four words in that address helped win over the Germans: *"Ich bin ein Berliner"* ("I am a Berliner"). JFK practiced at least ten minutes to master the German accent in its two-second delivery. And a half-million Berliners exploded with tumultuous approval during the speech.

---

[1]Ralph Waldo Emerson, "Power," *The Conduct of Life* (1860).

If you can't find a volunteer . . . .

Regarding your delivery, remember, if there are students in the class who are still learning English, be sure to speak slowly and try to maximize your eye contact. In an attempt to better understand you they may be closely watching the movements of your lips as you form your speech sounds and, at the same time, studying your facial expressions while you speak.

COPING WITH NERVES

Whichever method of speaking you select, one condition is predictable—you'll suffer the jitters: butterflies in the stomach, trembling knees, parched mouth, sweaty palms, and thumping heartbeat. But don't be alarmed, because these are normal reactions that grip most speakers, even seasoned ones.

If the jitters torture you, then shake hands with Michael Douglas, superstar actor-producer. When he was a college student, like you, and studying acting, he suffered such intense nervousness that he kept a wastebasket offstage; he used to vomit in it and then continue acting.

"I've worked hard," he said, "both as a person and as an actor, to fight my way through stage fright."[2]

It might be helpful for you to know that other famous people who have been struck by nervousness, stage fright, speaker apprehension, or whatever you want to call it, include Franklin Roosevelt, Ronald Reagan, Lily Tomlin, and Sir Laurence Olivier. There! Don't you feel better already?

Many students have confided to me that while they were speaking they were so nervous at times that they didn't think they could finish their talks. But in most cases they never looked one-quarter as nervous as they felt. Many speech instructors from all over the country have conveyed similar experiences, and fellow students generally agree that their classmates don't look even half as nervous as they claim to be.

Many communication scholars believe that stage fright, or speech tension, is the result of anxiety rather than fear.[3] Fear is a spontaneous reaction to a present negative event, whereas anxiety involves the anticipation of a future event. How many times can you recall being upset over something you had to do or that you expected to take place, only to find the actual situation was nowhere near as negative as you had anticipated? For example:

- Perhaps when you were in junior high school, one Friday afternoon your teacher told you that the principal wanted to see you first thing on Monday morning. Can you recall that ruined weekend, during which you conjured up all of the worst scenarios possible, only to find out that the principal wanted to ask you if one of your parents could accompany the class on a field trip?
- Just before going to lunch you receive a telephone message from your boss's secretary stating that your boss would like to see you at 2:30 P.M. to discuss an important matter. Instead of enjoying lunch (if you even have one), you spend the time upsetting yourself to the point of indigestion, only to discover that your boss merely wants to discuss the vacation schedule.
- You're one of three finalists for a job you want very much. The salary is generous, the hours are compatible with your school schedule, and the location is close to home. You have been told that a final decision will be made in a few days and you will be notified by phone. Will you experience any anxious moments waiting for the call?

Being anxious is a common and normal reaction to certain situations. By now you have probably found that the degree of anxiety you experienced while waiting to give your first talk was far worse than actually giving it.

---

[2]*Parade Magazine*, 14 February 1988, 5.
[3]J. A. Daly and J. C. McCrosky. *Avoiding Communication: Shyness, Reticence, and Communication Apprehension* (Beverly Hills, CA: Sage, 1984), 188.

Some Suggestions for Relieving Your Tension Before Speaking

1. Be sure that you're deeply interested in your topic.
2. Prepare thoroughly so that you know your topic very well. Most professional speakers master much more information than they need.
3. Think positively. As you prepare and practice your talk, keep telling yourself that you will do a good job and that the audience will be deeply interested in what you have to say.
4. As soon as your name is called, take a few very deep breaths while you're still sitting and a few more while walking to the front of the class. It helps to get a healthy supply of oxygen into your system.
5. Just remember, your audience wants you to succeed.

Some Physical Exercises to Help Alleviate Tension Before Speaking

1. Sit straight in your chair and relax your head letting it droop forward until your chin is touching your chest (or is as close to it as possible). Then s l o w l y move your head to the left and upward as you continue moving it to the right in a circular motion; then lower it to its original position with your chin resting on your chest. Pause about five seconds then repeat the exercise two or three times. After the third time, pause for about five seconds then repeat the exercise three more times but in the opposite direction. Take long deep breaths during this exercise.
2. Sitting upright and relaxed, lower your head so your chin is resting on your chest. Then, as you slowly inhale, slowly raise your head to an upright position. Then, as you slowly lower your head, slowly exhale until your head is resting in its original position. Repeat this exercise several times making sure that you are taking deep breaths as you slowly raise your head and slowly exhaling while lowering your head.
3. Sitting straight up, let your shoulders slump forward and let your arms hang loosely at your side. While taking slow deep breaths, shake the fingers on your hands as though you're trying to free them from something sticky.

To obtain the maximum benefit from your deep breathing, you want to be sure that you're breathing from your diaphragm, which is the muscle that separates your chest cavity from your abdominal cavity. By placing both hands flatly and firmly on your abdomen, you should be able to feel your abdomen expand when you inhale and contract as you exhale. If you have any questions regarding diaphragmatic breathing, don't hesitate to ask your professor.

The following exercises can be conducted while breathing normally.

4. While sitting relaxed in your chair, clench your fists and hold them tightly for about three or four seconds, then relax. (If you have long fingernails, WHOA!!) Repeat this exercise several times.
5. Repeat the above exercise using one fist at a time.
6. While sitting relaxed, firmly push down on the seat of your chair with both hands for several seconds and then relax. Repeat this exercise several times.

Exerting physical pressure and expending your energy should result in eventual and dramatic reduction of your body tension. I think that you'll find these exercises to be quite helpful.

Some Suggestions for Relieving Your Tension While Speaking

1. Just before you begin to talk, place your notes on the speaker's stand; look around at the entire class, take another deep breath, and, with a smile, greet your audience.
2. Use vigorous, but not constant, gestures with your hands, arms, shoulders, head, and body. Such physical actions will channel your nervous energy constructively, attract attention, and fortify your oral message.
3. As you look around the class, don't just scan the audience with your eyes. Move your entire head to the left, then to the right, and back to center. Fully moving your head in this manner should considerably ease neck tension.
4. Don't rivet yourself behind the lectern. Take a few steps to the left and remain there for 10 or 15 seconds before returning to the center position. Then, after a while, repeat this movement in the opposite direction. Deliberate movement is an excellent aid in lessening tension.
5. Focus on your message and audience. Try to become message-conscious, not self-conscious, and your nervousness should diminish, allowing you to communicate more effectively.
6. If you suddenly feel tension building or muscles tightening while you're at the lectern, try gripping the sides of the lectern and squeezing, then slowly releasing the grip and squeezing again. Repeating this exercise several times can be quite effective and hardly noticeable to the audience.
7. Act confident and you'll begin to *feel* confident.
8. Many students find it helpful to admit their nervousness at the beginning of their talk. There's nothing wrong with doing so. Such an admission to your classmates can gain you sympathy and understanding because soon it will be their turn to speak.

DEVELOPING STYLE AND CONFIDENCE AS A SPEAKER

The way you deliver a speech is critical to its total effectiveness. Poor delivery can largely negate the many long hours that you've invested in researching, planning, organizing, and outlining your talk. Someone once said: "Speeches are like babies—easier to conceive than to deliver."

get off to a flying start—begin in a positive way

You can begin immediately to develop your speaking style and confidence. You don't have to wait until you've finished this exciting course. Putting into practice the following suggestions can help you to *get off to a flying start:*

- Speak at every opportunity.
- Observe capable speakers and learn from them.
- Read good literature.
- Use a dictionary and thesaurus to strengthen your vocabulary.
- Practice writing, including your talks.
- Know your subject and feel deeply about it so that you can speak with enthusiasm.

Speak at Every Opportunity

strike up—start, initiate

Each day and evening of your life present countless opportunities for you to converse. Talk to members of your family about the kind of day they had at work or at school. Discuss their successes, failures, and accomplishments. Share yours with them as well. On the way to and from school or work and while you're there, *strike up* conversations with your instructor, classmates, supervisor, colleagues, friends, and acquaintances. *This is particularly important if you're a foreign student trying to improve your American grammar and pronunciation.* (You may find Chapter 15 on conversation especially helpful.)

If you belong to a club, organization, or community group (if you don't, join one), speak whenever you can. Whether in your community or on campus, volunteer to become a member of a committee, or campaign for a friend who's running for office. Better yet, run for an office yourself. Within a short time, you'll realize that speaking often can not only be fun but a learning experience as well. And really, isn't that what a fruitful life should be all about?

Aristotle put it wisely back in 4 B.C. when he said, "To learn is a natural pleasure, not confined to philosophers, but common to all men." You only need the will and the motivation.

Observe Capable Speakers and Learn from Them

Another superb learning exercise is to observe and listen to outstanding speakers. Speeches given by many great orators that were originally recorded on film have been transferred to videotape. Such invaluable collections are available at many libraries, perhaps even on your campus. Here you can witness some excellent examples of orators such as Winston Churchill, Franklin Delano Roosevelt, and Adolph Hitler (although he spoke German, watch his fiery delivery and dramatic gestures). Other great speakers of the past include Everett Dirksen, John F. Kennedy, Martin Luther King, Jr., Adlai Stevenson, and Harry S Truman. Some contemporaries include Mario Cuomo, Geraldine Ferraro, Billy Graham, Jesse Jackson, Barbara Jordan, Ann Richards, Elizabeth Dole, Bill Clinton, and Hillary Rodham Clinton.

Your librarian or instructor will be able to recommend other well-known communicators, past and present, who may be found on videotape. Look around your local video store and watch the TV listings, including PBS and cable. Take the initiative to *look*, *listen*, and *learn*.

Read Good Literature

Again, your school or local library can ***dish up*** an excellent menu of literature from which you may select, savor, and digest. Taking certain "lit" courses can quickly dispel the idea that literature is dull and boring.

dish up—make available

With a little inquiry and some independent research, you can experience the fulfillment of enjoying some of the greatest works of the literary masters, both prose and poetry. Avail yourself of some of the writings of such masters as Aristotle, Cicero, Confucius, and Shakespeare. Turn the pages of some of the masterpieces by authors such as Jane Austen, Rudyard Kipling, Robert Louis Stevenson, and John Keats. Why not sneak a peek at some of the works of Louisa May Alcott, Henry Thoreau, Walt Whitman, Emily Dickinson, Herman Melville, and Edgar Allan Poe? And don't forget titans of this century—William Faulkner, Ernest Hemingway, F. Scott Fitzgerald—and those still living—John Updike, Joyce Carol Oates, Ann Beattie, and Saul Bellow.

Referring to the reading of fine writings, someone said, "that man is known by the company his mind keeps." Particularly poignant is the quotation from the philosopher Francis Bacon who said, "Some books are to be tasted, others to be swallowed, and some few to be chewed and digested." Please, help yourself, and ***bon appétit***.

bon appétit—enjoy yourself

Use a Dictionary and Thesaurus

We cannot overemphasize the importance of expanding your vocabulary. We feel so strongly about this that we have incorporated vocabulary development as an integral part of this book (in the "Vitalize Your Vocabulary" sections in all but the first chapter). A strong, descriptive vocabulary indicates an educated (formally or not) person who usually draws praise and admiration. One of the surest ways to expand your present knowledge of words is to use an authoritative dictionary and **thesaurus** frequently.

You're bound to hear unfamiliar words every day. Start carrying a small notebook, one that can easily fit into your pocket or pocketbook. Whenever you hear a new word, write it down. You may hear such words in conversation, listening to a lecture, watching TV, listening to the radio, or you may see them in print. Jot them down, look them up in a dictionary, record their meanings, and most important, use your new words whenever you can. You'll be amazed how quickly your vocabulary will flourish. There are also a number of helpful paperback vocabulary development books available.

While a dictionary basically contains an alphabetized list of words with definitions, etymologies (if you don't know the meaning of this word, here's a good place to start—look it up and write down its definition), and pronunciations, a thesaurus is a book containing synonyms, antonyms, and, in some instances, slang, idioms, and colloquialisms (aha, another new one). A thesaurus can help you find the exact word to express your exact meaning. For example, in one such publication, the word "student" has over one hundred different classifications.

Words can announce life. Words can execute death. Words can bring happiness. Words can instill misery. Words can declare war. Words can welcome peace. Words can announce success. Words can proclaim defeat. Be sure of not only what you want to say but the words you choose to say it. And you gotta love this quote from Adlai Stevenson in a 1952 campaign speech: "Man does not live by words alone, despite the fact that sometimes he has to eat them."

Practice Writing, Including Your Talks

Another excellent exercise for developing your style and confidence as a speaker is to practice writing, including your talks. By writing your talks you'll be able to revise, change, or make any necessary improvements in language and content before making out your note cards. But remember, you don't want to read your talks verbatim.

Effective writing requires a great deal of effort and discipline, as many of you already know from having taken some writing courses. Writing requires you to think and evaluate and may also involve research, note taking, summarizing, paraphrasing, quoting, outlining, drafting, editing, and rewriting.

Writing can also help further develop your grammar and syntax skills as you sharpen your ability to communicate orally more accurately, clearly, coherently, understandably, informatively, and persuasively. From experience and research, we believe that a good writer has a better chance of becoming a good speaker, rather than vice versa.

Know Your Subject and Feel Deeply about It So That You Can Speak with Enthusiasm

Giving a talk is much easier when you have something worthwhile to say. If you have strong opinions based on personal experience that are contrary to the speaker's or if someone belittles or insults you or a member of your family, the chances are *pretty solid* that you would have little difficulty in counterattacking swiftly and with a vengeance.

This is how you should approach and prepare for every speaking assignment. Consider it a crusade and believe that what you will say to your listeners will be the most important or most inspirational message they will ever hear.

Knowing your topic inside out, researching and preparing more than you think you'll need, and being firmly convinced that your message will be entertaining, informative, or persuasive should enable you to deliver your talk with a degree of enthusiasm that may even surprise you. Don't *sell yourself short.*

pretty solid—very good, excellent

sell yourself short—underestimate your abilities

If you have believed, as many people do, that great speakers are born and not made, we hope that reading this chapter has changed your mind. For one final example of a speaker being made through years of effort, let's flash back to Boston in 1947. Sometime in that year, one of your authors was in a small audience of World War II veterans listening to a speech on foreign policy by freshman Congressman John F. Kennedy. He was witty and knowledgeable, but his voice lacked depth and variety, his language contained *er's* and *ah's*, his Boston accent was strong, and his hands were stuck in his pockets much of the time.

JFK was aware of his limitations. He knew that great speakers are made, not born. He knew that President Franklin D. Roosevelt and Prime Minister Winston Churchill struggled for years before they reached their full potential as speakers. He knew what he had to do and he did it.

Kennedy gave speeches often, read good literature to strengthen his vocabulary, and received coaching from a Boston University speech professor. In addition, he rehearsed his speeches, used a tape recorder to improve his voice and diminish his Boston accent, observed competent speakers, and wrote newspaper articles on social and political problems. He spoke before live audiences, on radio, and on television. As a result of his strenuous efforts, by 1960 he was ready for the crucial television debates with Vice President Richard Nixon. Many historians agree that Kennedy's performance won the presidential election for him.

Granted, JFK had many things going for him—wealth, education, family contacts, a brilliant mind, a sense of humor, good looks, personal drive—but if you do half of what he did, you will greatly improve as a communicator.

THINGS TO DISCUSS IN CLASS

1. Which methods of delivery do you think are used by political campaigners? Discuss this.

2. As a listener, which method of delivery do you prefer? Why?

3. Cite two speakers you've recently heard, and discuss their methods of delivery. In your opinion, which delivery was the most effective? Why?

4. Select a short passage and read it aloud in your normal delivery. Then, try reading the same passage aloud with enthusiasm, using inflection, feeling, and excitement in your delivery. Notice the vast improvement. Use of a tape recorder would be invaluable.

5. Recall for the class several instances in your life in which anticipating an event was far worse than the actual event.

6. If you've ever seen a speaker deliver a presentation without benefit of a lectern, tell the class how the speaker used his hands and notes.

7. To develop your ability to speak with enthusiasm and to improve your interpretation of the spoken word, read poetry and children's stories aloud and record them.

WHAT DO YOU REMEMBER FROM THIS CHAPTER?

1. List four methods of delivering a talk.
2. Explain the advantages and disadvantages of each method of delivery.
3. Is it permissible to use more than one method of delivery in the same talk?
4. Explain two differences between extemporaneous and impromptu talks.
5. Is it possible to prepare for an impromptu talk? Explain.
6. Why is practicing a talk important?
7. Is it a good idea to memorize the introduction and conclusion of a talk? Explain.
8. What role, if any, does enthusiasm play in speech delivery?
9. List three suggestions for relieving tension prior to speaking.
10. List three ways to help develop your speaking style.

VITALIZE YOUR VOCABULARY

Government and Politics

bipartisan (adj.) Representing members of two parties.
bureaucracy (n.) The whole body of nonelected government officials, often accused of red tape and insensitivity to human needs.
caucus (n.) A closed meeting of a political party to decide policies.
conservative (adj.) Tending to oppose change and to favor traditional ideas and values; (n.) a person who holds such views.
constituent (n.) A voter in a politician's district.
electorate (n.) The people qualified to vote in an election.
grass roots (n.) The local level, as opposed to the centers of political power.
gubernatorial (adj.) Pertaining to the governor.
impeach (v.) To legally charge a public official with misconduct in office.
incumbent (n.) The current holder of an office.

independent (n.) A voter who does not belong to a political party.

left wing (adj. and n.) See "liberal."

legislate (v.) To enact laws.

liberal (adj.) Favoring civil liberties and the use of government power to promote social reforms; (n.) a person who holds such views.

lobby (n.) Usually a group of people trying to influence lawmakers in favor of the group's special interest.

plank (n.) An article or principle in the platform of a political party.

platform (n.) A formal statement of a political party's goals and principles.

primary (n.) When voters select candidates from a field of candidates to run in the final election.

radical (adj.) Extreme, as in an approach to social, economic, and political problems; can be either left wing or right wing; (n.) one who holds such views.

referendum (n.) The practice of submitting a measure to the voters rather than to the legislature.

registration (n.) The official enrollment of citizens eligible to vote; if not registered, they cannot vote.

right wing (adj. and n.) See "conservative."

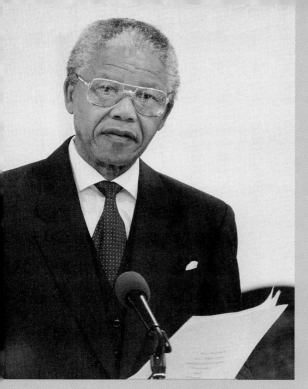

10

BE INFORMATIVE

To live effectively is to live with adequate information.

Norbert Wiener, *The Human Use of Human Beings* (1954), 1

After reading and understanding this chapter you should know:

- **The purposes and types of informative talks.**

- **Four principles that help people learn better.**

- **How to use statistics effectively.**

- **How to prepare the introduction, body, and conclusion of an informative talk.**

In this age of widespread college education, of national computer networks, and of endless research into the unknown, information has evolved into a national resource. By the same token, information has become an invaluable asset to individuals who can absorb it and share it through talking with their peers. In other words, speaking to convey knowledge and understanding can help you advance your career.

Adapting the knowledge level of your talk to the knowledge level of your audience is of supreme importance. Three kinds of audiences are described from this viewpoint, and, in order to help you meet their needs, various types of informative talks are explained.

Certain principles of learning that help you are discussed briefly. If you apply them, your informative talks will get better results, but applying these principles is not enough.

First you need to acquire knowledge, information, and understanding in order to flesh out your talk. And that means doing your homework.

Many down-to-earth suggestions are given for preparing the introduction, body, and conclusion of your informative talk. After you finish your presentation, a question-and-answer period is an excellent way to tie up loose ends.

The chapter ends with a speech by Nelson Mandela.

Appearing in this (and every) chapter is the feature "In Other Words," which will greatly benefit foreign and ESL students. To aid in their understanding of common American idioms and phrases, these expressions will be defined in the margin of the page on which they are introduced.

KNOWLEDGE IS POWER

Because the words *information* and *knowledge* appear throughout this chapter, let's define our terms:

> **information** (n.) Facts, data, news; knowledge communicated by others or obtained from study, instruction, or investigation.
>
> **knowledge** (n.) Comprehension, learning, information, an organized body of facts, or ideas inferred from those facts.

Americans have always set a high value on knowledge. We believe that democracy functions best when its citizens are armed with sound knowledge on which to base intelligent decisions. Because of this belief, the United States has developed the most extensive system of public education that the world has ever known. Because of this belief, the United States has more colleges and universities than do England, France, Germany, and the Commonwealth of Independent States combined. Because of this belief, the United States has more newspapers, magazines, book publishers, radio stations, television channels, computer networks, and public libraries than those same four countries put together.

Such media, both here and abroad, have created a revolution in the handling of information and an explosion of knowledge in countless specialized areas. As a result, information is now regarded as "a new basic resource that supplements the familiar natural resources of matter and energy."[1] Matter and energy change with use, while knowledge does not. On the contrary, the more that knowledge is used and shared among people, the more valuable it becomes; for example, the knowledge needed to produce and use penicillin and other miracle drugs has probably saved millions of lives.

Information is more accessible today than at any other time in our history, and our quest for it is insatiable. We have desktop, laptop, and notebook computers; the Internet; World Wide Web sites; e-mail; cell phones (both analog and digital, yet); pagers; faxes; and even hand-held organizers.

In a *Newsweek* article by Jennifer Tanaka, she writes that a single daily edition of the *New York Times* newspaper contains more information than the average person living in the seventeenth century would have been exposed to in a lifetime. She also writes that the average employee of a large corporation sends and receives an incredible 177 messages a day via cellular phone calls, e-mail, pager blips, Post-its® and faxes.[2] I bet that you can't wait to graduate and go to work for a large corporation.

---

[1] *Encyclopedia Britannica*, 15th ed., s.v. "information processing."
[2] Jennifer Tanaka, "Drowning in Data." *Newsweek*, 28 April 1997, 95.

America's continued commitment to this philosophy is clearly visible by our global dominance in such high-tech informational industries as computers, software, fibre optics, HDTV (high-definition television), and telecommunications. The world sees the United States ignoring all speed limits on the Information Super Highway. As one economist noted, "We're in the midst of the third industrial revolution."

SOME PURPOSES OF INFORMATIVE TALKS

Despite the multiplying numbers of computers (personal, business, and scientific) and databases, we still exchange astounding quantities of information orally. Much of our talking—on the job, in politics, at home, or in social contacts—is focused on one major objective: to present information so that it will be understood, remembered, and possibly utilized.

open new horizons—present new areas of interest

Briefly, you want to *open new horizons* for your listeners, to give them new perspectives and understanding. In light of this goal, most audiences fall into three categories that may overlap: not informed, generally informed, and well informed.

talk down—speak in a degrading manner

cover too much ground—overwhelm, present too much material

With listeners who are not informed, you should deal in elementary matters and explain any jargon or specialized concepts. Here's where relevant comparisons and statistics (discussed later in this chapter) can help your audience understand your presentation. Just be careful not to *talk down* to them and not to *cover too much ground* at one time.

With a generally informed audience, you should use fundamental knowledge sprinkled with advanced material. The perplexing question is this: How much of each is appropriate? (For ideas on researching your audience, see Chapter 6.) Since some of your listeners may resent basic information as an onslaught against their egos, you may explain that you're simply laying a foundation on which to build deeper understanding. Another diplomatic *"out"* for you is that you're reviewing fundamentals for a few people whose memories may need refreshing.

(an) "out"—way of escaping from a difficult situation

With well-informed listeners, you're free to skip fundamentals and plunge into advanced information in depth. Listeners armed with knowledge are usually easy to handle, but a warning belongs here—know your subject, or a few sadistic members of the audience may revel in *"showing you up."*

"showing (you) up"—trying to embarrass you

Some common types of audiences you are likely to address include:

- classes in school
- decision-making individuals or groups on the job
- voters assessing candidates at an open forum
- consumers listening to purchasing experts for tips on stretching the dollar or conserving energy
- people listening to radio and television newscasts, documentaries, and so on

Be careful not to talk down to your audience.

Someday, at school, on the job, in your community, you may find yourself giving an informative talk to one of these audiences and attempting to describe a person or place; to report an event, a problem, or a situation; or to explain a concept, device, process, theory; or giving directions.

An evaluation guide for **informative talks** appears near the end of this chapter. Since the guide reminds you to include important items in your informative talk, you should consult the guide before you speak.

SOME MAJOR TYPES OF INFORMATIVE TALKS

Among the major categories of speeches—those to entertain, to inspire, to persuade, to actuate, and to inform—by far the most often presented is the speech to inform. What does this mean to you? Simply that the way you handle your storehouse of information and share it with others can have a significant impact on the direction of your career.

Let's clarify the use of speech categories. Because a speech is labeled "informative" doesn't mean that it's boxed in a neat compartment called "information." An informative speech may contain elements of persuasion, entertainment, or both, and those extras will, very likely, make it a more effective speech. The point is that, although speeches belong primarily to one category, they often include elements of other categories.

The general objective of the informative speech is to convey understanding and knowledge, because humans have an instinctive need to understand themselves and their surroundings. And remember, to be successful this must be done in clear, understandable language. From that general objective, let's now focus on some of the more common types of speeches to inform: reports, instructions, demonstrations, and lectures.

Reports

A chief function of committees in business, education, politics, the armed forces—you name it—is to give reports on projects and problems. A neighborhood committee, for example, may investigate the need for traffic lights at a dangerous intersection, report its findings, and make a recommendation for or against traffic lights. At the other end of the spectrum, the president of the United States reports, once a year, on the State of the Union. Oral reporting goes on in all walks of life. How many oral reports have you given or heard in and out of school?

Instructions

Today you may tell an out-of-state tourist how to find the new shopping mall at the other end of town. Tomorrow your instructor may explain how to do a research paper. Handouts with specific steps to follow may supplement the oral instructions. Very often, written instructions help clarify the oral how-to-do-it phase. If you're a parent or grandparent—need I say more about the frequency of giving instructions?

Demonstrations

When you show someone how to use a camera, how to perform a card trick, or how to operate a computer terminal, you are demonstrating. This kind of informative speaking is so important that it rates a chapter of its own—Chapter 12.

Lectures

In addition to class lectures, this type of informative speaking includes talks at professional seminars, radio and television talks on travel and politics, and book reviews at club meetings. These talks are often given after luncheon or dinner; their prime purpose is to enhance the listeners' knowledge and appreciation of a particular subject.

SOME PRINCIPLES OF LEARNING

Before you embark on your first informative talk, let's review some key findings on how people learn. Teachers in the past few thousand years and psychologists in the past hundred or so years have discovered that the following principles, when applied, speed the learning process.

■ **People learn better when you, as a speaker, involve as many of their senses as possible.** For example, suppose that you're demonstrating how to make a new kind of spaghetti sauce. You cut and mix the ingredients (seeing), fry them (smelling), explain the procedure (hearing), and then hand out samples to your listeners (tasting). With four of their senses involved in this learning experience, your listeners will remember far more than if you used only words to convey the message.

Involve as many of their senses as possible.

Of course, this example is an extreme case because you won't always be able to involve four senses in the same talk. Often, however, you'll be able to involve the sense of seeing (with movies, filmstrips, photographs, maps, and models) and the sense of hearing (through the spoken word), and the sense of feel as you pass out objects.

■ **People learn better when salient points of information are repeated a few times or are restated in different words.** Here is an example of this principle:

> Doctors and dieticians tell us that breakfast is the *most important meal* of the day. Yet, millions of Americans skip this *crucial meal* daily, to save time, to pare off pounds, or both. After seven to nine hours in bed, these people may be rested sufficiently, but physically and mentally they need the *energy*—"fuel," if you don't mind—that a *well-balanced breakfast* can provide. Without that *energy*, their bodies and minds cannot operate at top efficiency through the morning. That is why, for most people, a *good breakfast* is a *key element* in nutrition that can lead to a healthy and more productive life.

Notice that the significant idea (italicized) in the preceding paragraph is mentioned seven times.

■ **People learn better when they're motivated to do so.** Your listeners pay close attention to you when you answer the often unspoken question that most people ask: "What's in it for me?" Tell them how to get a better job, reduce their income taxes, be healthier, live longer, or be more attractive to the opposite sex, and you can be sure that they will *hang on* every word you utter.

hang on—listen
very closely to

■ **People learn better when new, relevant information is presented in small, well-organized amounts.** If you're explaining the basic causes of World War II to an audience that knows little about the subject, you might organize your material according to political, economic, and military causes. You could discuss each category separately but not deeply, and in your conclusion, you could point out how all three types of causes combined to trigger the most devastating war in history.

How to Select a Topic

Although this subject is pretty well covered in Chapter 7, a couple of ideas bear repeating. Choosing a topic that interests you will enable you to better communicate your message with enthusiasm, credibility, and confidence. And, if you're excited about your topic, the chances are your audience will be, too.

From the moment you start considering potential topics you should start flashing positive messages across your mind such as, "My audience will find my topic interesting" and "My audience will benefit from what

I plan to say." Positive messages can greatly enhance your confidence in the topic selection–research–planning–delivery process.

Obviously, the best place to start your search is with yourself. Conduct an inventory of your experiences. Your work. Your travels. Your hobbies or your goals may make for interesting listening. You might have read a best-selling book, seen a memorable movie, attended a cacophonous (head for the dictionary) concert, or heard a lofty lecture. Perhaps, you met a celebrity or someone with an unusual occupation . . . all good topic possibilities.

A fruitful source that many students overlook—and that could provide very helpful information—is the number of student-related activities, programs, and services that your college offers. These include: student athletic activities and various clubs, advising and counseling, career services and, perhaps, internships and cooperative education, the Learning Center and External Studies. What about the Financial Aid office? (Yes, what about it?)

And don't forget the source of sources . . . the library with its multitude of books, magazines, newspapers, and electronic reference material. This might be a good time to quickly review the sections "What's This about Ethics" in Chapter 1 and "Doing Research" in Chapter 7.

No matter what topic you finally choose, be sure that:

- It's not too broad (limit your main points to four or five).
- You've established the specific purpose and thesis statement. (See Chapter 8.)
- You're able to present your message in the allotted time.

GETTING INTO YOUR INFORMATIVE TALK

The talk to inform, by its very nature, dictates that you do your research and that you know your subject. After all, your primary purpose is to convey information and understanding that your listeners didn't have before.

Because a strong introduction is crucial to any talk, before you plan your opening remarks you should review the ideas listed in Chapter 8. Most of those ideas apply to introductions to all kinds of talks. At the very least, in the introduction to your informative talk, you should:

- State the purpose of your talk.
- List the three or four main points orally and, if possible, write them on a chalkboard. However, if writing takes unduly long, your listeners' attention may wander. You may consider highlighting the main points on a poster, which is excellent visual reinforcement for your oral listing.
- Stress the subject's importance to your listeners; if it will save them time or money, make their lives easier, or help them get better grades, say so immediately.

Because first impressions are powerful and lasting, you should practice your introduction aloud many times so that you can deliver it fluently and still maintain eye contact. A well-spoken introduction can perform miracles for you in one or two minutes.

MOVING INTO THE MAIN DISCUSSION

You're now ready to launch into a discussion of the main points mentioned in your introduction. As you know from Chapter 8 (organizing your information), each main point requires subpoints for support: facts, examples, quotations from authorities, incidents, anecdotes, comparisons, statistics, and so on. Ample research should provide you with many of these supports (which, except comparisons, are illustrated in Chapter 8). Now let's look at comparisons, statistics, audiovisual aids, and questions as supporting elements for your informative talk.

Comparisons

If you're explaining concepts that are new to an audience, try to compare them with something familiar to the audience. A few apt comparisons can bring your explanation to life. For example, let's assume that you plan to give a talk about the importance of saving for the future. (Something that should be of interest to everyone.) Your *chances of connecting* with your audience would be greatly enhanced if you included some of the following observations:

chances of connecting—chances of your audience being interested in what you're saying.

- If you went out for dinner and a movie twice a month at a cost of $75 each time, that would total $1,800 a year. If, instead, you invested that money over 30 years and received 10 percent interest per year, you would have $339,073.[3] If you splurged only half as much, you would have $169,536.
- By spending just $1 a day (whether on a soft drink, gum, or a candy bar) for 40 years, by the time you're ready to retire you'll be short about $190,000.[4]
- Smoking a pack of cigarettes a day could burn a hole in your retirement account to the tune of $330,000.[5]

Here's another example of how money can quickly multiply (although not too many of us could completely participate): if you took 1 penny and doubled it each day of the month for 30 days you would

---

[3]Ric Edelman, *The Truth About Money*, (Washington, DC: Georgetown University Press, 1996), 299.
[4]Ric Edelman, "The No-Spending Plan." *U.S. New & World Report*, 20 October 1997, 82.
[5]Ibid, note 5.

have $5,368,709.12—that's 5 million, 368 thousand, seven hundred nine dollars and 12 cents. What would you have if there were 31 days in the month?

The following are two concise comparisons, one dealing with specific amounts of money and the other with imagery and science; both can be grasped easily:

1. In 1984 the federal government spent $2.6 billion daily. "Piled flat, one atop the other, 2.6 billion $1 bills would stack 176 miles high—745 times as tall as New York's Empire State Building."[6]
2. Sun flares sprayed streams of particles into space, sweeping the solar system *like streams of water from a revolving lawn sprinkler.*

Statistics

The use of statistics supplies concrete information that may perk up your audience's interest and, at the same time, may help establish you as a credible speaker. Try to observe the following cautions in using statistics:

- Don't throw reams of figures at your audience; they're too difficult to remember.
- In addition to giving statistics orally, present the key figures with a visual aid—a chalkboard, flip chart, poster, or slide.
- Repeat the most important figures at least once.
- Round off long figures. Instead of saying "$1,000,359," say "a little over a million dollars." Your audience will appreciate it. (The exception, of course, would be if you intend to be very specific in order to make a dramatic point as illustrated in the previous section when I discussed saving money.)
- Use only the most accurate and most recent statistics.

Notice how the following example dramatizes and clarifies the distance of the moon from the earth, about 239,000 miles:

If you could drive your car nonstop to the moon at 55 MPH, you'd get there in 182 days.

Here's a comparison among one million, one billion, and one trillion:

One million seconds is about 12 days.

One billion seconds is about 31 years.

One trillion seconds is about 31 thousand years.

Notice how effective the following comparisons are regarding waste product statistics:

---

[6]*U.S. News & World Report,* 24 December 1984, 25.

Recycling is gaining popularity, but currently only 11 percent of U.S. solid waste lives again as something else. And still the volume of garbage keeps growing—up by 80 percent since 1960, expected to mount an additional 20 percent by 2000. Not including sludge and construction wastes, Americans collectively toss out 160 million tons each year—enough to spread 30 stories high over 1000 football fields, enough to fill a bumper-to-bumper convoy of garbage trucks halfway to the moon.[7]

getting your message across—communicating so people will understand you

Another effective method of *getting your message across* is to use short, factual statements, such as:

1. The amount of energy that escapes through our doors and windows each winter is equal to all the oil that flows through the Alaska pipeline each year.
2. The average American uses the equivalent of seven trees in packaging and paper products each year.
3. In two weeks we throw away enough trash to fill both towers of New York's 110-story World Trade Center.[8]

What do you say we conclude this section on statistics with one that you may have helped to make possible? That is, if you wear Levi's. According to Levi Strauss, the largest manufacturer of jeans in the world, the company uses about 1.25 million miles of thread each year, or enough to wrap around the world more than 50 times.

Audiovisual Aids

Be sure to "spice up" your informative talk with audiovisual aids, such as recordings, CDs, videos, multimedia graphics, photographs, and maps (see Chapter 12). Say, for example, you were discussing the various types of automobile antitheft devices. Photographs and, perhaps, even a video would certainly be interesting and effective, but the most compelling visual aids would be to display the actual pieces of equipment. Reality "grabs" people.

Questions

A foresighted tactic to use while researching and preparing for your speech is to anticipate relevant questions that your listeners may want to ask at various stages of your talk. Asking such questions and answering them during your talk often stimulates your audience to think along with you and to bring up new ideas. If your talk is a lecture, you may wish to allow questions during your presentation. Then again, you may decide only to

---

[7]"Buried Alive," *Newsweek,* 27 November 1989, 67.
[8]*Masspirg Report,* September 1991.

accept them after your talk during the question-and-answer session. Be sure to clearly state the *ground rules* in your introduction.

ground rules— format of the presentation

WINDING UP YOUR INFORMATIVE TALK

At the end of your main discussion, you might pause a few seconds and move a step or so to either side. The pause and movement signal that your talk is about to end. Then you may say something like:

- In conclusion (or before concluding), I would like to emphasize the following points.
- If you leave with only one thought, I hope that it would be . . . .
- And now I would like to close with a quotation from . . . (an anecdote about . . . , a comparison between . . . , a poem about . . .).
- Let me briefly summarize . . . .

Again, you may stress the importance of the subject and the benefits that the listeners may derive from the knowledge you've shared with them. Remember that a conclusion should be brief and to the point. Don't drag it out or trail off by muttering, "Well, I guess that's about it."

Another idea for your conclusion is to encourage listeners who want to learn more about the subject. You can list, on the chalkboard, relevant titles of magazine articles or books. Better still, prepare this information as a one-page **handout** that you can distribute on the spot. Most people like handouts because they're free and can be useful as lasting reminders of your key points.

Whereas other categories of talks seldom require a question-and-answer period, the informative talk does for these practical reasons: (1) if your treatment of a particular topic was foggy or incomplete, you have a second chance to clarify it; and (2) if you omitted a facet of the subject that concerns some of the listeners, you can supply the missing information.

Former President Harry S Truman summed up the value of the question-and-answer session in these words: "I know of no way of communicating more information in shorter time than the question-and-answer method."

Sometimes question-and-answer periods begin with a resounding silence that embarrasses both speaker and listeners. Almost everyone *shies away* from being the first to ask questions for fear of sounding stupid. Planning can avert this silence. Ask a few questions—thought out beforehand—and answer them yourself if nobody in the audience cares to try.

shies away—to hesitate or to withdraw

Or you can do what many professional speakers do—"plant" a question or two with a friend in the audience; it's perfectly legitimate. If nobody speaks up, your friend can *"break the ice."* Then other listeners will very likely pop questions at you.

break the ice— start asking questions

If you've done enough research, you'll be able to answer almost all queries, which should give you a feeling of accomplishment for a job

"Of course, (gulp) I know the answer to your question . . . but first let's hear what you think."

well done. If a question stumps you, don't try to bluff around it. Admit that you don't know the answer but that you will try to find it. Most of your listeners will appreciate that you're an honest and ethical human being who doesn't pretend to be a know-it-all.

A SAMPLE INFORMATIVE SPEECH AND OUTLINES

As mentioned earlier, it is common that the various types of speeches do intertwine. An informative talk could contain elements of persuasion, and motivation, as well as inspiration. And such a speech took place on May 10, 1994, when Nelson Mandela, newly elected president of South Africa delivered his inaugural address to the people of South Africa and the world at Pretoria. This historic event, for the first time, proclaimed the end of apartheid.

After you read Mandela's stirring speech, review the two outlines—sentence and topic—to see how it might have been constructed.

Glory and Hope[9]

Let There Be Work, Bread, Water, and Salt For All

1 Your majesties, your royal highnesses, distinguished guests, comrades and friends: Today, all of us do, by our presence here, and by our celebrations in other parts of our country and the world, confer glory and hope to newborn liberty.

2 Out of the experience of an extraordinary human disaster that lasted too long must be born a society of which all humanity will be proud.

3 Our daily deeds as ordinary South Africans must produce an actual South African reality that will reinforce humanity's belief in justice, strengthen its confidence in the nobility of the human soul and sustain all our hopes for a glorious life for all.

4 All this we owe both to ourselves and to the peoples of the world who are so well represented here today.

5 To my compatriots, I have no hesitation in saying that each one of us is as intimately attached to the soil of this beautiful country as are the famous jacaranda trees of Pretoria and the mimosa trees of the bushveld.

6 Each time one of us touches the soil of this land, we feel a sense of personal renewal. The national mood changes as the seasons change.

7 We are moved by a sense of joy and exhilaration when the grass turns green and the flowers bloom.

8 That spiritual and physical oneness we all share with this common homeland explains the depth of the pain we all carried in our hearts as we saw our country tear itself apart in terrible conflict, and as we saw it spurned, outlawed and isolated by the peoples of the world, precisely because it has become the universal base of the pernicious ideology and practice of racism and racial oppression.

9 We, the people of South Africa, feel fulfilled that humanity has taken us back into its bosom, that we, who were outlaws not so long ago, have today been given the rare privilege to be host to the nations of the world on our own soil.

10 We thank all our distinguished international guests for having come to take possession with the people of our country of what is, after all, a common victory for justice, for peace, for human dignity.

Mandela gets to the point immediately, with no long-winded introduction.

He provides a stirring use of parallelism: "reinforce humanity's belief . . . , strengthen its confidence . . . , sustain all our hopes . . . ."

He links the reactions of South Africans to those of the rest of the world, establishing a common response from all listeners.

He paraphrases the U.S. Declaration of Independence by using the phrase. "We, the people of South Africa . . . ."

Having linked South Africa with the other nations of the world, he invites the latter to share in his country's destiny.

[9]President Nelson Mandela, "Glory and Hope," speech delivered to the People of South Africa, Pretoria, South Africa, 10 May 1994.

He wins support by acknowledging the efforts of those who brought about the achievement being celebrated.

11   We trust that you will continue to stand by us as we tackle the challenges of building peace, prosperity, nonsexism, nonracialism and democracy.

12   We deeply appreciate the role that the masses of our people and their democratic, religious, women, youth, business, traditional and other leaders have played to bring about this conclusion. Not least among them is my Second Deputy President, the Honorable F. W. de Klerk.

13   We would also like to pay tribute to our security forces, in all their ranks, for the distinguished role they have played in securing our first democratic elections and the transition to democracy, from bloodthirsty forces which still refuse to see the light.

The appeal to healing wounds and the promise to consider amnesty help to overcome the resistance of those who in the past have been adversaries and thereby enlist their participation in the new government.

14   The time for the healing of the wounds has come.

15   The moment to bridge the chasms that divide us has come.

16   The time to build is upon us.

17   We have, at last, achieved our political emancipation. We pledge ourselves to liberate all our people from the continuing bondage of poverty, deprivation, suffering, gender and other discrimination.

18   We succeeded to take our last steps to freedom in conditions of relative peace. We commit ourselves to the construction of a complete, just and lasting peace.

The evocation of the Declaration of Independence is reinforced with the use of the term "inalienable rights."

19   We have triumphed in the effort to implant hope in the breasts of the millions of our people. We enter into a covenant that we shall build the society in which all South Africans, both black and white, will be able to walk tall, without any fear in their hearts, assured of their inalienable right to human dignity— a rainbow nation at peace with itself and the world.

Mandela demonstrates humility, portraying himself as servant of the people whose action placed him in his present position.

20   As a token of its commitment to the renewal of our country, the new Interim Government of National Unity will, as a matter of urgency, address the issue of amnesty for various categories of our people who are currently serving terms of imprisonment.

21   We dedicate this day to all the heroes and heroines in this country and the rest of the world who sacrificed in many ways and surrendered their lives so that we could be free.

22   Their dreams have become reality. Freedom is their reward.

He uses slightly unnatural expressions to elevate his statements to a loftier rhetorical level: "We understand it still . . . ," "We know it well that . . . ."

23   We are both humbled and elevated by the honor and privilege that you, the people of South Africa, have bestowed on us, as the first President of a united, democratic, nonracial and nonsexist South Africa, to lead our country out of the valley of darkness.

24   We understand it still that there is no easy road to freedom.

25   We know it well that none of us acting alone can achieve success.

He again uses repetition and parallelism: "for national reconciliation, for national building, for the birth of a new world."

26   We must therefore act together as a united people, for national reconciliation, for nation building, for the birth of a new world.

27   Let there be justice for all.

28   Let there be peace for all.

29   Let there be work, bread, water and salt for all.

30   Let each know that for each the body, the mind and the soul have been freed to fulfill themselves.

31   Never, never and never again shall it be that this beautiful land will again experience the oppression of one by another and suffer the indignity of being the skunk of the world.

32   The sun shall never set on so glorious a human achievement!

33   Let freedom reign. God bless Africa!

Analysis

To an American ear, this speech is suggestive of such prominent American documents as The Declaration of Independence, Lincoln's "Gettysburg Address," and the speeches of Franklin D. Roosevelt and John F. Kennedy—and especially Martin Luther King, Jr.'s, "I Have a Dream" speech, which is presented in Appendix A and which you will want to compare to Mandela's address to discover the striking similarities of both content and style.

Throughout the speech, Mandela uses simple but eloquent language; short, cadenced, epigrammatic sentences that have the ring of slogans—saved from monotony by interspersed longer sentences of more fluid rhythm. Forceful one-syllable words predominate.

He makes frequent use of the "We" structure to establish a oneness between himself and the rest of the South African people. Like Lincoln, he knows that repetition can be highly effective rather than boring, especially when wrapped in parallel structure.

The style will also suggest a Biblical tone to many listeners.

You can no doubt identify other ways in which this speech achieves its special effect.

Now, here's a sentence outline of the speech:

Title

Glory and Hope: Let There Be Work, Bread, Water, and Salt for All

Purpose

To celebrate the birth of a new South Africa and to inspire confidence in its future

Thesis Statement

Through the efforts of many, a new order for South Africa has arisen out of the pain of the past; though the future will not be easy, it holds the promise of fulfillment, dignity, and freedom for all

The repetition and parallelism continue in a stirring litany: four successive sentences begin with "Let," following the model of King's speech. Three of these "Let . . ." sentences end with "for all." (Is this suggestive of "with liberty and justice for all"?) He also repeats the words "again" and "never."

He offers a juxtaposition of opposites: the high-level abstractions of "justice," "peace," and "work" against the basic physical elements of "bread," "water," and "salt."

The parallel to King's speech is carried out at the end, where Mandela refers to a well-known patriotic American song, as King ends with the words of a famous spiritual.

Introduction

I. Welcome guests
II. Acknowledge significance of the occasion and issue challenge to South Africans

Body

I. Establish inclusiveness of the new order
II. Describe pain of the past
III. Acknowledge South Africa's return to the community of nations, welcome participation of other countries in sharing this historic event, and invite their support in South Africa's struggle to meet the challenges of the future
IV. Give credit and express gratitude to the masses of South Africans, to F. W. de Klerk, and to our security forces
V. Call for national healing
VI. Pledge ourselves to liberation of our people, to peace, to a secure society for both black and white
VII. Promise to address the issue of amnesty
VIII. Dedicate the day to those who made freedom possible
IX. Express awareness of the difficulties awaiting us

Conclusion

I. Call for justice; peace; work, bread, water, salt; self-fulfillment; and freedom from oppression
II. God bless Africa!

Here is a topic outline of President Mandela's talk.

Title, Purpose, Thesis Statement

Same as in sentence outline.

Introduction

I. Welcome
II. Significance of occasion and challenge

Body

I. Inclusiveness
II. Pain of the past
III. Role of other nations
IV. Credit and gratitude
　　A. To masses of South Africans

B. To F. W. de Klerk
C. To security forces
V. National healing
VI. Pledges
A. To liberation
B. To peace
C. To security for all
VII. Amnesty
VIII. Dedication
IX. Difficulties of the future

Conclusion

I. Goals for the future
II. Benediction

SOME SUGGESTED TOPICS FOR INFORMATIVE TALKS

1. Some of the effects of El Niño
2. The difference between inflation and stagflation
3. Some of the laws from which members of Congress are exempt
4. The high cost of education
5. What is the taxpayers' cost to support one member of Congress?
6. Voter apathy at election time
7. What is safe sex?
8. How to avoid date rape
9. What is political pork?
10. Buying versus leasing a car
11. The voucher system of education
12. Global Warming: Fact or Fiction?
13. Children murdering children
14. How secure is Social Security?
15. Ethics in the media
16. The latest electronic gadgetry
17. Why are the public schools flunking?
18. What is a financial planner?
19. Domestic abuse
20. The double standard of our judicial system
21. The demise of the daily newspaper
22. Genetic cloning
23. The right to bear arms
24. Dyslexia
25. Alternative health care

26. The Libertarian philosophy
27. Doublespeak or gobbledygook
28. Does the return of prayer in the public schools have a prayer?
29. Teen suicide
30. Anorexia nervosa and bulimia
31. What is sexist language?
32. When is a lie not a lie?

For more suggested topics, see Appendix B.

Figure 10.1 **Evaluation Guide for Informative Talks**

Name of Speaker: _____

Title of Talk: _____

	E				P
	5	4	3	2	1

Introduction

Did the speaker:

	E 5	4	3	2	P 1
1. State the purpose of the talk and explain the importance of the subject?					
2. Ask a challenging question or two or use a relevant quotation(s) or a startling statement to stimulate the audience?					
3. Pique your interest and desire to listen?					

Body

Did the speaker:

4. Use effective transitional words or phrases to get into the Body smoothly?					
5. Enhance the main ideas with appropriate supporting details?					
6. Effectively use audiovisual aids (recordings, videotapes, charts, photographs, objects, etc.)?					
7. Have eye contact with entire audience (referred to notes only occasionally)?					
8. Move around a bit and gesture?					
9. Have proper posture and poise (did not lean on lectern or fidget)?					

EVALUATION GUIDE FOR INFORMATIVE TALKS

If your instructor wants you to evaluate a speaker, this evaluation guide (see Figure 10.1) will be discussed, in detail, in class. You may be asked to make copies of this guide for class use or your instructor may hand them

---

Figure 10.1 Continued

	E				P
	5	4	3	2	1
10. Speak clearly using understandable language?					
11. Speak loudly enough without many pauses?					
12. Speak with inflection and enthusiasm?					
13. Present statistics and figures in an interesting manner (numbers rounded off and repeated for emphasis; sources quoted)?					
14. Try to relate the subject directly to the audience?					

Conclusion

Did the speaker:

15. Indicate by transitional words or phrases that the talk was about to end?					
16. Summarize the key ideas?					
17. Handle questions competently during the question-and-answer session following the talk?					
18. Repeat or rephrase questions that some listeners might not have heard or understood?					
19. Successfully present a worthwhile learning experience?					
20. Present a well-organized and cohesive message?					

Additional comments

_____

_____

_____

_____

out to you. This guide enables you to evaluate the speaker and rate the speech from Excellent (5) to Poor (1). The specific areas to be considered are numbered 1 through 20. If you wish to present the speaker with a numerical grade, then add the corresponding number above each check mark for each of the twenty areas evaluated and total them. You can give more feedback in the Additional Comments section.

THINGS TO DISCUSS IN CLASS

1. Prepare a short informative talk on one of the following:
   a. a concept or device
   b. a process or theory
   c. an event
   d. a problem
   e. a situation
2. Be prepared to discuss some principles that speed the learning process.
3. Prepare a short talk (a minute or two) giving specific directions on how to get somewhere. Be as concise and explicit as possible.
4. Prepare a five- to ten-minute talk on one of the following topics:
   a. the organizational structure of a business
   b. the organizational structure of an educational facility
   c. the organizational structure of a political campaign

WHAT DO YOU REMEMBER FROM THIS CHAPTER?

1. What are the prime purposes of informative talking?
2. List several categories of speeches. Which one is presented most often?
3. List some principles which, when applied, speed the learning process. Give examples of these principles.
4. What are some elements that should be included in the introduction of your informative talk?
5. What cautions should you observe when you use statistics?
6. Is it a good idea to follow an informative talk with a question-and-answer period? Explain.
7. Can an informative speech contain elements of persuasion or entertainment? Explain.
8. When explaining concepts that are new to an audience, what type of comparisons should you make?

VITALIZE YOUR VOCABULARY

Present-day English includes thousands of words based on roots from the ancient Greek language. The following is a sampling of roots, along with their meanings and some relevant English words:

Roots	Meanings	English Words
anthrop	human being	anthropology, philanthropy
arch, archi	rule, govern	anarchy, monarchy
auto	of oneself	autonomy, autograph
bio	life	biology, biography
biblio, bibl	book	bibliography, bibliophile
chron	time	chronicle, chronology, synchronize
dyn	power, force	dynamite, dynamo
geo	earth	geology, geography
gon	angle, corner	Pentagon, trigonometry
gram, graph	write, draw, record	autograph, telegraph
hydr	water	dehydrate, hydrant, hydroplane
metr, meter	measure	diameter, metronome, geometry
onym	name, word	anonymous, pseudonym, synonym
orth	straight, correct	orthodox, orthodontist, orthopedic
phil	like, love	anglophile, bibliophile (see biblio)
phon	sound	euphory, phonetics, telephone
pod	foot	tripod, podium
poly	many	polygarny, polytechnic
scop	look at, watch	microscope, periscope
syn	together, at the same time	synchronize, synthesis
tele	distant, far	telephone, telescope (see scop)
theo	god	theocracy, theology
tom	cut, split	appendectomy, atomize

BE
PERSUASIVE

People are generally better persuaded by the reasons which they
have themselves discovered than by those which have come into
the minds of others.

Pascal, *Pensées* (1670), 10, tr. W. F. Trotter

After reading and understanding this chapter you should:

- **Appreciate the importance of speaking to persuade.**

- **Know the purposes of speaking to persuade.**

- **Be familiar with methods of analyzing an audience.**

- **Know how to use statistics effectively.**

- **Understand the meaning of facts, opinions, "expert" opinion and inferences.**

- **Understand the various strategies and principal methods to help you persuade an audience to accept your views.**

- **Understand the Motivated Sequence of persuasion.**

CHAPTER PREVIEW

A form of communication crucial to the achievement of your career goals is persuasive speaking. Several examples of persuasive speaking are listed to show how practical and how valuable it can be to you.

Persuasive speaking has three purposes: to convince people to take action that you want them to take, to change radically their attitudes or beliefs, and to strengthen or weaken their current attitudes or beliefs.

Before you can persuade your listeners to change their stance and do what you want them to do, you must analyze your audience. Several relevant questions are asked; if you can find answers, you'll stand a good change of winning the audience to your side.

Armed with some understanding of your audience, you're now in a position to plan strategy. Two types of audiences are considered: (1) friendly and (2) neutral or passive.

Authorities on persuasion, starting with Aristotle 2200 years ago, agree on three ways to persuade:

1. Through logical argument by using evidence and reasoning.
2. Through speaker credibility.
3. Through appealing to basic social, biological, and psychological needs and desires.

Another method of persuasion—the Motivated Sequence—is also discussed. Each of the four methods is highlighted, and specific examples are given.

The chapter ends with a an electrifying speech by Elizabeth Dole at the 1996 GOP National Convention in San Diego on behalf of her husband, Senator Bob Dole, who was chosen to be the Republican Party presidential nominee.

Appearing in this (and every) chapter is the feature "In Other Words," which will greatly benefit foreign and ESL students. To aid in their understanding of common American idioms and phrases, these expressions will be defined in the margin of the page on which they are introduced.

In Other Words:

THE IMPORTANCE OF PERSUASIVE SPEAKING

Is the ability to persuade important to you, your family, your career? Instead of simply answering "yes," we'll list some examples of **persuasive speaking** that occur all around you. Maybe you've already been involved in one or more of the following situations:

- representing yourself in Small Claims Court
- persuading a professor to admit you into her already over-enrolled course
- convincing your manager that you should be chosen for a promotion to a position that has *just opened up*
- presenting your case to borrow the family car
- presenting your case for denying the request for use of the family car
- selling yourself during a job interview
- listening to political candidates ask for your vote
- strongly presenting your views, as a parent, on the subjects of sex education and condom distribution in the public schools

just opened up— just became available

We're sure that you get the point that persuasive speaking is a valuable skill to develop. Although there are no magic formulas or *rules of thumb* to transform you overnight into an accomplished persuader, there are several suggestions in this chapter to help you sharpen your ability. Of course, before you can convince anybody of anything, your body, your voice, your facial expressions, and your gestures should reflect the fact that you yourself are convinced. Audiences sense whether speakers are convinced of the truth of their arguments or are faking it.

rules of thumb— certain rules based on experience or common sense

The Stanford University Graduate School of Business, perhaps the foremost school of its kind in the world, conducted research on successful managers and found that they have five major characteristics in common. "Oral persuasiveness" leads the list because "the successful manager is primarily an effective speaker . . . he is interested in persuading others to his point of view."[1]

Before we begin, remember these powerful words from Lord Chesterfield, written in 1739, but still true today, "To please people is a great step towards persuading."

THE PURPOSES OF PERSUASIVE SPEAKING

All the examples of persuasive speaking listed in the previous section have one common aim: to convince people to take a form of action.

---

[1] *Nation's Business*, June 1976, 6.

The importance of persuasive speaking

Therefore, they're called speeches to **actuate,** and the best way to accomplish that is through motivation (discussed later in the chapter).

Another purpose of talks to persuade is to reinforce or strengthen, listeners' existing attitudes, beliefs, behavior, opinions, or values. Let's say, for example, that you strongly oppose the distribution of condoms (birth control devices) in the public schools and you're to speak to a group whose views coincide with yours. You would simply reiterate a few powerful arguments to reassure your listeners and fortify their position.

A third purpose of persuasive speaking is to convince people to *change* their attitude toward a particular subject. Suppose you're speaking to a group that is neutral on the subject of condom distribution in the public schools and open to discussion. In your introduction, try to capture their goodwill immediately (see the section on introductions in Chapter 8). You would now follow with some strong arguments for your position and elaborate on them. Then you might introduce statistics and other evidence accompanied by visual aids as you discuss ethics, morality, parental responsibility, health issues, etc.

ANALYZING YOUR AUDIENCE

In order to persuade your listeners, it is crucial that you learn as much as possible about your audience's beliefs and attitudes toward your topic and your position. If your listeners' beliefs and attitudes are fixed, perhaps you should settle for a chance to speak your piece and hope that they'll give you a fair hearing. Realistically, you cannot expect to change their minds with just one speech, no matter how convincing you are. If, however, your listeners are open minded, you may be able to swing some moderates among them to your banner.

Figure 11.1 shows the range (from strongly opposed to strongly favorable) of audience feelings, attitudes, and beliefs toward any speaker and subject. Sometimes an audience is polarized at one inflexible position, especially on emotional issues that cut deeply into their lives, such as unemployment, busing, gun control, abortion, and the high cost of energy. At other times an audience may be so fragmented that its members span the entire spectrum from strongly opposed to highly favorable.

No question about it—it's important to study your audience beforehand. (Refer to Chapter 6.)

turning an audience around—getting the audience to agree with your position

Turning an audience around is a devilishly difficult task, much tougher than selling an automobile or a house. Convincing an audience to make even a slight change in direction requires a carefully planned approach, anchored in a shrewd assessment of the audience's position. Before you can make that assessment, however, you should try to answer the following questions and any others that pertain to your particular situation.

1. What are you trying to accomplish? In other words, what is your specific purpose in speaking?
2. How does your audience feel toward your purpose and position?
3. What emotional or psychological appeals will move these people? (This is discussed later in this chapter.)
4. What logical reasoning will "reach" them?
5. Are they willing to accept new ideas?
6. Why should this audience listen to you?
7. Do you know anyone who has had previous experience with this audience? Can that person help you answer these questions?

After you've analyzed your audience in terms of these questions, you will better understand their attitudes, feelings, and motives. Only then will you be prepared to plan your overall strategy.

Figure 11.1 The Range of Beliefs and Attitudes of Listeners

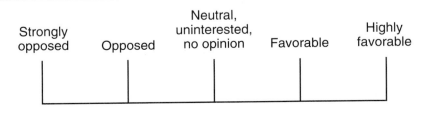

Turning an audience around can be a difficult task.

SPEECH STRATEGY

Because this is a basic speech guide, we will delve into strategy just deeply enough to help you cope with some typical situations. For example:

■ If the audience agrees with your position, discuss a few major issues so that you will reinforce your audience's position and erase any doubts that may plague them.

■ If the audience is interested but undecided, use a few of your strongest arguments, both logical and emotional, to **nudge it over the line** into your territory. If an audience is *"sitting on the fence,"* sometimes a gentle prod is all that is needed to spur them to make a decision favorable to your point of view.

■ If your audience is not interested in your subject, try to appeal to some aspects of their self-interest (discussed later in this chapter).

■ If your audience disagrees with you, don't be aggressive in the introduction. Instead of using a strong, positive statement, phrasing your proposition or solution in the form of a question or two may be a more tactful approach. Let's say that you're to speak to hard-pressed taxpayers (is there any other kind of taxpayer?) in your town about raising taxes to finance a cleanup of the town's polluted lake. You might start by asking, "Do you want your children to have a safe, healthful place to swim, fish, and sail? Or do you want them to hang around street corners, pizza parlors, pool halls, or video game arcades?"

nudge it over the line—move it in your favor

"sitting on the fence"—undecided

- Under the same circumstances, another approach would be to discuss areas of agreement first—if there are any—and then move to areas of disagreement. You might start like this: "We taxpayers all agree on the need for a family recreation area in town. Fortunately, we have a lake and we should use it for family fun. After we clean up the lake, our taxes will return to normal. In other words, this proposed tax increase will last only as long as the cleanup project lasts."

- If your audience understands the problem, spend less time on it and more time on your solution. Let's continue with the lake situation. Since your listeners, the taxpayers, understand the problem, you should devote most of your efforts to describing the benefits that they will enjoy from the restored lake. Be sure to stress that the tax increase is temporary and will stop after the lake is cleaned up.

- Spot your most convincing arguments at the beginning and end of your speech. Arguments in the middle tend to be forgotten. Playwrights know this, which is why the best plays usually open with a bang and close with a crash.

- Try to anticipate questions and objections. Plan your answers beforehand. This tactic applies to all speech situations, not just to persuasive speaking, and it can spare you many a headache.

- The opportunity to participate in a question-and-answer session may win over some hostile listeners. If you've studied your audience, you know who its influential members are. While you're speaking, focus special attention on them, because the other members tend to follow their lead.

Try to anticipate objections.

How to Select a Topic

Although this subject is pretty well covered in Chapters 7 and 10, several ideas bear highlighting. Obviously, selecting a subject about which you feel very strongly will enable you to better communicate your position with confidence and credibility.

Remember, that in a speech to persuade, nothing is more essential than transmitting credibility; because you're not only offering your audience *accurate* information but you're trying to:

■ convince them to take a form of action
■ reinforce or strengthen their existing attitudes, beliefs, behavior, opinions, or values
■ change their attitudes or opinions to agree with your position

Let's start by looking at some of the resources available to you.

Personal

As I mentioned in Chapter 10, an excellent starting point in selecting a topic is with yourself by reviewing your own experiences.

■ Perhaps you applied for a job and were turned down because of Affirmative Action policies in place at the company or public institution.
■ Maybe you were told that the neighborhood school within walking distance from your home is full and your children must be bused across the city to another school.
■ Maybe you have a ***real beef*** about the registration process at your college or the college's policy of canceling classes due to low enrollment even though that particular class may be required in order for you to graduate.
■ If you're from another country, perhaps you have a problem with our immigration laws or our foreign policy in general.

real beef—gripe

Print Media

Another rich source of acquiring ideas is from the print media.

■ All major newspapers offer editorials as well as a section on Letters to the Editors, where anyone can express his or her opinion simply by writing to the newspaper.
■ Equally as prolific as a source for topic selection are the weekly news magazines such as *Newsweek, U.S. News & World Report,* and *Time* as well as various liberal and conservative publications.
■ And, of course, the omnipresence of national and local radio and television talk shows.

Electronic Media and Library

- Don't forget the inexhaustible resources available on the Internet.
- And the good old reliable (always-there-when-you-need-them) source . . . your college or public library staff.

coming up with—
deciding on

By now, you should, at least, have a pretty good idea on how to get started on *coming up with* a topic to persuade.

No matter what topic you select, remember the previously mentioned triad for an effective persuasive performance.

- Narrow the topic and present four or five main points.
- Clearly establish your specific purpose and thesis statement.
- Be sure you're able to present your message in the allotted time.

METHODS OF PERSUASION

Speech authorities, psychologists, politicians, trial lawyers, and master salespeople know that there are four principal methods of changing people's attitudes or actuating people to do what you want:

1. Persuading through evidence and **reasoning.** (The formal term for this action is **argument.**)
2. Persuading through speaker credibility or **ethos.**
3. Persuading through appeals to basic social, biological, and psychological needs, wants, and desires.
4. Persuading by using the Motivated Sequence (MS, explained on pages 255–257.).

In most cases of successful persuasion, all four methods are mixed in varying degrees, depending on the speaker's analysis of the audience and on the speaker's character and style.

How to Persuade Through Evidence and Reasoning

Let's consider these methods, starting with argument and its components, evidence and reasoning. **Evidence,** as you know, consists of facts and expert opinions.

A fact is information that can be proved, is documented, and can be verified. Here are some examples.

Fact: Some of the highest paid people in the country are professional athletes.

Opinion: Professional athletes are overpaid.

Fact: There is no human life on the moon.

Opinion: There is no human life in outer space.

Fact: Princess Diana was killed in an automobile crash.

Opinion: Princess Diana's death was the result of a foreign conspiracy.

Fact: *The New York Times* has one of the largest circulation figures of any newspaper in the United States.

Opinion: No question, *The New York Times* is a great newspaper.

Using Opinions Wisely   Opinions may be either your own or those of other people. As with facts, some opinions are convincing and others are not, depending on their sources. Your opinion of the causes and probable cure of inflation will carry weight only if you're an expert economist who has a reputation for sound thinking. Therefore, if you're using opinions in your speech to persuade, identify the sources and their qualifications.

The most valid type of opinion is the **"expert opinion."** This is expressed by a recognized authority in a particular field. Expert "testimony" may differ but, nonetheless, is admissible in a court of law. (And you can't get much more valid than that.)

On the other hand, using "nonexpert" opinion can jeopardize your talk. In a presidential TV debate, watched by 90 million people in October 1980, President Carter committed a gaffe that cost him dearly. During an exchange with California's Governor Reagan, the Republican nominee, on whether or not to increase our stock of nuclear arms, he mentioned his daughter Amy's fear of nuclear proliferation. That statement not only *turned people off,* but it made President Carter the butt of countless cutting comments. The voters couldn't have cared less about 11-year-old Amy's opinion on nuclear weapons. The President should have quoted a world-famous nuclear physicist; that opinion would have been credible and persuasive.

turned people off—made people angry or disinterested

At the close of that same debate, Governor Reagan showed how to use people's own opinions to win votes by asking questions that hit Americans where it hurt most—in their pocketbooks: "Is it easier for you to go and buy things in the stores than it was four years ago? Are you better off now than you were four years ago?" That masterful use of questions to persuade an audience helped catapult Reagan into the White House.

Such a key question helped another presidential candidate capture the White House. In 1960 Senator John F. Kennedy faced a formidable obstacle—prejudice against Catholics. Never in 180 years had the United States elected a Catholic president, and JFK was determined to alter the course of history. In a landmark speech to a prejudiced audience—the Ministers' Association in Houston, Texas—he made this persuasive point:

Today I visited the Alamo where, side by side with Davy Crockett and Sam Bowie, died Bailey and Carey and McCarthy. . . . But no one knows whether they were Catholic or not, because there were no religious tests at the Alamo.

"Why, then," JFK asked, "should there be a religious test for the White House?"[2]

Inferences mean drawing a conclusion or generalization based on observation, experience, and/or logic. *In other words,* when you infer something, you come to a conclusion or generalization based on what you see, hear, or read, but which may not be specifically evident or stated. For example, let's say you're driving home late one night after studying at the library. As you approach your house, you observe a police car in your driveway. Whoa! As a result you may conclude one or several theses (inferences). A member of your family is ill and they're waiting for the ambulance. Perhaps there was a burglary. Maybe your kid sister got into *a little jam* and the police took her home. It isn't until you enter the house that you learn (with great relief) that the police officer is a friend of your dad's and he stopped in to say hello.

in other words— say in another, more understandable way

a little jam—a little trouble

As you can see, when you make an inference it isn't necessarily a valid one. Inferences may prove to be correct, false, or elsewhere in between.

To sum up, remember that **facts** are statements that are documented and can be verified. Everyone is entitled to his or her opinion but the only authoritative ones are offered by experts or authorities in their specific fields. And inferences are conclusions or generalizations based on your experience, observation, and/or logic which may be true or, best, an educated guess.

Types of Reasoning   If you have facts and authoritative opinions, you're in a position to carry out some reasoning. So now let's discuss some common types of reasoning: deductive, inductive, causal, and analogic.

Deductive reasoning is the type of reasoning that moves from a general premise, or principle, to a specific conclusion. If the premise is true, then the conclusion is most likely true. As we mature over the years, we learn lessons of life from which we make deductions. For example, we may deduce, from experience, that people who smoke in elevators and other closed-in places are more concerned with their own immediate satisfaction than with the comfort of others.

In formal terms, deductive reasoning is structured as a *syllogism* that consists of a major premise, a minor premise, and a conclusion. The classical syllogism is this:

Major premise:	All men are mortal.
Minor premise:	Socrates is a man.
Conclusion:	Socrates is mortal.

---

[2]*Boston Globe*, 20 November 1983. A37.

"Relax, son—I'm just delivering tickets to the Police Benefit Show."

Here's another example of deductive reasoning:

Major premise:	People who eat fatty, cholesterol-laden junk food are asking for health problems.
Minor premise:	The Smith family lives on that kind of diet.
Conclusion:	The Smith family will face health problems.

Sometimes in conversation or in a talk, one of the parts of a syllogism may be omitted. Consider these statements, for instance: "Whenever tuition and fees at colleges are raised, many students drop out. Next year the tuition and fees at this college will go up 25 percent." The conclusion implied, but not stated, is that a lot of students will be forced to leave college.

Beware of one potential pitfall in using deductive reasoning: You must be certain that both premises are true. If they're not, the conclusion will be unreliable, as in this syllogism:

Having a college degree is the surest way to get a well-paying job.

Charles Ross will soon have a college degree.

Charles Ross will get a well-paying job.

As we all know, having a college degree is only one factor in achieving a well-paying job and, therefore, the conclusion is invalid.

Inductive reasoning, the reverse of deductive reasoning, starts with specific *examples* or *cases* and ends with a general *conclusion* based on the examples or cases. For instance, much American food lacks taste and food value; canned produce and packaged bread are notorious in this respect. Compared to European breads, most American bread is flat, tasteless, spongy mush. In addition, most of our canned fruits and vegetables are "embalmed" with chemical preservatives and additives that may cause serious health problems. Most of these foods are produced, processed, and packaged by giant farm corporations. From these examples, we may draw the general conclusion that these farm corporations are impairing the health of the American people.

This discussion of American food can be condensed in the following syllogism:

Much American food (bread, canned fruits and vegetables) lacks taste and nutritional value. (specific example)

Most of these foods are produced by giant farm corporations.

These corporations are harming our health. (general conclusion)

Here's another example of inductive reasoning:

Some federal laws and regulations promote clean air and water. (specific example)

Clean air and water are essential to good health.

Therefore, we should support these laws and regulations. (general conclusion)

A common weakness in inductive reasoning is illustrated in the following generalization.

The Professional Air Traffic Controllers Organization and another union went on strike in violation of their contracts.

Therefore all unions are bad and should be outlawed.

That generalization is weak and invalid because it is based on a very limited number of examples. There is no rule about how many examples you need, but the more you can cite, the stronger your case will be.

Causal reasoning, also discussed in Chapter 8, moves from cause to effect (result). For instance, doctors and scientist have proved, through thousands of experiments, that smoking heavily (cause) shortens your life by a certain numbers of years (effect).

Here's another common-sense example of causal reasoning:

When mortgage rates decline, people are more willing to buy homes. (cause)

Mortgage rates are now declining.

Sales of homes will soon increase. (effect)

The danger in causal reasoning is to oversimplify, to rely too heavily on one cause; in the real world, most effects are brought about by several causes. In the smoking example, it is important to consider that other factors—heredity, environment, and lifestyle—influence longevity.

To avoid oversimplification in causal reasoning, keep the following two questions in mind:

1. Did the alleged cause, in fact, result in or contribute to the effect?
2. Is the alleged cause the only cause of the effect?

In **analogic reasoning** (reasoning based on analogy), you predict that, because two things or situations are similar in several important respects, they will be similar in other respects and will therefore produce similar results. For example, suppose you argue that a one-way traffic system in your city would relieve congestion and reduce the number of injuries and fender-benders because that system achieved these results in another city. To make a convincing case, you must prove that the two cities are alike in most vital aspects: number of vehicles and traffic officers, weather, population, condition of streets, traffic lights, and so on.

Experts who try to predict the behavior of the stock market will sometimes warn that stock can be expected to decline because the prevailing economic conditions are comparable to those that existed just prior to some past major decline. The success rate of such predictions is not very good, usually because even though there may be many similarities between economic conditions of two different periods, there are always other conditions that are not the same. Similarly, a baseball fan might predict that a particular team will win the pennant because it bears a striking resemblance to some other team that won in some past season. Such a prediction is not likely to come true, because there are many variables—including the other teams—that are not comparable.

We can see that analogic reasoning is often subject to error because the things compared may be too different. We must remember that no two things are identical. The persuasiveness of any argument based on comparison depends on very close similarity between the things compared. In other words, the points of similarity must far outweigh points of dissimilarity.

If analogic reasoning is of limited value as a form of proof, it can be useful as description or explanation. A good way to describe something your audience is not familiar with is to compare it to something that they know well. You could, for example, prepare someone who is going to a hockey game for the first time by explaining that hockey is a lot like basketball. Similarly, you could describe the British system of government by pointing out the many ways in which it is similar to our own.

Neither of our descriptions would be complete, however, unless we pointed out the differences between hockey and basketball and between the British and American systems of government. This realization suggests a very useful variation of analogic reasoning. The *comparison and contrast* form of reasoning combines similarities and differences and is a more accurate way to describe most things.

Whichever type of reasoning you choose to use—deductive, inductive, causal, or analogic—you should be able to handle your evidence (facts and authoritative opinions) effectively.

How to Persuade Through Statistical Credibility

firing off—stating or saying many

If you think that statistics (see statistics in Chapter 10) play an important role in the informative talk (and you do think that, don't you?), then *firing off* statistics in a persuasive speech can be crucial. Although Mark Twain is credited for espousing, "There are three kinds of lies—lies, damn lies, and statistics,"[3] they are only as effective as they are accurate.

When searching for statistics, keep the following three points in mind:

secondhand—not from the original source

1. *Sources.* Does the information come from the original source such as a governmental or private agency/study or is it second-hand such as from a newspaper or a news magazine quoting from the original source? If it's **secondhand,** be sure it's complete and accurate.
2. *Reputation of the source.* Is the source a recognized authority in the field, reflecting credibility? In other words, are you quoting from the U.S. Bureau of the Census, the *Wall Street Journal,* or the *National Enquirer*?

pay off—bring results

3. *Recency of data.* Be sure to document the latest statistics. And you do this by researching several sources. This extra effort will *pay off.*

Statistics alone can be boring and dry. Inject life into them. Paint them in language that is understandable. For example, if you're talking about the astronomical 4 trillion (that's with 12 zeros) dollar national debt,[4] you could spark your audience by declaring that it would take the U.S. Mint approximately 114 years, 4 months, and 3 weeks just to print that sum.

Another approach to grab an audience's attention is to "telegraph" a litany of short, pungent statistics.

Every five seconds of the school day a student drops out of public school.

Every 34 seconds a baby is born to a mother who did not graduate from high school.

Every five minutes a child is arrested for a violent crime.

Every seven minutes a child is arrested for a drug crime.

---

[3]Mark Twain, *Autobiography* (1924), v. 1, ed. A. B. Paine.
[4]Executive Office of the President and Office of Management and Budget, 1993.

"Statistically speaking, 50% of all married people are women."

Every two hours a child is murdered.

Every four hours a child commits suicide.

Every nine hours a child or adult under 25 dies from HIV.

Every day 3 children die from abuse.

Every day 13 children die from guns.

Every day 1115 teenagers have abortions.

Every day 7945 children are reported abused or neglected.

Every day 100,000 children are homeless.

Every day 1,200,000 latch-key children come home to houses in which there is a gun.[5]

The final example of statistics below would forge an extremely persuasive argument in a talk on gun control. These statistics headline the dramatic difference between handgun control in seven countries and no handgun control in the United States.

In 1992 handguns killed:

    13   in Australia

    36   in Sweden

---

[5]*Boston Globe*, 6 February 1994, 94.

60	in Japan
97	in Switzerland
128	in Canada
33	in Great Britain

Total 367   people as compared to 13,220 in the United States.[6]

As we conclude this section on statistics, remember—their efficacy is only proportional to their accuracy.

How to Persuade Through Speaker Credibility

During the Watergate crisis in the 1970s, the credibility of the White House plummeted to its lowest ebb in American history. The word "credibility" was bandied about daily—in newspapers, in magazines, on television, on radio, and in conversations everywhere. The scandal had reached such alarming proportions that people no longer believed any statements issued from the White House. Its credibility, an intangible but vital resource, was utterly destroyed.

When an audience believes a speaker and has faith in him or her, the speaker enjoys **credibility.** Credibility doesn't just happen; it has to be earned through such personal characteristics as:

- sincerity and concern for listeners
- tact and friendliness
- reputation and character
- self-confidence and poise
- experience and special knowledge of the subject

A crisis reminiscent of Watergate was the 1987 Iran-Contra scandal, in which it was revealed that members of the Reagan administration had made arms deals with Iran and had used the proceeds to finance the Contra rebels in Nicaragua. At congressional hearings, the key figure was Marine Lt. Col. Oliver North, who admitted carrying out the highly questionable deals. It appeared that North was slated to be the scapegoat for his superiors, the hapless victim of his congressional inquisitors.

What actually happened? After four days of testimony, North emerged a folk hero. He became as famous as Lee Iacocca, who, as president of Chrylser Corporation, saved the company from bankruptcy and possible extinction, and better known than Secretary of State George Schultz. He drummed up more support for the Contras in four days than President Reagan had done in six years. For a short time, at least, "Olliemania" gripped the nation; T-shirts, bumper stickers, and even pop music sang his praises.

---

[6]Personal communication from Handgun Control, Washington, DC, 3 June 1994.

He really enjoys credibility.

How can we account for this sudden reversal in which the expected victim became the victor? It was, in fact, a triumph of overwhelming credibility. We Americans admire and respect a man of courage. Colonel North appeared in uniform, wearing a chestful of combat medals and decorations. We also admire and respect a man who is dedicated to his wife and family. Colonel North insisted that not only had he been a faithful husband, he had accepted the gift of a home security system only in order to protect his loved ones. We admire and respect a man who shows loyalty to his superiors, especially if one of those superiors is the president. Colonel North made it clear that his loyalty was absolute. And finally, abandoning both military and bureaucratic jargon, Colonel North spoke in simple, folksy English that proclaimed him to be "one of us."

In short, Colonel North fully understood the elements that impart credibility to a speaker and exploited them to his advantage. We're certainly not recommending that you use a manipulative approach when you speak in private or in public—but you would be foolish not to consider the impression you're making. (This would be an excellent time to review the section on ethics in Chapter 1.)

How to Persuade Through Appeals to Basic Human Needs, Wants, and Desires

We all have a certain amount and degree of basic needs, wants, and desires. And these important ingredients of life have no age barrier. Many older people wish to be younger, and many younger people wish to be older. People seek a higher standard of living, ways to live longer, ways to enjoy greater health, ways to make more money, ways to be more socially acceptable and respected, and ways to be more appealing to the opposite sex.

Audience members are more easily persuaded when you can suggest ways to fulfill their basic needs, wants, and desires, such as those that follow.

Self-Preservation   We all need food, clothing, and shelter. We want to escape accidents, fires, violence, and other risks to our well-being and our family's well-being. These needs are reflected in the escalating sales of fire and smoke detectors as well as hurricane and flood insurance. In the same vein, the demand for burglar alarms and other security systems in motor vehicles, as well as in homes and industry, has prompted some manufacturers to include them as standard equipment.

In a persuasive appeal to this need, you can assert that your position fulfills your listeners' need for self-preservation. For example, you might try to persuade the audience to buy smoke detectors by pointing out their life-saving feature.

Sexual Attraction   Most of us want to be admired and fulfilled by the opposite sex. It's a normal desire that lasts a lifetime. This sexual need is responsible for the multibillion-dollar-a-year cosmetic and apparel industry supported by both sexes. These industries are able to persuade potential customers (audience members) that their cosmetics and apparel satisfy customers' desire to be attractive. How else can you explain the popularity of such services as mate-matching, computer dating, singles clubs and trips, and male and female escort services?

Feeling Good and Looking Good   Again, this is a universal want, and if you can unlock the secrets of good health and grooming, you will always have an audience. Today more and more men go to hair stylists, enjoy facials, and seek the services of plastic surgeons, once patronized mainly by women. According to *Fortune* magazine, each year men spend 9.5 billion dollars on face lifts, eyelid lifts, hair pieces, make-up, and (are you ready for this?) even girdles.[7]

---

[7]Margery Eagan, "Quest for Body Beautiful Crosses the Gender Line." *Boston Sunday Herald,* 15 September 1996, 6.

You may also be aware of the dynamic growth in the number of health clubs and weight salons that welcome both sexes and the rising consumption of fresh and natural foods, herbs, and vitamins to improve health and looks. Interest in nutrition has never been higher. At the same time, people are drinking fewer alcoholic beverages and smoking less than they used to.

Social Acceptance   Most people crave acceptance by their peers at school, at work, and in social activities. Some people continually strive for acceptance and **don't "make it"**; other people bask in acceptance without appearing to exert much effort. Some individuals would go to any length to become members of exclusive clubs, societies, or organizations or to have their children attend "very" private schools. This strong desire for social acceptance is probably the reason that so many people are taking self-help courses and purchasing record numbers of self-development books. Such resources offer ways to become socially acceptable; you can use the same technique in your persuasive speech.

don't "make it"— don't succeed

Acquisition of Wealth   Just about everyone wants wealth in some form—jewels, stocks, land, real estate, art objects, or just plain old cash. Tell your listeners how to acquire wealth and you'll have them *eating out of your hand.*

eating out of your hand—completely captivated

Many best-selling books have targeted the subject of financial security. Titles such as *How to Make a Fortune in Real Estate, How to Invest Wisely, The Fortune to Be Made in Penny Stocks, Investing in Gold and Other Precious Metals,* and *Create Your Own Treasure with Paintings and Other Artifacts* are not only being gobbled up by a hungry public, but many of the authors are attracting standing-room-only audiences at their public lectures and seminars.

Curiosity   People need knowledge about many topics—science, business, sports, government, entertainment, other people, and especially themselves. If you can answer their questions, audiences will be mesmerized by your every word. This curiosity accounts for the popularity of biorhythms, psychics, numerologists, tea leaf and palm readers, and astrology. Radio and TV talk shows, as well as newspaper and magazine columns featuring these topics, enjoy large participatory audiences.

Altruism   Altruism is the generous urge to help others without any motive of self-gain. It is on this basic urge that the United Fund, Heart Fund, Salvation Army, and various cancer research funds base their appeals for financial aid and the Red Cross bases its appeal for blood donations. The desire to be altruistic also explains why such programs as the Peace Corps and VISTA have been so successful. Fortunately, many people feel a compulsion to help others—to do something for humanity. Many of them remain anonymous.

Patriotism   Many people who don't respond to other appeals may react generously when asked to help their country. This is especially true in times of war or other national disasters. Although our sense of patriotism dipped to a low ebb during and after the Vietnam War, that antipatriotic mood reversed itself sharply during the Persian Gulf War. A tremendous surge of men and women volunteered to serve in Operation Desert Storm. This patriotism is further documented by the increasing number of public and private colleges offering ROTC military training programs and some high schools offering Jr. ROTC programs.

Identification of Speaker with the Audience   Let's say you're going to speak to a gathering of farm workers about joining a union. If you once spent a summer picking lettuce or grapes, you should mention that experience in your introduction. Then you could relate to the farm workers, and they would more likely feel that you understand their day-to-day problems and that you're concerned about their welfare. They would be far more inclined to accept your ideas than if you had never experienced their long hours, meager pay, and spartan housing.

Belonging   We all belong to a family and feel loyal to it as well as to friends, schools, social clubs, political parties, and neighborhood organizations. Most of us feel a very strong loyalty to our profession and place of employment. These networks of loyalties and interrelationships strongly influence our actions and attitudes. Most people want to belong.

So compelling is this burning need to belong that many people escape society's mainstream to join communes and cults. And some have even voluntarily participated in group-suicide rituals.

Adventure   Traveling to faraway, exotic places or experimenting with a new sport (bungee jumping, sky diving or hang gliding) are examples of fulfilling the desire for adventure. Some people feel a compulsion for adventure laced with clear-cut danger—for example, climbing a challenging mountain or exploring a fearsome glacier, big game hunting in Africa, diving perilously deep for ship wreckage or treasure, or sailing across the Atlantic singlehandedly. To exploit this urge for adventure, travel agencies publish vivid advertisements that show people climbing mountains or hiking across glaciers. Our history is distinguished by families and individuals with a penchant for adventure—from our early pioneer settlers to our pioneers in space travel.

Since all these motives (needs, wants, desires) affect people in different ways, when you speak to persuade, you should try to appeal to your listeners through as many motives as possible.

This very basic discussion of human needs, wants, and desires merely *touches the surface* of the vast, tremendously complex subject of human motivation and persuasion. It is a fascinating area with endless frontiers.

touches the surface—only approaches the subject; lacking in depth.

Who would imagine, for example, that even the *locale* (where the speech is given) of a persuasive speech could influence its outcome? Yet this happened in the 1976 presidential primary campaign. Governor Jimmy Carter, a Southerner born and bred, won the black vote consistently (except in Maryland), and thereby won some crucial primary elections. One tactic distinguished Governor Carter from all the other Democratic candidates—he spoke to black audiences in their churches.[8]

Remember this—to convince people, you should appeal to their minds and emotions; one reinforces the other.

How to Persuade by Using the Motivated Sequence

The Motivated Sequence (MS) of persuasion was created by Alan Monroe, late professor of communication at Purdue University. He distilled this method of persuasion from many years of conducting sales

---

[8] *Boston Sunday Globe*, July 1976, 33.

training programs in the business world. Basically, the MS method consists of five steps:

1. *Arouse attention to the need or problem.* State how this problem affects your listeners—their health, happiness, security, financial savings, etc.
2. *Describe the need or problem in its various facets.* Explain to your listeners the reasons why they should be concerned about the problem and the urgent need for its resolution.
3. *Satisfy the need.* Present a plan of action that will meet the needs or solve the problems of your audience. Provide evidence that the plan of action has helped others.
4. *Visualize the results.* Show listeners how adopting your plan of action will change their lives for the better. On the other hand, if they reject the plan, show how their lives will get worse.
5. *Call for action.* Challenge your listeners to take action, if possible, right then and there, to start changing things. Since getting started is usually hard, try to get them to take one specific step—such as signing a protest statement or making a pledge not to smoke anymore—and the next step will be easier.

CAUTION
You must know where your listeners stand on the problem or issue. They may need reinforcement or encouragement on just one or two of the five steps. If that's the case, concentrate your efforts there.

Let's see how the Motivated Sequence can be applied to a speech. You will remember that in Chapter 8, we presented the skeleton of a talk attempting to persuade the audience to visit The Culinary House restaurant. Here is another perspective on that same talk showing how it can be adapted to follow the steps of the Motivated Sequence:

Introduction

[Arouse attention to the need or problem.]

You've just come home from an exceptionally difficult day. You're exhausted, your blood sugar is low, and you're starved. But the last thing you want to do is go out to the kitchen and slave over a hot stove to prepare dinner.

[Describe the need or problem I its various facets.]

You need to be pampered. Your jaded appetite requires a special treat and your jangled nerves need to be soothed—but an inspection of your wallet reveals that you don't have very much money to last you until payday.

Body

I know just the solution: go out for dinner at The Culinary House. I recommend The Culinary House because the food is outstanding, the atmosphere is charming, and the prices are right. [Describe the food, the atmosphere, and the prices.]

[Satisfy the need.]

Conclusion

Picture yourself relaxing while you and the special someone in your life feast on your favorite meal in the tastefully decorated, romantically lit dining room to the accompaniment of soft background music—without having to be nervous about the inevitable arrival of your check.

[Visualize the results.]

If the picture I've just painted appeals to you, pay a visit to The Culinary House. You'll be glad you did!

[Call for action.]

A SAMPLE PERSUASIVE/NOMINATING SPEECH AND OUTLINES

Just because we categorize a speech as entertaining, informative, persuasive, nominating, actuating, or inspiring doesn't necessarily mean that it is boxed in a neat compartment and features only elements of that particular category. Categories can and do overlap.

For example, a major nominating speech would include some elements to persuade as well as to inform because, obviously, you're trying to convince your audience not only to look favorably on your nominee, but actually to vote for him or her. The speech may also include elements to entertain as well as to inspire.

I am not saying that all these elements should be included in one speech but, when you think about it, you can see how such overlapping can and does occur.

Can you imagine the reception of a speech that effectively includes most or all of the above categories and is brilliantly delivered? Well . . . that's exactly what happened on August 14, 1996, at the National Republican Convention when Elizabeth Dole nominated her husband Senator Robert Dole as the Republican candidate for president of the United States.

To personalize her speech and maximize its emotional content, she delivered it from the convention floor among the delegates rather than behind a lectern on stage. To say that her speech literally held the audience spellbound would be an understatement.

Before I present Elizabeth Dole's speech "This Is a Defining Moment in Our Nation's History," here's a brief analysis of it for you to study and use as a guide as you read over her speech.

In nominating her husband, Bob Dole, to be the Republican candidate for the presidency, Elizabeth Dole chose not to give a traditional speech stressing his qualifications for the office. Instead, she opts to humanize a man who had been widely perceived as austere and unemotional. Through a series of human-interest anecdotes, she portrays Bob Dole as compassionate and deeply concerned for the less-privileged members of society.

In addition, she focuses on the "character issue" by presenting an extensive series of testimonials to her husband's integrity. Throughout the speech she also invokes themes that appeal to large segments of the Republican party. Her extended reference to Bob Dole's serious war-inflicted injuries maintains a tone of patriotism, while references to his humble origins and the final mention of his relationship with her own mother play up the "family values" theme so popular with many Republicans.

Here, now, is Elizabeth Dole's speech followed by a sentence and topic outline.

"This Is a Defining Moment in Our Nation's History"

1   Tradition is that speakers at National Republic Conventions remain at this imposing podium. I'd like to break with tradition for two reasons. I'm going to be speaking to friends and secondly I am going to be speaking about the man I love. Just a lot more comfortable for me to do that down here with you.

2   Now for the last several days a number of men and women have been painting a remarkable portrait of a remarkable man. A man who is the strongest, the most compassionate and tender person, I've ever known. A man who is quite simply my own personal rock of Gibraltar. Tonight I want to put the finishing brush strokes on that portrait, if you will.

3   Bob Dole, if you're watching, let me warn you that I may be saying some things that you in your modesty would never be willing to talk about. I think the people you've been serving all these years in America deserve to know, they have the right to know.

4   This is not a time to be silent. This is a defining moment in our nation's history. This election is about the vision and values that will shape America as we move into the next Century; about the character of the man who will lead us there.

5   Now Bob Dole, as you know, was born in a small Kansas town. His parents were poor, in fact at one point, when Bob was a boy, they had to move their family, parents and four children, to

the basement and rent out the small home upstairs, just to make ends meet.

6 But while they were poor, perhaps, in material things, they were rich in values—values like honesty, decency, respect; values like personal responsibility, hard work, love of God, love of family, and patriotism. These are the values that led Bob on the battlefields of Italy. These are the values that helped sustain him in over three years in the hospital.

7 Now I didn't know Bob back then, but Pat Lynch did. Pat stand a moment if you will. Pat Lynch is from Boone, Iowa. Pat was one of Bob's nurses in Percy Jones Hospital, Battle Creek Michigan. Pat has told me about Bob's good humor and how they would wheel him from ward to ward to cheer up other soldiers. She also told me that Bob was very patient, and that he tapped his inner resources so that he could endure not just day after day but month after month.

8 Also, Pat told me that when Bob was totally paralyzed and people thought he would never walk again, he willed himself to walk. He was a person of great perseverance and determination and drive. He recovered fully except for the use of his right arm, in his three years in the hospital.

9 During that period of time I think Bob's sensitivity to problems of others was certainly deepened as well, because he's been there, he's been through adversity, he's known pain and suffering.

10 It was at this time in his life that he got to know Dr. Kelikian. Dr. Kelikian was a great surgeon of Chicago, Illinois. Dr. Kelikian had fled war-torn Armenia as a young man. Three of his sisters were not so fortunate. But he came to the United States with only $2.00 and a rug from his home land under his arm. Dr. K, at that time a young boy, worked on a farm. The owner of that farm was so impressed that he paid his way through college. He went to medical school and became a great surgeon, a master of bone and joint surgery.

11 Bob Dole went to Dr. Kelikian looking for a miracle because he wanted to be the person he was before the war, a great athlete, a person that was on his way to study medicine. Dr. Kelikian performed a number of operations and then administered tough love. He had to say to Bob, "you are not going to find a miracle. Now the choice is up to you, Bob, you can continue to feel sorry for yourself or you can get on with your life and work to make the most of what you do have.

12 Dr. Kelikian would not take a penny for any of the operations and did the same for many young veterans coming back from the war who couldn't afford the medical care they needed. So you can imagine how we cherish the friendship of Dr. Kelikian's widow Alice Kelikian and her daughter Alice.

13   Certainly Bob has known the struggle of making ends meet and he couldn't have had a college education if it were not for the GI bill. So he is going to protect and preserve and strengthen that safety net for those who need it. Also he has dedicated his life to make a difference, a positive difference for others, because of his own experience. Whether it's on the battlefield, on the Senate floor, or whether it's in his personal life. He is going to make that difference for others.

14   You know it was only about 12 years ago that I recall so well Bob coming home from a trip to Kansas. We were sitting in the bedroom talking and he said, "Elizabeth my plane was late and they were trying to rush me into a meeting out there and there were these two young people who were waiting outside the door to talk to me. They were severely disabled and they were there with their parents, Tim and Carla were their names. Tim said to me 'Senator Dole, we found a source of help for people that have a disability such as ours in another state, can you help us get there?'"

15   As Bob was telling me about it, I can't stop thinking about Tim and Carla. "Elizabeth, I have been meaning to start a foundation for people with disabilities for years and I haven't done it yet." Well, very soon thereafter the Dole Foundation was up and running and Bob has raised millions of dollars to help people with disabilities. Tim, thank you for inspiring Bob Dole to start the Dole Foundation for people with disabilities. Tim, I want to thank you for your courage and your spirit. Thank you, and we love you.

16   I remember about 10 years ago Bob and I were about to celebrate our birthdays, which are 7 days apart in late July. Bob suggested a reverse birthday party. He said, "Let's go to Sara Circle," which is a very special place in inner-city Washington that houses and administers to elderly poor. He said, "Let's find out what the 30–40 residents most need and want and give them the gifts, and give them the party.

17   So that is what we did, and we have had many wonderful visits there with cherished friends, the most recent about three weeks ago. And I remember a Thanksgiving about three or four years ago. Bob called up and he said, "You know, Elizabeth, I would like to do something different this Thanksgiving," and he sounded kind of sheepish, because he had already put the plan in motion. I said "Bob, what would you like to do?" He said, "I have invited 25 young people and their church sponsors to have Thanksgiving dinner with us." He had already reserved places for us and he had TVs put in so the kids could watch the Redskins game.

18   But I think what touched us so deeply was after they had finished their Thanksgiving meal and they had finished watching

the game, they began to talk about their life stories. The common thread that ran through so many of their stories was that these kids had until recently never heard someone say, "I care about you. I care about you.

19 Ladies and Gentleman you never read about that Thanksgiving dinner in the paper or heard about it in the media, because Bob Dole never told anyone about it. He did it from his heart. He wants to make a difference, a positive difference for others because he cares. Because that is who he is.

20 I will certainly not forget his last day as majority leader of the United States Senate. I was seated up in the balcony, you know, and I was watching as Senator after Senator, Democrat and Republican, stood and paid tribute to my husband on the Senate floor.

21 They talked about his countless legislative achievements. How he had led the United States Senate to successfully pass the largest tax cut in the history of the United States of America. They talked about how he saved Social Security. I want to quote from a letter.

22 This is Claude Pepper, as you know he was champion of seniors. He wrote to Bob on May 11, 1983, and thanked Bob for his extraordinary contributions, saying, and I quote, "You never lost hope and faith in our accomplishing the immeasurable task in saving Social Security. We could never have produced these results without your skill and sincerest desire to make a meaningful contribution.

23 That's leadership ladies and gentleman.

24 They also talked about how Bob had led the Senate just last year to save Medicare, to increasing spending 62%, only to have the White House veto the legislation, providing no other alternative for saving the system, except a multi-million dollar ad campaign to scare our senior citizens.

25 They talked about Bob's incredible ability to bring people together and his sense of humor. That reminds me of the time I was up for confirmation hearings before one of the committees of the Senate for Secretary of Transportation and my husband introduced me.

26 You know what he did to me? He sort of did a take-off on Nathan Hale, 'And I regret that I have but one wife to give for my country's infrastructure!' That's Bob Dole. But above all these, Senators, Democrats and Republicans talked about Bob's character, his honesty, his integrity.

27 I remember Senator Pete Domenici, the beautiful speech that you gave and when you concluded your speech you said, "The next majority leader of the United States Senate had better know that he had better be honest, he had better tell the Senate the

truth because Bob Dole knew no other way." Remember that Pete?

28   Diane Feinstein, Democrat of California said that "Bob Dole's word," listen to this now, "Bob Dole's word is his commitment and his commitment is a matter of honor and we often disagree on issues," she said, "but even when we disagree I know where I stand with Bob Dole and I know I can trust his word."

29   And that is why ladies and gentlemen, why Bob Dole's fellow Senators elected him 6 times to be their leader. Because they know he is honest and trustworthy, a man of his word, and his word is his bond, and they know he has exceptional leadership skills.

30   Isn't that exactly what we want in the President of the United States? You see these are the people, just think about this, these are the people who know him so well that they have worked with him day after day, year after year. They know what his judgment is like under pressure, that is why they continued to put their faith and trust in him, making him the longest serving Republican leader in Senate history, 11 years.

31   I am also very proud of the fact that the employees of the United States Senate, the waiters and waitresses, and others who work there, voted Bob twice—4 years apart—two surveys—as the nicest, friendliest Senator of all 100 Senators.

32   These are employees like Trudy Parker, who is a member of the United States Capital police. Trudy, bless your heart, Trudy was the first person that Bob saw on his way to work every morning while he was in the Senate.

33   On that final day, I can still see you and I will always remember it forever. You threw your arms around my husband with tears streaming down your face and you said, "Elizabeth, everywhere you go people tell you that they love Bob Dole because he always had a kind word for everyone," bless you Trudy, thanks.

34   Now let me just say I could go one and on sharing stories about this loving husband and father, this caring friend, please indulge a very proud wife this one final story that neither I nor a 95-year-old mother will ever forget.

35   When Bob was dating me, he used to go to North Carolina a lot and visit my parents. One morning unbeknownst to me he left his bedroom and went down to where my mother was fixing breakfast in the kitchen. He had a towel over his arm and shoulder that had been disabled in the war. He said, "I think, Mrs. Hanford, you ought to see my problem." Mother said, "Bob, that is not a problem, it is a Badge of Honor."

36   My fellow Americans I believe that in the years to come future generations will look back to this November, and say, "Here is where America earned a Badge of Honor.

37   Here is where we elected a President who gave us more opportunity, a smaller and more efficient government, and stronger and safer families.

38   Here is where we elected a better man who led us to a better America, because here is where we elected Bob Dole.

39   God Bless You All.

Her speech was a great success, prompting many columnists to proclaim that it was one of the greatest speeches ever delivered at any national political convention.

Here is a sentence outline of that speech:

This Is a Defining Moment in Our Nation's History

Purposes

I. To support the nomination of Bob Dole as the Republican candidate for the Presidency
II. To humanize a man frequently perceived as severe
III. To emphasize the "character issue" in the 1996 presidential campaign

Thesis Statement

As we move into the next century, America needs a president who has vision and character; a president rich in in values like honesty, decency, respect, and patriotism; a president who accepts personal responsibility and has an enviable record of extraordinary leadership.

Introduction

I. Because the content of my remarks is intimate, I am going to speak down here with you, away from the podium.
II. I am going to fill in the details of a remarkable portrait of a remarkable man.
III. This is a defining moment in our nation's history.

Body

I. Bob Dole comes from humble origins: poor in material things but rich in values.
II. Bob spent three years in the hospital recuperating from war injuries.
   A. Through that ordeal, he demonstrated his good humor, strength, determination, and sensitivity to others.
   B. He was fortunate enough to come under the care of Dr. Kelikian.

1. Dr. Kelikian had transformed himself from a penniless immigrant into a great surgeon.
        2. After his surgery on Bob, Dr. Kelikian challenged him: "Get on with your life and work to make the most of what you . . . have."
   III. Since Bob took advantage of the GI Bill to pursue his education, his gratitude ensures that he will protect and preserve and strengthen the safety net for those who need it.
   IV. Bob's compassion can be seen in several typical acts:
        A. His encounter with two disabled young people led Bob to establish the Dole Foundation to help people with disabilities.
        B. He once held a "reverse birthday party" at Sara Circle.
        C. Another time, he invited twenty-five young people and their church sponsors to join us for Thanksgiving dinner.
    V. Bob's integrity and determination to make a difference are revealed by numerous testimonials:
        A. His Senate colleagues credited him with passing the largest tax cut in history and enacting legislation to save Medicare.
        B. Claude Pepper thanked Bob for saving Social Security.
        C. Diane Feinstein cited his honesty and trustworthiness.
        D. The U.S. Senate elected him six times to be its leader.
        E. Employees of the Senate twice voted Bob the nicest, friendliest of all 100 Senators.
   VI. One final story: Bob once showed my mother his badly injured arm and shoulder, telling her "you ought to see my problem."

Conclusion

Future generations will look back on this election and say, "Here is where America earned a Badge of Honor."

Here is a topic outline of the same speech:

Title, Purpose, and Thesis Statement

(Same as in the sentence outline)

Introduction

   I. Speak away from podium to be intimate
  II. Portrait of a remarkable man
 III. Defining moment

Body

   I. Humble origins but rich in values
  II. Hospitalized for war injuries
      A. Courage through his ordeal

   B. Under the care of Dr. Kelikian
       1. Doctor's background
       2. Doctor's advice to Bob
  III. Bob's education and caring philosophy
  IV. Examples of compassion
       A. Establishment of Dole Foundation
       B. Birthday party anecdote
       C. Thanksgiving dinner anecdote
   V. Integrity and determination shown by testimonials
       A. Largest tax cut in history and Medicare legislation
       B. Claude Pepper tribute
       C. Accolade from Diane Feinstein
       D. Six times was elected leader
       E. Tribute from Senate employees
       F. Final story of Bob and my mother

Conclusion

  VI. Future generations and "Badge of Honor"

SOME SUGGESTED TOPICS FOR PERSUASIVE TALKS

1. HMOs need regulation.
2. Are equal rights and Affirmative Action one and the same?
3. Juveniles who commit adult crimes should be prosecuted as adults.
4. What is sexual harassment?
5. We should do away with plea bargaining.
6. Smokers should (not) have rights, also.
7. Do we need more gun control legislation?
8. Students should (not) be allowed to see their professors' evaluations.
9. Does a politician have a right to a "private" life?
10. Gay and lesbian couples should (not) be able to adopt children.
11. Why the government should (not) continue to subsidize private industry with our tax dollars to advertise their products overseas.
12. Middle-class America is slowly vanishing.
13. All foreigners living/working in this country should (not) be required to become U.S. citizens.
14. Term limitations for elected officials.
15. Abortion.
16. Convicted drug dealers should receive the death penalty.
17. The demise of the Social Security program is (not) a hoax.
18. The answer to our public education debacle is vouchers.
19. Why should our public schools be allowed to hand out condoms but forbid prayers?
20. Global warming is (not) a lot of hot air.

21. You can (can't) be an effective mother and have a full-time career at the same time.
22. The United States should (not) continue its role as international police officers.
23. A president of the United States who deliberately lies to the people should (not) be forced to resign or be impeached.
24. The morals of our country are headed for the sewer.
25. Don't use sexist speech.

For more suggested topics, see Appendix B.

EVALUATION GUIDE FOR PERSUASIVE TALKS

If your instructor wants you to evaluate a speaker, this evaluation guide will be discussed, in detail, in class. You may be asked to make copies of this guide for class use or your instructor may hand them out to you. This guide enables you to evaluate the speaker and rate the speech from Excellent (5) to Poor (1). The specific areas to consider are numbered 1 through 25. If you wish to present the speaker with a numerical grade, then add the corresponding number above each check mark for each of the 25 areas evaluated and total them. You can give more feedback in the Additional Comments section.

Figure 11.2 Evaluation Guide for Persusaive Talks

Name of Speaker: _____

Title of Talk: _____

	E				P
	5	4	3	2	1

Introduction

Did the speaker:

1. Get the audience's attention?

2. Clearly state the reason for selecting the topic?

3. Identify self and subject with the audience?

4. Reveal understanding and knowledge of listeners' beliefs and attitudes toward subject?

Body

Did the speaker:

5. Use effective transitional words and phrases to get into the Body?

	E				P
	5	4	3	2	1
6. Place the most convincing arguments at the beginning and then repeat them at the end of the main Body?					
7. Use factual evidence and logical reasoning?					
8. Use logical arguments?					
9. Use audiovisual aids effectively?					
10. Overpower the audience with statistics and facts?					
11. Show strong knowledge of the subject?					
12. Achieve credibility by citing sources for information presented?					
13. Get the most possible "mileage" by appealing to the audience's social, biological, and psychological needs, wants, and desires?					
14. Maintain eye contact with everyone (referring to notes only occasionally)?					
15. Move around and gesture meaningfully?					
16. Display proper posture and poise (did not lean on lectern or fidget)?					
17. Speak clearly using understandable language?					
18. Speak loudly enough without many pauses?					
19. Speak with inflection and enthusiasm?					

Conclusion

Did the speaker:

	E				P
20. Indicate by transitional words or phrases that the talk was about to end?					
21. Briefly present convincing closing remarks?					
22. Convince, stimulate, or motivate the audience to take some form of action?					

Continued

Figure 11.2 Continued

	E 5	4	3	2	P 1
23. Handle questions competently during the question-and-answer session following the talk, providing answers that were short and to the point?					
24. Repeat or rephrase questions that some listeners might not have heard or understood?					
25. Offer a worthwhile learning experience?					

Additional Comments

_____

_____

_____

_____

_____

_____

_____

_____

_____

_____

_____

_____

THINGS TO DISCUSS IN CLASS

1. List two topics for a persuasive speech that would affect members of your class. Explain what methods you would use to win their sympathy and motivate them to react the way you want them to.

2. Excluding the topics previously listed, give two topics for speeches to persuade.

3. Evaluate two TV commercials as to their intended audience and the persuasive appeal(s) used. Did the commercials accomplish their purpose?

4. Prepare a five-minute gripe talk about something at your school or place of employment. Present a solution to the situation and conclude by suggesting a form of action for your audience to take.

5. Give an example of how you would persuade an audience using appeals to self-preservation and sexual attraction.

6. Give an example of how you would persuade an audience using appeals to feeling and looking good and social acceptance.

7. Give an example of how you would persuade an audience using appeals to acquisition of wealth and curiosity.

8. Give an example of how you would persuade an audience using appeals to altruism and patriotism.

9. Bring to class two newspaper or magazine advertisements and discuss the appeal(s) used to influence the intended audience.

WHAT DO YOU REMEMBER FROM THIS CHAPTER?

1. List three purposes of talks to persuade.
2. What is the benefit of anticipating questions and objections?
3. Name three ways to persuade people.
4. List three elements that contribute to a speaker's credibility.
5. Is credibility the sole requirement for persuading people? Explain.
6. Name three basic needs of individuals to which speakers might appeal.
7. List three questions that you should ask yourself concerning an audience for whom you are planning a persuasive talk.
8. List two speakers you consider to have credibility and defend your choices.
9. Give an example of deductive reasoning.
10. Give an example of inductive reasoning.
11. Give an example of causal reasoning.
12. Give an example of analogic reasoning.
13. Explain the Motivated Sequence.
14. Explain fact, opinion, and inference.
15. List two things to keep in mind when researching statistics.

VITALIZE YOUR VOCABULARY

When you communicate, you often use number words or number ideas, but did you ever wonder where the numbers come from? Most English number words derive from either Latin or Greek (L or G). For example:

Source Words	Meanings	Number Words
semi (L)	half	semicircle, semicolon
hemi (G)	half	hemisphere
uni, from unus (L)	one	unit, union, unison, unilateral
primus (L)	first	primary, primate
monos (G)	single, solitary	monarch, monocle, monogamy, monolog
sesqui (L)	one and a half	sesquicentennial
bi, bin (L)	two	bigamy, binary, binocular
tri (G)	three	tripod, triad, trilogy
quadr, quadri (L)	four	quadrangle, quadrant, quadrille
penta (G)	five	pentathlon, Pentagon, pentateuch
quin, quint (L)	five	quintet, quintuplets
decem (L)	ten	decade, decathlon, December
deca, deka (G)	ten	decalogue
decimus (L)	tenth	decibel, decimal
centum (L)	100	centennial (see "Bi"), centipede
mille (L)	1000	millennium
kilo (G)	1000	kilometer, kiloton
mega (G)	1,000,000, extremely large	megaton, megabuck
myriad (G)	a large, indefinite number	myriad is used as an English word
micro (G)	1/1,000,000, extremely small	microscope, microeconomics

12

FIRST AID ON USING AUDIOVISUAL AIDS

In one of the most famous and fateful incidents in the Bible, the Lord summoned Moses to the top of Mount Sinai. There He appeared to Moses in the form of a fiery cloud, and there— to the appropriate accompaniment of thunder and lightning— He presented Moses with the Ten Commandments. That, so far as I know, is the earliest recorded use of audiovisual techniques for mass education.

Harold Howe II, former U.S.
Commissioner of Education, addressing
the National Audiovisual Association

After reading and understanding this chapter, you should:

- **Understand the power of audiovisual aids to persuade an audience.**

- **Understand the value of using audiovisual aids to enhance and complement your talk.**

- **Become familiar with the various types of audiovisual equipment and basic computer technology and know what to be aware of when using them.**

- **Be able to select a topic and present a demonstration talk on it.**

Specialists in modern educational psychology agree on at least one principle: the more senses involved in learning, the greater the learning. That is a convincing reason to use audiovisual aids whenever you think they will enhance your presentation.

This chapter reviews historic events that graphically display the power and impact of audiovisual media.

Audiovisual aids described in this chapter include charts and graphs, flip charts, photographs, chalkboards, slides, overhead transparencies, audiotapes and videotapes, records, models, and maps. Several points on how to use and operate projectors and similar equipment are presented. Among the most significant are computers. Advances in technology make it practical and convenient to integrate live online materials as well as prepackaged segments to many types of presentations, including multimedia.

Also discussed is the demonstration talk: what it is, how to prepare for it, and how to present it.

Appearing in this (and every) chapter is the feature "In Other Words," which will greatly benefit foreign and ESL students. To aid in their understanding of common American idioms and phrases, these expressions will be defined in the margin of the page on which they are introduced.

How Visuals Can Aid You

You may recall that in Chapter 10, the first principle of learning that we discussed was that people learn better and retain information longer when you, the speaker, involve as many of their senses as possible. This chapter is solely devoted to adding visuals to your speech to help make your presentation more interesting, educational, memorable, and even, perhaps, more entertaining. Using visual aids effectively can help capture and hold your audience's attention, create a pictorial image in their minds, and greatly enhance their ability to retain what they're viewing.

If your primary language is not English, visual aids can provide additional meaning and value as you speak. If you are concerned that you may not be completely understood, you can fortify your message and your confidence by displaying key or troublesome words along with your visuals to enable your audience not only to *hear* what you have to say but also to *see* what you're saying. In other words, allow the visuals to share the spotlight so that all the attention won't be exclusively on you.

Consider the Impact of Audiovisual Aids

The power of pictures to persuade can be overwhelming. (You may have viewed on TV some of the following events. If not, grab this opportunity

"Let's talk about the great floods of 1993."

to do a little research to expand your knowledge of history. Any one of these events could be "pictured" in an interesting and dynamic speech.) Indelibly stamped in the memories of millions of people throughout the United States and the world are vivid photographs, films, or videos of such tragedies as:

- the death camps and crematoriums of Nazi Germany, in which millions of Jews and others were murdered during World War II
- the shoot-out and total destruction by fire of the Branch Davidian's cult compound in Waco, Texas, where at least 72 men, women, and children were consumed by the inferno in 1993
- the first nuclear power plant "meltdown" in history at Chernobyl in the Ukraine in 1986
- the explosion of a powerful bomb in an underground parking garage under the World Trade Center in New York City in 1993, which left five dead, a crater about 200 feet wide and several stories deep and a grotesque portrait of twisted steel. Almost 50,000 people had to evacuate the 110-story twin towers by walking down stairwells while blinded by smoke.
- the massacre of Chinese students who raised the Statue of Liberty during a prodemocracy demonstration in Tiananmen Square in Beijing, China, in 1989
- the "Great Flood of 1993" in nine midwestern states that left at least 50 people dead, 70,000 homeless, and $12 billion in property damage
- the mass slaughter and massive starvation in such global spots as Sarajevo, Bosnia and Herzegovina, Mogadishu, Somalia, Rwanda, and Kosovo between 1992 and 1999
- the assassination of President John F. Kennedy in Dallas in 1963
- D-Day, June 6, 1944
- the car crash in Paris, France, in August 1997, which took the life of England's Princess Diana and the billions who mourned at her globally televised funeral
- the grotesque sight at the California compound where thirty-nine members of the Heaven's Gate religious cult were found dead on March 26, 1997, after a ritual suicide
- the incomprehensible destruction of Papua New Guinea, by giant tidal waves, resulting in over 2000 deaths

And what television viewer can ever forget that Tuesday morning, January 28, 1986, at Cape Canaveral? Despite problems with weather conditions, the space shuttle *Challenger* was scheduled to blast off with an unusual crew member on board—Christa McAuliffe, a high school teacher selected to become the first teacher-astronaut to fly into space.

Sixty-three seconds after takeoff, ten miles high, and at a speed of almost 2000 miles per hour, *Challenger* exploded and became engulfed in a raging orange cloud of flames. McAuliffe and the *Challenger* crew entered history as victims of the worst space disaster the world had ever seen. People everywhere, including many schoolchildren, witnessed this incredibly chilling event televised live, many viewers were not only shocked but required emotional counseling. The effect of the TV image of the disaster is a striking example of how the power of pictures can have a jolting impact on an audience. (See former President Reagan's moving eulogy in Chapter 13.)

And speaking of experiencing a "jolting impact" from visuals, here's one more event easily classified by the media as among the most startling and memorable news events in American TV history. It took place at approximately 1 A.M. on March 3, 1991. Rodney King had led the police on a high-speed chase on the freeway, at times exceeding 100 miles per hour before he was finally apprehended by police.

What followed next was videotaped by a bystander who just happened to have his camcorder. The 81-second videotape showed Rodney King being unmercifully beaten with batons by arresting officers of the Los Angeles Police Department. In all, King received 56 blows. In the following days and weeks a shocked nation gasped as it looked incredulously at the frame-by-frame replay on television.

If watching this spectacle was shocking, how many millions of viewers will ever forget the numbing verdict, a little over a year later, when a jury found all police officers involved in the beating "not guilty." Surpassing the incredulous verdict was what happened in the next 72 hours in South-Central Los Angeles when frenzied protesters and looters unleashed the deadliest riot in 25 years "that left 44 dead, 2000 bleeding, and $1 billion in charred ruins."[1] All this violence, blood, and destruction viewed from the comfort of your living room. Talk about the awesome power of visuals!

Now, let's explore how to use this incredible power in your presentations.

SPARKING UP YOUR PRESENTATIONS

After speaking with numerous business executives and managers, I learned how amazed they are at the huge number of sales presentations that fizzle. Yet, with a little more effort and imagination in the use of **audiovisual aids,** such presentations can convince associates at a business conference, win over potential clients to the speaker's viewpoint, or close a crucial sale. Remember, hearing and seeing fortify believing. (That rhymes.)

---

[1]*Newsweek*, 11 May 1992, 30.

In Other Words: Fortunately, more and more companies are realizing the importance of making presentations with audiovisual aids and have established in-house media departments. Some of the larger insurance, utility, and industrial companies have media production studios that rival commercial radio and TV stations. Although you may not have access to such a first-class team of media production professionals, with some preparation, imagination, and knowledge of visual aids, and computer graphics you can offer a successful audiovisual presentation or demonstration talk.

Because of the increase in TV viewing, acquiring information visually is, to a disturbing extent, replacing reading. This fact is substantiated by the dismally low reading scores in the public schools. Another depressing fact is that many adults rely so much on their TV sets for news and informational programs that the degree of illiteracy in this country is growing at an alarming rate.

ring some bells—
become alerted or
to take notice

How alarming? This should *ring some bells.* In a survey involving 180 million adults, most of whom attended 12 years of public school, over 95 percent (or 174 million) couldn't read, write, and figure well enough to go to college; two-thirds (or 120 million) didn't have the "literacy proficiency" to go to high school; and nearly 25 percent (one-quarter or between 40 and 44 million) just couldn't read.[2] Another survey entitled *Adult Literacy in America,* reports (and I'm glad that you're sitting down) that approximately 90 million Americans over the age of 16 are, according to most workplaces, basically unfit for employment.[3]

what's going on—
what's happening

Just so that you'll know *what's going on* in some other countries, consider these further facts. In Japan, there is virtually no illiteracy. In West Germany, the school year is two months longer than ours. And in South Korea they go to school on Saturdays.

Most American high school graduates have seen 15,000 hours of TV and, as a result, expect speakers to use visual aids.

The addition of a few graphs (see Figure 12.1), charts, pictures, models, slides, movies, videotapes, audiocassettes, or records, together with a dash of creativity, can transform an average presentation, whether in the classroom or at a sales meeting or business conference, into an exciting and highly motivating event.

The use of audiovisual aids is supported by an established principle of psychology: People learn far more through two senses-hearing and seeing, for example—than through one (hearing or seeing) alone. A study by psychologists shows that 85 percent of what we learn comes through our eyes and only 11 percent through our ears.[4] If some of your aids—for example, models or small objects—can be handled by your audience, then the sense of touch reinforces hearing and seeing.

---

[2]Regina Lee Wood, "Our Golden Road to Illiteracy," *National Review,* 18 October 1993, 54.
[3]*Time,* 20 September 1993, 75.
[4]Robert L. Montgomery, *A Master Guide to Public Speaking* (New York: Harper & Row, 1979), 36.

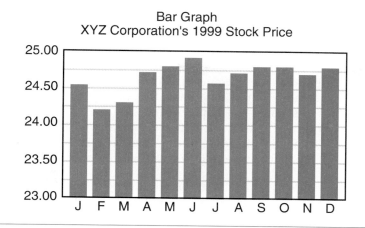

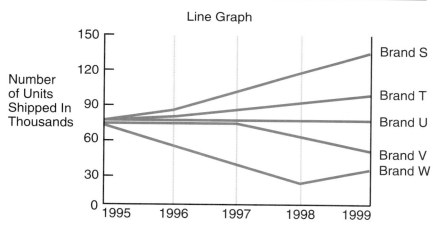

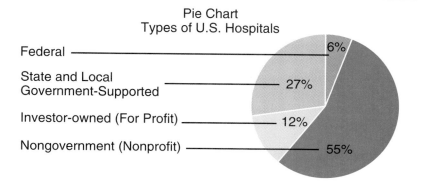

Figure 12.1 Graphs Like These Make Very Effective Visual Aids

The American Management Association, which conducts management training sessions worldwide, tells us that from an average lecture we retain about 10 percent of the information. Using visual aids, the retention jumps to 50 percent. And, when we combine visual aids with audience participation, our retention capability soars to 70 percent. Remember, the more senses involved, the greater the learning. (This principle is also discussed in Chapter 10.)

Another powerful reason for using visual aids is that they arouse and maintain audience interest and reinforce the message. There's no question that the effort you put into preparing visual aids pays off handsomely.

ADDING SIGHT AND SOUND TO YOUR PRESENTATIONS

If you're required to give a presentation that involves using audiovisual aids, you'll probably find it challenging and rewarding, because it is informative and, in some cases, entertaining. Using audiovisual aids requires planning and practice and can result in a performance that will be a credit to you. It will afford you a rich opportunity to further develop your self-confidence, for it will place you in the role of expert lecturer.

Computers are among the easiest tools to use for delivering effective audiovisual aid. Although we'll explore the use of slides, transparencies, and audio and video materials individually, you may decide to use several of these at once. If you do, then a computer—laptop or PC—and specially designed software programs can save you a lot of time and work and, at the same time, inject more life and excitement into your presentation.

Be sure that the physical surroundings are adequate for your audiovisual aids. If a table is needed to hold your models, be sure one is there. Check that an electrical outlet (with sufficient power) for your projector is within reach, or that you have an extension cord. Computers don't require any special electrical connectors, however, a power strip with a built-in surge protector is a good idea. If the room is wired with a jack to connect to a telephone line, or better yet a digital line, (*you're golden*) then you might consider including an online portion to your presentation. You can be sure that your class will be very impressed.

you're golden— you're making the most of a situation

Try to avoid displaying visual aids before you refer to them in your presentation. If you're going to use charts, graphs, photos, and so on, set them up beforehand but keep them covered or out of view so that your listeners will not get a sneak preview and be distracted.

Always rehearse your presentation a few times, using the same equipment you plan to use in your talk. The key to a flawless performance is practice, practice, practice. It's the only way to counter

"Murphy's law": If anything can go wrong, it will. Nothing is more embarrassing in the middle of a presentation than fumbling with a piece of equipment because you haven't practiced using it.

Of course, no one is immune from the plague of Murphy's Law. Not even the "high and mighty" of government. Early in his administration, President Clinton was scheduled to deliver one of the most important speeches of his young presidency to a joint session of Congress. Because of last-minute editing changes, a top aide rushed the final version of the speech to the operator of the TelePrompTer just moments before speech time. In his haste, he inadvertently hit the wrong button on the computer and combined the new speech with an old one already in the system.

No one realized the blunder until President Clinton himself reached the podium, looked at the TelePrompTer, saw the old speech, and with stricken terror turned to Vice President Gore and declared, "We have to get this fixed."

It took almost seven minutes (which I'm sure seemed like hours) to correct the problem. Meanwhile, the eloquent and confident (and, we might add, well-prepared) Chief Executive started his critical speech on National Health Care to Congress and the nation using only his rough

If anything can go wrong, it will.

"cool"—in complete control

notes until the TelePrompTer caught up with him.[5] A looming disaster was averted by a calm, *"cool,"* and confident president.

Would you like another classic example of Murphy's Law at work? Bill Gates, the founder and chairman of the giant computer software company Microsoft was planning to unveil his new Windows 98 software to a large and major computer show audience in Chicago. After a brief introduction extolling the virtues of his new product, and right on cue, one of his assistants went to plug in a scanner when, you guessed it, the system crashed. Zero, nada, blank, poof! A very confident Mr. Gates quipped without missing a beat, "I guess we still have some bugs to work out. That must be why we're not shipping Windows 98, yet."[6] He, then, proceeded to another computer to complete his demonstration.

Now, allow me to present "Vasile's Law." Vasile's Law states that to break Murphy's Law, you should perform a full-dress rehearsal of your presentation. In other words, plan, prepare, and practice—several times, if necessary—to avert delay and embarrassment. Bill Gates's being prepared by having standby equipment *on hand* and displaying a quick sense of humor averted what could have been a humiliating experience, which can work for you, too.

on hand—nearby and available for use

Consider Using an Easel

Easels are useful for displaying a variety of visual aids, including large cards or poster boards bearing charts, graphs, or other information; flip charts; and photographs.

To Display Large Cards   Charts, graphs, simple statistical tables, and the like may be prepared in advance using pieces of poster board about three feet by four feet. Place all of your cards on the easel, and as you finish with each card, remove it and place it on the floor. When preparing these cards or boards, use stiff paper that won't curl down and fall off the easel. If the cards are thin, glue or tape two of them together. Number them in case they get out of sequence, and use two or more colors for a more eye-catching presentation. You can also use different colors for headings, subheadings, and overall emphasis.

Since the audience will tend to direct its attention to portions of the visual aid that you're not discussing, prepare the material in a way that allows you to cover what is not being currently discussed. Each unit can be covered with a strip of paper or a piece of cloth that can be removed when you're ready to discuss that point.

To avoid blocking people's view, use a three-foot pointer or a telescopic one. This will enable you to remain at arm's length from the cards

---

[5]*Newsweek,* 4 October 1993, 4.
[6]Cliff Edwards, AP, "Windows 98 Crashes During Gate's Show." *Boston Globe,* 21 April 1998, C7.

and still reach the material comfortably with the pointer. But, remember to hold the pointer with the hand closest to the easel and never turn your back on the audience.

And, now here are some pointers when using your pointer. As tempting as it may be, don't play with the instrument. In other words, don't tap or slap the pointer against your leg, don't rub or stroke it, don't swing it between your legs and don't continually drop it on your foot or on the floor. Remember, the purpose of the pointer is to point *at* and not play *with*. I hope you **get the point.**

get the point—
understand

To Use a Flip Chart   A flip chart is a pad of paper approximately 27 inches by 33 inches, normally containing about 50 sheets. This form of visual aid allows you to flip each page up and over the easel when you're finished with it. You may prepare it in advance of your presentation or write on it during your talk. In either case, be sure to use a marker that won't bleed through to the pages underneath. Large blotches on pages are distracting and look amateurish.

Don't talk to the pad of paper while writing on it. Keep your attention focused on the audience. Again, the information you're putting on the pages can be made more interesting and emphatic by using more than one color.

If there's a "bleed-through" problem, use two sheets at a time.

To Display Photographs   Photographs are an excellent medium for conveying information, especially to a small group. Size is a critical element; make sure that the photographs are large enough to be seen by everyone. For a larger group, you may need to have enlargements made (this can be quite expensive).

A famous example of the persuasive power of photographs took place during the Cuban missile crisis in October 1962, before the United Nations Security Council. The U.S. ambassador, Adlai Stevenson, confronted the Soviet ambassador, showing him and the world enlargements of aerial photographs which proved that the Soviet Union was building offensive missile bases in Cuba. In light of this overwhelming evidence, world opinion forced the Soviet Union to dismantle the missiles and bases, thus averting a possible nuclear war.

Consider Using a Chalkboard

A chalkboard is a simple visual aid that is readily available in most classrooms. Before you write on it, be sure that it's completely erased. If possible, write before you give your presentation and cover your material with a large piece of paper or cloth so that the audience is not distracted by it. For added effectiveness and interest, use a second color of chalk along with the traditional white. Headings and major points, for example, may be written in either yellow, pink, orange, blue, or purple. You can purchase a box of chalk in mixed colors. Again, a little imagination can produce a more interesting and memorable presentation. We suggest, however, not using more than two colors.

If your presentation requires writing on the chalkboard, try to minimize the amount of writing so that you can devote maximum attention to your audience. Don't speak while writing on the board. Speak either before or after, and when you do, use a pointer and stand sideways so that you can look at your listeners.

"classy"—a bit showy, feeling you're better than average

Speaking of pointers, if you really want to be *"classy,"* instead of using a wooden or metal retractable one, use a **laser pointer.** This state-of-the-art piece of equipment emits a beam that produces a red dot on surfaces up to a couple of hundred feet away. Although I doubt you'll ever be that far from your visual, you can appreciate the advantage of mobility between you and your audience.

CAUTION
When using a laser pointer, never point it at the audience and, above all, avoid direct eye exposure because laser radiation can be dangerous.

Although we've advised you not to speak while writing on the chalkboard, also try to avoid long periods of silence, because silence causes interest to lag. Remember to write clearly and large enough for all to see—and try to write on a straight line. Be sure to hold the chalk at a sharp angle (30 to 40 degrees) to the board; otherwise, the moving chalk will cause nerve-wracking squeals and make your audience want to run for cover.

Consider Using a Projector

Many schools have audiovisual departments that are well stocked with various types of projectors and other equipment and usually are staffed by professionals. In a short time, staff members can teach you to operate the equipment. Knowing your audiovisual staff and the equipment can be very helpful to you.

Slide Projector   If you're using slides, be sure that they're arranged beforehand and locked in trays or in a carousel. If you don't, you'll waste time holding slides up to the light to try to figure out how to place them in correct sequence. Remember that color slides are more compelling than black-and-white ones. Also, slides combine well with audio aids. For example, you can either speak while showing slides or record your narrative onto an audiocassette and play it while the slides are being shown. To avoid a *"migraine,"* be sure that all your slides are numbered and titled. These two hints will enable you to present them easily and keep them in the right order.

migraine—a very bad headache

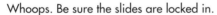

Whoops. Be sure the slides are locked in.

Opaque Projector   An opaque projector can project the image of a book or magazine page, of the pages of a report, or of a diagram (usually no larger than 10½ by 10½ inches). Although this machine tends to overheat and the fan may blow your material around a bit, it does permit you to display material in the detail and color of the original source.

Overhead Projector   An overhead projector requires overhead **transparencies,** thin sheets of clear plastic (acetate) on which information has been printed or on which you may write information before or during your speech. Transparencies are very popular because they can be made fairly easily at your local photocopy shop. For example, you can make full-color prints and transparencies from paper originals in a matter of minutes. Since you can photocopy onto acetates, you can prepare the text or figures on a word processor/desktop publishing computer. If you're familiar with this electronic equipment, the possibilities are unlimited. In addition, your school's audiovisual library may have transparencies on a multitude of subjects.

An overhead projector transfers information from an overhead transparency or a computer monitor using an **LCD panel** to a screen or a blank wall.

CAUTION

Most overhead and opaque projectors have extremely short focal length lenses that necessitate their being placed close to the screen and, therefore, in front of the audience. Since you'll be standing behind or beside the machine, be sure that the image is projected high enough so that everyone can view it easily. Although slide "carousel" and movie projectors produce some noise while in operation, they usually have zoom lenses and can be easily placed at the rear of the audience, where they are less distracting. Remember to set up your equipment beforehand to ensure proper focus and sound level.

Movie Projector   There are various types of movie projectors—8 or 16 millimeter (mm), sound or silent. When you use sound, be sure to check the volume before the audience arrives. Having the volume too low is as annoying as having it too high. If you use silent film, remember that operation of the equipment produces a hum and that you must speak loudly enough to overcome the hum. Have the film already threaded so that all you have to do is flick a switch to start it.

Filmstrip Projector   A filmstrip projector guides a strip of 35-mm film past the lens by a series of sprocket holes. This type of projector has no feed or take-up reel and is very easy to operate. Since most filmstrips usually run between two and ten minutes, they're perfect for presenting short segments in a visual talk. Again, your school's audiovisual department may have a large supply of filmstrips on various subjects from which you may select.

Consider Using Laptops or Personal Computers, LCD Panels, and Presentation Software

The multimedia capabilities of computers make it easier than ever to include audiovisual materials in your presentation. You don't have to be a wizard of technology to put sound and images into your talk.

Presentation software programs like Microsoft's PowerPoint (see Figure 12.2) include templates that can be easily customized to serve a range of projects. For example, you can create a slide show to display on your computer as a prompt to keep you on track. You can also project those same slides onto a screen or wall to support what you're saying visually for your listeners. If you wish, you can print copies of your slides to use as handouts. This will allow your audience to hear and consider your words while, at the same time, supplying them a place to *jot down* a few additional ideas from your presentation. Pretty fantastic isn't it? But, we're not through yet.

jot down—write down

For the more creative and adventurous presenters, live, online demonstrations and examples can be produced if there's a telephone or

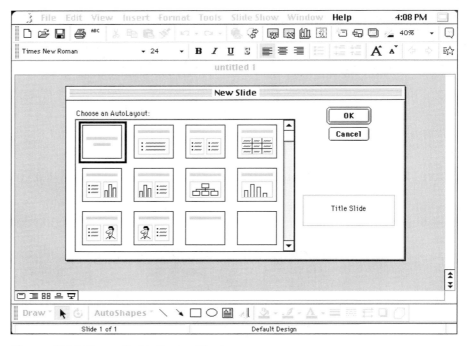

Figure 12.2 PowerPoint Screen Display.
You can create, store, and project a slide presentation right from an average PC.

breaking news—news that is happening as you speak

digital line jack within reach of your computer. *Breaking news,* maps and photos, video and audio resources are all there at your fingertips on the World Wide Web via the Internet. Integrating live elements into your talk can bring a spontaneity and immediacy than can help keep your audience attentive and educationally informed and entertained. Just be sure that the material you select and your methods of presentation are

go overboard—be excessive

appropriate to the topic and that you don't *go overboard.* Sights and sounds are not a substitute for facts, accuracy, and continuity of ideas, but rather are an enhancement to them.

keep this in mind—remember this

I know I'm repeating myself, but you will do well to *keep this in mind:* do not fall into the trap of relying too heavily on one tool. Always be prepared with options if the power should go out or a connection can't be established. Have a backup plan in case the file you stored on a floppy disk suddenly can't be retrieved, or a web server you've connected to goes down without warning. Remember what happened to President Clinton and Chairman Bill Gates. Now go and be as creative as you can be.

Consider Using Recorders and Record Players

Audiotapes, records, and compact discs can add another dimension to your presentation. For example, you might use tapes with a silent film or slides or use records to illustrate a talk on music appreciation. Small cassette tape recorders are convenient to carry and to operate if you plan to interview people, to record statements, or to record sounds to enhance your presentation.

Videocassette Recorder (VCR)   Many how-to videotapes can be rented to enhance your presentation on how to do something like a particular craft, hobby, or trade. Be sure to preview the tape to decide what segment(s) you plan to use. If you want to do your own videotaping, you may be able to borrow equipment from your school.

If you plan to use a VCR, be sure that everyone in the class can see the monitor clearly. If the audience is large, consider setting up monitors on both sides of the room for maximum viewing capability. Again, your school's AV department can probably help you set up the equipment if you make arrangements beforehand. Don't wait until presentation day.

Consider Using Objects

Displaying objects (for example, tools or pieces of equipment) is an excellent way to explain how something operates. If you can't bring in life-sized objects (for example, an auto engine or Stealth Bomber), bring in scale models, but be sure that they are large enough to be seen. Always stand behind or beside the object, never in front of it or between it and the audience. To sustain audience attention, it's a good idea to keep objects out of sight until the point in your presentation at which they're

A VCR can be a very useful aid. Be sure to position the monitor so that everyone can see it.

needed. If they're on display at the start of your talk, the audience may be more interested in the objects than in what you're trying to convey. Until you need them, they can be hidden in the recess of the lectern, in a box or bag on a nearby chair, or on the floor. If you're using more than one object, display and discuss them one at a time so that all the attention will be focused on the item under discussion.

Passing objects around the class can be tricky. If all the listeners receive the same objects at the same time, they'll be better able to follow you than if you pass around several different objects at different times. Audiences can become more engrossed in looking at objects in their hands than in what you're saying. After your talk, you might consider displaying the objects on a table so that your audience can inspect them closely.

Consider Using Handouts

follow your talk—proceed along with the speaker

Handouts—maps, charts, tables, photographs, and diagrams—are very effective because everyone in the class gets one, and your listeners can *follow your talk* more closely. Again, if you're planning to pass around several handouts, don't do so all at once because the audience may pay more attention to them than to what you're saying. Hand them out individually at the appropriate time during your talk, and be sure to allow the class enough time to become familiar with the contents before you resume speaking. To save time, several members of the class can assist in distributing the handouts. If you're planning to distribute handouts to be taken home, rather than pass them out during your talk, mention to your audience that they will be available following your presentation.

Preparation of handouts can be considerably simplified if you have access to a computer. Computer graphics now make it possible for the operator to create and print out many unique and imaginative visuals such as line graphs, bar graphs, charts, drawings, and three-dimensional illustrations in both black and white or color. Once you have the finished product, you can easily have copies made for projection or for handouts.

run the risk—take the chance

Using more than one type of visual aid is not only acceptable, but can greatly complement your overall presentation. However, if you select too many types, you *run the risk* that they will overpower your message.

THE DEMONSTRATION TALK

One type of talk that particularly lends itself to the use of audiovisual aids is the **demonstration** (demo) **talk.** The practical value of using audiovisual aids, particularly in a demo talk, is beautifully expressed in an ancient proverb, a masterpiece in three short lines:

What I hear, I forget.

What I see, I remember.

What I do, I know.

In other words:

Hearing is good.

Seeing is better.

Doing is best.

And now back to the demo talk. The objectives are:

1. To show the class how to do or how to make something. For example,
   - how to create a flower arrangement
   - how to prepare a financial aid form
   - how to make a wreath from pine cones
   - how to decorate a cake
   - how to identify counterfeit money
   - how to perform cardiopulmonary resuscitation (CPR)

2. To explain to the class how something operates. For example,
   - how a standard transmission functions
   - how a word processor works
   - how a solar panel gathers energy
   - how rack and pinion steering works
   - how a microwave oven works
   - how an electric car runs

Without question, the demonstration talk ranks number one among students. In most cases it truly adds up to a genuine learning experience. A demonstration talk should generally take between 10 and 20 minutes. A shorter time will not give you a worthwhile experience in using audio-visual aids, and your audience may just be *getting warmed up* to your subject when—poof, it's all over.

getting warmed up—starting to become interested

Consider Involving Members of the Audience

Whenever you can get a member or members of your class to participate in your demonstration talk, your effort will involve your audience more deeply. For example, if you're to demonstrate how to manicure fingernails, use a volunteer as a model. If your topic is sketching, use a student from the class as your model rather than drawing from a picture or photo. One student showed the Heimlich maneuver for aiding a choking victim. Following the lecture portion of his presentation, he demonstrated the method on a class volunteer. He then had the entire class pair off, and every member performed this life-saving technique on another.

The class selected this talk as its favorite. So remember, if possible, involve members of the audience.

If you're planning to use a volunteer as a part of your demonstration talk, arrange this in advance. Why? Because you want to be sure that you have a volunteer, willing and able, when the time arrives. Incidentally, most professionals who need a volunteer for their presentation "plant" one in the audience.

Consider Yourself as a Visual Aid

Remember, the most effective visual aid can be you. You can add spice and additional interest to your presentation by playing the role. For example, if you plan to show the class how to create a Caesar salad, wear a white apron and a chef's hat. If you plan to show how to set a table professionally, wear a waiter's outfit. To show the class how to take a blood pressure, wear a medical uniform. If you're a police officer or firefighter and you plan to talk about some aspect of your job, wear your uniform or fire outfit. With a little imagination, you can significantly enhance your visual presentation by "dressing the part."

How to Select a Topic to Demonstrate

You're probably scratching your head now and wondering, along with many others in the class, what you can demonstrate. This is a common

reaction, but from years of experience we've found that those who encounter difficulty in selecting a topic usually end up with a satisfactory one. If you're having a problem, tell your instructor; a five-minute chat may turn up an answer for you.

You can approach this talk from one of two directions. You can either select a topic that you know or one that you know little about but would be interested in researching. If you choose the latter, you'll become involved in a solid learning experience.

A Topic You Know   The natural choice is a topic you know something about. You should take inventory of your knowledge, experiences, and skills to decide which topic you will present. Did any of your jobs, full-time or part-time, require special skills? Did you receive special training in the service? What about your hobbies? Are you involved in any of the following: rollerblading; collecting CDs, sports cars, matchbook covers, wines, or stamps; cycling; shopping; or aerobics/physical fitness? Do you like to cook or bake? You'll probably be astonished at some of the things you've done or are interested in that would make worthwhile presentations. Don't *sell yourself short.*

The following are some topics that resulted in successful presentations by students whose initial reaction was "There's nothing I can do."

sell yourself short—underestimate your abilities

- A student who had worked in an ice cream parlor demonstrated how to make several types of sundaes.
- A football enthusiast gave an excellent presentation and explanation of the various signals used by referees. He even wore an official black-and-white striped shirt.
- A woman intrigued the class with her talk about—and demonstration of various positions in—yoga.
- In a presentation on self-defense, a woman effortlessly flipped several male students on a mat.
- A student who was a police officer demonstrated the art of fingerprinting by using classmates for subjects.

Without question, the most memorable demonstration talk was by a student who was a rather good magician. In fact, he was working his way through college by performing at children's birthday parties, bar mitzvahs, and other occasions. Well, while demonstrating his "prestidigitational" skills, he made the class disappear and I never saw them again. (Did I have you going there for a minute?)

A Topic You Know Little About   If you're ambitious about learning, you may select a topic that you're not too familiar with, conduct research on it, probably receive instruction, and then give the presentation. This approach requires considerable preparation, but it will be rewarding.

NOTICE TO STUDENTS FROM OTHER COUNTRIES
Here's a wonderful opportunity to share with us some of the culture of your native country (customs, traditions, religions, clothing, language, etc.).

SOME SUGGESTED TOPICS FOR DEMONSTRATION TALKS

Here is a list of topics for demonstration talks. For further suggestions, see Appendix B.

1. Forecasting the weather
2. Types and uses of sporting equipment
3. Photography
4. Collecting (coins, stamps)
5. Playing a musical instrument
6. Firefighter and police equipment
7. Performing a native dance
8. Show clothing from your native country
9. Assembling terrariums
10. Planning a garden
11. Making balloon animals

"Step three in making a pizza is very tricky."

12. Framing a picture
13. How to install a light dimmer
14. How to pack a parachute
15. What to look for when reading a wine label
16. How to make an antipasto
17. How to communicate by sign language
18. Basic self-defense for women
19. Some basic carpentry tools and how to use them
20. How to gift wrap a package and make bows.
21. How to pack a suitcase
22. How to coordinate a wardrobe (male or female)
23. Applying make-up
24. Performing card tricks
25. Handicrafts (knitting, macramé, découpage, crochet)
26. Giving first aid to a choking victim (Heimlich maneuver)
27. Art (sketching, collage)
28. How to read the stock market page
29. How to score a tennis match
30. Making a lamp out of a bottle

EVALUATION GUIDE FOR DEMONSTRATION TALKS

If your instructor wants you to evaluate a speaker, this evaluation guide will be discussed, in detail, in class. You may be asked to make copies of this guide for class use or your instructor may hand them out to you. Evaluate the speaker by checking Yes or No for each of the nineteen specific areas listed. You will also have a chance to grade the Overall Performance and give more feedback in the Additional Comments section.

Figure 12.3 An Evaluation Guide

Name of Speaker: ————————————————

Title of Talk: ————————————————

	Yes	No
Introduction		
Did the speaker:		
1. Greet the audience?		
2. State the purpose for selecting the topic?		
3. Explain exactly what was to be demonstrated?		

Continued

Figure 12.3 Continued

	Yes	No
Body		
Did the speaker:		
4. Present the talk in a logical sequence?		
5. Define any technical terms used?		
6. Maintain eye contact with the audience?		
7. Display objects one at a time?		
8. Have the objects placed so that everyone in the class could see them?		
9. Use too many audiovisual aids, thereby causing confusion?		
10. Have the audiovisual equipment present and ready for use?		
11. Know how to operate the audiovisual equipment?		
12. Have enough handouts for everyone in the class?		
13. Use the handouts effectively?		
14. Prepare visuals (posters, charts, etc,) large and clear enough to be seen and understood by the entire class?		
15. Use the aids in any way that was distracting to the presentation?		
Conclusion		
Did the speaker:		
16. Accomplish the purpose of the talk?		
17. Clearly answer the questions from the audience during the talk or after it?		
18. Show strong knowledge of the subject?		
19. Offer an interesting, entertaining, or learning experience? (Were you glad you attended class today?)		

Overall Performance: Excellent _____ Good _____ Fair_____ Poor_____

Figure 12.3 **Continued**

Additional Comments

_____

_____

_____

_____

_____

_____

_____

THINGS TO DISCUSS IN CLASS

1. Visit your audiovisual department and become familiar with its equipment.
2. Tell about a recent talk (presentation) in which audiovisual aids were used—for example, a commercial or a how-to project on TV or a class lecture.
3. Name a profession or occupation in which audiovisual aids play an important role.
4. Select a topic you'd like to talk about and explain which audiovisual aids you'd use and how you'd use them.
5. List a topic that would require the use of audiovisual aids. Explain.
6. Bring three types of graphs to class and explain the differences among them.
7. Watch a news program and weather report on TV and be prepared to discuss the types of visual aids used and their overall effectiveness to the "message."

WHAT DO YOU REMEMBER FROM THIS CHAPTER?

1. How can the use of audiovisual aids help get your message across to the audience?
2. Is it permissible to use more than one aid in a presentation? Explain.
3. Explain the impact of pictures.
4. What must you be careful of when you use handouts?
5. What should you keep in mind when you write on a chalkboard?
6. What's a good technique for preparing large cards to be placed on an easel?

7. Explain several advantages of using transparencies during your presentation.
8. If you show objects or scale models, where should you stand in relation to the audience?
9. What's a good thing to remember if you're planning to use a volunteer during your demonstration talk?
10. Explain the persuasive power of videotapes.
11. Explain the ancient proverb:

   What I hear, I forget.
   What I see, I remember.
   What I do, I know.

12. Explain the difference between an overhead and an opaque projector.
13. What would be the best location in a room for a projector? Explain.
14. What must you be careful of when preparing a flip chart?
15. Is it a good idea to have a member of the class participate in your presentation? Explain.
16. Explain some of the capabilities of PowerPoint.
17. Explain several multimedia applications that your computer can perform.

VITALIZE YOUR VOCABULARY

Dining Out, or As You Peruse the Menu

The following words and terms may be found on menus at many popular restaurants:

á la carte Each individual item listed on the menu is separately priced.
al dente Firm, not soft or mushy, to the bite. Refers to vegetables or pasta.
appetizers Certain dishes (small portions) served prior to the main meal or entree.
au gratin (oh grah tan) Having a browned or crusted top, often made by topping with bread crumbs, cheese, and/or a rich sauce and passing under the broiler.
au jus (oh zhoo) Served with its natural juices.
bisque A cream soup.
canapé (can ah pay) A tiny open-faced sandwich, served as an hors d'oeuvre.
consommé A rich, flavorful, seasoned broth that is perfectly clear and transparent.
coq au vin (coke oh van) A French dish of chicken braised in wine.
crêpe (krepp) A very thin pancake, often served rolled around a filling.
florentine With spinach.

hors d'oeuvre (or durv) An appetizer or canapé served with cocktails, usually before dinner.

jardinière (zhar din yair) Garnished with fresh "garden" vegetables, such as carrots, green beans, peas, or cauliflower.

julienne Cut into thin strips.

maître d'hotel (may truh doh tell) Also called the maitre d'; the head steward of the dining room.

mousse A light, soft, creamy dessert made so by the addition of whipped cream or beaten egg whites or both.

oscar With crabmeat and asparagus, as in Veal Oscar.

princesse Garnished with asparagus.

provençale (pro vahn sal) Garnished with or containing tomatoes, garlic, parsley, and sometimes mushrooms and olives.

purée Mashed or strained to a smooth pulp.

sorbet (sor bay) French word for sherbet, usually made with fruit juices and no milk products or eggs.

table d'hote (tobble dote) Referring to a menu on which prices are listed for complete meals rather than for each separate item. The opposite of à la carte.

torte German word for various types of multilayered cakes.

vin (van) French word for wine.

Various Types of Sauces

alfredo A basic white sauce made with cream, butter, and cheese slowly stirred together over heat to a smooth texture.

béarnaise (bare nez) A sauce made of butter and egg yolks and flavored with vinegar, shallots, tarragon, and peppercorns.

béchamel (bay sha mel) A sauce made by thickening milk or cream with flour and butter.

hollandaise A sauce made of butter, egg yolks, and lemon juice or vinegar.

mornay A sauce made of béchamel and Gruyère cheese.

supreme A cream sauce made of chicken stock and heavy cream.

13

SAYING A FEW WORDS . . . VERY FEW!

Let thy speech be short, comprehending much in a few words.

Ecclesiastes 32:8

After reading and understanding this chapter, you should be able to:

- Make an announcement.
- Introduce a speaker.
- Present an award.
- Give a thank-you talk after receiving an award.
- Make a nominating speech.
- Give an installation speech.
- Propose a toast.
- Utilize a public address microphone.

CHAPTER PREVIEW

Since you probably already belong to or are likely to join some organizations, you may be called on to introduce a speaker, present an award, nominate someone for office, make an announcement, or give a report. You may even be asked to propose a short toast. If you're lucky, you may be elected toastmaster or function chairperson, and in that position you may present some or all of the special types of speeches explained in this chapter. As an active member of your organization, you may also be called on to respond to any of these speech situations.

This chapter briefly touches on these special-occasion talks from the standpoints of the introducer (function chairperson, toastmaster, master of ceremonies) and the person giving the response. Some examples of these talks are included.

Appearing in this (and every) chapter is the feature "In Other Words," which will greatly benefit foreign and ESL students. To aid in their understanding of common American idioms and phrases, these expressions will be defined in the margin of the page on which they are introduced.

In Other Words:

GIVING A SHORT TALK

As you mature and start your ascent in the business or social community, the odds are that you will be called on "to say a few words." Industry executives agree that there is no surer way for an employee to earn recognition in the company than to display an ability to communicate effectively before an audience. The same holds true for your fraternal, political, or other social activities. You'll be amazed at the respect and admiration you earn when you can comfortably give a short talk.

No set of rules encompasses all the situations that may surround a **special-occasion talk.** Many factors impinge on the talk: your personality and position, the circumstances of the occasion, the time element, the type of audience, the main speaker, and the reason for the particular talk. All these factors must be considered.

The most important characteristic of these talks is brevity. Usually the talk ranges from one to five minutes except for the toast, which is usually less than a minute. If you're the chairperson, your function is to be an intermediary between the head table and audience. You're not expected to give a *long-winded* speech or to poke fun at the guest of honor. Your job is to move the proceedings along quickly and smoothly, with dignity and professionalism.

long-winded—a talk that is too long

Whenever you have the opportunity to "say a few words" and the first thought that *crosses your mind* is, "How much could I possibly say in a short time?" Then, carefully consider the following:

crosses your mind—comes to mind

- The Lord's Prayer has 71 words.
- The Ten Commandments has 297.
- The Gettysburg Address has 266.
- General McAuliffe clearly got his message across during the Battle of the Bulge with one word: "Nuts!"
- A modern record for brevity took place in 1945 when one of President Roosevelt's wartime speeches lasted only six minutes.
- The all-time record goes to George Washington, whose second inaugural speech contained 135 words and lasted only two minutes.
- In Genesis, the story of the creation of the world is told in 400 words.
- For your information (and not necessarily a warning), the longest inaugural speech on record was delivered by William Henry Harrison and it contained 8445 words. (At the inauguration, he caught a cold, which developed into pneumonia, and died precisely one month later.)[1] *So, watch it.*

so, watch it—so, be careful (like a warning)

There are many types of special-occasion talks ranging from announcements, to sales talks, **eulogies,** retirement testimonials, dedications, and after-dinner talks; you have commencement addresses, pre-

---

[1] *U.S. News & World Report,* 28 December 1992, 32.

senting and accepting awards as well as welcoming speeches, and there are more. However, this chapter focuses on the talks that are most likely to be of immediate concern to you.

How to Make an Announcement

At most organizational meetings, time is set aside to ask for help with a future event and to announce its time and place. **Announcements** should be short and carefully prepared, and they should include all pertinent information.

It's amazing how many announcements exclude an important bit of information—for example, the date or time of the event. Perhaps you can recall attending a meeting in which a committee chairperson announced an upcoming event, only to be asked, "What was that date again?"

How to Get the Facts

If you're responsible for gathering information for an announcement, seek an authoritative source (the president of your organization, the chairperson of a committee, or the member designated by the chairperson). Get the source's phone number so that you can check information or any changes that occur before the announcement has to be made. In preparing your announcement, include as many of the five W's (who, what, when, where, why) as possible and the H (how).

When you've prepared the announcement, check it for all details. Ask yourself:

1. What is being planned?
2. When and where will the event be held and what about parking?
3. Do the day and date of the event coincide on the calendar?
4. Will tickets be necessary? If so, how much will they cost?
5. Where will the proceeds go?
6. Is the event open only to members?
7. What is the reason for the event?
8. Who is responsible for the event?
9. Are volunteers needed? If they are, who should be contacted?
10. If there's to be a speaker, what is his or her name?

Gather as much correct information as possible and present only vital information. Most organizations publish newsletters or bulletins that include additional details. Because of this, your announcement need not give telephone numbers of people to contact.

How to Deliver the Announcement

Delivering your announcement with enthusiasm can bolster interest and positive reaction from your audience. You may conclude your announcement by repeating key facts—for example:

The Boston College High School Parents' Club will hold its annual May Festival on Saturday, May 18, from 9 A.M. to 4 P.M. on the school grounds. As you know, all proceeds will go toward the scholarship fund.

We can still use some volunteers for an hour or two. Please check in with one of our volunteer coordinators, Mr. Joseph Robert or Ms. Deborah Grilli, right after this meeting. We would appreciate a little of your time and effort.

Remember, our annual May Festival will be held all day Saturday, May 18, right here on the B.C. High School grounds, and we need more volunteers. Thank you.

How to Introduce a Speaker

The main problem with introducing a speaker is that, all too often, the introducer talks far too long. This situation was highlighted in an anecdote told by President William Howard Taft.

Once he presided at a meeting at which a number of distinguished guests were to give five-minute talks. The young chairman of the event rose to say a few words and rambled on for 45 minutes. After he sat down, President Taft stood up and said: "I remember once when I was in politics, we had a meeting at which there was to be one of these preliminary addresses. One guest captured and held the platform and when he finally finished, I remarked, 'I will now present Mr. So-and-So, who will give you his address.' Mr. So-and-So arose and stated, with some heat, 'My address is 789A 22nd Street, New York City, where my train goes in fifteen minutes. Good night.'"

In sharp contrast to that angry reply is the humorous response (to a long-winded introduction) made by Alabama Senator Howell Heflin at a meeting of the American Bankruptcy Institute. "I believe," he said, "that was the most comprehensive introduction I have ever received. You omitted one thing—that in 1974 I had a hemorrhoidectomy."[2] (Now, go to your dictionary and learn a new word!)

If you're responsible for introducing a speaker, consider the following guidelines.

Be Aware of Your Responsibility

Your primary function is to prepare and motivate your audience to listen to the featured speaker. If you can instill such interest, you've done your job.

---

[2]*Newsweek*, 20 May 1991, 19.

Be Familiar with the Speaker and the Topic

As soon as you know who the speaker will be, find out as much as possible about his or her background and the subject of the speech. If she is well known, information about her will be available through her press office or in newspapers. If he is not well known, call him for a profile.

If possible, try to meet the speaker before the event to ensure that your information is accurate and current and that you know the speaker's topic. You don't want the speaker to have to correct you during his or her opening remarks. Sometimes the title of the speech will suffice; at other times it may be appropriate to mention the subject matter.

Be Brief

How often have you heard an **MC** (master of ceremonies) say, "Our speaker this evening needs no introduction," and then give a biography from birth to the present? If the speaker needs no more than a short introduction, then give it.

One of the briefest and most humorous introductions was given many years ago by former U.S. Representative Morris "Mo" Udall (D-Arizona). As master of ceremonies at a dinner, he presented Adlai Stevenson (twice governor of Illinois, twice Democratic presidential nominee in the 1950s, and U.S. ambassador to the United Nations) in one unique sentence: "This man needs no introduction and I'll be damned if I'll give him one."[3]

The length of your introduction should not exceed two or three minutes. No better example of brevity and simplicity exists than the introduction you've heard many times, "Ladies and gentlemen, the President of the United States."

Be Careful Not to Embarrass the Speaker

Sometimes a chairperson can go to extremes in praising the speaker as one of the most brilliant, eloquent, and humorous orators of the day. This is embarrassing for three reasons: (1) the speaker very likely cannot *live up to* such an introduction, (2) the speaker probably *realizes* that, and (3) the chairperson may be preparing the audience for a resounding letdown.

live up to—fulfill the expectations of

Be Natural

If you're good at telling anecdotes and jokes or at being humorous, great. Nothing sets an audience more at ease and puts them in a receptive mood than a few laughs. It will benefit you to spice your introductory remarks with humor that directly links the speaker, the subject, and the

---

[3]*The Boston Globe,* 17 February 1988, 29.

Be brief in your introduction.

occasion. However, if you're not a naturally humorous person, *don't try to be.* Humor in the wrong hands can be disastrous. As any professional comedian will tell you, trying to make people laugh is a very serious business.

Be Informative

It's important to know and present a balanced blend of the following pieces of information: the speaker's background, the subject of the message, the specific occasion, and the audience. Ponder each of these items separately and completely when you're preparing your introduction.

Be Careful Not to Make Personal Comments about the Speaker's Subject

This is not the time and place to **editorialize.** When you introduce the speaker's topic to the audience, don't elaborate on the topic. That is the speaker's job. You may mention the importance of the subject, its relationship to the audience, and the speaker's knowledge of it, but leave the contents to the speaker.

Be Sure to Pronounce the Speaker's Name Correctly

The most famous slip of the tongue was uttered by radio announcer Harry Von Zell when he proclaimed to the nation, "Ladies and gentlemen, the president of the United States, Hoobert Heever." Clearly, in his mind, the announcer knew how to pronounce the name; but, at that moment, his tongue thought differently and out came the blooper. There are no sweeter sounds to reach a person's ears than those of her or his name. It's worth getting it right.

If you're not positive about the exact pronunciation of the speaker's name, ask how to pronounce it in advance. If you have to, write it down phonetically.

Present the Speaker to the Audience

If you feel that the speaker is not well known to the audience, you may mention her name several times during the introduction. If she is known to the audience and you want to use a dramatic approach, you may announce her name at the very end of your introduction. After you've presented the speaker, face her and in a warm, welcoming manner, wait until she arrives at the speaker's stand; then return to your seat. (You start the applause.)

The following is an example of a speech of introduction.

> Good evening and welcome to our annual Media Awards Banquet. It is such a pleasure to see so many past recipients of these awards in our audience . . . a special welcome to all of you.
>
> It is, indeed, a rare privilege for me to have the opportunity of introducing our guest speaker for this evening.
>
> Prof. Joan Murray enjoys an international and distinguished reputation as a speaker, educator, writer, and communications consultant. She frequently appears as a guest on the nation's most popular radio and TV interview programs.
>
> During her tenure as chairperson of the Communication Department at Regis College in Weston, Massachusetts, Prof. Murray is responsible for developing media curricula in radio and television, public relations, photography, and motion picture production.
>
> Under her direction and leadership, the college's studio-classrooms, production facilities, and equipment represent the ultimate in state-of-the-art design and operation. Students enjoy individualized as well as small group learning experiences.
>
> Since Prof. Murray's many innovative approaches in media education and curriculum development have attained national prominence, she is a constant recipient of invitations to speak or conduct communication workshops not only in academe but also in private industry. As a matter of fact, she has just returned from a lecture tour in England,

Germany, France, and Italy, where she discussed "International Communication," which is also her topic this evening.

We are extremely fortunate to have her here this evening, and I'm delighted to introduce our featured speaker, Prof. Joan Murray.

How to Present an Award

In planning to present an award you should keep in mind the following key points.

Refer to the Award Itself

It is important in your opening remarks to call attention to the award that is about to be presented. What is its significance; when and why was it founded? Who was its first recipient? Is it presented annually or only on special occasions? These are some questions to consider, and you may think of others.

Refer to the Occasion

This will prepare your audience for what is about to take place. You will attract the audience's attention and interest.

Refer to the Recipient

Explain why and how this individual or group was selected. Be sure to point out the achievements that led the recipient to this honor.

Refer to Those Whom You Represent

Mention if the award is being presented on behalf of a lodge, council, club, or company. The source of the award is of vital interest to the recipient and to the audience. The source certainly deserves praise. Express the sincere goodwill of the source and its satisfaction with the person chosen.

Make the Presentation

For the sake of building interest and including an element of mystery, you may wish to mention the name of the recipient last. Then, if the award can be handled easily, hold it up for all to see, read the inscription on it, present it, and congratulate the recipient. Then allow the recipient the opportunity to respond.

The following is an example of a speech used in presenting an award.

As you know, the highlight of today's annual dinner is the announcement of the CHEF OF THE YEAR. This is the highest honor that a member can receive because the honoree is selected by his or her peers of the Massachusetts Chefs de Cuisine by secret ballot.

This award is presented annually in memory of Peter Berrini, a well-known and respected executive chef and one of the original founders of the American Culinary Federation. It is presented to a member "for years of dedicated and distinguished service and for exemplifying the highest standards of character and unselfish devotion" not only to this organization but to the culinary arts profession as well.

This year's gold medal winner is a very special person. He is a member of the American Academy of Chefs, of which there are only 650 throughout the United States and Puerto Rico, and is a Certified Executive Chef, of which there are only 1500 nationwide. As a past president of the Massachusetts Chefs de Cuisine he has held office for four consecutive years, the longest in the 14-year history of this organization. During his first term as president, he was personally responsible for the largest enrollment of new members of any chapter in the United States, for which he received a special national citation from the prestigious American Culinary Federation.

The eighth recipient of the CHEF OF THE YEAR award is a full professor and is department chairperson of the Culinary Arts and Hotel/Restaurant Management programs at Bunker Hill Community College in Boston for both day and evening divisions. He is a food service consultant, lecturer, and writer. And you may have heard or seen one of his many appearances on radio and television programs.

It's a distinct honor and privilege for me to announce that the members of the Massachusetts Chefs de Cuisine have unanimously voted Arthur P. Buccheri as their CHEF OF THE YEAR.

HOW TO ACCEPT AN AWARD

Sometimes when an award is presented, no formal reply is needed or expected. If that's the case, a simple, sincere "thank you" is sufficient. At other times a reply might be appropriate or called for by audience cheers of "speech, speech." If you're going to a function and there is the slightest possibility that you may be given an award, prepare a thank-you statement. In preparing a speech of acceptance, use the following techniques.

Be Honest

If the award comes as a total surprise, your facial expression may attest to the fact, but don't hesitate to express your surprise orally. The audience will be more delighted. You should have no difficulty expressing your sincere gratitude. Sometimes a heartfelt "thank you very much" will suffice.

Call Attention to the Award

Explain what the award means to you. (You might want to refer to others who have received the award previously and you may want to mention how pleased you are to join their esteemed company.)

Be Generous in Your Praise

If you're accepting an award on behalf of a group or team, be sure to share the honor with them. If it was a singular effort and someone inspired you, don't keep it a secret. If appropriate, mention the future and how this honor may affect your efforts and plans. Don't forget to thank those responsible for presenting you with the award. It may also be appropriate to thank the individual who made the presentation. The following is an example of a speech to accept an award.

> There are two things I will always remember this evening for. One, I'm at a loss for words, and two, I'm deeply moved to receive this plaque naming me the recipient of your "Outstanding Member of the Year Award."
> I know what this award represents, because I have actively participated in the voting for our first two recipients. It is indeed a thrill for me to join their elite company.
> The honor you have presented me with this evening will always remain very special. I wish to thank the members of the nominating committee and each and every one of you for your most generous expression of recognition.
> I will always cherish this award and the precious moments of this evening. Thank you very much.

HOW TO MAKE A NOMINATING SPEECH

As you become more involved in organizations, whether scholastic, business, or political, you may have the opportunity to nominate someone for office. If you belong to an organization, perhaps you recall a meeting when nominations for offices were called for. ***Someone from the floor,*** after being recognized by the chairperson, may say, "I would like to place in nomination the name of Mrs. Eunice Flagg" or "I would like to nominate Mr. Vincent Shea." What you heard were *names* placed in nomination. Following are some suggestions to use if you want to nominate not just a name, but a person worthy of the office.

someone from the floor—a person from the audience

Describe the Responsibilities of the Office

build a powerful case—make a strong argument

Mention the specific requirements attached to the office. Include its duties, importance, and broad responsibilities. (Remember that you want to ***build a powerful case*** for your nominee.)

Be generous in your praise, but . . . .

Name the Candidate

In a voice so that all can hear *clearly*, announce your candidate and then explain to the gathering why he is the right person for the office. Mention the candidate's background, experience, and other offices held. How long has she been a member and did she serve on any committees? Now's the time to *fire all cannons*.

fire all cannons— mention with great enthusiasm; use everything at your disposal

Place the Name in Nomination

Conclude your nomination talk by formally announcing the full name of your candidate—for example, "Therefore, ladies and gentlemen, it is with a great deal of pride that I place in nomination for the office of president of local 2259 the name [loud and clear] of Marion Zulon." At this point your fellow supporters should explode with approval. The following is a sample speech to nominate a candidate.

I am very proud to place in nomination for president of our alumni association the name of one of our most active members, Mr. Andrew Aloisi.

We all know the demanding responsibilities that this office bears . . . leadership qualities, the talent to select chairpersons of important committees, the ability to look ahead, the gift to motivate, and certainly the love of his alma mater.

"answered the call"—volunteered

Mr. Aloisi possesses all these attributes and more. During the last few years he has *"answered the call"* many times from this organization, and with distinction. As chairman of the membership committee, he was responsible for significantly increasing our active rolls. As program director, he brought many new and interesting events to this organization. Last year he was chairman of the Fund Raising Committee, and our coffers were swelled by the most successful year ever enjoyed by our association. He has also served with credit on our travel committee.

Mr. Aloisi, a successful businessman, has, at the request of this association, generously made himself available to talk and meet with recent graduates and help them in launching their careers.

He is an executive with understanding and compassion and that special talent of being able to get things done. Those of us who have had the good fortune of working with Andrew know only too well his executive ability and devotion to his duties.

This coming year we will be celebrating our 100th anniversary. It is a special occasion that promises to attract renowned educators and political leaders from all parts of the world. This special time warrants special leadership, and with that in mind I take great pleasure to place in nomination for the office of president of our alumni association . . . Mr. Andrew Aloisi.

HOW TO GIVE AN INSTALLATION SPEECH

Congratulations, you've been elected to office. You've worked hard for the victory and you deserve it; however, you must now plan to make your first speech before the group. The following are some helpful ideas.

Express Your Gratitude

The first order of business is to express your sincere thanks for the vote of confidence bestowed on you, particularly by your supporters. You should also assure your nonsupporters that you will represent them fairly.

Accept the Challenge

You may wish to mention what the office is all about and enumerate some significant responsibilities. Explain that you accept all of the challenges the office has to offer and that you look forward to the coming term.

Admit That It's Not a Job for One Person

Tell the group that getting the job done requires more than one person and that you're looking forward to working closely with the other officers and various committees. It's also appropriate (and could win goodwill) to refer to the past president in a complimentary fashion and indicate that you would like to call on him or her occasionally for advice.

Look Ahead

The group will be anxious to hear something about your future plans. You can motivate your audience by outlining some of the steps you plan to take in the coming term. It is not necessary to detail every program, plan of action, or all you hope to accomplish. Brevity is important. You'll have many other opportunities to address the group. The following is an example of an installation speech.

> I wish to express my sincere thanks for the honor you have bestowed on me this evening. Our association is well known in the community not only for its active membership, but also for the many acts by its members in and for our community. It is a privilege to have been elected to its highest office.
>
> This organization—and we are all proud of it—achieved many milestones during the past year. It comforts me to know that I will have the full support and cooperation from our now past president, Charlie Flagg, as I begin my new term.
>
> Shortly, I will be calling on you for your assistance—to head committees, to become committee members, and to fulfill other important duties. I know your response will be as generous as it always has been.
>
> This organization, as any organization, is only as effective as the involvement of its members. We have one of the largest memberships of any organization in the state. And we have a record of accomplishments that speaks for itself.
>
> The two major goals I have established for the coming year are to increase our membership and to become more involved in our community. A high-priority item on our agenda will be the establishment of a special fund-raising committee to help us further meet special community needs.
>
> This will be a year of commitment, challenge, and participation. I will furnish that commitment. I will accept that challenge. I now ask for your participation.
>
> Again, I thank you for your vote of confidence and the opportunity to serve you.

NOTE
Be careful not to say anything critical of the preceding year that will reflect unfavorably on your predecessor.

THE EULOGY OR SPECIAL TRIBUTE SPEECH

Although giving a eulogy or special tribute speech isn't exactly the type of talk that would most likely be of immediate concern to you, I am including a most eloquent tribute delivered by one of the most outstanding communicators ever to reside in the White House for you to study, analyze, and appreciate.

On January 28, 1986, the space shuttle *Challenger* blasted off from Cape Canaveral, Florida, carrying six astronauts and an unusual crew member—Christa McAuliffe, a high school teacher selected to become the first teacher-astronaut to fly into space.

Sixty-three seconds into the flight the space craft exploded before a watching nation, including thousands of horrified schoolchildren.

Instead of delivering his annual State of the Union Address that evening, President Ronald Reagan presented a very moving, emotional, and memorable eulogy to the fallen "heroes."

The impact of this speech was best illustrated by *New York Times* columnist Anthony Lewis, a constant critic of Reagan's policies, when he wrote:

> In a few words, simple and direct, the President gave meaning to the deaths of the seven astronauts. He spoke to their families with consoling respect. He expressed our inchoate feelings. He was touching without being mawkish. He was dignified. Listening to Mr. Reagan, I thought I understood better than ever before the mystery of his enormous popularity as President.[4]

Here is Ronald Reagan's Tribute to the *Challenger* Astronauts.[5]

------

1   Ladies and gentlemen, I'd planned to speak to you tonight to report on the State of the Union but the events of earlier today have led me to change those plans. Today is a day for mourning and remembering.

2   Nancy and I are pained to the core by the tragedy of the shuttle *Challenger*. We know we share this pain with all of the people of our country. This is truly a national loss.

3   Nineteen years ago, almost to the day, we lost three astronauts in a terrible accident on the ground. But we've never lost an astronaut in flight; we've never had a tragedy like this. And perhaps we've forgotten the courage it took for the crew of the shuttle; but they, the *Challenger* Seven, were aware of the dangers, but overcame them and did their jobs brilliantly. We mourn seven heroes: Michael Smith, Dick Scobee, Judith Resnik, Ronald McNair, Ellison Onizuka, Gregory Jarvis, and Christa McAuliffe. We mourn their loss as a nation together.

4   For the families of the seven, we cannot bear, as you do, the full impact of this tragedy. But we feel the loss, and we're thinking about you so very much. Your loved ones were daring and brave, and they had that special grace, that special spirit that

------

[4]Anthony Lewis, "The Dignified Part." *New York Times*, 30 January 1986, p. A21.
[5]Ronald Reagan, Tribute to the *Challenger* Astronauts, White House Address to the Nation, Washington DC, 28 January 1986 (Weekly Compilation of Presidential Documents, Vol. 22, No. 5, pp. 104–105).

says, "Give me a challenge and I'll meet it with joy." They had a hunger to explore the universe and discover its truths. They wished to serve, and they did. They served all of us.

5   We've grown used to wonders in this century. It's hard to dazzle us. But for 25 years the United States space program has been doing just that. We've grown used to the idea of space, and perhaps we forget that we've only just begun. We're still pioneers. They, the members of the *Challenger* crew, were pioneers.

6   And I want to say something to the schoolchildren of American who were watching the live coverage of the shuttle's takeoff. I know it is hard to understand, but sometimes painful things like this happen. It's all part of the process of exploration and discovery. It's all part of taking a chance and expanding man's horizons. The future doesn't belong to the faint-hearted; it belongs to the brave. The *Challenger* crew was pulling us into the future, and we'll continue to follow them.

7   I've always had great faith in and respect for our space program, and what happened today does nothing to diminish it. We don't hide our space program. We don't keep secrets and cover things up. We do it all up front and in public. That's the way freedom is, and we wouldn't change it for a minute.

8   We'll continue our quest in space. There will be more shuttle flights and more shuttle crews and, yes, more volunteers, more civilians, more teachers in space. Nothing ends here; our hopes and our journeys continue.

9   I want to add that I wish I could talk to every man and woman who works for NASA or who worked on this mission and tell them: "Your dedication and professionalism have moved and impressed us for decades. And we know of your anguish. We share it."

10   There's a coincidence today. On this day 390 years ago, the great explorer Sir Francis Drake died aboard ship off the coast of Panama. In his lifetime the great frontiers were the oceans, and an historian later said, "He lived by the sea, died on it, and was buried in it." Well, today we can say of the *Challenger* crew: Their dedication was, like Drake's, complete.

11   The crew of the space shuttle *Challenger* honored us by the manner in which they lived their lives. We will never forget them, nor the last time we saw them, this morning, as they prepared for their journey and waved goodbye and "slipped the surly bonds of earth" to "touch the face of God."

How to Propose a Toast

There are many occasions when proposing a toast is appropriate and desirable: births, birthdays, graduations, bar mitzvahs, weddings, anniversaries, promotions, and so on. The occasion could be a large gathering or simply an evening with a companion. No matter what the occasion, the toast should be brief, meaningful, and sincere.

A good exercise is to try to write down as many short toasts for as many situations as possible and keep the list handy for various occasions. Whenever you hear a clever toast, *jot it down,* perhaps rewording it to fit your own personality.

jot it down—
write it down

Another excellent source for getting ideas for "toasts" is from greeting cards. Save them or visit the greeting card section in many stores. The following are examples of toasts for various occasions:

■ **Births**

To Kaitlyn Elizabeth
    . . . You're so delicate and beautiful
     From your head to your toes
To your parents, you'll always be
     Their American Beauty Rose. Welcome.

"Cheers . . . prost . . . a vôtre santé . . . saluto . . . and . . . here's looking at you, kid . . . ."

■ **Birthdays**

Another candle on your cake
    is really no reason to pout,
Give thanks to God that you have the breath
    To blow the damn thing out. Happy Birthday, Kevin.

■ **Graduation**

May your achievements on campus easily transfer to the world of industry as you matriculate to a new and exciting adventure. We wish you great success . . . and congratulations, Janet.

■ **Bar Mitzvahs**

May the helping hand of God be always near to guide you on your adventurous journey from boyhood to manhood. Shalom.

■ **Weddings**

To Patty and Wally. Two very special people.
    May this day so filled with love, friendship and laughter,
Be the way of life you both enjoy happily everafter. Saluto.

■ **Anniversaries**

To Barbara and Albie. May the special joy and happiness that you share with us today, intensify with loving abundance in the many years to follow. Congratulations.

■ **Job promotions**

Brian, your company has an enviable reputation for making solid business decisions. Like the one they just made—your promotion. Congratulations.

■ **Retirement**

May the years that you've spent laboring be doubled as you work on your years in leisure, pleasure and, hopefully, just plain fun. Congratulations Bob, you deserve it.

■ **A toast to you**

Here's to the student who's almost completed this course
    I hope you experience no feelings of remorse
But when the opportunity arises for you to get up to speak
    You'll have all my best wishes that you perform at your peak.

TESTING . . . 1 . . . 2 . . . 3 . . . 4

Unless you plan a career in radio or TV, the chances are slim that you'll ever appear before a radio microphone (mike) or a television camera to express your views. It's far more likely that you'll appear before a **public**

address (PA) microphone at a school, fraternal, or social gathering. Let's discuss some testing and speaking techniques that you may find helpful.

Before you speak, you should test the mike to be sure it's working and at the proper level (volume). To test a mike, *speak* into it. The most common testing phrases are "Testing 1 . . . 2 . . . 3 . . . 4" and "Hello, testing. Can you hear me OK in the back of the hall?"

Above all, never test a mike by slapping it or blowing into it, because it is a very delicate, sensitive instrument. Doing either may damage it and annoy your audience.

Being the right distance from the mike is important. If you're too close, your voice will boom at everyone and your *P*'s and *B*'s (**plosives**) will sound like explosions. However, if you're too far away from the mike, the audience will have to strain to hear you and may then tune you out.

The best way to know the correct distance from the mike is to test it. If the level has been set correctly, your mouth should be three to five inches away from the mike. If your voice is strong, move back from the mike. If your voice is soft, move closer. It's important to listen to yourself and to look at your audience. You can hear yourself from the loudspeakers in the hall, and you can receive feedback from observing your audience.

When speaking over a PA system, be sure to slow your delivery so that every word can be heard clearly and distinctly. Otherwise, your words may sound jumbled. Because you'll hear yourself over the loudspeakers a split second after you've spoken, you shouldn't speak too rapidly.

Speak directly into the mike and don't move your head from left to right, or the audience will miss half of what you're saying. This guideline applies particularly to MCs who may be introducing head table guests. After you've introduced someone, you may look in his or her direction for a second or two; introduce the next person, speaking directly into the mike; then glance at that person. Face the person you're introducing only if you can speak directly into the mike at the same time.

Above all, speak in your natural voice. For many people, this is the hardest thing to do. It seems that whenever people appear before a microphone, they try to lower their voices, sound dramatic, or start to over-e-n-u-n-c-i-a-t-e. Speak as you always do. Remember, the microphone is like a magnifying glass and will detect and amplify flaws in delivery.

Always treat a microphone with respect and always assume it is "on" (live). Otherwise, you could experience a few humiliating moments.

If you have to sneeze, cough, or blow your nose, be sure to turn your head as far away as possible from the mike. Finally, don't grab or hold onto the mike that you're speaking into. Doing so could produce an annoying hum or static over the loudspeakers.

In Conclusion

Now that you are all experts in the art of small talks, perhaps you will enjoy the following amusing anecdote.

Once upon a time, in the days of the Roman Empire, a mob was gathered in the Coliseum to watch as a Christian was thrown to a hungry lion. The spectators cheered as the wild beast went after its prey. But the Christian quickly whispered something in the lion's ear and the beast backed away with obvious terror on his face. No amount of calling and foot stomping by the audience could get the lion to approach the Christian again. Fearlessly, he walked from the arena.

The Emperor was so amazed at what had happened that he sent for the Christian and offered him his freedom if he would say what he had done to make the ferocious beast cower in fear. The Christian bowed before the Emperor and said, "I merely whispered in the lion's ear: 'After dinner, you'll be required to say a few words.'"[6]

THINGS TO DISCUSS IN CLASS

1. Get some news of an upcoming event either from your school newspaper or from the student activities center, and make an announcement of the event to the class.

---

[6]S. H. Simmons, *New Speakers' Handbook* (New York: Dial Press, 1972), 22–23.

2. Introduce a classmate who's prepared to give a talk.

3. Prepare and deliver a one- or two-minute talk to present an award.

4. Prepare and deliver a one- or two-minute talk after receiving an award.

5. Make a one- or two-minute nominating speech.

6. Give a one- or two-minute installation speech.

7. Give a short toast for a wedding, birthday, job promotion, bar mitzvah, or christening.

8. From your library research, find a good example of one of the special-occasion talks discussed in this chapter. Read it to the class, and explain the reason for your selection.

What Do You Remember from This Chapter?

1. What information should be included when you make an announcement?

2. Mention two valid sources of information for an announcement.

3. What is a common problem when someone introduces a speaker?

4. When you introduce a speaker, why should you be careful not to over-praise him or her?

5. Why should you try to inject some humor in your comments?

6. Name two elements to include when you present an award.

7. Name two important elements of a speech to nominate.

8. What information should an installation speech contain?

9. When giving an installation speech, what must you be careful of regarding the preceding officers?

10. List two occasions when a toast would be appropriate.

11. How should you test a microphone for operation and level?

12. While speaking into a PA mike, how can you be aware of the right volume?

13. What is the most important characteristic of a special-occasion talk?

Vitalize Your Vocabulary

Health Care

acupuncturist A professional who practices a traditional therapeutic technique whereby the body is punctured with very fine needles in the treatment of certain diseases and pain.

allergist A physician who specializes in the treatment of allergies.

cardiologist A physician who specializes in the diagnosis and treatment of heart disease.

chiropodist A physician specializing in the diagnosis and treatment of hand and foot problems.

chiropractor A doctor who treats specific ailments by performing manipulative adjustments to the spinal column. Chiropractic treatment excludes medicine and drugs.

dentist A doctor involved in the diagnosis, prevention, and treatment of diseases of the teeth.

dermatologist A physician specializing in the treatment of skin problems.

dietitian A professional specializing in the field of diet as it relates to one's health.

geriatrician or **geriatrist** A physician whose practice is devoted to patients of old age.

gynecologist A physician specializing in women's health problems.

immunologist A physician specializing in the study and prevention of certain diseases.

internist A physician specializing in internal medicine but not surgery.

neurologist A physician specializing in the diagnosis and treatment of disorders of the nervous system.

obstetrician A physician whose practice is devoted to the care of women during and after pregnancy.

oncologist A physician specializing in the study and treatment of tumors.

ophthalmologist A physician specializing in the treatment of eye diseases.

optician A professional who makes lenses and eye glasses.

optometrist A professional involved in the examination and treatment of certain visual defects by prescribing corrective lenses.

orthodontist A dentist specializing in correcting misaligned teeth.

orthopedist A physician who performs surgery or manipulative treatment of disorders of the skeletal system.

otolaryngologist A physician who treats diseases of the ear, nose, and throat.

pediatrician A physician specializing in the care of infants and children.

periodontist A dentist who treats problems concerning tissue surrounding the teeth, bone structure, and gums.

pharmacist A professional who prepares and dispenses drugs.

psychiatrist A physician trained in treating mental illnesses.

psychologist A Ph.D. professional who deals with mental and emotional processes and problems.

radiologist A physician trained in radiography or X-ray as a means of diagnosis.

urologist A physician specializing in the treatment of urinary tract problems.

14

LET'S MEET AND DISCUSS IT

Men are never so likely to settle a question rightly as when they discuss it freely.

Thomas Babington Macaulay, *Southey's Colloquies*, 1830

After reading and understanding this chapter you should know:

- **Some elements of the Reflective Thinking Process.**

- **Some characteristics of a panel discussion, symposium lecture, round-table discussion, brainstorming session, buzz session meeting, and committee.**

- **Some responsibilities of a panel moderator.**

- **Some responsibilities of a panelist.**

- **Some responsibilities of an audience.**

- **Some responsibilities of a member attending a meeting and of a meeting chairperson.**

- **Some main qualities of a group leader or chairperson.**

CHAPTER PREVIEW

The environment, the consumer movement, health care, and education are just a few areas of public concern in which Americans are demanding and getting a voice. They are serving on more and more committees, participating in forums, on panels, and in symposia. They are interacting in groups to solve problems, to make decisions, and to carry them out.

This chapter explains the Reflective Thinking Process as well as the more common types of group discussion: panel, symposium, lecture, round-table, brainstorming, buzz session, general meeting, and committee. These various groups consist of moderators, chair-people or leaders, panelists or participants, and sometimes audiences. The significant responsibilities of these people are listed in detail. Also included in this chapter are diagrams of suggested seating arrangements for these major types of group discussions.

Appearing in this (and every) chapter is the feature "In Other Words," which will greatly benefit foreign and ESL students. To aid in their understanding of common American idioms and phrases, these expressions will be defined in the margin of the page on which they are introduced.

In Other Words:

GETTING INVOLVED

If you're an active member of a business, political, religious, educational, civic, or fraternal organization—congratulations. You're an activist and enjoy getting involved. On the other hand, maybe you would like to participate in an organization but you lack self-confidence. Becoming involved can be a gratifying, rewarding experience and can lead to unexpected opportunities.

in tune—in agreement

sound off—voice an opinion.

Perhaps there's a local group that is *in tune* with your way of thinking; maybe a local issue has you so aroused that you feel compelled to *sound off;* perhaps you would like to volunteer for a worthy cause within your community. If you feel the desire to get involved, go for it.

A trend toward increased activism in America began in the 1980s, when the consumer movement, spearheaded by Ralph Nader's Raiders, emerged as a vibrant force in the nation and in our lives. As the 1980s ended, more and more Americans displayed and vented their anger and frustrations over local and national issues by becoming involved in local, statewide, and national affairs. The impact of this voter anger was especially evident during the November 1991 national and state off-year elections, when many insiders were voted out and many outsiders were voted in. And in 1992, dozens of congressmen, guilty of bouncing checks, quit politics rather than face the likelihood of being *"bounced" out* of office by *teed-off* voters.

"bounced" out—voted out

teed-off—very angry.

These days, average consumers not only are running for political office, but also are being appointed to state and local regulatory boards and commissions. Parents, many from single-parent homes, are participating in advisory councils involving the operations of their children's schools/daycare facilities. Concerned and eager citizens are being selected as trustees and advisors to state-supported colleges and universities. No matter how diverse their personal views are, they all have one thing in common—they are all participants in some form of **small-group discussion.** No longer is the average voter a passive one. Many are now ready, willing, and able to "meet and discuss it" with the powers to be.

More than just being present at hearings or large meetings in which they might ask a question or two, citizens are now becoming members of symposia, panels, and committees to communicate, interact, and make decisions. In the business and professional worlds, you may be asked to, or may wish to, participate in a convention, conference, department or committee meeting, seminar, brainstorming or buzz session, or any one of the other types of group communication.

Most small-group communication is either public (open) or private (closed). *Public* discussions take place before an audience, which may or may not be allowed to participate, whereas *private* discussions are open only to group members. (See Figure 14.1.) Federal and state legislation increasingly tends to favor public meetings for government activities.

A Private/Closed Discussion

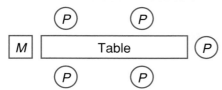

A Public/Open Discussion

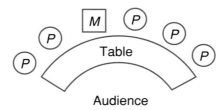

Figure 14.1 Suggested Seating Arrangements for a Private/Closed Group Discussion and a Public/Open Group Discussion. M Signifies the Moderator and P Signifies the Participants.

The group's private or public status depends on certain considerations:

- How many group members will participate?
- What is each member's rank and influence?
- What is the subject to be discussed?
- Is the subject confidential?
- How soon must a decision or solution be reached?
- Will the decision affect a small or a large group of people?
- When and where will the meeting be held?

REFLECTIVE OR CRITICAL THINKING

Among the reasons for the various formations of small-group interactivity are to inform, to persuade, to gather facts and information, to propose some type of action, to resolve a problem, or a combination of these.

Finding a solution to an existing problem is a common objective of most small-group efforts, and how each member of the group approaches that objective can determine the success or failure of that solution. Before a problem-solving discussion takes place, group members should agree on the approach that the dialogue should follow. Doing so will ensure a more productive, orderly, intelligent, and time-saving exercise where group members stay on the subject.

"I've already arrived at the consensus that I'm expecting all of you to reach."

One of the most popular approaches is the **Reflective** or **Constructive Thinking Pattern** developed by educational philosopher John Dewey in 1910.[1] Dewey's method consists of five steps:

1. Identify the problem.
2. Analyze the problem.
3. Offer possible solutions to the problem.
4. Evaluate and select the best solution(s).
5. Implement the solution.

Step 1. Identify the Problem

It's critical that all the participants agree not only that a problem *does* exist but also what the actual problem is. The goal to be achieved must be established and clearly understood by all members of the group so that they will know in what direction the discussion is headed. To avoid any misunderstandings, all terms that may come up during the discussion must be clearly defined.

Step 2. Analyze the Problem

The problem must be specifically stated, clearly defined, and completely understood. Once the problem is fully recognized, the members must dis-

[1]John Dewey. *How We Think* (Lexington, MA: D.C. Heath, 1910).

cuss such questions as, "How long has the problem existed?" "Have any previous attempts been made to address the problem?" If so, "What were the results?" "Is the problem worth attempting to solve or is it beyond our authority?" "What are the causes of the problem?" Once these and other questions are answered, you're ready to begin the solution process.

Step 3. Offer Possible Solutions to the Problem

Now's your chance to be creative as members of the group offer as many solutions as possible. This stage should focus more on quantity of solutions than on quality. Don't stop to criticize every suggestion made; evaluation comes next. Right now you want to list as many practical solutions as possible so that you'll have a large pool of ideas from which to draw.

Step 4. Evaluate and Select the Best Solution(s)

This step evaluates the *pros and cons* of each suggested remedy. Will it work? Would a combination of suggestions be more practical? Is it the most expedient method(s) of producing the desired effect? How difficult is it to implement and receive feedback about its effectiveness? After these important questions are discussed, analyzed, debated, and answered in detail, a solution can be adopted through **consensus.**

pros and cons— positions for or against a particular issue

Step 5. Implement the Solution

Your final effort is to decide the best way to implement the course of action in order to solve the problem. An important consideration is that, after the solution(s) is carried out, its effectiveness should be tested, if possible. This testing can be done by telephone inquiry, mail questionnaires to be returned, or by face-to-face polling. If the desired effect is not being attained, you would have to return to one of the previous steps and repeat part(s) of the five-step approach.

Reflective or Critical Thinking is a developing process that progresses from problem identification to a practical solution and its implementation. It is, therefore, paramount that you thoroughly complete each step before going to the next one.

TYPES OF SMALL-GROUP DISCUSSION

Some of the more popular types of small-group discussion in which you may likely participate on or off campus include:

- panel
- symposium
- lecture

- round-table
- brainstorming session
- buzz session
- meeting
- committee

The Panel Discussion

The **panel** discussion is perhaps the most popular type of group communication and the one you'll most likely become involved in, either as a moderator, panelist, or audience member. A panel usually consists of four to six members and a moderator seated at a table and facing the audience. Figure 14.2 shows the customary seating arrangement for a panel discussion.

The primary purpose of a panel discussion is for the panelists to explore different aspects of a subject or problem through interaction. The panelists individually express their views on the topic under discussion, interact with each other, and then answer questions from the audience. The interaction among the panelists may result in a spirited, intellectually stimulating discussion. Whenever the audience is allowed to participate, regardless of the type of discussion, it is called a **forum**.

Some Responsibilities of the Panel Moderator

in your grasp— within your capability

As a panel **moderator**, you have *in your grasp* the power to conduct either a smooth, meaningful discussion or one fraught with chaos.

Figure 14.2 Two Ways to Set Up a Panel Discussion. A Semicircular Arrangement Is Preferred so that Panelists can Easily See Each Other. M Signifies the Moderator and P Signifies the Panelists.

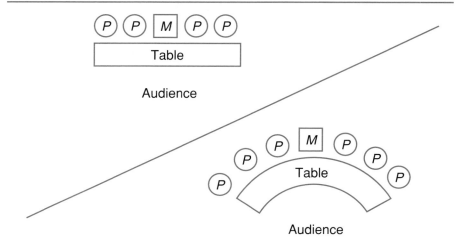

1. Be sure that the panelists have name cards on the table in front of them so that the audience will know their names. If the room is large, and those in the rear have difficulty reading the names, you might put each panelist's name on the chalkboard directly behind the panel.
2. Greet the audience and introduce yourself.
3. Briefly tell the audience the topic to be discussed.
4. Inform the audience when it may question the panel.
5. Introduce each panel member. You may also mention whether the panelist's position is pro or con.
6. Allow each panelist to make an opening statement of a minute or two.
7. After the opening remarks, allow the panelists to talk and question each other.
8. Be prepared to throw a question or two at the panelists to trigger discussion in case interaction is not immediate.
9. Remain impartial, but be ready to question individual panelists if the discussion starts to lag or veer off course or if an opinion needs clarification.
10. Be sure to give each panelist a chance to express his or her views.
11. When you feel that the discussion has just about run its course, or if a time limit has been established, ask the panelists to summarize their views; allow one to two minutes for each.
12. Present a summary of major ideas or concepts expressed from both viewpoints.
13. Open the discussion to the audience.
14. Call only on those who raise their hands. Again, be aware of time monopolizers.
15. Don't hesitate to declare anyone out of order if the situation warrants.
16. When the time is up, thank the audience and the panel.
17. Be tactful but firm if you have a panelist who's monopolizing the floor. Try to spark some response from the more reticent members.

Being a moderator is an assignment that can be extremely rewarding when the result is a smoothly run interactional experience, followed by a spirited but orderly response from the audience.

Some Responsibilities of the Panelists

As a member of a team, your attitude and participation are vital to the overall success of the discussion.

1. Be informed and prepared to become totally involved in the discussion. In other words, *do your homework.*
2. Keep your opening remarks and summary to a minute or so.

do your homework—thoroughly prepare

Be tactful, but firm.

3. If a panelist falters, help out by immediately picking up the discussion and sustaining it. Perhaps the panelist just needs a minute or two to regain composure.
4. Have supporting material with you and be prepared to identify your sources.
5. Don't monopolize the floor; give others a chance to speak.
6. Don't interrupt another speaker.
7. Be tolerant and understanding; don't be overpowering and overbearing.
8. Be brief and to the point; don't ramble.
9. Don't become personal and sarcastic.
10. Always respect the moderator and the other panelists.
11. *Keep cool,* no matter how heated the exchange becomes.

keep cool—maintain your composure

Some Responsibilities of the Audience

Psych yourself for a learning experience and be prepared to jot down questions to ask panelists during the question-and-answer period.

1. Give undivided attention to the discussion and to the participants' views.
2. When you wish to ask a question, raise your hand and wait for recognition by the moderator.
3. *Keep an open mind* until you've heard all of the views. Remember the words of engineer-inventor-author Charles F. Kettering: "Where there is an open mind, there will always be a frontier."
4. You may direct your question to the panel in general or to a specific individual.

keep an open mind—avoid prejudice; don't make a decision before you've heard everyone speak

Keep cool, no matter how heated the exchange.

5. Keep your question short and to the point; don't make speeches.
6. Don't question or enter a discussion with another member of the audience.
7. Don't antagonize or embarrass anyone.
8. Remember that you can disagree without being disagreeable. "We owe almost all our knowledge not to those who have agreed, but to those who have differed."[2]

THE SYMPOSIUM

A **symposium** usually consists of three to five members and a moderator. It differs from the panel discussion in that each participant of a symposium covers only one specific phase of the topic being discussed. The remarks should be well planned, prepared, and practiced before the discussion.

The symposium format is very common at large conventions, at business meetings, and in education in which experts are invited to speak on specific phases of a subject, question, or problem. A good example of an educational symposium takes place annually in high school auditoriums across the country as students ponder matriculating to college. (You may have attended one or more such functions yourself and probably never realized that you were present at a symposium.) At such an event several college representatives would discuss his or her expertise in such areas as:

---

[2]Charles Caleb Colton, *Lacon* (1825), 2.121.

Figure 14.3 Examples of Symposia Seating Arrangements. M Signifies the Moderator and P Signifies the Panelists.

1. a four-year college vs. a two-year college
2. a state-supported college vs. a private college
3. the admissions process
4. applying for financial aid

The moderator introduces the participants and the subject and maintains control over the presentation. He or she informs the audience of the procedure to be followed and whether there will be a forum after the talks. The moderator should also be very much aware of the time element so that the symposium does not interfere with other presentations on the program.

The seating arrangement of a symposium is similar to that of a panel discussion, except that the moderator may sit or stand on one side of the participants instead of in their midst. Figure 14.3 shows the arrangement.

THE LECTURE

The **lecture** panel is one form of public discussion in which a recognized authority on a specific subject presents a lecture and then is questioned by a panel. A variation is the *lecture panel forum* in which the audience is allowed to participate once the lecture and questions from the panel are over. Another variation is the *lecture forum,* in which the audience is allowed to ask questions of the lecturer after he or she finishes.

A **chairperson** presides over the lecture and introduces the guest lecturer, subject, and the panel if there is one, and states the format to be followed. Figure 14.4 illustrates the seating arrangement.

Figure 14.4 Example of a Lecture Seating Arrangement. C Signifies the Chairperson; L, the Lecturer; and P, the Panelists.

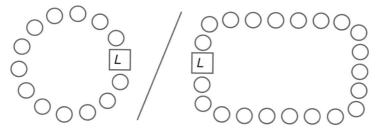

Figure 14.5 The Choice of a Seating Arrangement for a Round-Table, or Group, Discussion Depends on the Number of Participants. L Signifies the Group Leader.

THE ROUND-TABLE DISCUSSION

The **round-table discussion** method is prevalent in classes where discussion and total group interaction are emphasized, as well as in many other settings. The unique feature of this discussion is that there are only participants; there is no audience. Circular seating allows for maximum informality and a sense of closeness.

The leader introduces a subject or question, calls on individuals to present their views, and then invites all members to express themselves freely. This is perhaps the most intimate form of group communication. The seating arrangement for a round-table discussion is shown in Figure 14.5.

The discussion is a learning experience for all participants if they make the effort to prepare and participate, keep an open mind, and are ready to inquire. The words of Joseph Joubert, French moralist and essayist, sum up this topic: "The aim of argument, or of discussion, should not be victory, but progress."[3]

THE BRAINSTORMING SESSION

Brainstorming is a creative, freewheeling, no-holds-barred approach to solving problems. Participants—usually 5 to 10 in the business world and up to 20 in a class—should be given a few minutes of silence to think and unleash their imaginations. They should spout anything and everything that comes to mind, while a recorder lists all the ideas on paper or on a chalkboard. Quantity, not quality, of ideas should be emphasized.

---

[3]Joseph Joubert, *Pensées* (1842), 7.31, tr. Katherine Lyttelton.

The crucial principle behind brainstorming is this: No matter how preposterous an idea may sound, there must be no criticism or evaluation of it or its contributor. Participants must be free to say anything.

screen the ideas—evaluate them

This also means that you must control your nonverbal communication, as well, so as not to convey any negative messages such as raising your eyes and head, frowning while spreading your closed lips, or shaking your head. No criticism means nonverbal as well as verbal.

After about 15 minutes of brainstorming, *screen the ideas;* then evaluate, expand, and refine them. Next, sift through the surviving list, focusing on the advantages and disadvantages of each; then reduce the list to the best two or three ideas.

Incidentally, brainstorming can be an excellent way to find speech topics.

THE BUZZ SESSION

The **buzz session** is a problem-solving process that demands a knowledgeable discussion leader who is thoroughly familiar with the problem and who can conduct the entire discussion process. He explains the discussion format and the problem to the audience and divides the audience into clusters of four to six individuals. Each cluster functions indepen-

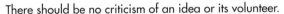

There should be no criticism of an idea or its volunteer.

dently and may take 10 to 15 minutes to come up with solutions. Someone in each cluster should record them.

At the end of the discussion period, the leader asks each cluster recorder to present a one- to two-minute summary of the cluster's recommendations. The responses are then combined and written on the chalkboard. The results are finally discussed either by a preselected panel or by the entire audience.

Buzz sessions are an outstanding mode of group communication, although some participants tend to *clam up* in big groups, everyone usually contributes to a buzz session. These sessions may have various formats depending on the people and problems involved, the time constraints, and the location. Buzz sessions are particularly effective if you have a large audience.

clam up—be quiet, do not speak

THE MEETING

Two components of any organization are **meetings** and committees. The most popular type of group encounter that you'll experience even more than the panel discussion is the meeting. Take a moment or two to reflect on the many meeting situations in which you've recently participated . . . at home, at school, at work, at your health club or day care center. We could consider these types of meetings small and informal. Maybe you were involved in a discussion with your family about a vacation destination; or with fellow students, airing complaints about the school cafeteria or discussing the need for more school funding for women's athletic programs.

At these types of meetings, because of the limited number of participants, you were able to interact either one-on-one or intragroup rather informally . . . like an extended conversation. You could supply input without being officially recognized—that is, you didn't need permission from a group leader to speak. In other words, the type of discussion in which you were participating was unstructured. You were free to ask questions, respond to the statements of others, agree or disagree, as long as you didn't monopolize the time or become disagreeable and personal.

On the other hand, organizations such as labor, civic, fraternal, social, or business-related organizations have large memberships, making it necessary for meetings to be conducted in a stricter and more formal manner to avoid inequities and chaos. As a member, you're entitled to know the organization's constitution and by-laws; its officers; all the working committees and their members; and the time, place, and agenda of each meeting. Of course, you also have the right to speak, to vote, and to run for elective office.

on the other hand—from another point of view

Most large meetings agree to operate by **parliamentary procedure** which is guided by the authoritative and internationally respected *Robert's Rules of Order* and employ the following **agenda:**

1. *Call to order*—The chairperson calls the meeting to order to officially begin proceedings.
2. *Reading of the minutes*—The secretary reads an accounting of the previous meeting and, if necessary, corrections are made and approved.
3. *Committee reports*—Reports from the various committee chairpersons/officers are presented to the membership.
4. *Action on old or unfinished business*—Unfinished business from the last meeting or from other previous sessions are now acted on.
5. *Action on new business*—Members can now introduce, discuss, and act on new business.
6. *Announcements*—Brief announcements are now made to the membership concerning events and functions directly related to the organization.
7. *Adjournment*—After the motion to adjourn (to conclude the meeting) has been presented and seconded by another member, the chairperson declares the meeting formally adjourned. (At this time you may either go home or continue socializing.)

You've been given a rather basic explanation of how a formal meeting is conducted. For a more complete understanding of parliamentary procedure see Henry M. Robert's, *Robert's Rules of Order*. I'm sure there's a copy in your library.

Some of Your Responsibilities When Attending a Meeting

- *Be on time.* Not only is it rude to be late for a meeting, but it can be disruptive. Continual tardiness can weaken your image and effectiveness among your peers.

done your homework—been thoroughly prepared

- *Be prepared.* If you're planning to speak, be sure you've **done your homework.** Be clear, concise, and correct, and be sure to speak so that everyone can hear you.
- *Be open-minded.* Don't expect everyone to be agreeable or ecstatic about what you have to say. Accept opposing views objectively.
- *Be courteous.* If you disagree with what's being said, don't interrupt the speaker. Wait for your turn to be recognized and don't get personal.
- *Be attentive.* Listen carefully to speakers so you'll understand what's being said. It's embarrassing to respond to or inquire about something that has already been discussed. Also, refrain from talking while someone else **has the floor.**

has the floor—is speaking

- *Be serious.* The temptation to be humorous at times can be overpowering but, generally speaking, keep your remarks sober and pertinent. Most people frown on a constant joker.
- *Be sensitive.* Be aware of other members' needs and anxieties and never try to advance your cause at the expense of others. Hurt feelings can leave deep scars.

■ *Be responsive.* Offering suggestions and being sympathetic don't get things done. Organizations not only need talkers, they need doers. In order to pursue ideas or implement courses of action, you should be prepared to offer your services. Perhaps you could volunteer to serve on a committee.

THE COMMITTEE

A **committee** is a small group consisting of five to nine members. (An odd number is usually chosen to avoid tie votes.) It is headed by a chairperson who establishes an agenda and keeps members *on course.* The organization's president may name the chairperson, or members of the committee may select their own. Committee members can be appointed or elected, or they may volunteer.

on course—focused on the subject being discussed

Organizations and action groups may have such committees as:

Entertainment	Health and safety
Fund-raising	Building
Scholarship	Retirement
Membership	Student activities
Budget and finance	Taxation
Awards	Education
Political action	Nominations

A member of a committee should exercise the same responsibilities as members attending a meeting and should ideally possess the following qualities:

■ *Commitment.* You should be a dedicated individual who can place the group's objectives and best interests above your personal feelings. Your presence and promptness can always be counted on. If you're going to be absent, notify the chairperson well in advance.

■ *Intelligence and experience.* You should be an informed individual who knows how to track down information, digest it, and communicate it so that everyone can understand it. You can be depended on to have more than one perspective on the subject and to make positive contributions. If you plan to supply your colleagues with reports, memos, or other types of handouts, do it.

■ *Personality.* You should be an even-tempered person who can take as well as give constructive criticism. You can disagree without becoming disagreeable, and your friendliness allows you to get along easily with other committee members. You are quick to compliment and offer support.

■   *Integrity.* You should not intentionally belittle or degrade colleagues or their opinions, and you should be mindful of other people's feelings, especially when responding to a questionable viewpoint. You can be relied on for honesty and a high standard of ethics.

YOU AS THE GROUP LEADER

made your mark—earned the reputation; become known

Suppose that you have ***made your mark*** as an active and responsible participant in your organization, and you have just been selected to play a leadership role. It may be to conduct a large meeting or to chair a committee. For a large gathering (over 20 people), you should prepare and complete a premeeting checklist. (See Figure 14.6.) Nothing can destroy the momentum and effectiveness of a meeting more easily than the lack of proper accommodations, equipment, and supplies. Investing the time to establish and check off such a list will pay dividends.

Also, as an effective leader you should be sensitive to the needs and demands confronting not only the group, but each member as well. You should be able to guide the group and, at the same time, be flexible enough to adapt to changing needs during the meeting. And, finally, you should radiate confidence and authority.

The following are some suggestions for acting as group leader:

■   Mention any rules of procedure.
■   Announce the topic and goal of discussion.
■   Help group members get to know each other (if size permits).
■   Encourage maximum participation.
■   Allow those with opposing views equal time to speak.
■   Encourage, but don't force, a silent member to speak.
■   Refer questions back to the group instead of answering them yourself.
■   Ask questions to clarify meanings.
■   Ask questions that cannot be answered by just a yes or no.
■   Keep the discussion on track.
■   Be impartial, yet question logic and validity.
■   Avoid personality clashes.
■   Be complimentary whenever possible.
■   Don't permit private conversations while a person is speaking.
■   Don't allow a speaker to monopolize the floor.
■   List important points on the chalkboard if doing so would benefit the group.

run out of time—use up your allocated time

■   Watch the clock so you won't ***run out of time.***
■   Take notes so that you can present a salient summary after the discussion ends.
■   Make announcements pertaining to a recommended course of action, information regarding next meeting, and so on.

Figure 14.6 Premeeting Checklist

Reason for Meeting:
Day and Time of Meeting:
Name(s) and telephone number(s) of person(s) to contact in the event of problems:

Check When
Completed   Comments

Room (Name or Number)
   Reserved
   Tables
   Chairs
   Sign designating room
   Name cards
   Lectern
   Seating arrangement
   Refreshments

Audiovisual Equipment
   Public address system
   Tape recorder
   Presentation tapes
   Microphones
   Chalkboard
   Chalk
   Easel
   Flip chart
   Overhead projector
   Other projectors
   Broad felt-tip pens
   Television monitor(s)
   VCR
   Screen

Printed Material
   Agenda
   Other handouts (list them)

Supplies for Participants
   Paper
   Pens or pencils
   Pitchers of ice water and glasses

Be aware of the time element.

- Accept only one question per person so that as many as possible may speak.
- Thank all participants and praise their contributions.

The position of group leader, or chairperson, is a responsible, challenging one that can also be rewarding and personally gratifying.

THINGS TO DISCUSS IN CLASS

1. Weigh the advantages and disadvantages of a strong discussion leader.
2. Assume the responsibility for selecting a small group and prepare a 15-minute panel discussion. Then, as moderator, present it to the class.
3. List one topic for each of the following:
   a. A panel discussion.
   b. A lecture.
   c. A symposium.
   d. A round-table discussion.
   e. A forum.
   f. A brainstorming session.
4. Assume that you are a panel moderator. Introduce yourself and briefly tell the audience the topic to be discussed. Then introduce each member of the panel and explain the format and ground rules.

WHAT DO YOU REMEMBER FROM THIS CHAPTER?

1. List two of the more common types of group discussion.
2. Explain the Reflective Thinking Process.
3. How should a panel be set up for maximum impact?
4. Explain two responsibilities of a panel discussion moderator.
5. Explain two responsibilities of a panelist.
6. Explain two responsibilities of an audience.
7. What is a discussion called when the audience is allowed to participate?
8. Briefly explain the symposium.
9. How does the symposium differ from the panel discussion?
10. What is brainstorming?
11. What is a buzz session?
12. Name two qualities that a committee member should have.

VITALIZE YOUR VOCABULARY

Common Banking Terms

ATM (n.) Automatic teller machine; a banking machine where customers may receive cash from their existing accounts by inserting a bank card and entering a special code.

assets (n.) Things of value that are owned and can be turned into cash.

balance (n.) The amount of money that you have in your savings or checking account.

C.D. (n.) Certificate of deposit; a specified amount of money deposited for a certain length of time that cannot be withdrawn earlier without paying a penalty. The interest rate, which remains constant, is higher than a regular savings or passbook account.

checking account (n.) An account established at any financial institution from which you may withdraw money on demand by writing checks. Some checking accounts earn interest.

collateral (n.) Money or other assets that you pledge as security to protect the interests of the institution that lends you money.

co-sign (v.) When you borrow money, another person may be required to sign along with you; the co-signer would be responsible for the repayment of the loan if you should default.

credit line (n.) A sum of money that a bank makes available to a customer or company from which they may draw as needed.

credit rating (n.) A rating based on a person's history of repaying loans or charges on time.

deposit (v.) Putting money into a savings or checking account.

direct-deposit (n.) An agreement between your employer and your bank that your paycheck will automatically be deposited in your bank account; on payday you receive a statement of the transaction rather than a paycheck.

joint account (n.) A bank account in two peoples names, each of whom may withdraw funds.

loan (n.) Money lent at a certain rate of interest with a written agreement to repay it.

money market account (n.) An account requiring a minimum deposit that may have limited monthly check-writing privileges; the interest rate exceeds that of a regular savings account but fluctuates monthly; withdrawals may be made anytime.

overdraw (v.) Write checks for money that you don't have in your account; these checks are rejected and returned to you for "insufficient funds," and you are charged a penalty.

penalty (n.) An extra charge for any infraction against any of the agreed-on rules or regulations stipulated by the bank.

reconciliation (n.) Balancing your checkbook; a monthly activity you should perform to ensure that the balance in your checkbook is equal to the amount shown on your monthly bank statement.

savings account (n.) An account at a bank in which you have money that earns interest; also known as a passbook account; you may withdraw funds anytime without penalty.

service charge (n.) A fee that banks charge customers for certain services; fee(s) may vary at different banks.

teller (n.) A bank employee who performs various banking services for customers such as cashing checks, selling traveler's checks, accepting deposits, etc.

withdraw (v.) Take money from an account.

15

WHAT DO YOU SAY AFTER YOU SAY "HELLO"?

The art of conversation is the art of hearing as well as of being heard.

William Hazlett, *The Plain Speaker* (1826)

After reading and understanding this chapter, you should know:

- Some keys to good conversation.

- Some preconversational tips.

- How to improve your conversational ability.

- How to start a conversation.

- How to remember names.

- How to express sympathy and emotional support.

- How to talk on the telephone.

CHAPTER PREVIEW

Almost all oral communication involves speaking face to face with one or a few persons. It's a daily activity in which you can improve a great deal if you try.

One of the keys to becoming a good conversationalist is to be genuinely interested in people. This interest is reflected by your attitude, eyes, smile, and handshake. Another key is to have many activities or hobbies and to be able to discuss them knowledgeably. Keeping up with the daily news in various fields by means of newspapers, magazines, and radio and TV broadcasts is a third way to help make you a more interesting person to talk with.

You can develop your conversational ability if you practice the suggestions given. For example, you should be sincere and listen attentively; you should not interrupt, monopolize, offend, complain, or pry; and you should not be a know-it-all.

There are also suggestions for initiating a conversation and keeping it moving—for example, how to introduce people and yourself, how to compliment people sincerely, how to discuss politics and religion, how to ask provocative questions, and how to express sympathy.

Since many people have trouble remembering names, we briefly discuss some psychological principles that can be applied to help you remember names.

Lastly, in todays fast-paced world, making contacts is a significant aspect of getting ahead, so there are suggestions that can help you advance your career.

Appearing in this (and every) chapter is the feature "In Other Words," which will greatly benefit foreign and ESL students. To aid in their understanding of common American idioms and phrases, these expressions will be defined in the margin of the page on which they are introduced.

CONVERSATION

So far, our emphasis has been primarily on how to prepare and deliver a talk confidently on a specific topic. Another more common but crucial aspect of communication is one that you engage in daily. It's a skill that you should master—the art of conversation.

You will engage in conversation countless times each day for the rest of your life. As far as making an impact on your daily life, there is perhaps nothing more important than the way you converse with people. At home; at work; at school; at a business, social or community gathering; in dealing with your spouse, your roommate, your children, or your neighbor; in interacting with your bank, utility company, or IRS agent; and in person or over the telephone, conversation plays a vital role in your life.

Conversational skill can be indispensable on the job. Let's look at an incident in the career of Sergeant Paul Crow, a homicide detective with the Daytona Beach (Florida) Police Department. He was investigating a case in which a woman had been stabbed to death. A second woman had been stabbed in a similar manner, but had survived to identify her assailant. Sgt. Crow interviewed the suspect repeatedly, won his confidence and trust, and encouraged him to *"open up."* "Then he would go on and on," said the sergeant, *"to get it off his chest."* I had to talk on his level, laugh at his jokes, talk about things he knew about." In the end, the prisoner confessed to murdering 27 women. He is now serving a life sentence.[1]

"open up"—freely express himself

to get it off his chest—openly express himself and talk about things that may have bothered him

Think for a moment. Can you recall social or professional conversations that you wanted to leave (or actually did leave) because you felt the experience was a waste of time? Perhaps the person who spoke the most was boring and conceited and monopolized the conversation, or a tedious know-it-all, or engaged in malicious gossip.

There is no question that interesting conversation is an art that can and should be developed. And that's what this chapter is all about. "Conversation is an art in which a man has all mankind for his competitors, for it is that which all are practicing everyday while they live."[2]

SOME KEYS TO GOOD CONVERSATION

Some of the most delicious moments of life blossom in conversation. The art of swift and witty response is universally admired and enjoyed.

---

[1] *Boston Sunday Globe*, 24 October 1982, 12–13.
[2] Ralph Waldo Emerson, "Considerations by the Way." *The Conduct of Life* (1860).

Sarah Bernhardt, who reigned as the queen of the English- and French-speaking theater from about 1880 to 1920, was as skillful at dialogue off-stage as on. In her later years, she lived high up in an apartment building in Paris. One day an elderly admirer arrived at her door, gasping for air after the long climb. When he recovered his breath, he asked, "Madame, why do you live so high up?"

"My dear," replied the divine Sarah, "it is the only way I can still make the hearts of men beat faster."[3]

You may recall conversations with people who were captivating, people who made you feel that you were part of the action and who listened to you with as much interest as you listened to them. If you're genuinely interested in others, the conversation stands an excellent chance of being absorbing. There's nothing like a stimulating conversation; in fact, a good conversationalist is usually popular and well received. Such people know how to communicate confidently with others. To be well liked, admired, and respected and to feel that you're making a contribution to society, no matter how infinitesimal, is an unequaled experience.

You can become a better conversationalist, a more appealing person, and a more respected and admired individual. You can, that is, if you have the determination to work at it. And what's even better, you're not on a stage or under a magnifying glass, but among friends. Every day you'll have a multitude of opportunities to practice, to experiment, and to evaluate yourself.

If you blunder, so what? In a few moments you'll have another chance. You won't be graded, criticized, or evaluated. You're free to progress as much as you want, at your own pace. You have your friends, even strangers, classrooms, home, work, the beach, social clubs, and meetings. We all make mistakes. That's a fact of life. There's nothing wrong with that, provided we learn from them and don't repeat them. The only person who never makes mistakes is the person who never tries anything. What a dull and boring existence. You can make your life more interesting, exciting, adventurous, and fulfilling. It's up to you.

Conversation begins even before you speak. As we mentioned in Chapter 2, your physical presence and expression transmit impressions, favorable or unfavorable, to those around you. Before engaging in conversation, consider these four nonverbal elements: your attitude, your eyes, your smile, and your handshake.

Your Attitude

You must look forward to conversation. It can be challenging, rewarding, and informative if you allow it to be. Have an open, unbiased mind and

---

[3] *The Little, Brown Book of Anecdotes*, ed. Clifton Fadiman (Boston: Little, Brown, 1985). 60.

You're not on a stage or under a magnifying glass.

be ready to listen to all. Be eager to see what you can derive from this experience and what you can contribute to it.

A burning positive attitude is volatile fuel for the ignition of stimulating conversation. If you're shy, quiet, or reserved, "The important thing is to pull yourself up by your own hair, to turn yourself inside out and see the whole world with fresh eyes."[4] And if you really want some words on which to chew and digest then savor the following gem from Harvard psychologist William James who said, "The greatest discovery of my generation is that a human being can alter his life by altering his attitudes of mind." Powerful, powerful words. If you really want to do something then you must believe that you *can* do it. *Go for it.*

Go for it—take a chance and try it

---

[4]Peter Weiss, *Marat/Sade* (1964) 1.13, Geoffrey Skelton and Adrian Mitchell.

Your Eyes

Your eyes will reflect if you're genuinely interested. "The eyes have one language everywhere,"[5] and it's understood everywhere. Look people in the eye to communicate your friendliness and sincerity; otherwise you exclude them. This is particularly true when conversing with two or more people. Looking into the eyes of each person present will help bring reciprocity into the discussion. *In other words,* looking at all present can't help but motivate them to look at you. As far as eye contact and conversation go, remember the old adage, "the eyes have it."

In other words— to say it another way

Your Smile

Can you think of a better way to communicate nonverbally with someone than with a sincere smile? Smiling can be contagious. Try it on the next acquaintance you see; you both may be surprised at the results from something that requires so little effort—just spontaneity.

Wilber D. Nesbit put it quite beautifully when he said,

The thing that goes the farthest towards making life worth while,
That costs the least, and does the most, is just a pleasant smile.

Your Handshake

Shake hands with a grip firm enough to convey a meaningful expression. If you're a strong person, don't use your strength for squashing knuckles. By the same token, people turn away from a lifeless, dangling handshake. When you can greet someone with responsive eyes, a friendly smile, and a warm; meaningful handshake, you've mastered the first step in learning to communicate interpersonally with purpose.

SUGGESTIONS TO IMPROVE YOUR CONVERSATIONAL ABILITY

Are there any secrets, special formulas, or rules that can make you a more effective conversationalist? No, but you must have a burning desire and a total commitment to the effort. Let's look at some suggestions that can help you sharpen your conversational ability.

---

[5]George Herbert, *Jacula Prudentum* (1651).

Try to avoid the "wet-fish" handshake.

Be Interested

The right attitude is a prerequisite for participating in conversation. Try to be interested not only in all the topics but also in each participant. If you're not interested in the participants, they'll respond in the same way. So, when someone is speaking focus your entire attention on him or her. Bernard Baruch, a former great statesman once said, "You can win more friends in two months by showing interest in others than you can in two years by trying to interest others in you."

Have Varied Interests

One of the secrets of stimulating talkers is to have varied interests and to be knowledgeable about them. A good conversationalist can discuss (with reasonable confidence) local, state, and national politics and knows something about the economy; sports; and the social, educational, and entertainment world. Relying on information from the daily newspaper, a weekly news magazine, radio talk shows, TV news, movies, and books and magazines, good conversationalists talk with people and *listen critically*. They're generalists.

Hobbies, travel experiences, sports, jobs, military service, and people you've met or work with are all possibilities for stimulating topics of conversation. If you make the effort to expand your horizons, you can become more interesting to others.

Be Sincere

put on airs—sound phony, conceited

In conversation, don't try to *put on airs* and don't bluff, lie, or brag. An insincere person usually ends up with no audience. There is no substitute for sincerity. Remember Lincoln's statement: "You may fool all the people some of the time; you can even fool some of the people all the time; but you can't fool all of the people all the time."

Be a Good Listener

get wrapped-up in—become very enthusiastic about

There is no greater compliment to a speaker than a listener's total absorption in what he or she is saying. Listen with your eyes, your ears, your mind—your total self—with intensity. You'll be amazed at how much you can *get wrapped up in* an individual and how much information you can acquire, which may ultimately enhance your contribution to the exchange. In the process of communication listening is as important as speaking.

President Franklin D. Roosevelt once received an official visitor who immediately commented on one of the ship models on his desk. FDR took the bait and devoted most of the 30-minute visit to discussing ships and the Navy. When the visitor left, the Chief Executive said to his secretary, "That man is one of the best conversationalists I have ever met."

You can almost be guaranteed popularity when you can enjoy the reputation of being a good listener.

Don't Interrupt

An easy way to turn people off or to anger them is to interrupt them often while they're speaking. It's a rude thing to do. The guilty person can't wait to finish someone else's story, to correct a speaker, or to announce a punch line prematurely. Interrupting is justified only when a speaker is boring the audience or becoming offensive (using profanity, bigotry, or insults). If you must interrupt, be as tactful as possible to avoid a scene, but do it.

broke in—interrupted

A classic example of "uncontrollable" interruption occurred between the two female members of the U.S. Supreme Court, no less. As Justice Sandra Day O'Connor was questioning an attorney during oral argument before the full bench, just-appointed Justice Ruth Bader Ginsburg rudely *broke in* with her own question. This brought an immediate acrid stare accompanied by the incisive, "Excuse me! Just let me finish," from an irate O'Connor.[6]

As difficult as it may be, at times, try not to interrupt someone until that person finishes speaking. Not only will you be appreciated, but you will also gain respect.

---

[6]*Newsweek*, 11 April 1994, 6.

On occasion, it's okay to interrupt.

Don't Be a Bore

We all know one-track people who discuss the same old topics: job, hobby or sport, house, car, or boat. It might have been interesting the first or second time, but the third time is boring. Family and relatives can be boring topics, especially discussed by a person who can't wait to extract a wallet bursting with children's pictures or to incessantly babble about their offspring at college or about their "prestigious" jobs. Winston Churchill felt that the subject of children was inappropriate for adult conversation. At one particular gathering, an ambassador said to him, "You know, Sir Winston, I've never told you about my grandchildren." The old warrior chomped on his cigar, dragged deeply, and exhaled, "I realize it, my dear fellow, and I can't tell you how grateful I am."

Here's how another international statesman handled boring situations. Prince Otto Bismarck of Prussia had been conversing for rather a long time with the English ambassador when the latter posed the question: "How do you handle insistent visitors who take up so much of your valuable time?" Bismarck answered, "Oh, I have an infallible method. My servant appears and informs me that my wife has something urgent to tell me." At that moment there was a knock at the door and the servant entered with a message from his wife.

Know When to Conclude

Once your turn has come to talk, don't act as though it may be your last chance on earth and go on and on and on. If you have something to say, say it. Then give others the opportunity to express themselves; listen to them, and respond. That's the essence of conversation.

Unfortunately, long-winded speakers have always assailed our ears and taxed our patience. Claude Swanson, a well-known national politician from Virginia during the turn-of-the-century, one evening presented a long and rambling speech. Following his talk, an elderly woman approached him to shake his hand. "How did you like my speech?" asked Swanson. "I liked it fine," she replied, "but it seems to me you missed several excellent opportunities." A puzzled Swanson then queried, "Several excellent opportunities for what?" "To quit," she snapped.[7] I once heard someone give some excellent advice: It's okay to hold a conversation, but you should let go of it now and then.

Don't Be Offensive

rub people the wrong way—irritate them

There are many ways to offend people—for example, by making derogatory remarks about their dress, physical appearance, voice, accent, religion, or politics. These remarks cause two negative results: They anger the recipient and they brand the offender as a person to be avoided. It's far better to say nothing than to *rub people the wrong way.* Remember the words of Darius Lyman who said, "I have often regretted my speech, never my silence."

Don't Be a Constant Complainer

Everyone has problems and, as a rule, would rather not hear yours. A brief mention of your problem might be acceptable to your listeners, but don't dwell on it for the entire conversation. Some people always complain, no matter what the subject is. Since their negative attitude can be contagious, you'd be wise to avoid them.

Don't Pry

Nobody can be more offensive than one who persists in prying for personal information. Following are some typical questions followed by some apt retorts which may produce some interesting facial expressions. (But be sure you retort with a smile.)

Why don't you have any children?

We don't want any . . . We hate kids. . . . Or: *I give up . . . why?*

---

[7]*The Little, Brown Book of Anecdotes*, 530.

Your drapes are beautiful. They must be expensive; are they?
Thank you. Yes, they are, and very.
And how old might you be, my dear?
I might be 25, 30, 31.

A super reply was once returned by my wife when a busybody asked about the family income. My wife leaned toward the questioner and whispered, "Are you good at keeping secrets?" "Oh yes, certainly," was the reply, to which my wife answered, "So am I."

Don't Be a Know-It-All

Obnoxious people in conversation are experts on everything—politics, labor problems, social problems, religion, family affairs. No matter what the topic of discussion may be, they have the answers. Being knowledge-able is a tremendous asset when you participate in conversation, but sometimes discretion and good taste are greater virtues.

Don't Be a Gossip

Unfortunately, many people enjoy gossip and rumors. It's very tempting and so easy to say things just for attention and recognition. This activity is not only cruel, but it can inflict irreparable damage to another person's character. And, let's face it, no one really trusts or respects a gossip.

As the Greek dramatist Sophocles said in the fifth century B.C., "A short saying oft contains much wisdom." Actually, I have two for you and they're both proverbs that solicit your contemplation:

Whoever gossips to you, will gossip about you.

Spanish proverb

What you don't see with your eyes, don't witness with your mouth.

Jewish proverb

Disagree Without Being Disagreeable

Nothing is more stimulating than a conversation sparked with disagree-ment, provided it remains on a rational, friendly level. There is much to gain from hearing opposing viewpoints, plus the challenge of persuading or being persuaded. Whenever disagreement is introduced into a conversation, everybody's interest perks up. Don't shout or lose your temper if someone gets the better of you. If you feel embarrassed at losing an argument, per-haps you could have been better prepared. There will be a next time. No one likes to lose, but accepting it gracefully could earn respect for you.

A wise old speech professor of mine once said, "It is better to stir up a question without deciding it, than to decide it without stirring it up." Go for it.

Include Everyone

When you're involved in conversation, be sure to direct your remarks to everyone. Look at each person as you make your points. Then they'll be more apt to pay attention to you and to respond. Interest shown by eye contact, a nod of the head, and an occasional gesture toward an individual will do it.

Try to Be More Outgoing

In every conversation there are speakers, listeners, and speaker-listeners. Perhaps you're the kind who'd rather remain in the background and just listen to what's going on. But that's only half the fun. If you tend toward shyness, you belong with the majority of the human race. (This topic is discussed in detail in Chapter 1.)

TV commentator Barbara Walters used to be one of that majority. Some years ago, she and her husband attended a Fourth of July party, where they were introduced to novelist Truman Capote. His book *In Cold Blood* had just been published and was zooming to the top of the bestseller list. ". . . I was yearning to talk with him about it," she confessed, "but I couldn't cross the barrier of my own shyness and my fear that Capote must be fed up with people asking about his work."[8]

If you're a listener or a speaker-listener, you may find that small groups (four or five people) are easier to break into than large groups (ten or more). But you must *want* to engage in conversation. An exercise is to observe good talkers in action and to adopt some of their methods.

In some situations, reluctance to speak up can be dangerous—even fatal. In February 1982, at Washington National Airport, two pilots of a Boeing 737, about to take off, saw snow and ice building up on the wings and engines even after their plane had been de-iced twice. Both pilots were deeply worried—the audiotapes revealed later—but instead of questioning the control tower about the advisability of takeoff, they said nothing. They crashed into the Potomac River, killing 74 aboard and four passing motorists.[9] It pays to speak up, even if you may be ignored or wrong.

As we said earlier, since the whole world is your laboratory, experiment with these techniques. You have a great deal to gain, and when you start to participate more in conversation, it will become easier and will do wonders for your self-confidence. Since improvement depends on active participation, the sooner you start, the better.

---

[8]Barbara Walters, *How to Talk with Practically Anybody About Practically Anything* (New York: Dell, 1971), xiii.
[9]"We're Going Down, Larry," *Time*, 15 February 1982, 21.

HOW TO START A CONVERSATION

Let's now look at some ways to help you start a conversation and keep it going.

"I'd Like You to Meet . . . ."

Assume that you're being introduced to a small group. Your introducer may mention something about you—your background, experience, or job—and perhaps even tell you some unusual tidbits about individual members of the group you're meeting. During this time you can decide to whom you would like to return for conversation because of a possible common interest.

"Hello, I'm . . . ."

If there's no one to introduce you, you should introduce yourself. Since nearly everyone at a gathering enjoys meeting the other guests, take a deep breath, approach someone, and introduce yourself. In addition to your name, give some information that might be interesting to the person and that might allow him or her to respond in kind. After a handshake, repeat her name aloud. Then you might say something about the host and hostess, your work, your home, sports, or the latest headline news. Then *toss the ball* to the other guest and see what happens.

toss the ball (to someone)—allow the other person to respond

"Excuse Me, But Didn't I Hear You Mention . . . ?"

On occasion you may overhear a topic of interest from someone in a small group. Nothing could be more complimentary, at your first opportunity, than to approach the person with something like, "Excuse me, but I couldn't help hearing you mention. . . . That sounds fascinating. Could I ask you . . . ?" The fact that you're interested in someone enough to pursue his line of conversation will *open the door for you,* and a lively meeting could ensue.

open the door for you—allow you the possibility of continuing your conversation

"Say, I Like Your . . . ."

Nothing is easier to accept than a sincere compliment. Perhaps you admire someone's jewelry, shirt, tie, blouse, hairdo, or suit. If you do, say so. Again, since bringing positive attention to someone's abilities or possessions is highly satisfying, you're almost guaranteed an interested listener. Paying a genuine compliment is an excellent springboard for starting a conversation.

"Crummy Weather We're Having, Eh?"

Discussing the weather or natural disasters can serve two purposes: It can fill a silent period between people, and it can be an interesting subject if you're on top of the news. What about the devastation in California caused by the 1998 El Niño, which resulted in pounding rains, mudslides, high winds, record surfs and . . . deaths; or the relentless fires that hungrily consumed hundred of thousands of acres and threatened homes and lives in Florida due to a record drought?

"I Never Discuss Politics and Religion."

Although some people will not discuss politics and religion, these subjects can lead to a stimulating, informative give-and-take. For that to happen, however, the participants must not become hotheaded, irrational, or belligerent. There perhaps has never been a time in our country's history when so much controversy surrounds so many political and religious issues. For that reason alone, we should talk over those subjects more than ever. Exploring them intelligently can be a beneficial experience that could lead to better understanding among people.

"How do you like this weather?"

Play the Role of Interviewer

Although some people find this technique difficult, it can be most rewarding. It requires discovering someone who has an unusual lifestyle or profession, someone who may be quietly sitting in the background. Get the person to talk. This technique involves asking questions (how? what? why? and when?) and could result in an exhilarating experience for all those present.

A few years ago I attended a large social gathering where I knew only the host and hostess. From talking with the hostess, I learned that one guest—the hostess pointed him out—was a senior design engineer in a company that produced and tested missiles. She added that he was not only brilliant and had a sense of humor, but he could also translate difficult scientific concepts into common language.

At the first chance, I introduced myself to the engineer and started questioning him about his early start in mechanics and electronics, about some design challenges and solutions, about his travel overseas, and so on. As the conversation warmed up, more and more guests began to ask questions and contribute comments. When a lull occurred, I revved up the proceedings with another pertinent question. By the time the conversation ended three hours later, practically all 40 guests had participated in this informative and sometimes entertaining experience.

An excellent way to learn this technique is to listen to radio and TV talk shows and to read interviews in the news media. Notice how questions are begun and followed up, how they're developed from answers, and how they're phrased so that they don't elicit one-word responses. Notice how interviewers leave a particular line of questioning and start another and when and how they *wrap it all up.*

wrap it all up—
conclude

"I Never Forget a Face . . . But Names?"

How often have you heard that? Some people can remember names but can't match them with faces; others can remember faces but can't recall names. One way to impress people is to remember their names. To most of us, nothing is more important.

Memory can be strengthened if you're willing to work at it. The following are some elements involved in developing your memory for names and faces.

1. *Attention.* Whenever you meet people for the first time, pay strict attention to their appearance, because you want to remember their names. Observe facial features—eyes, hair, ears, dimple, nose—for something striking or peculiar that may make it easier for you to recall the person later.
2. *Association.* Is there any way you can associate the name with the person's features or occupation? Perhaps Ms. Smiley has a beautiful smile. Perhaps Mr. Pearlman is in the jewelry business

or his teeth resemble pearls. It's amazing how, with effort and imagination, you can associate a name with a physical feature, occupation, or hobby. Be on the lookout.

3. *Comparison.* Perhaps a person has a name similar to that of a very good friend of yours. Visualize this person in comparison with your friend. Compare their features. Search for a resemblance or vast difference that might make it easier for you to remember your new acquaintance's name. Again, you may be amazed at what you can *come up with.*

come up with—
discover

4. *Repetition.* When you meet a person for the first time, repeat the person's name as often as possible so that it is firmly implanted in your mind. Be sure that you hear the correct pronunciation of the name. If necessary, have it repeated and spelled; then you repeat it. Repetition is one of the keys to memorizing. But be sure to pay undivided attention to the person and the person's name. I recall a rather embarrassing situation when I was introduced to a gentleman and, due to inattentiveness, I didn't catch his name and replied, "That's an unusual name; how do you spell it?" He obliged with "S-M-I-T-H."

Samuel Johnson put it best when he said, "The true art of memory is the art of attention."

How to Make Social and Business Contacts

One of the more pragmatic aspects of life is making business and social contacts. Let's not kid ourselves; the more people we know, the more progress we may make in our careers. You may have friends who were promoted or got jobs because they knew certain people. Others may have received benefits or special treatment because they had contacts.

Getting to know people is very important, but first you have to meet them. An excellent place to do this is at school. Try to get along with as many people as possible by being friendly and helpful and by keeping in touch. You never know who may be able to assist you in the near future or after graduation. If you're in a position to do someone a favor, do it. The day may come when you'll need a favor in return.

If you have a goal to achieve, make it a point to associate with people who can help you. Associate with people you admire and respect; some of their talents may *rub off on you.* Whether in your business or social environment, there are always key people, leaders, who get things done. If you can help them in any way, volunteer. Do more than is expected, and that alone will set you apart from the masses. When people in authority can depend on you, you're beginning to build a future for yourself.

rub off on you—
be transferred to you

HOW TO EXPRESS SYMPATHY AND EMOTIONAL SUPPORT

We all occasionally find ourselves in situations when some comforting words or actions must be expressed. Perhaps a loved one or a friend has died, your spouse was laid off work after 15 years with the company, a close relative is diagnosed as having a terminal illness, or your closest friend's teenager was arrested for injuring an elderly person while driving under the influence of alcohol.

Perhaps the most difficult situation to be confronted with is someone's death. How often have you heard people ask, "What do you say?" It would be impossible to list all of the appropriate things to say to cover specific situations, but the following suggestions may help make your presence a little more comforting and, at the same time, offer a grieving person some emotional support.

Be an Active Listener

Listening attentively to a bereaved person can be very supportive and therapeutic. If the individual wishes to talk about the situation, listen with all the love and understanding *at your command.* Often, just listening without interrupting or pontificating can provide that person with the needed comfort. If he or she doesn't wish to talk and would rather be alone, respect that decision, but indicate clearly that you'll be available whenever he or she feels like talking.

at your command—in your power

Empathize

Be sure to communicate that you understand how the person feels by nodding or saying such things as, "I can understand your feelings," "I know what you're going through," "Yes, it is tragic," or "I know what you mean." It's important that the person feels that other people understand, sympathize, and care, even though they might not have actually experienced the same loss. But, showing your genuine concern can be therapeutic.

Express Nonverbal Support

At times, just touching is the most eloquent message that you can communicate to a distressed person. A hug, an arm around the shoulder, the squeeze of a hand, or a kiss says it all. If you honestly feel that you are at a complete loss for words, don't attempt any.

Don't Platitudinize

Sayings like "Well, everything happens for the best," "God works in strange ways," or "Think of the good times" are usually not what a grieving person wishes to hear. Your sensitive caring and understanding are far more important than your philosophizing. A sincere "If there's anything you need" or "If there's anything I can do, please let me know," or "I'll call you tomorrow" can be very comforting.

Trying to think of just the right words to say to a grieving person can be quite uncomfortable and embarrassing—but it needn't be. You know the situation and the person(s) involved. As long as you are sincere with your expression of understanding, whether verbal or nonverbal, you can feel confident that your presence will be appreciated.

HOW TO TALK ON THE TELEPHONE

For most people, talking on the phone is an important means of developing and carrying on one-to-one relationships. Talking on the phone is something you do regularly, perhaps many times daily, at home and on the job. The following are some suggestions to help you become more proficient at it.

Courtesy

Always treat telephone callers courteously, not only because it's the right thing to do but because your response colors their impression of both you and your company or organization. If you've had a rough day and your nerves are rubbed raw, don't let your voice and words show it. That's easy to say but hard to do. If you're too pressured to talk at the moment, say so, get the caller's name and number, and call back in 15 minutes, a half-hour, or whenever you can. But do what you said—call back.

Too many people today answer the phone, "Just a moment, please," and then keep the caller hanging for three or four minutes. It's far more considerate and businesslike to get the caller's name and number and return the call a few minutes later.

This approach especially applies if you have "call waiting," which allows you to answer an incoming call while you're speaking on the phone. If the incoming call is more urgent than your present conversation, politely say so to the first caller and state that you'll call right back. Courtesy and tact on the phone *pay off* in the long run.

pay off—eventually bring positive results

Voice

Your voice will come through more warmly if you remember that you're not talking to a piece of office equipment, but to another human being. If you feel what you're saying and visualize the other person (see "Oral Visualization" in Chapter 5), you'll probably even use gestures, such as nodding your head, shrugging your shoulders, and smiling, and your voice will reflect that. As a result, you won't sound mechanical; you'll sound human.

Always treat telephone callers courteously.

For most people, the transmitter, or mouthpiece, should be held one or two inches away from the mouth and at the same level. If you tend to talk softly, keep the mouthpiece less than an inch away; if you blast, three or four inches would be better.

Pronunciation

Don't chew gum, smoke, or clench a pencil between your teeth. Any of those actions will result in slurred words so that your listener may have to keep asking, "What did you say?" or "Pardon me?" And be sure to speak slowly so that you will be understood. The most common speech problem by telephone users is that they talk too fast.

Brevity of Calls

At work it's a sensible idea to keep most of your calls short, say, five minutes or less. Plan your statement beforehand, and once on the phone, explain the reason for your call and its importance. Then close with a few words on the course of action you or the other person is going to take. Avoid rambling endlessly; someone else, with an urgent message, may be trying to reach you or the person you're speaking with.

Expressions of Goodwill

Certain expressions "stroke" most people soothingly. Some of these are:

"You have a very pleasant voice."

"Thank you."

"I appreciate that."

"I'm glad to help you."

"If you have any questions, be sure to call me."

When said sincerely, these expressions can build goodwill for you and your company.

Identification

At work, rather than answering with "Hello," you should immediately identify yourself and your department. Not only does this save time, but callers will know that they have the right party and, in that case, will most likely identify themselves. Whenever you make a call regarding a serious complaint or problem, be sure to note the date and the other person's name and number for future reference.

Security

Once you pick up the receiver, don't make side remarks to anybody nearby. Even if you cup your hand over the mouthpiece, the callers may hear information through the earpiece that they shouldn't know. In a social sense that could be embarrassing; in the business or professional world, it could be costly to your organization or to your career.

Memory Aids

Always have a pencil and notepad near the phone so you can take messages promptly. Keeping on hand a list of frequently used numbers and emergency numbers can save precious time.

Taking Messages

When you answer for someone who's not in the office, avoid statements like:

"She's having coffee now."

"She's late today."

"She's in the ladies room"

A more tactful approach would be to say, "She's out of the office. May I take your name and number so she can call you when she returns?"

Leaving Messages

When phoning people who don't know you and who are not able to take your call, be sure to give your name and number including area code and extension to the person answering. Then repeat that information slowly, because too many of us zip off the phone number before it can be jotted down.

Answering Machines

Some people get startled when the numbers they've dialed yield a recorded announcement. They hesitate, then fumble through a some-what incoherent message. Since answering machines are quite common, you'd be wise to anticipate hearing one when calling someone and to pre-pare a short message. Oh, another thing: It's advisable to wait for at least five rings before hanging up because that's when some machines start to record your message.

THINGS TO DISCUSS IN CLASS

1. Before class, in the cafeteria, or at your next social function, select a per-son you've seen before but never talked with. Introduce yourself and start a conversation. Tell the class of your experience.

2. List a few different sections of a newspaper and tell the class some news items you discovered in each section.

3. Listen to a radio talk program and take notes. Then tell the class about the talk show host and the line of questioning. Was he or she fair? probing? interesting? a good listener?

4. Try one or more of the techniques of starting a conversation discussed in this chapter and tell the class about your experience(s).

5. Tell the class how you feel about discussing politics and religion.

6. What methods do you use to remember names and faces? Share your methods with the class.

7. How do you rate yourself as a listener? Tell the class how you can be-come a more effective listener.

8. Your closest friend didn't get a much-desired job. Tell the class what you would say to comfort him or her.

9. List several "prying" questions, and suggest some suitable responses to them.

10. You're at a party, conversing with someone who doesn't agree with you. Suddenly, the other person becomes loud and disagreeable. Tell the class what your response would be.

WHAT DO YOU REMEMBER FROM THIS CHAPTER?

1. What are some ways to develop your conversational ability?
2. How can you become a more interesting person?
3. List a few good conversational habits.
4. When is it permissible to interrupt someone?
5. Comment on this statement: "I never discuss politics or religion."
6. Explain several ways to start a conversation.
7. What are some elements involved in memory development, especially regarding people's names?
8. What is the key to making business and social contacts?
9. How can you disagree without being disagreeable?
10. When answering a question, should you look only at the questioner or at every member of the group? Explain.
11. Can you express sympathy nonverbally? Explain.
12. When talking on the telephone, how far should your mouth be from the mouthpiece?

VITALIZE YOUR VOCABULARY

Phobias

A phobia is an irrational and exaggerated fear of an object or situation. The word *phobia* is derived from the Greek word *phobos,* which means "fear," "terror," or "panic."

phobia	Fear of
auto or monophobia	being alone
acrophobia	heights
agoraphobia	open or public places
androphobia	men
ailurophobia	cats
anthophobia	flowers
anthropophobia	people
aqua or hydrophobia	water
arachnophobia	spiders

astraphobia	lightning
aviophobia	flying
brontophobia	thunder
claustrophobia	closed or small places
cynophobia	dogs
demonophobia	demons (suffered by some children at Halloween)
electrophobia	electricity (especially from getting a shock)
ergophobia	work
equinophobia	horses
ereuthophobia	blushing
genophobia	sex
graphophobia	writing
gynophobia	women
hemophobia	blood
herpetophobia	lizards or reptiles
hodophobia	traveling
homophobia	homosexuals
hypnophobia	sleep
kakorrhaphiophobia	failure
logophobia or phonophobia	public speaking (The author is sure that this term doesn't apply to anyone taking this course. Not too much!)
microphobia	germs
mysophobia	dirt
numerophobia	numbers
nyctophobia	darkness or night
ochlophobia	crowds
ophidiophobia	snakes
pathophobia	disease
pyrophobia	fire
tachophobia	speed
thanatophobia	death
triskaidekaphobia	the number 13
xenophobia	strangers/foreigners

A Word from the Author

Hi! Since most people experience some type of phobia to some degree, even though they may hesitate to admit it at first, you might consider introducing this subject the next time you encounter a lull in the conversation at your next social engagement. The subject of phobias could also produce a most interesting, revealing, and enlightening class discussion. And don't forget to use the dictionary to learn the correct pronunciations of the words listed above.

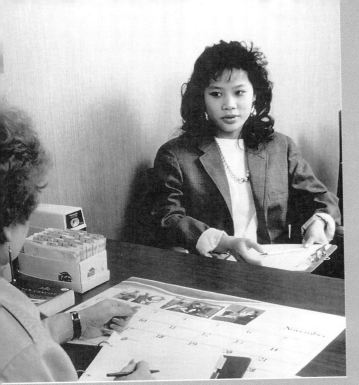

LET'S GO TO WORK

Too many job seekers expect other people to find a job for them. They don't do their homework. They don't evaluate what they have accomplished and figure out where their talent and experience might be most valuable.

Business Week, 23 March 1974, 73

After reading and understanding this chapter, you should know:

- What employers look for in applicants.

- How to "sell yourself" to a prospective employer.

- The most effective ways to find a job.

- How to set your job objectives.

- How to prepare a résumé.

- How to write an application letter.

- How to research a company before an interview.

- How to contact a company.

- How to prepare for a job interview.

- What to wear to an interview.

- How to handle yourself during an interview.

- How to discuss and negotiate a starting salary.

- How and when to ask for a raise.

- Which questions may be discriminatory and illegal.

- How to follow-up a job interview.

CHAPTER PREVIEW

This chapter is a culmination of the authors' combined 55 years of business experience, especially in regard to job searching and interviewing. Applying the suggestions in this chapter should help make you job hunt more efficient and productive.

Your first step in finding employment is to determine your objective, without limiting your marketability to one type of job. Second, prepare a one-page résumé that summarizes your education, experience, and capabilities. (Although résumés are primarily a writing task, this chapter on the interviewing process would not be complete without a brief mention of them, as well as of an application letter and a thank-you letter.)

Third, get job interviews and learn as much as possible about the companies that will interview you. Many ideas are given to help you land interviews and to find information on the companies.

The three phases of an interview—before, during, and after—are dealt with in depth. Numerous practical suggestions and cautions are presented, and they merit hard study. For example, an interviewer cannot legally ask about many aspects of your life, and you need not answer such questions.

The last topics discussed are the importance of dressing correctly, negotiating a starting salary, and asking for a raise.

Appearing in this (and every) chapter is the feature "In Other Words," which will greatly benefit foreign and ESL students. To aid in their understanding of common American idioms and phrases, these expressions will be defined in the margin of the page on which they are introduced.

In Other Words:

WORDS OF WISDOM

You've almost completed the course and many of you may soon embark on a new and exciting venture of seeking full-time employment. If this is your first such voyage, the thought of leaving the secure environment of the campus to enter the cold and competitive arena of the business world could be a little unsettling; but I'm sure that you're **up to it**. After all, isn't this exactly what you've been preparing for?

up to it—able to cope with the situation

At this point, I feel a lot like a concerned coach just before a crucial game—compelled to give his players a "pep" talk to bolster their spirits, to inflate their self-confidence, and to inspire them to excel in their expectations. So, before we actually get into the chapter, I think that you'll find it very helpful to review some of the highlights that you may have already covered regarding specific areas of verbal communication which, when applied, can be crucial during your job interview.

First, let's see what employers look for in speaking skills in applicants, then let's review how you can give them what they want. The most vital skill in getting any job is the ability to **"sell yourself."** You may possess excellent academic credentials and job experience, but unless this can be convincingly communicated to your interviewer, you've failed a critical test.

"sell yourself"— present your qualifications in a convincing manner

The ability to sell yourself

WHAT EMPLOYERS LOOK FOR

Fact: Employers look for people who can communicate in clear and understandable language and who are in command of a fairly good vocabulary.

Fact: Employers look for applicants who appear confident, poised, and orally persuasive.

Fact: Employers look for applicants who enjoy interacting with co-workers and who can intelligently express their views, opinions, and ideas.

Fact: Employers look for candidates who are conscious of current events: people who read newspapers and watch news programs and who can intelligently discuss *what's going on.*

what's going on— what is happening

Fact: Employers look for job seekers who are able to express exactly what type of job they're interested in, why they want to work for that company, and be able to explain certain goals and objectives they wish to achieve once they're hired.

Fact: Employers look for job candidates who can clearly state their value to the company.

Fact: Employers look for job applicants who not only have researched the company, but are comfortable discussing it.

Fact: Employers are always looking for prospective employees who are ENTHUSIASTIC. Being enthusiastic means speaking slightly faster, having noticeable inflection in your voice, occasionally smiling, being animated, using gestures and, of course, maintaining that all-important eye contact.

In other words, show and sound like you're genuinely happy to be there and you would love to work for that company.

in other words— saying it another way

HOW TO SELL YOURSELF TO A PROSPECTIVE EMPLOYER

Some of the oral skills you'll want to review and master in order to present yourself as a positive, confident, and persuasive candidate include.

- Be sure to speak with inflection and not in a monotone. A colorful delivery sparks interest and creates a positive image.
- Be sure to speak in complete sentences without any unnecessary pauses or hesitations, which convey a lack of credibility.
- Speak in a firm and deliberate tone to convey authority.
- Be sure to enunciate and articulate all syllables within a word as well as word endings.

- Be sure to *drop* your voice at the end of sentences to sound confident. (This is especially directed to women.)
- Be sure to pronounce words correctly. Think before you speak.
- Avoid slang and clichés. They indicate a lack of vocabulary.
- Refrain from the constant use of words and phrases such as: "OK," "You know," "wicked," "awesome," "cool," "well," "right," and "super."
- Be careful not to use sexist language. Instead of policeman, fireman, and mailman; say police officer, firefighter, and mail carrier. And remember that not all elementary school teachers, nurses, secretaries, and flight attendants are women and not all doctors, lawyers, airline pilots, and heavy equipment operators are men. (See Appendix C for a list of common sexist words and their suggested nonsexist alternatives.)
- Keep your words and sentences short to be better understood.
- Don't speak too slow or too fast.
- Use as many concrete and dynamic words as possible. (See the lists of action words that appear later in this chapter.)
- Keep your eyes on the interviewer to show your interest.
- As you speak flash an occasional smile to convey warmth and friendliness.
- And, whenever you open your mouth be sure to . . . Speak With Confidence.

SOME WAYS TO FIND A JOB

These are the most common ways to find a job:

1. A friend tells you there's an opening at work and, if you're interested, he or she could set up an interview.
2. Someone tells you that Arthur's Restaurant is looking for waitstaff. You telephone and are asked to come in for an interview.
3. You read an advertisement that representatives of a certain company will be in town, and if you're interested, you're to call for an interview.
4. A close relative owns a company and offers you a position—no interview required!
5. You contact your college placement office.
6. You contact state and private employment agencies.
7. You consult your computer. With the explosion of the World Wide Web (www) listing thousands of career-related sites on the Internet, an invaluable source for job listings is literally at your fingertips. But, remember, this option could be extremely time-consuming and expensive if you don't know exactly what you're looking for (unless, of course, you use the library). You want to be

as specific as possible in your search before tapping out on your keyboard or manipulating your mouse. The more precise the keyword, the more efficient your effort will be. A visit with your campus or local public librarian could be immensely productive. Some web sites for use when job searching might include, Career-Builder, CareerMart, CareerSite, E.Span, IntelliMatch, and 4Work.com.

No matter how you learn of a job opening, you are likely to be engaged in one or more interviews before you make a final decision. Just as in preparing a speech, the more you prepare for an interview, the better your chances for success will be.

SET YOUR JOB OBJECTIVES

According to a national expert on career planning, employers say that the number-one problem with people coming in for their first job is that they don't know what kind of position they're looking for.[1] On the basis of your education and experience, you should know what type of work you

[1]Peggy J. Schmidt, "That First Job: Finding it and Getting Ahead," *U.S. News & World Report*, 6 July 1981, 67–68.

wish to pursue. It may be to your advantage to broaden your range of choices. If, for example, you're interested in becoming a police officer, don't confine your search exclusively to police departments. If there are no openings there, you may consider private investigative work or positions in a penal institution or in industrial and commercial security. By accepting a job in an allied field, you'll shorten your job-hunting time and make yourself more versatile.

During your job interview, you may be told that the position you're specifically applying for has been filled and asked if you would consider a related position. Even though you might be disappointed, it may be wise to consider the second option because (1) you may get the job, (2) after you prove yourself, that job may enhance your opportunity for upward mobility, and (3) if you're not happy with your job, at least you're working and it's much easier job searching while employed than unemployed.

How to Prepare a Résumé

A **résumé** is a one- or two-page (preferably one-page) summary of your qualifications. It is your "ad," your foot in the door. It can either get you an interview of land in the wastebasket.

A résumé serves a twofold purpose: (1) It is a significant communication between you and your potential employer. (2) It can be helpful when you're filling out a job application, especially for dates, a list of jobs held, and your social security number.

Whether you're offered a position might depend on how well you prepare your résumé. It is important that a résumé present all necessary, pertinent information clearly and neatly.

What Information to Include in Your Résumé

The following elements usually comprise a résumé: personal data, job objectives, educational background, work experience, community activities, military service, and perhaps references.

Personal Data   Give your name and address (include zip code), telephone number (include area code), date of birth (not required legally), and marital status (also not required).

Job Objectives   Name the position you're seeking. If you don't have a specific position in mind, then be general.

Educational Background   Include the schools you've attended and years of graduation, your major and minor fields of study, your degrees, any certificates or awards received, and activities you engaged in. Start with the most recent schooling first. If you ranked scholastically in the top quarter of your graduating class, state that fact; otherwise, don't.

Work Experience   List the more recent jobs you've held (full-time and part-time). Include dates, responsibilities, achievements, and any suggestions or improvements you contributed.

When describing your job duties in your résumé, use as many action verbs as possible, such as:

achieved	directed	originated
administered	documented	performed
analyzed	expedited	persuaded
coordinated	generated	planned
conceived	implemented	produced
conducted	increased	proposed
decreased	initiated	recommended
delegated	launched	reduced
demonstrated	managed	researched
designed	monitored	saved
developed	motivated	solved
devised	organized	supervised

More and more larger companies are using computers to scan résumés and store their data for future reference. These computers are programmed to "sight search" for "key words" that are directly job-related so it's important to include on your résumé a generous helping of such nouns or "key words," which the computer will instantly recognize. For example:

- If you're applying for a position in the travel industry, you'd want to include such nouns as travel, booking, ticketing, schedule, documents, itinerary, reservations, and confirmation.
- For an accounting position, you may want to include accounting, payroll, accounts receivable, accounts payable, quarterly reports, audits, and billing.
- As an applicant for an administrative assistant position, the following words should catch the computer's eye (and memory): telephone, computer, software, word-processing, correspondence, FAX and copy machines, meetings, confidential, and executive.
- For a job in the advertising/marketing area, you'd want to include on your résumé words like advertising, marketing, schedule, buying, demographics, copy, production, proposal, presentation, print media, electronic media, client, logo, trade, and slogans.

Obviously, action verbs are important for sentence flow and impact when being read by the human eye, but, also remember that job-related descriptive nouns on your résumé can be most appealing to the "electronic" eye. Be sure to visit your college's career services center for any assistance you may need in résumé preparation.

Community Activities   You may list organizations and clubs to which you belong and any offices you held.

Military Service   Military experience is especially important if your job or your training in the military service relates to or supports your job objectives. Be sure to include any awards, commendations, and the type of discharge or separation received.

References   If you are asked for references, supply their names; otherwise, state that their names are available on request. Be sure to get permission from your references in order to avoid embarrassment. Give your references copies of your résumé so that they'll know your qualifications.

How to Produce Your Résumé

Once you have compiled your information, show it to someone who knows how a résumé should be set up and ask for constructive criticism. If you do not type well, have a competent typist type the résumé and then have clear photocopies made.

You may also visit your local copy or quick-print center and have your résumé produced on a desktop publishing system. Most quick-print shops can show you several standard formats from which to choose. A professionally designed computer-set résumé will attract more favorable attention than a typed one.

If you're into computers, and you should be, there's no reason why you can't produce a professionally prepared résumé. Between what's already in your computer and the large selection of software and CD-ROMs available, your toughest decision just may be deciding which format to use.

Production of your résumé can be a crucial factor. For example, presenting your résumé on off-white (or pastel, light blue or gray) paper instead of on plain white can increase *its* chances of being noticed and *your* chances of landing a particular job tenfold, according to Walter Lowen, one of the nation's leading personnel experts.

As mentioned earlier, résumés may take many formats; Figure 16.1 and Figure 16.2 show two acceptable formats.

WRITE AN APPLICATION LETTER

When you mail your résumé, be sure to paper-clip a short **application** (cover) **letter** to it. This letter should tell your prospective employer two things: what you have to offer the company and why you feel you're qualified for the position. (See Figure 16.3.)

Walter A. Bryant

88 North Central Avenue • Greensboro, NC 27410 • (919) 555-1936

Job Objective

To work in the office of comptroller or treasurer of a small manufacturing organization in order to qualify for general management responsibilities.

Education

1995 to 1997

Central Piedmont Community College, Charlotte, NC. Received Associate's Degree, June 1997. Majored in Business Administration with several courses in economics, including industrial organization and public policy. Was president of Delta Kappa Epsilon fraternity. Financed expenses partially through scholarship, summer jobs, and part-time work as a sorter at the First National Bank Computer Center, Charlotte, NC.

Experience

1999 to Present

Barbara Callaway Investment, Inc., Greensboro, NC 27410. Security Analyst: Report to Director of Research. Duties involve analyzing current stock issues and industry trends, preparing weekly market letter for customers, and writing reports on specific stocks or situations as requested by partners.

Summer Work

Summer jobs during college years included camp counselor, construction laborer, and carpenter's helper.

Military Service

1997 to 1999

U.S. Marine Corps. On graduation from college, entered Marine Officer Candidate School, Camp Lejeune, NC. After completing four-month program, was commissioned 2nd lieutenant and assigned to U.S. embassy in Rome as security officer. I was responsible for a 15-person 24-hour security force assigned to protect the embassy and its grounds. Received commendation and was released from active duty in June 1999.

Interests

Swimming, tennis, music, and photography.

References

Available on request.

Figure 16.1 Sample Résumé of a Student with Diversified Experience

Patty Kaitlyn
1994 Seventh Avenue
South Boston, MA 01993
(617) 246-8101

Professional Goal   To become a high school teacher of
computer science and programming.

Education
1996 to 2000   Regis College, B.S. in Business
Administration, with a major in marketing
and minor in computer science. Graduated
with high honors. Extracurricular activities:
Senior Class President, President of
Speech Club, and Public Information
Director of campus daycare center.

Work Experience
Summers   AT&T, Boston. I started as an intern in the
1997 to 1999   management training program. During the
second summer, I was promoted to
Assistant to the Director of the Northeast
Marketing Division.

Summers and   Eva Bot'Elle Fashions, Newton, MA.
Weekends   I worked in sales.
1995 to 1996

References   The above two companies

Figure 16.2 Sample Résumé of a Student with Limited Experience

---

The main objective of your application letter is to interest the reader
to the point that you will be invited for an interview. Never start this letter with "To Whom It May Concern," "Dear Sir," or "Dear Ms.," unless
you're answering a blind ad (an ad that instructs you to reply to a PO box
number or address instead of to an individual). Remember, whenever
possible, it's your responsibility to find out who will receive your letter
and address it to that person. This information will also be useful in your
follow-up phone call.

November 3, 1998

Mr. Albert W. James
Personnel Supervisor
Midwest Telephone Company
85 North Central Avenue
Chicago, IL 60603

Dear Mr. James:

In reference to your advertisement in the Quincy
Sun on November 1 for a junior accountant, I am
enclosing my résumé.

In college I majored in accounting and finance and
ranked in the top ten percent of my class. I also
worked as an accountant for three summers and
part-time during my last two years of college. I
feel confident that my education and experience
qualify me for the position.

I would appreciate an opportunity to discuss this
position with you, and I will phone you in a few
days to arrange an interview at your convenience.

                    Sincerely,

                    Nancy Shea
                    37 Rangeley Street
                    Chicago, IL 60603

Figure 16.3 Sample Application Letter

RESEARCH THE COMPANY AND POSITION

Finding out as much as possible about a company and the position you seek can pay off for you during the interview. How old is the company? What products or services does it provide? What is its geographical area of sales? If it has branch offices, where are they? Is the company growing or standing still? (Refer to the text on research in Chapter 7.)

If you're looking for a specific position (for example, sales), you may want to know the present size of the company's sales staff. How much

Try to learn as much as possible about the company.

traveling is involved? How large is the average territory? As a new member of the sales staff, will you be selling the whole line of products or just a portion of it? What is the company's promotion policy—is it usually from within the company or does the company bring in outsiders? What are your chances for advancement?

The more you know about the company and the position, the better you'll be able to respond during the interview. If you can't find all the answers you'd like to have, ask questions when the right opportunity occurs during the interview. Informed questioning will demonstrate that you *did your homework* and are genuinely interested in the company.

Many sources of information are available about your prospective employer and the position you seek—for example, the public library and the college placement office and library, as well as company folders, newsletters, magazines, and annual reports. If possible, talk to employees, visit a brokerage office, and look through business publications and the business section of your newspaper.

No question, browsing the World Wide Web (www) using CD-ROM indexes, or searching an online database can supply enormous amounts of information useful for company research. Again, if necessary, visit your campus or local public library for any assistance in locating specific electronic information sources.

did your home-work—are thoroughly prepared

Contact the Company

Now that you know the direction in which you're heading, it's time to contact the company and arrange an interview. You have two courses of action: conventional and unconventional.

Conventional

You can mail your résumé and application letter either to the Human Resources office or to the appropriate individual responsible for hiring. You can appear in person with your résumé to inquire of possible openings, or you can telephone the Human Resources office. Other means of communication could be by FAX or E-mail.

Unconventional

Perhaps you have a friend already working for the company who may be able to deliver your résumé and say some good words on your behalf. Any action on your behalf by a contact within the company can expedite matters and *give you an edge* over the competition.

give you an edge—give you an advantage

Job Interviews

While job searching, your day could be considerably brightened by a company's invitation to come in for an **interview.**

You've Been Granted an Interview

You'll be notified of your forthcoming interview by telephone, by letter, or by your company contact. Be sure to write down the exact time, date, place (specific building or office), and the correct name (and its pronunciation) of the person you're to meet. You'll find it useful to take along a pen and a small notebook.

You should put together some questions you may wish to ask at the appropriate time during the interview. Remember that it will be a conversation in which both of you will participate, even though the interviewer will most likely take the initiative, at least in the beginning. Your questions may run something like this: What exactly would my duties be? Is there a probation period, and if so, how long is it? When is the starting date? What are the company's prospects? What would be my chances for advancement? Does the company have an educational program for self-development? The interviewer may answer some or all of these questions during the interview, but if not, then you ask them.

How to Dress for the Interview

What you wear to the interview can play a significant role in your creating a positive first impression. As you learned in Chapter 3 (on nonverbal communication), you transmit messages even before you say a word. Interviewers receive an impression of you as soon as they see you, and if you neglect your appearance, they may assume that you will neglect your work. Don't take chances with your image.

In a survey of over one-hundred top executives of major corporations, 84 percent said they turned down people who dressed improperly for job interviews; 96 percent answered that their firm's employees had a much better chance of getting ahead by dressing well; and 72 percent indicated they would hold up the promotion of a person who didn't dress properly.[2]

Guidelines for attire may vary from company to company or from one state to another, but generally it is wise to dress conservatively and not wear anything that would boldly call attention to you.

A woman should consider either a tailored suit in a neutral shade with a neutral-colored tailored blouse or a blazer and skirt with a tailored blouse. Wear a simple, well-groomed hairdo and avoid gaudy jewelry, excessive make-up, revealing clothes, and strappy shoes. Keep away from vibrant and clashing colors. Wearing a watch could signal your interviewer that you're aware of the importance of time.

A man should select a tailored, well-fitting, conservative suit in a neutral or dark color and a white or light blue shirt with a straight, spread, or buttoned-down collar. His tie should be either striped or small-patterned, but conservative. Don't mix clashing colors, and avoid plaids and checks. Don't overlook important "messages" from your grooming such as clean, manicured fingernails and polished shoes.

The Day of Your Interview

When the big day finally arrives, you'll probably be nervous—a normal reaction. Just remember that you've come a long way from your first talk in class. You've done your homework, you're confident, and you know what you want. You're ready. The following are some helpful suggestions:

1. Plan to arrive five or ten minutes early. Sitting in the reception area and reading or talking with the receptionist or secretary may relax you and may provide additional information about the company.
2. If you're asked to bring additional information (references or another copy of your résumé), put them in a briefcase, large folder, or manila envelope. Don't fold them or stuff them into your purse or pocket.

---

[2]John T. Molloy, *Dress for Success* (New York: Warner Books, 1982), 36.

You're probably nervous.

3. Be sure to have a pen or two in case you're asked to fill out additional forms, and don't forget a notebook.

The moment of truth has arrived. The administrative assistant or receptionist announces, "Mr. Bryant will see you now. Go right in." Or the interviewer may come out to greet and escort you into the office. Your job interview has begun.

The interviewer plans to find out as much about you as possible. Since the task will be simpler if you're relaxed, the interviewer will most likely try to put you at ease quickly. After the initial introduction ritual (shaking hands firmly and offering you a seat), the interviewer may ask if you'd like a cup of coffee. When it arrives, if there's no napkin with it, tear a sheet of paper from your notebook and put the cup on it. By not placing your cup of coffee on the interviewer's desk or other furniture, you automatically gain a few points. Your notebook will serve additional purposes, as you'll see later.

The purpose of the job interview is twofold: (1) The interviewer has a position to fill with the best qualified individual in terms of education, intelligence, ambition, imagination, appearance, dependability, and moral character. (2) You want to convince the interviewer you are that individual.

Your Nonverbal Behavior During the Interview

What you do during the interview may be just as important as what you say and how you say it. Here are ten points to ponder:

1. Maintain the **communication cycle.** Focus your eyes and mind on the interviewer and when he or she speaks, listen. If a reply is in order, respond. Total concentration will pay dividends.
2. Avoid distractions. The office may be laden with many interesting objects (on the interviewer's desk, on shelves, on walls, and so on). Although they may make for interesting conversation, remember that the primary purpose of your visit is to be interviewed, not to chat about curios. Obviously, if the situation calls for you to comment on an interesting piece, keep the comment brief. Don't digress from the main reason for your visit.
3. If you're sitting on a sofa or soft easy chair, don't relax into the contours or stretch out. While seated, don't fidget or change positions often because it can be distracting.
4. If you brought a briefcase or manila envelope, place it on your lap or beside your chair, not on a desk or table.
5. Keep your shoes away from furniture.
6. Keep hands away from your hair and face. Constantly brushing hair aside from your eyes may annoy the interviewer.
7. If there's a confidential folder or papers on the interviewer's desk that look interesting, mind your own business!
8. Don't smoke.
9. Don't play with your tie clip or tie, necklace, earrings, or other pieces of clothing or jewelry.
10. Don't chew gum or anything else.

The Verbal Side of the Interview

At this point you should review Chapters 5, 10, and 15.

Although you may be sitting during the interview, *"be on your toes"* for a question (or two or three) that might *catch you off guard.* It's not unusual for an interviewer to *toss at you* one or more of the following questions. (To help you prepare for the "unexpected," I've included some possible responses for you to *mull over.*)

1. *"O.K., Nancy, what can we do for you?"* This type of question is a good *ice breaker,* in that the interviewer will probably be just as interested in your immediate reaction as she or he would be in your response. You might *come back with* something like, "First of all, I want to thank you for granting me this interview. I am applying for the position of Developmental Editor, which I saw advertised in the *San Diego Chronicle.* From the job description in

"be on your toes"—be alert, be prepared

catch you off guard—find you unprepared

toss at you—ask you

mull over—think about

ice breaker—a good way to start

come back with—reply with

Don't be too relaxed.

the ad, which I have with me, I feel that I have the qualifications and skills for that position."

2. *"Why do you want to work for us?"* Your reply could greatly benefit from your research of the company and/or from **firsthand** information from friends or contacts who may work there. For example, "A couple of things really impress me about your company. Although you're one of the largest software companies in the country, I recently read in *Business Week* that you plan to expand to foreign markets, which interests me. Also I particularly like the fact that it's your company's policy to **promote from within.**" (Mentioning the fact that you recently read about the company in a national business magazine is, indeed, a plus in your favor.)

3. *"Tell me something about yourself."* Remember what you read about "brevity." As tempted as you might be to "chronicle" your life history, here's an excellent opportunity to display your oral skills in highlighting and summarizing some key accomplishments. If the interviewer wants more information he or she won't hesitate to ask follow-up questions. You might answer this inquiry by saying, "I've always enjoyed being a student and being involved in student activities. In college, not only did I maintain a 3.5 average, but I was responsible for increasing the memberships in the Computer and Public Speaking Clubs. I helped pay my tuition by working a couple of nights a week, weekends and summers at Computer Land as a sales clerk. I thoroughly enjoy interacting not only with my co-workers but with customers, as well."

firsthand—direct

promote from within—promote from among those who are presently working there

a great opener—a good opportunity

"sound all your trumpets"—emphasize all your positive qualities

overdo it—do it to excess

"throws"—catches unprepared, confuses

4. *"What is your greatest strength?"* Here's **a great opener** to *"sound all your trumpets,"* but be careful not to **overdo it.** No one is impressed with a braggadocio or an egotist. You might respond with, "I feel my greatest strength is accepting whatever assignment is handed me and to complete that assignment to the best of my ability and as quickly as possible. I take great pride in completing jobs that I have started."

5. *"What major weakness do you have?"* This common question *"throws"* a lot of job applicants because no one wants to confess to having any faults. We all have weaknesses because we're human. Someone once said, "If we had no faults, we would not take so much pleasure in noticing them in others," which is true. Obviously, you don't want to say anything that could hurt you like, "Well, to be honest with you, I find it very hard getting up in the morning and, as a result, I'm often late." A more positive response might be, "Many of my colleagues tell me that I'm somewhat of a perfectionist, which means it usually takes me a little longer to complete assignments. But, frankly, I strongly feel that although it may take longer to get something done, I really try to get the job done "right" the first time. However, I am trying to work faster and not sacrifice quality."

6. *"Why should we hire you?"* A good reply might be, "Because I like your company. I like the fact that you're still growing and I would like to grow with you. With growth comes opportunities, I like that. I like to work and I like to learn . . . and I am not a clock watcher. With my education, experience, and enthusiasm I know

"My major weakness is that I'm financially challenged and employment impaired."

that I can be a benefit to your company." (And, besides, I need a job.)

7. *"Tell me exactly what you're looking for."* There's nothing wrong with being brief and direct. "I'm looking for the position that I'm being interviewed for. My education and experience convince me that I can do the job. I hope that I can convince you."

8. *"Where do you see yourself five years from now?"* Again, researching the company or talking to some friends who are presently employed there could help your response considerably. Ask yourself, "What would be a realistic goal in this time frame?" If you were applying for a position in the personnel department, don't try to impress your interviewer by smugly stating, "In five years I hope to be sitting in your chair." Your interviewer may not be planning to vacate his or her chair in five years . . . and you may **come across** as too pushy. A better reply might be, "In five years I would hope to have demonstrated my commitment and ability to perform my job well enough to be accepted into your Management Training Program where I would earn a position with more responsibilities and opportunities for leadership."

come across—appear to be

9. *"Tell me of some of your accomplishments at school."* Again, here's your opportunity to highlight some of your achievements without sounding conceited. You might reply, "Needless to say, I'm very proud of the fact that I maintained a 3.5 average while working about twenty hours a week and was still able to participate in several student activities including the college newspaper. Another thing that gave me great satisfaction was being a volunteer tutor and aide in the college's writing lab during my junior and senior years."

10. *"What do you consider a fair starting salary?"* The question of money or one's worth is always a difficult one, especially, for first-time job seekers. But, it needn't be. Remember, the company's goal is to hire a person for as *little* as possible and your goal is to receive from the company as *much* as possible. That's business. Obviously, the company is in a much better position. A fairly good reply might be, "I'm sure that you can appreciate how difficult that question is to answer, especially from the standpoint of someone who's looking for a job. I have no idea if you have a minimum–maximum range for entry-level positions, a basic starting salary, or if the salary is negotiable. I, therefore, can only rely on the fairness of your company's policy on starting wages and, perhaps, your recommendation. If the starting salary isn't negotiable, I'd be willing to consider your recommended offer."

This type of response lets the interviewer know that you know you're at a disadvantage, but at the same time letting him or her know that you're willing to have the company make a fair and reasonable offer. (More on talking money appears in the next section.)

"My accomplishments at school? Funny you should ask."

In my many years as a job seeker and Oral Communication Consultant, I have found the responses to the preceding ten questions effective. Read them over again, perhaps several times, and don't hesitate to vary or adapt them to your own personality and style. And remember to Practice, Practice, Practice.

Worth Remembering

turn off—cause to lose (someone's) interest

According to a number of interviewers, many job applicants just don't listen to the questions asked and frequently provide responses to questions not asked. Nothing will *turn off* an interviewer quicker than an applicant who doesn't listen and respond directly to questions asked. Remember:

- Don't digress.
- Don't offer more information than is necessary.
- Don't supply information that is not germane (Do you have your dictionary handy?) to the specific topic being discussed.

---

how you handle yourself—what your reaction will be

A practical way to prepare for these questions is to ask yourself this question: If you were in the interviewer's place, what answers would impress you? The reason you may be confronted with such questions is that the interviewer wants to see *how you handle yourself*. Although most interviewers don't ask more than one or two such questions, you'd be wise to prepare answers to them, since there is no way of knowing which ones you'll be asked. A popular approach is for the interviewer to ask a question about current events. A person who's interested in what's happening in the world will probably be interested in the company and in the job.

Here are some other topics and questions you should be prepared to answer:

- Place of birth and where you grew up
- Schools attended, courses of study, favorite subjects
- Why you selected the schools and what extracurricular activities you engaged in
- Do you want to continue your education?
- Did you work while going to school and to what extent?
- Military service and present status
- What do you know about the company?
- Your immediate and long-range goals
- Do you know anyone who works for the company?
- Present occupation and why you left other jobs
- What specific job do you want?
- A question or two about politics and current events
- Do you have any hobbies?
- Do you like to travel?
- Are you willing to relocate?
- Are you involved in community activities and to what extent?
- What can you do for the company?
- How much money do you need as a salary?

Let's Talk Money

For some strange reason many people, including some employment counselors, consider the discussion of salary during an interview as risky and questionable. It shouldn't be, because most people work for one reason—to earn money.

Most companies usually classify positions with specific job descriptions, including minimum and maximum salary ranges. It's only natural for an employer to try to hire someone for as little as possible. That is business.

During your first interview, the chances are slim that the subject of salary will emerge. If the company representatives are interested in you, they'll ask you to return for a second interview; then they may offer you the position and announce the starting salary. At this point you can either accept the figure or try to negotiate a higher one. If you feel confident and *have good vibes* about the situation, then *shoot for* the higher salary.

Let the person know that you want the job, that you can do it well, and that you would be an asset to the department and the company. There's nothing wrong in asking if the salary offered is entry level or if the position carries a minimum and maximum salary range. You could state that, based on your academic credentials and previous job experience, you were hoping for a higher starting salary—and name a figure.

have good vibes—to feel good and confident

shoot for—try to get

Some individuals may find it more comfortable, if they're offered a position and a figure, to simply ask, "Is the salary negotiable?" If the answer is no—then, that's it. Obviously, whatever strategy you choose will depend on how much you want and need the job.

During your negotiations, explore the company's policy regarding raises, promotions, vacations, medical and dental coverage, and other fringe benefits, such as tuition reimbursement, profit sharing, and 401-Ks (if they haven't already been discussed). There's a good chance these may more than compensate for a lower starting salary.

close the door on yourself—eliminate yourself from consideration

And be careful not to *close the door on yourself.* Don't say things like "Although I would like the job, I must have more money" or "I couldn't take the job at that low figure." Always leave room for possible negotiations.

Some Questions That May Be Illegal or Discriminatory

Since passage of the Age Discrimination in Employment Act of 1967, Title VII of the Civil Rights Act of 1964, the Equal Pay Act of 1963, and executive orders related to such legislation, an interviewer must be very cautious about his questions.

Any questions pertaining to age, sex, color, race, religion, or national origin could be discriminatory and unlawful. Other topics that may be il-

"With all the lovely fringe benefits we offer, you'll have very little need for money."

licit include questions about your marital status, spouse, dependents, credit status, home ownership, personal savings, experiences with the law and litigations, questionable experiences while in the military, present salary, bondability, and health problems or handicaps. If such questions are asked and the applicant is not hired, the applicant could file a complaint at the local office of the Commission Against Discrimination or the Equal Employment Opportunity Commission. Prior to a job interview, it would be wise to make an appointment with your school's Career Development or Job Placement office for guidance in this *ticklish area.*

ticklish area— very sensitive or controversial subject

The Interviewer's Approach

The interviewer will probably use one of the following approaches.

1. He or she may do most of the talking and questioning to see how you respond. Your poise, patience, and immediate reaction to questions, as well as how well you handle difficult ones, will be carefully observed.
2. He or she may say very little so that the burden of sustaining the interview will be on you. This approach is the most difficult for the new job seeker, but the interviewer may be looking for someone who is determined and well prepared and who can communicate intelligently.
3. He or she may employ a give-and-take technique in which both of you contribute equally to the conversation.

How to Behave During the Interview

The way in which you behave, verbally and nonverbally, during the interview may or may not clinch the job for you. The following tips may help ensure your success.

1. Try not to respond to questions with one- and two-word answers. An average reply should be between one and two minutes long. Occasionally, however, a yes or no answer is perfectly acceptable.
2. Your answers should contain only the information sought by the question. One exception would be some valuable information that would benefit your cause and that you hadn't yet had the opportunity to mention. If the questioning allows you to *slide in* the information without being too obvious, do it. For example, if you were asked about part-time employment and you wanted to mention that you paid for 80 percent of your education, you could say something like "Yes, I feel that working while going to school is worthwhile. For some of us it is a necessity. I've worked nights and weekends during the school session and full-time during the summers. Not only did this work enable me to complete my education, but the experience was invaluable, especially for the position I'm now seeking."
3. Look for nonverbal signs. If the interviewer's eyes wander around the office or to some things on the desk, perhaps you've been

*slide in—*introduce, mention

rambling on without substance. Glancing at a clock or gathering papers together may indicate that the interviewer is about to terminate the interview. If the interviewer tilts the chair back while still looking at you, that could mean that he or she is interested in your response. Therefore, you should keep going.

4. When answering tough questions, it's permissible to pause a second or two to gather your thoughts. Then look the interviewer straight in the eye and respond as confidently as possible.

5. Never offer confidential information about a competitor for whom you worked. It could weaken your chances for employment because the interviewer may feel, and rightfully so, that you might reveal company secrets if you're hired. If you have any business or professional secrets, keep them locked up. If your prospective employer enters into this delicate area, he or she could be testing your integrity.

6. Don't criticize former employers. If you've had an unpleasant experience on a job, admit that it may have been a personality conflict and share some of the blame.

7. Be honest in your answers and careful in your exaggerations because the interviewer is a pro who may spot phony talk. Personnel specialists in the same area usually know one another on a first-name basis. If the interviewer doubts the truth of some of your statements, he or she can easily phone the personnel di-

Look for nonverbal signs.

rector of your former employer and check you out. "Honesty is the best policy" is still the best policy to practice.

8. Don't beg for the position. Don't say, "I'll do anything just to *get my foot in the door"* or "I'll work for nothing to get a start." Your interviewer may feel that if you're willing to work for nothing, that's all you may be worth. No respectable employer expects anyone to work for nothing.

get my foot in the door—obtain any job as a starting point

9. The last thing you need is an argument. If you find that you must disagree, be as tactful and as brief as possible. On the other hand, don't always agree just to be sociable.

10. If you're being considered by other companies, don't pressure your interviewer by comparing conditions and offers. Negotiate terms at your second meeting. If you *play games* during your initial interview, you could lose.

play games—act less than sincere, try to manipulate

11. Keep your options open. There's always a possibility that the interviewer might feel that you're better suited for another available position rather than the one you're applying for. Listen closely to all aspects of the other position because it may prove more challenging and rewarding than the original one.

12. If you're offered a position then and there and you have no doubts or questions, accept it and ask when you can start. If you have some doubts or would like to compare some of the other offers, then thank the interviewer for the offer but explain you'd like some time to think it over. Ask if you can call in a few days, and regardless of your decision, be sure to call at the appointed time. Requesting time to think over acceptance of a position is common. If the interviewer wants a definite answer immediately, you're faced with a major decision. Before the interview you might think about such a possibility so that you'll be prepared if a decision is expected. An immediate answer, however, is rarely requested. Almost all companies will give you up to a week to decide.

13. If you feel that the interview is not going well and that you're really *blowing it, don't give up.* Do your best and *keep your cool.* Many people tend to underrate themselves and be too self-critical. Have you ever taken an exam and felt that you did poorly, only to be pleasantly surprised later? It could happen again. Even if you did botch the interview, so what? You've gained valuable experience, and you'll have other opportunities.

blowing it—not doing well at all

keep your cool—continue to act calm and confident

14. No matter how much at ease your interviewer sets you, don't get overly chummy. Remember, putting you at ease and in a relaxed mood is one way the interviewer can see the real you. Always refer to the interviewer by Mr., Miss, Mrs., or Ms. Reply with a "yes sir" or "yes ma'am."

15. Be alert not to oversell yourself. If, either by facial expression or by words, the interviewer appears impressed with your qualifications, leave it at that. Don't ramble on and on about your abilities.

16. At the end of the interview you should be told when a decision will be made. If the interviewer doesn't tell you, ask. It's a reasonable request.
17. Before you leave, smile, shake hands (but only if the interviewer extends a hand first), and thank the interviewer for the chance to discuss the job.

Some Tips for Following Up the Interview

Now that the interview is behind you, can you sit down and relax? No, not yet. There are still things to do. For example:

jot down—write

1. At the earliest opportunity after leaving the office, take out your trusty little notebook and *jot down* notes and impressions you wish to remember. Since you may be invited back for a follow-up interview, these notes can play an important role at future meetings. In fact, keeping notes on all interviews should help you compare offers and make a final decision.
2. Should you send a thank-you note to the interviewer? Why not? It'll give you favorable attention and another opportunity to make a subtle pitch—"after having the opportunity of speaking with you and learning more about the company and the position, I'm more convinced about wanting to work for your company and making a contribution to it." Figure 16.4 shows an acceptable thank-you note.

follow-up—find out more

3. Would a telephone *follow-up* be proper? Certainly. Showing your further interest by a short phone call will, more often than not, make a positive impression. Do one or the other—a note or a phone call—but not both.
4. If you don't receive an offer, *don't get discouraged.* The more interviews you have, the more experience you'll acquire, and just by the law of averages, you're bound to find a job. Although the legendary Babe Ruth chalked up an enviable home run record, he also struck out often. It takes no talent to quit, but if you believe in yourself and your abilities and are determined to succeed, then you eventually will.

Your college placement office is there to help you and your career. Get to know the director and members of the staff. They have a great deal to offer you, but it is *you* who must take the initiative and it is *you* who must sell yourself. Good luck.

HOW ABOUT A RAISE?

Let's assume that you've been on the job ten months to a year and haven't received a pay increase. You feel that you should be getting more money and you decide to ask for a raise, but how and when should you do it?

```
                                    116 King Street
                                    Avon, MA 02173
                                    July 24, 1999


Mrs. Patricia Bitsy
Supervisor, Department of Nursing
Brian Walter Medical Center
Boston, MA 09111

Dear Mrs. Bitsy:

Thank you for the opportunity to meet with you
today to discuss one of the openings on your staff.

The position appeals to me very much and sounds
exactly like what I'm looking for. I am more eager
than ever to join your staff.

I appreciate your kind comments regarding my
qualifications and look forward to hearing from you.

                        Sincerely yours,


                        Evelyn Elisav
```

Figure 16.4 Sample Thank-you Note

Before you ask for a raise, be sure you've ***done your homework.*** Be prepared to justify your request with documented facts and figures. Being on time, never being absent, and doing a good job are not valid reasons for a raise. These qualities are expected of you and may very well prompt your boss to declare, "That's what you're getting paid to do."

done your home-work—prepared

On the other hand, if, during a special project, you've often stayed late in order to finish the job on time, if you're always willing to assist others to benefit the company, if you have established an impressive sales record, if you have exceeded your quota or your department's expectations of you, if you have displayed leadership qualities, if you have willingly accepted additional responsibilities, if you have either implemented or suggested to management ways to increase productivity—in other words, if your performance is above and beyond what is normally expected of you, then you would have a powerful case for a raise. But be sure to document all your facts and be prepared to state the amount of increase you feel you deserve. Be confident and realistic with your request or you may find yourself negotiating a starting salary with another company.

It may be worthwhile to find out what mood your boss is in before asking for a raise. Clearly, your chances would be better if he or she were in a positive mood. If you know that someone plowed into his or her new car on the way to work, postpone your visit.

In conclusion, ***keep in mind*** a couple of things regarding wages.

keep in mind—
remember

1. Very few workers (your author included) honestly feel that their salary represents the true worth of their labor and . . .
2. The less money that a company expends on its average employees, the more money it has for its executives and shareholders. And that's why it's so important to thoroughly understand the meaning and application of the words *compromise* and *negotiate*.

THINGS TO DISCUSS IN CLASS

1. If you haven't already done so, visit the placement office at your school and become familiar with its function.
2. Either from your audiovisual library or from the placement office, get and study a videotape or film on interviewing procedures and demonstrations.
3. Visit your school's placement office, gather the latest information on types of questions that should not be asked in an employment interview, and discuss them in class.

Find out what mood your boss is in.

4. Select a company that you'd like to work for and conduct some research on it. Discuss your findings in class.

5. Assume that you're currently working and you feel that you deserve a raise. Tell the class how you would approach this topic and what you would say to your boss.

6. Select a personal subject that you feel would be inappropriate to discuss with an interviewer. Explain to the class how you would handle this delicate situation if the interviewer raised the subject.

7. If the interviewer asked you questions about your previous employer, explain to the class what your response should be.

WHAT DO YOU REMEMBER FROM THIS CHAPTER?

1. What is a résumé and why is it important?
2. What is an application letter and what is its purpose?
3. When you research a company, what information should you look for?
4. What would be appropriate dress for you to wear to a job interview?
5. Should you prepare some questions to ask the interviewer? Explain.
6. List some important tips to keep in mind about your conduct during the interview.
7. What are some questions that could catch you off guard but that you should be prepared to answer?
8. What areas of questioning during an interview could be discriminatory and illegal?
9. What's a good policy to follow regarding criticism of former employers?
10. List two things to think about and do after the interview.
11. List three ways to find a job.
12. Explain two ways to contact a company to arrange for a job interview.

VITALIZE YOUR VOCABULARY

Economic and Financial

Here is a partial list of the most commonly used words you'll find when reading the business and financial sections of your newspaper or news magazine.

acquisition (n.) The purchase of one company by another.
balanced budget (n.) When receipts equal current expenditure.
balance of payments (n.) The difference between all payments made to and from foreign countries over a specific period of time based on imports and exports.

bear market (n.) A market in which prices are falling.

bond (n.) A written promise by an issuer to repay a fixed amount of borrowed money at a specified time.

bull market (n.) A market in which prices are rising.

capital gain or **loss** (n.) A profit or loss from the sale of assets such as stocks, bonds, or real estate.

common stock (n.) Share of ownership in a corporation that entitles you to vote.

conglomerate (n.) A large corporation consisting of many other different companies.

cost of living (n.) What a person or family spends on necessary goods and services such as food, clothing, and rent to maintain a certain standard of living.

deficit spending (n.) Government spending in excess of revenues.

depression (n.) An extended period of economic decline when unemployment is high, prices are low, and there are many business failures.

disposable income (n.) Personal income available to spend after taxes and expenses are paid.

dividend (n.) A sum that is paid by a company to shareholders in the form of cash or shares of stock.

Dow Jones Industrial Average (n.) An index of stock market prices, based on the prices of 30 leading companies on the New York Stock Exchange.

Federal Deposit Insurance Corporation (FDIC) (n.) A U.S. government–sponsored corporation that insures individuals up to $100,000 in any account they may have in a national bank or other financial institution.

full employment (n.) Theoretically, when everyone who wishes to work is gainfully employed.

golden parachute (n.) Provisions in the employment contracts of executives guaranteeing substantial financial benefits if they lose their positions due to a corporate takeover.

gross domestic product (GDP) (n.) The market value of all goods and services that have been bought for final use during a specific period of time. It is a measure of the economy.

individual retirement account (IRA) (n.) A self-funded retirement plan that allows employed individuals to contribute up to a maximum annual amount toward their retirement while deferring taxes until retirement.

inflation (n.) An increase in the level of prices resulting in a loss of currency value.

insider information (n.) Important facts about the condition or plans of a corporation that have not been released to the general public.

interest (n.) What you pay for borrowing money.

junk bonds (n.) Bonds that are issued by companies with low credit ratings and usually pay high interest rates because of their relatively high risk.

leading indicators (n.) A series of eleven indicators from different segments of the economy that the U.S. Commerce Department uses to predict when changes in the level of economic activity will occur.

liquid assets (n.) Assets that include cash or other things of value that can be easily converted to cash.

merger (n.) When two or more companies get together and operate as one.

money supply (n.) All of the currency held by the public, plus checking accounts in commercial banks and savings institutions.

mutual fund (n.) A portfolio of professionally and managed financial assets into which you pool your money along with thousands of other investors.

national debt (n.) The debt of the federal government.

prime interest rate (n.) The rate charged by banks on short-term loans to large commercial customers with the highest credit rating.

recession (n.) A period of economic decline when production, employment, and earnings fall below normal levels; usually lasts from six months to a year.

supply-side economics (n.) The belief that lowering income tax rates will inevitably lead to the increase of economic growth and the revitalization of the economy in general.

takeover (n.) Acquisition of one company by another company or group by sale or merger. When management is agreeable to this action, it is a "friendly takeover." When management is opposed to this action, it is an "unfriendly or hostile takeover."

A more complete listing of economic and financial terms can be found in *The 1999 World Almanac and Book of Facts* published by World Almanac Books.

APPENDIX **A**

SPEECHES TO STUDY

Here are six speeches for you to enjoy, study, and analyze. The first three are not only historical but are, indeed, excellent examples of true oratorical genius. They merit reading and digesting more than once. The fourth, by Mark Twain, is not only classic in its own right, but one with which you should easily be able to associate—the possible apprehension over giving your first talk. The fifth speech, by former First Lady Barbara Bush, appeared in Chapter 11 of the seventh edition. Because of its wonderful reviews and its "down-to-earth" contents, I've decided to include it again in this eighth edition. And, finally, President Bill Clinton's so-called contrition speech following his unprecedented sworn testimony before a Federal Grand Jury. On December, 19, 1998, the U.S. House of Representatives voted in favor of two of four articles of impeachment against President Clinton. The first alleging that he committed perjury in his August, 17, 1998 grand jury testimony and the second that he obstructed justice. Bill Clinton became only the second president and is the first in 130 years to face a legal trial in the U.S. Senate which began January 11, 1999. On Friday, February 12, 1999, the U.S. Senate voted to acquit President Clinton on the two articles of impeachment, permitting the president to complete his second term in office.

To further help you in the study and analysis of these speeches, each one, with the exception of the president's address, includes a sentence and topic outline along with its commentary.

GENERAL NORMAN SCHWARZKOPF

One of the truly great American speeches of this century was delivered by General H. Norman Schwarzkopf in May 1991 to the U.S. Congress. This 20-minute speech was "interrupted by applause 14 times, often with standing ovations"[1] because it was highly inspirational and emotional, especially when he answered the question "who were we?"—that is, who made up the American Armed Forces. Here is his blockbuster answer to that question: "We were men and we were women . . . Protestants and Catholics and Jews and Moslems and Buddhists . . . black and white and yellow and brown and red, and we noticed that when our blood was shed in the desert, it didn't separate by race."

Without question, this speech "stands by itself on a mountain-top" for several reasons: its inspirational content; its clear, down-to-earth language fortified with parallel structure and repetition; its facts about our Armed Forces; and the general's powerful delivery.

Here is his speech, as recorded in the *Congressional Record*.[2] Because the paragraphs in the *Congressional Record* are overly long, we've altered the paragraphing of the speech according to a nearly illegible copy of the speech received from the general's headquarters in Tampa, Florida. That copy also noted occasions of applause.

General Schwarzkopf's Speech to the U.S. Congress

1   (Applause) Mr. Speaker, members of Congress and distinguished guests. It's a great day to be a soldier and it's a great day to be an American. (Applause)

> The dramatic opening sentence grabs your attention instantly.

2   I want to thank you for the singular distinction of being allowed to speak to a special session of the Congress of the United States of America. Indeed, I am awed and honored to be standing at the podium where so many notable men and women have stood before me. Unlike them, I don't stand here today for any great deed that I have done. Instead, I stand here because I was granted by our national leadership the great privilege of commanding the magnificent American service men and women who constituted the armed forces of Operation Desert Shield and Desert Storm. (Applause)

3   And before I go any further, I must—through their representatives who are here today—tell each and every one of those extraordinary patriots that I have no idea what the future holds in store for me. But I do know one thing: I will never ever in my entire life receive a greater reward than the inspiration that I received every single day as I watched your dedicated performance, your dedicated sacrifice, your dedicated service to your country. (Applause)

> The general is very generous in giving credit to the service men and women who served in Operation Desert Shield and Desert Storm. We Americans admire a public figure who doesn't "hog" the limelight and take all the credit.

4   Since I was fortunate enough to command these great Americans and since you are the elected representatives of the

---

[1] *Boston Globe*, 9 May 1991, 23.
[2] *Congressional Record—House*, 8 May 1991, H2814.

American people, I would presume today to speak for our service men and women through you to the people of our great nation.

5   First of all, who were we? We were 541,000 soldiers, sailors, airmen, Marines, and Coast Guardsmen. We were the thunder and lightning of Desert Storm. We were the United States military and we're damn proud of it. (Applause)

6   But we were more than that. We were all volunteers. And we were regulars, we were reservists, we were national guardsmen serving side-by-side as we have in every war, because that's what the United States military is. And we were men and we were women, each of us bearing our fair share of the load and none of us quitting because the conditions were too rough or the job was too tough, because that's what your military is. And we were Protestants and Catholics and Jews and Moslems and Buddhists and many other religions fighting for a common and just cause, because that's what your military is. And we were black and white and yellow and brown and red, and we noticed that, when our blood was shed in the desert, it didn't separate by race; it flowed together. (Sustained applause) You see, that's what your military is.

7   And we fought side by side with brothers and sisters at arms who were British and French and Saudi Arabian and Egyptian and Kuwaiti and members of many other Arab and Western nations. And you know what? We noticed the same thing when their blood was shed in the desert. It did not separate according to national origin.

8   We left our homes, our families, and traveled thousands of miles away and fought in places with names we couldn't even pronounce, simply because you asked us to, and therefore it became our duty, because that's what your military does.

9   We now proudly join the ranks of Americans who call themselves veterans. We're proud to share that title with those who went before us. And we feel a particular pride in joining the ranks with that special group who served their country in the mountains and the jungles and the deltas of Vietnam. (Sustained applause) They served just as proudly in Vietnam as we served in the Middle East.

10   And now that we've won a great victory, we dare to ask that, just as we were willing to sacrifice and fight to win the war, you be willing to sacrifice and search to win the peace. (Applause)

11   We would like to offer our thanks. First, we'd like to thank our God for the protection He gave us in the deserts of Kuwait and Iraq. Most of us came home safely. We ask Him to grant a special love to all of our fallen comrades who gave their lives for the cause of freedom, and we ask that He embrace to his bosom not only the 147 of us who were killed in action, but also the 188 of us who gave their lives before the war, during Operation Desert Shield, and since the termination of Desert Storm. They, too, no less than our killed in action, died for the cause of freedom.

The general asked the question: "First of all, who were we?" It's the kind of question that arouses interest. His answer was striking— "We were the thunder and lightning of Desert Storm. We were the United States military and we're damn proud of it."

The general portrayed the U.S. military and made his points stick by using repetition. Four times he ended statements with the words, "because that's what your military is."

The general paid respect and recognition to the veterans of the Vietnam War who, when they returned home, were treated much differently. Many of the emotional and psychological wounds and scars of those veterans still fester.

The general thanked God "for the protection He gave us in the deserts of Kuwait and Iraq." This is an especially emotional paragraph.

12   We also ask that God grant special strength to our comrades who are still in the hospitals with wounds and injuries they received during the war. By their example, we should all remember that the freedoms we enjoy in this great country of ours do not come without a price. They are paid for and protected by the lives, the limbs, and the blood of American service men and women.

13   We would also like to thank our Commander-in-Chief for his wisdom and courage and the confidence he demonstrated in us by allowing us to fight this war in such a way that we were able to minimize our casualties. (Sustained applause) That is the right way to fight a war. (Applause)

More thanks, this time to our Commander-in-Chief, Congress, comrades who stayed behind, our families, and the American public. Again, a deeply emotional statement.

14   We'd like to thank the Congress and former administrations for giving us the finest tanks, the finest aircraft, the finest ships, and the finest military equipment in the whole world without question. (Applause) Without question, that is what gave us the confidence necessary to attack into the teeth of our enemy with the sure knowledge that we would prevail. And we would ask that in years to come, as we reduce the quantity of our armed forces, that you never forget that it is the quality of the armed forces that wins wars. (Sustained applause)

15   We want to say a special thanks to our comrades in uniform who stayed behind. You backed us up so we could carry the fight to the enemy. You maintained the peace so that we could win the war. We never could have done our job if you hadn't done yours.

16   We also want to thank the families. It's you who endure the hardships and the separations, simply because you choose to love a soldier, a sailor, an airman, a Marine, or a Coast Guardsman. But it's your love that truly gave us strength in our darkest hours. (Sustained applause) Military families are the wind beneath our wings.

17   Finally, and most importantly, to the great American people. The prophets of doom, the naysayers, the protesters, and the flag burners all said that you wouldn't stick by us. But we knew better. We knew you'd never let us down. By golly, you didn't! (Sustained applause) Since the first hour of Desert Shield until the last minute of Desert Storm, every day and every way, all across America you shouted that you were with us. Millions of elementary school, high school, and college students, millions and millions of families, untold numbers of civic organizations, veterans organizations, countless offices, factories, companies, and work places, millions of senior Americans, and just plain Americans never let us forget that we were in their hearts and you were in our corner. Because of you, when that terrible first day of the war came, we knew we would not fail. We knew we had the strength of the American people behind us, and with that strength, we were able to get the job done, kick the Iraqis out of Kuwait, and get back home. (Sustained applause)

A brief conclusion that is pure dynamite because of parallel construction.

18   So for every soldier, thank you America. For every sailor, thank you America. For every Marine, thank you America. For every airman, thank you America. For every Coast Guardsman, thank you America. From all of us who proudly served in the Middle East and your armed forces, thank you to the great people of the United States of America. (Sustained applause)

Sentence Outline of General Schwarzkopf's Speech to the U.S. Congress

Introduction

I. It's a great day.
II. Thank you for the privilege of speaking to you.
III. On behalf of the great Americans who fought in Operation Desert Shield and Desert Storm, I speak to the people of our great nation through you.

Body

I. Who were we?
   A. We were 541,000 soldiers, sailors, airmen, Marines and Coast Guardsmen.
   B. We were all volunteers; regulars, reservists, national guardsmen; men and women; members of many religions and races.
   C. When our blood was shed in the desert, it didn't separate by race or nationality.
   D. That's what your military is.
II. We went to the Persian Gulf because you asked us to.
   A. That's what your military does.
III. We proudly join the ranks of American veterans.
IV. Now we ask you to sacrifice and search to win the peace.
V. We would like to offer our thanks—to God; to our Commander-in-Chief; to Congress and former administrations; to our comrades who stayed behind; to our families.

Conclusion

I. But most of all, we offer our thanks to the great American people.
   A. You didn't let us down.
   B. We derived strength from your support.
II. From all who fought, thank you to the great people of the United States of America.

Topic Outline

Introduction

I. A great day
II. The privilege of speaking to you
III. Congress as representatives of the people

Body

I. Who we were:
    A. 541,000 soldiers, sailors, airmen, Marines and Coast Guardsmen.
    B. All volunteers:
        1. Regulars, reservists, national guardsmen
        2. Men and women
        3. Members of many religions and races
    C. No separation of blood by race or nationality
    D. What your military is
    E. Response to what you asked of us
    F. What your military does
II. American veterans now
III. Admonition to win the peace
IV. Thanks:
    A. To God
    B. To Commander-in-Chief
    C. To Congress and former administrations
    D. To comrades who stayed behind
    E. To our families

Conclusion

V. Above all, thanks to the great American people for:
    A. Support
    B. Strength
VI. Thanks from all who fought to the great people of the United States of America

JOHN F. KENNEDY

The following three speeches were also given by men who spoke with eloquence, confidence and effectiveness. The first speech, delivered by President John F. Kennedy in Berlin in 1963, also ranks among the best of this century. Kennedy had gone to Europe to support democracy and freedom and to strengthen our commitment to Western Europe. He spoke to the people and reached them most effectively. The title won audience goodwill and interest because it is in German. His entire speech—note how short it is—appears below, followed by the outlines.

"Ich Bin Ein Berliner"

1 I am proud to come to this city as the guest of your distinguished Mayor, who has symbolized throughout the world the fighting spirit of West Berlin. And I am proud to visit the Federal

JFK's pride in visiting Berlin and his compliments to the Mayor and Chancellor further intensify his hold on audience goodwill and interest. His assurance of American military aid, if necessary, gives his listeners a feeling of security.

His knowledge of history enables him to compare Berlin with Rome. He identifies with his listeners by using their language.

Here is the President of the United States, the most powerful man in the world, poking fun at his German accent and at the same time complimenting the interpreter. Europeans are not used to this kind of humor from heads of state.

The President admits that democracy has its faults, but it does not have to erect walls to keep people as prisoners. Another compliment to West Berlin.

The President builds up powerful emotional impact through repeating "Let them come to Berlin," in German.

Now JFK reaches out emotionally and touches people—husbands and wives, brothers and sisters, families.

Germans have earned the right to be free, to unite their families, and to live in peace. These ideas appeal to West Europeans. Note the transition to the conclusion. "So let me ask you, as I close, . . ."

Republic with your distinguished Chancellor who for so many years has committed Germany to democracy and freedom and progress, and to come here in the company of my fellow American, General Clay, who has been in this city during its great moments of crisis and will come again if ever needed.

2   Two thousand years ago the proudest boast was *"civis Romanus sum."* Today, in the world of freedom, the proudest boast is *"Ich bin ein Berliner."*

3   I appreciate my interpreter translating my German!

4   There are many people in the world who really don't understand, or say they don't, what is the great issue between the free world and the Communist world. Let them come to Berlin. There are some who say that communism is the wave of the future. Let them come to Berlin. And there are some who say in Europe and elsewhere we can work with the Communists. Let them come to Berlin. And there are even a few who say that it is true that communism is an evil system, but it permits us to make economic progress. *Lass' sie nach Berlin kommen.* Let them come to Berlin.

5   Freedom has many difficulties and democracy is not perfect, but we have never had to put a wall up to keep our people in, to prevent them from leaving us. I want to say, on behalf of my countrymen, who live many miles away on the other side of the Atlantic, who are far distant from you, that they take the greatest pride that they have been able to share with you, even from a distance, the story of the last 18 years. I know of no town, no city, that has been besieged for 18 years that still lives with the vitality and force, and the hope and the determination of the city of West Berlin. While the wall is the most obvious and vivid demonstration of the failures of the Communist system, for all the world to see, we take no satisfaction in it, for it is, as your Mayor has said, an offense not only against history but an offense against humanity, separating families, dividing husbands and wives and brothers and sisters, and dividing a people who wish to be joined together.

6   What is true of this city is true of Germany—real, lasting peace in Europe can never be assured as long as one German out of four is denied the elementary right of free men, and that is to make a free choice. In 18 years of peace and good faith, this generation of Germans has earned the right to be free, including the right to unite their families and their nation in lasting peace, with good will to all people. You live in a defended island of freedom, but your life is part of the main. So *let me ask you, as I close*, to lift your eyes beyond the dangers of today, to the hopes of tomorrow, beyond the freedom merely of this city of Berlin, or your country of Germany, to the advance of freedom everywhere, beyond the wall to the day of peace with justice, beyond yourselves and ourselves to all mankind.

7   Freedom is indivisible, and when one man is enslaved, all are not free. When all are free, then we can look forward to that day when this city will be joined as one and this country and this great continent of Europe in a peaceful and hopeful globe. When that day finally comes, as it will, the people of West Berlin can take sober satisfaction in the fact that they were in the front lines for almost two decades.

8   All free men, wherever they may live, are citizens of Berlin, and, therefore, as a free man, I take pride in the words *Ich bin ein Berliner.*

and the emotional buildup using parallel construction, "beyond . . . to . . . ." The President expresses hope for a better tomorrow.

He builds his conclusion on the idea of a better future. Another compliment to Berlin.

An extremely moving conclusion in German words, the title of the speech. Note the conciseness of the last paragraph.

Sentence Outline of John F. Kennedy's "Ich Bin Ein Berliner"

Introduction

    I. I am proud to be here as the guest of your mayor and to be with the Chancellor and General Clay.
    II. "Ich bin ein Berliner."

Body

    I. Let those who want to know about the Communists come to Berlin.
    II. America's freedom presents a marked contrast to communism.
    III. West Berlin remains a city of vitality and force, hope and determination.
    IV. The Berlin wall symbolizes the failures of the Communist system and is an offense against humanity.
    V. Germany deserves to be free and united.

Conclusion

    I. I ask you to lift your eyes to the advance of freedom everywhere.
    II. Freedom is indivisible.
    III. When this city and country are joined as one, its people can be proud of having been in the front lines for two decades.
    IV. "Ich bin ein Berliner."

Topic Outline

Introduction

    I. Pride in being here in the company of the Mayor, the Chancellor, and General Clay
    II. "Ich bin ein Berliner."

Body

  I. Berlin as place to learn about Communism
  II. Contrast between Communism and America's freedom
  III. Tribute to Berlin's vitality and force, hope and determination
  IV. Symbolic significance of Berlin
  V. Germany's need to be free and united

Conclusion

  I. Anticipation of the advance of freedom
  II. Indivisibility of freedom
  III. Anticipation of Berlin's pride when the city and country are united
  IV. "Ich bin ein Berliner."

Martin Luther King, Jr.

On August 28, 1963, one of the nation's most eloquent voices, on behalf of the Civil Rights Movement, mesmerized and inspired almost a quarter of a million black and white peaceful demonstrators who were gathered at the Lincoln Memorial in Washington, D.C. The purpose of this massive rally was to draw attention to the black demands for equality in employment and civil rights.

The speech, which follows, was delivered by Martin Luther King, Jr., the recognized leader of the nonviolent Civil Rights Movement who, in the same year, was named "Man of the Year" by *Time* magazine and a year later received the Nobel Peace Prize. His speech, "I Have a Dream," also ranks among the finest of this century. Here is the speech and analysis, followed by the outlines.

"I Have a Dream"[3]

King opens his speech with references to two historic occasions: the signing of the Emancipation Proclamation and the one hundredth anniversary of that action.

1 Five score years ago, a great American, in whose symbolic shadow we stand today, signed the Emancipation Proclamation. This momentous decree came as a great beacon of light of hope to millions of Negro slaves who had been seared in the flames of withering injustice. It came as a joyous daybreak to end the long night of their captivity.

2 But one hundred years later, the Negro still is not free. One hundred years later, the life of the Negro is still sadly crippled by the manacles of segregation and the chains of discrimination.

[3]Linkugel, Allen, Johannesen, *Contemporary American Speeches,* 3rd ed. (Belmont, CA: Wadsworth, 1972), 289–93.

3   One hundred years later, the Negro lives on a lonely island of poverty in the midst of a vast ocean of material prosperity. One hundred years later, the Negro is still languished in the corners of American society and finds himself an exile in his own land. So we have come here today to dramatize a shameful condition.

4   In a sense we have come to our nation's capital to cash a check. When the architects of our republic wrote the magnificent words of the Constitution and the Declaration of Independence, they were signing a promissory note to which every American was to fall heir. This note was a promise that all men, yes, black men as well as white men, would be guaranteed the unalienable rights of life, liberty, and the pursuit of happiness.

5   It is obvious today that America has defaulted on this promissory note insofar as her citizens of color are concerned. Instead of honoring this sacred obligation, America has given the Negro people a bad check, which has come back marked "insufficient funds."

6   But we refuse to believe that the bank of justice is bankrupt. We refuse to believe that there are insufficient funds in the great vaults of opportunity of this nation. So we have come to cash this check—a check that will give us upon demand the riches of freedom and the security of justice.

7   We have also come to this hallowed spot to remind America of the fierce urgency of now. This is no time to engage in the luxury of cooling off or to take the tranquilizing drug of gradualism. Now is the time to make real the promise of democracy. Now is the time to rise from the dark and desolate valley of segregation to the sunlit path of racial justice. Now is the time to lift our nation from the quicksands of racial injustice to the solid rock of brotherhood. Now is the time to make justice a reality for all of God's children.

8   It would be fatal for the nation to overlook the urgency of the movement and to underestimate the determination of the Negro. This sweltering summer of the Negro's legitimate discontent will not pass until there is an invigorating autumn of freedom and equality. 1963 is not an end but a beginning. Those who hope that the Negro needed to blow off steam and will now be content will have a rude awakening if the nation returns to business as usual.

9   There will be neither rest nor tranquility in America until the Negro is granted his citizenship rights. The whirlwinds of revolt will continue to shake the foundations of our nation until the bright day of justice emerges.

10   But there is something that I must say to my people who stand on the warm threshold which leads into the palace of justice. In the process of gaining our rightful place we must not be guilty of wrongful deeds.

11   Let us not seek to satisfy our thirst for freedom by drinking from the cup of bitterness and hatred. We must forever conduct our struggle on the high plane of dignity and discipline. We must

He employs through the next three paragraphs an extended metaphor of cashing a check ("promissory note") and carries it through its bouncing and the bank's being bankrupt.

He establishes a compelling tone of urgency to heighten the force of his demand for Negro equality.

He then issues a calming, counterbalancing appeal for restraint—not in the struggle but in the manner in which it is carried out—by denouncing "wrongful deeds."

not allow our creative protest to degenerate into physical violence. Again and again we must rise to the majestic heights of meeting physical force with soul force.

He avoids alienating whites by acknowledging that many of them support the Negro's cause.

12   The marvelous new militancy which has engulfed the Negro community must not lead us to a distrust of all white people, for many of our white brothers, as evidenced by their presence here today, have come to realize that their destiny is tied up with our destiny and they have come to realize that their freedom is inextricably bound to our freedom. This offense we share mounted to storm the battlements of injustice must be carried forth by a biracial army. We cannot walk alone.

13   And as we walk, we must make the pledge that we shall always march ahead. We cannot turn back. There are those who are asking the devotees of civil rights, "When will you be satisfied?" We can never be satisfied as long as the Negro is the victim of the unspeakable horrors of police brutality.

Continuing a kind of contrapuntal effect he then arouses the indignation of his audience by offering a series of examples of injustice suffered by Negroes.

14   We can never be satisfied as long as our bodies, heavy with the fatigue of travel, cannot gain lodging in the motels of the highways and the hotels of the cities. We cannot be satisfied as long as the Negro's basic mobility is from a smaller ghetto to a larger one.

15   We can never be satisfied as long as our children are stripped of their selfhood and robbed of their dignity by signs stating "for whites only." We cannot be satisfied as long as a Negro in Mississippi cannot vote and a Negro in New York believes he has nothing for which to vote. No, we are not satisfied, and we will not be satisfied until justice rolls down like waters and righteousness like a mighty stream.

16   I am not unmindful that some of you have come here out of excessive trials and tribulation. Some of you have come fresh from narrow jail cells. Some of you have come from areas where your quest for freedom left you battered by the storms of persecution and staggered by the winds of police brutality. You have been the veterans of creative suffering. Continue to work with the faith that unearned suffering is redemptive.

17   Go back to Mississippi; go back to Alabama; go back to South Carolina; go back to Georgia; go back to Louisiana; go back to the slums and ghettos of the Northern cities, knowing that somehow this situation can, and will be changed. Let us not wallow in the valley of despair.

One of the most famous segments of American oratory, the "I have a dream" section of this speech appeals to the audience to share his faith that right will prevail.

18   So I say to you, my friends, that even though we must face the difficulties of today and tomorrow, I still have a dream. It is a dream deeply rooted in the American dream that one day this nation will rise up and live out the true meaning of its creed—we hold these truths to be self evident, that all men are created equal.

19   I have a dream that one day on the red hills of Georgia, sons of former slaves and sons of former slave-owners will be able to sit down together at the table of brotherhood.

20   I have a dream that one day, even the state of Mississippi, a state sweltering with the heat of injustice, sweltering with the heat of oppression, will be transformed into an oasis of freedom and justice.

21   I have a dream my four little children will one day live in a nation where they will not be judged by the color of their skin but by content of their character. I have a dream today!

22   I have a dream that one day, down in Alabama, with its vicious racists, with its governor having his lips dripping with the words of interposition and nullification, that one day, right there in Alabama, little black boys and black girls will be able to join hands with little white boys and white girls as sisters and brothers. I have a dream today!

23   I have a dream that one day every valley shall be exalted, every hill and mountain shall be made low, the rough places shall be made plain, and the crooked places shall be made straight and the glory of the Lord will be revealed and all flesh shall see it together.

24   This is our hope. This is the faith that I go back to the South with.

25   With this faith we will be able to hew out of the mountain of despair a stone of hope. With this faith we will be able to transform the jangling discords of our nation into a beautiful symphony of brotherhood.

26   With this faith we will be able to work together, to pray together, to struggle together, to go to jail together, to stand up for freedom together, knowing that we will be free one day. This will be the day when all of God's children will be able to sing with new meaning—"my country 'tis of thee, sweet land of liberty, of thee I sing; land where my fathers died, land of the pilgrim's pride; from every mountain side, let freedom ring"—and if America is to be a great nation, this must become true.

27   And so let freedom ring from the prodigious hilltops of New Hampshire.

He then issues a protracted call for action.

28   Let freedom ring from the mighty mountains of New York.

29   Let freedom ring from the heightening Alleghenies of Pennsylvania.

30   Let freedom ring from the snow-capped Rockies of Colorado.

31   Let freedom ring from the curvaceous slopes of California.

32   But not only that.

33   Let freedom ring from Stone Mountain of Georgia.

34   Let freedom ring from Lookout Mountain of Tennessee.

35   Let freedom ring from every hill and molehill of Mississippi, from every mountainside, let freedom ring.

36   And when this happens, and when we allow freedom to ring, when we let it ring from every village and hamlet, from every state and city, we will be able to speed up that day when all of God's children—black men and white men, Jews and Gentiles, Catholics and Protestants—will be able to join hands and to sing

He ends on a positive note by predicting victory for "all of God's children."

in the words of the old Negro spiritual, "Free at last, free at last;
thank God Almighty, we are free at last."

Analysis

To gain the acceptance of his audience, King appeals to quotes or paraphrasing well-known phrases of inspiration: Lincoln's Gettysburg
Address ["Five score years ago," "this hallowed spot"], the Declaration of
Independence ["We hold these truths to be self-evident . . ."], "America"
["My country 'tis of thee . . . ," "Let freedom ring . . ."], the Bible ["every
valley shall be exalted . . ."], and a famous Negro spiritual [Free at last,
free at last . . ."].

Throughout the speech, he also uses the technique of chant-like repetition: "One hundred years later," "Now is the time," "we must," "We
cannot be satisfied," "Go back to," "I have a dream," and "Let freedom
ring from . . . ."

Sentence Outline of Martin Luther King, Jr.'s, "I Have a Dream"

Introduction

    I. Cite the Emancipation Proclamation
    II. Describe the lack of freedom of the Negro one hundred years later

Body

    I. Describe the "promissory note" of the founding fathers
    II. Cite America's default on that note
    III. Call upon the nation to make good
    IV. Explain the determination of the Negro
    V. Caution against committing wrongful deeds: bitterness and ha-
       tred, physical violence, distrust of all whites
    VI. Exhort Negroes not to turn back from their present militancy
    VII. Acknowledge excessive trials and tribulations of many Negroes
    VIII. Assert faith in the future ["I have a dream"]
    IX. Show how that faith can bring about equality and freedom

Conclusion

Let freedom ring until we are all free at last.

Topic Outline

Introduction

    I. Emancipation Proclamation
    II. One hundred years later

Body

  I. "Promissory note" of founding fathers
  II. Default
  III. Challenge to make good
  IV. Negro's determination
  V. Avoidance of wrongful deeds
  VI. Militancy
  VII. Trials and tribulations
  VIII. My dream for the future
  IX. What faith can achieve

Conclusion

Call to action ["Let freedom ring"]

MARK TWAIN

The following speech was delivered on October 5, 1906, in Norfolk, Connecticut, by Mark Twain (Samuel Longhorn Clemens) to an audience following one of his daughter's singing recitals, her first public appearance. America's greatest humorist, raconteur, and author of such classics as *The Innocents Abroad*, *The Prince and the Pauper*, *The Adventures of Tom Sawyer*, and his masterpiece *Huckleberry Finn*, aptly chose to speak about his first public appearance giving a talk.

  You may find it somewhat comforting and, at times, humorous as you read his short talk to know that this literary giant also suffered pangs of stage fright.

  Note the brevity of his speech as well as his folksy style, delivery, and language. Here's his speech, "Mark Twain's First Appearance," with analysis and outlines.

"Mark Twain's First Appearance"[4]

1 My heart goes out in sympathy to any one who is making his first appearance before an audience of human beings. By a direct process of memory I go back forty years less one month—for I'm older than I look.

2 I recall the occasion of my first appearance. San Francisco knew me then only as a reporter, and I was to make my bow to San Francisco as a lecturer. I knew that nothing short of compul-

He opens with a personal reminiscence, adding a joke about his age [he was actually 70 when he made this speech, not 40].

[4]*Mark Twain's Speeches* (New York: Greystone Press, Mark Twain Company, 1923), 242–43.

In a humorous exaggeration, he compares his stage fright to his having been seasick, winning audience sympathy.

The details of the darkness and emptiness of the stage and theater heighten the sense of nervousness that he is trying to convey.

His use of people planted in the audience is a technique still widely used by speakers and entertainers to guarantee desired reactions. He shows how his vanity caused his momentary downfall. He was so proud of having awed the audience that he forgot his own prearranged signals and looked to the governor's wife, presumably in a gesture of self-satisfaction—thereby producing laughter at precisely the wrong time.

After mentioning his subsequent self-confidence, he refers back to his stage fright at the beginning, to tying together the introduction and conclusion of his talk.

He ends with a simple thank you on behalf of his daughter.

sion would get me to the theatre. So I bound myself by a hard-and-fast contract so that I could not escape. I got to the theatre forty-five minutes before the hour set for the lecture. My knees were shaking so that I didn't know whether I could stand up. If there is an awful, horrible malady in the world, it is stage-fright—and sea-sickness. They are a pair. I had stage-fright then for the first and last time. I was only seasick once, too. It was on a little ship on which there were two hundred other passengers. I—was—sick. I was so sick that there wasn't any left for those other two hundred passengers.

3   It was dark and lonely behind the scenes in that theatre, and I peeked through the little peek-holes they have in theatre curtains and looked into the big auditorium. That was dark and empty, too. By-and-by it lighted up, and the audience began to arrive.

4   I had got a number of friends of mine, stalwart men, to sprinkle themselves through the audience armed with big clubs. Every time I said anything they could possibly guess I intended to be funny they were to pound those clubs on the floor. Then there was a kind lady in a box up there, also a good friend of mine, the wife of the Governor. She was to watch me intently, and whenever I glanced toward her she was going to deliver a gubernatorial laugh that would lead the whole audience into applause.

5   At last I began. I had the manuscript tucked under a United States flag in front of me where I could get at it in case of need. But I managed to get started without it. I walked up and down—I was young in those days and needed the exercise—and talked and talked.

6   Right in the middle of the speech I had placed a gem. I had put in a moving, pathetic part which was to get at the hearts and souls of my hearers. When I delivered it they did just what I hoped and expected. Then I happened to glance up at the box where the Governor's wife was—you know what happened.

7   Well, after the first agonizing five minutes, my stage-fright left me, never to return. I know if I was going to be hanged I could get up and make a good showing, and I intended to. But I shall never forget my feelings before the agony left me, and I got up here to thank you for her for helping my daughter, by your kindness, to live through her first appearance. And I want to thank you for your appreciation of her singing, which is, by-the-way, hereditary.

Analysis

Mark Twain's speech is effective because of its simple narrative approach, its conversational tone, and its touches of humor. Twain pokes fun at himself, thus gaining the sympathetic understanding of the audience.

Sentence Outline of "Mark Twain's First Appearance"

Introduction

I empathize with anyone who makes a first appearance before an audience. [Twain's daughter had just made her first public appearance as a singer.]

Body

   I. I recall my own first appearance.
      A. I had to force myself by means of an iron-clad contract to go through with it.
      B. I was overcome by stage fright.
  II. The dark and emptiness exaggerated my fear.
 III. I planted people in the audience to make sure there would be laughter.
      A. Several men were to pound the floor with big clubs when I said something funny.
      B. The governor's wife, in a box seat, was to laugh whenever I looked up at her.
 IV. During a moment of touching silence, I ruined the effect by inadvertently looking up at the governor's wife.
  V. In conquering my stage fright, I learned that I had the ability to make a good showing in front of an audience.

Conclusion

Thank you all for helping my daughter to live through her first appearance.

Topic Outline

Introduction

Empathy regarding first appearances

Body

   I. My first appearance
      A. Need to force myself
      B. Stage fright
  II. Confrontation of empty, dark theater
 III. Plants in audience
      A. Men with clubs
      B. Governor's wife
 IV. Looking at governor's wife at the wrong time
  V. Overcoming stage fright and gaining confidence

Conclusion

Thanks on behalf of my daughter

BARBARA BUSH

The following speech was delivered by Barbara Bush, wife of then-President George Bush, at Wellesley College's commencement in 1990. The speech is extremely effective in persuading the graduates, all women, to make three vital decisions regarding family relationships, volunteer work, and personal growth. Each decision and its benefits to the graduates is explained clearly and fully.

Incidentally, the graduates had previously objected to Barbara Bush as commencement speaker for two reasons. First, they wanted Alice Walker, author of *The Color Purple*, because purple was the 1990 "class color." Second, they asked, "What has Barbara Bush ever accomplished on her own? Her position is a consequence of her marriage to George Bush."

Although Mrs. Bush was the graduates' second choice, she promptly accepted the invitation.

A powerful persuasive tool that highlights the speech is the frequent use of the key words *you* and *your*. They appear over 35 times and help to get the audience involved. As you might expect, the speech was such a smashing success that the graduates gave her a standing ovation.

Here is Mrs. Bush's commencement speech.

The First Lady wastes no time in informing the graduates that she has spoken at Wellesley before.

She indirectly acknowledges that her choice as speaker was controversial when she plainly declares that at Wellesley, diversity is not just tolerated, it is embraced. This forthright remark prompted the first of many rounds of applause, and from here on Mrs. Bush captivated her audience.

Choices and Change[5]

1   Thank you President Keohane, Mrs. Gorbachev, trustees, faculty, parents, Julie Porer, Christine Bicknell and the Class of 1990. I am thrilled to be with you today, and very excited, as I know you must all be, that Mrs. Gorbachev could join us.

2   More than ten years ago when I was invited here to talk about our experiences in the People's Republic of China, I was struck by both the natural beauty of your campus and the spirit of this place.

3   Wellesley, you see, is not just a place, but an idea, an experiment in excellence in which diversity is not just tolerated, but is embraced.

4   The essence of this spirit was captured in a moving speech about tolerance given last year by the student body president of

[5]Barbara Bush, "Choices and Change," speech delivered at Wellesley College, Wellesley, Massachusetts, 1 June 1990.

one of your sister colleges. She related the story by Robert Fulghum about a young pastor who, finding himself in charge of some very energetic children, hit upon a game called "Giants, Wizards and Dwarfs." "You have to decide now" the pastor instructed the children, "which you are . . . a giant, a wizard or a dwarf?" At that, a small girl, tugging on his pants leg, asked, "But where do the mermaids stand?"

5   The pastor told her there are *no* mermaids. "Oh yes there are," she said. "I am a mermaid."

6   This little girl knew what she was and she was not about to give up on either her identity *or* the game. She intended to take her place wherever mermaids fit into the scheme of things. Where *do* the mermaids stand . . . all those who are different, those who do not fit the boxes and the pigeonholes? "Answer that question," wrote Fulghum, "and you can build a school, a nation, or a whole world on it."

She tells an interesting anecdote about a child and identity that sets the tone and theme of her address.

7   As that very wise young woman said . . . "Diversity, like anything worth having, requires *effort.*" Effort to learn about and respect difference, to be compassionate with one another, and to cherish our own identity, and to accept unconditionally the same in all others.

8   You should all be very proud that this is the Wellesley spirit. Now I know your first choice for today was Alice Walker, known for *The Color Purple.* Instead you got me—known for the color of my hair! Of course, Alice Walker's book has a special resonance here. At Wellesley, each class is known by a special color, and for four years the class of '90 has worn the color purple. Today you meet on Severance Green to say goodbye to all that, to begin a new and very personal journey, a search for your own true colors.

Mrs. Bush directly recognizes the fact that she was not the first choice of the graduating class to be commencement speaker and injects a bit of personal humor referring to the color of her hair.

9   In the world that awaits you beyond the shores of Lake Waban, no one can say what your true colors will be. But this I know: You have a first-class education from a first-class school. And so you need not, probably cannot, live a "paint-by-numbers" life. Decisions are not irrevocable. Choices do come back. As you set off from Wellesley, I hope that many of you will consider making three very special choices.

10   The first is to believe in something larger than yourself, to get involved in some of the big ideas of your time. I chose literacy because I honestly believe that if more people could read, write and comprehend, we would be that much closer to solving so many of the problems plaguing our society.

She introduces the first of three choices that she challenges the graduates to make and, at the same time, reveals what her choice was.

11   Early on I made another choice which I hope you will make as well. Whether you are talking about education, career or service, you are talking about life, and life must have joy. It's supposed to be fun!

She talks about the second choice and, again, personalizes it.

12   One of the reasons I made the most important decision of my life, to marry George Bush, is because he made me laugh. It's

true, sometimes we've laughed through our tears, but that shared laughter has been one of our strongest bonds. Find the joy in life, because as Ferris Bueller said on his day off

> "Life moves pretty fast. If ya don't stop and look around once in a while, ya gonna miss it!"

In the third and strongest challenge. Mrs. Bush states that although a career is important, "you are a human being first—another thought-provoking observation.

13   The third choice that must not be missed is to cherish your human connections: your relationships with friends and family. For several years, you've had impressed upon you the importance to your career of dedication and hard work. This is true, but as important as your obligations as a doctor, lawyer or business leader will be, you are a human being first and those human connections, with spouses, with children, with friends, are the most important investments you will ever make.

The First Lady stresses what is and what is not regrettable when you look back over your life, giving the graduates more to think about.

14   At the end of your life, you will never regret not having passed one more test, not winning one more verdict or not closing one more deal. You will regret time not spent with a husband, a friend, a child or a parent.

She talks about a Wellesley tradition and brings it up to date, then refers back to the anecdote regarding the small child and the mermaids and, once again, introduces humor.

15   We are in a transitional period right now, fascinating and exhilarating times, learning to adjust to the changes and the choices we, men and women, are facing. I remember what a friend said, on hearing her husband lament to his buddies that he had to babysit. Quickly setting him straight, my friend told her husband that when it's your own kids, it's not called babysitting!

16   Maybe we should adjust faster, maybe slower. But whatever the era, whatever the times, one thing will never change: fathers and mothers, if you have children, they must come first. Your success as a family, our success as a society, depends *not* on what happens at the White House, but on what happens inside your house.

Mrs. Bush introduces the subject of family by emphasizing the fact that, as time goes on, one thing never changes—fathers and mothers. And if they have children, those children must come first because our success as a society depends on it. This comment leaves no doubt where she stands regarding the responsibilities of parents to their children and the importance of the family in our society.

17   For over 50 years, it was said that the winner of Wellesley's annual hoop race would be the first to get married. Now they say the winner will be the first to become a C.E.O. Both of these stereotypes show too little tolerance for those who want to know where the mermaids stand. So I offer you today a new legend: the winner of the hoop race will be the first to realize her dream, not society's dream, her own personal dream. And who knows? Somewhere out in this audience may even be someone who will one day follow in my footsteps, and preside over the White House as the president's spouse. I wish him well!

18   The controversy ends here. But our conversation is only beginning. And a worthwhile conversation it is. So as you leave Wellesley today, take with you deep thanks for the courtesy and honor you have shared with Mrs. Gorbachev and me. Thank you. God bless you. And may your future be worthy of your dreams.

Analysis

What started out as a negative situation (being turned down as first choice for commencement speaker) was converted into a positive experience by the classy speech of a classy lady.

Here's a sentence outline of the former First Lady's speech:

Sentence Outline of "Choices and Changes"

Purpose

To persuade, inspire, and motivate Wellesley graduates to make their lives personally fulfilling and to suggest guidelines for doing so.

Thesis Statement

To make the most of your life, you must decide on three courses of action: believe in and work for a great cause, have fun, and cherish your family and friends.

Introduction

   I. Thank Pres. Keohane, etc., and express excitement that Mrs. Gorbachev can join us today.

  II. Wellesley is a place of beauty, an experiment in excellence where diversity is embraced.

     A. Tell story about pastor and children and the game they played called "Giants, Wizards and Dwarfs." Mention the little girl "mermaid" who was different and didn't fit into the usual pigeonhole.

     B. You should be proud that the Wellesley spirit encourages respect for differences among us.

     C. Mention author Alice Walker and *The Color Purple*, the color that your class has worn for four years.

Body

  III. Today, enriched with your first-class education, you start a new, very personal journey that involves three very special decisions by you:

     A. First, believe in something larger than yourself and become involved in it. I chose literacy because if more people could read, write, and understand, we'd be closer to solving many problems plaguing society.

     B. Whether you're talking about education, a career, or community service, you're talking about life, and life must be joyful. Have fun. One of the reasons I married George is that he made me laugh.

C. Cherish your relationships with spouses, families, and friends. You're a human being first and your human connections are the most important investment you'll ever make. Families come first and our success as a society depends on what happens inside your homes.

Conclusion

IV. Closing remarks:
A. For over 50 years Wellesley tradition said that the winner of your annual hoop race would be the first to get married, and lately that she'll be first to become a CEO. Now I offer you a new approach—that she'll be the first to achieve her own personal dream, not society's dream.

B. "Thank you for the courtesy and honor you have shared with Mrs. Gorbachev and me. God bless you. And may your future be worthy of your dreams."

Topic Outline

Title, Purpose and Thesis Statement,

Same as in the sentence outline

Introduction

I. Greetings and welcoming remarks
II. Brief description of Wellesley College where diversity is embraced
A. Anecdote about "Giants, Wizards and Dwarfs"
B. Pride of Wellesley
C. The class color

Body

III. Life's journey involves three decisions
A. Involvement in a cause larger than yourself
B. Enjoyment of life
C. Appreciation of your relationships with family and friends

Conclusion

IV. Closing Remarks:
A. Traditional Wellesley dream versus your own personal dream
B. "Thank you. God bless you. And may your future be worthy of your dreams."

PRESIDENT WILLIAM JEFFERSON CLINTON[6]

Here is President Bill Clinton's so-called contrition speech to the nation delivered on August 17, 1998, following his unprecedented sworn testimony before a Federal Grand Jury. (See Chapter 6.) His speech was delivered from the Map Room at the White House.

Address to the Nation

Good evening.

This afternoon in this room, from this chair, I testified before the Office of Independent Counsel and the grand jury.

I answered their questions truthfully, including questions about my private life, questions no American citizen would ever want to answer.

Still, I must take complete responsibility for all my actions, both public and private. And that is why I am speaking to you tonight.

As you know, in a deposition in January, I was asked questions about my relationship with Monica Lewinsky. While my answers were legally accurate, I did not volunteer information.

Indeed, I did have a relationship with Ms. Lewinsky that was not appropriate. In fact, it was wrong. It constituted a critical lapse in judgment and a personal failure on my part for which I am solely and completely responsible.

But I told the grand jury today, and I say to you now, that at no time did I ask anyone to lie, to hide or destroy evidence, or to take any other unlawful action.

I know that my public comments and my silence about this matter gave a false impression. I misled people, including even my wife. I deeply regret that.

I can only tell you I was motivated by many factors. First, by a desire to protect myself from the embarrassment of my own conduct.

I was also very concerned about protecting my family. The fact that these questions were being asked in a politically inspired lawsuit, which has since been dismissed, was a consideration, too.

In addition, I had real and serious concerns about an independent counsel investigation that began with private business dealings 20 years ago, dealings, I might add, about which an independent federal agency found no evidence of any wrongdoing by me or my wife over two years ago.

---

[6]*Transcribed by the Federal Document Clearing House.*

The independent counsel investigation moved on to my staff and friends, then into my private life. And now the investigation itself is under investigation.

This has gone on too long, cost too much, and hurt too many innocent people.

Now, this matter is between me, the two people I love most—my wife and our daughter—and our God. I must put it right, and I am prepared to do whatever it takes to do so.

Nothing is more important to me personally. But it is private, and I intend to reclaim my family life for my family. It's nobody's business but ours.

Even presidents have private lives. It is time to stop the pursuit of personal destruction and the prying into private lives and get on with our national life.

Our country has been distracted by this matter for too long, and I take my responsibility for my part in all of this. That is all I can do.

Now it is time—in fact, it is past time—to move on.

We have important work to do—real opportunities to seize, real problems to solve, real security matters to face.

And so tonight, I ask you to turn away from the spectacle of the past seven months, to repair the fabric of our national discourse, and to return our attention to all the challenges and all the promise of the next American century.

Thank you for watching. And good night.

APPENDIX B

SUGGESTED SPEECH TOPICS

If you're having difficulty coming up with ideas on what to talk about, here are a number of suggestions to aid you in your selection.

MORE TOPIC SUGGESTIONS FOR A DEMONSTRATION TALK

1. Performing aerobics.
2. Various types of dancing.
3. Outdoor camping.
4. Taking your blood pressure.
5. How to fold a flag.
6. How to write a résumé.
7. Laptop computers.
8. How to analyze handwriting.
9. How to read a champagne label.
10. How to select a bottle of wine.
11. How to tape ankles to prevent injury.
12. Selecting sports equipment (football, hockey, skiing).
13. How to keep score (in bowling, tennis, baseball, etc).
14. How to read body language.
15. How to replace a broken window.
16. How to refinish furniture.
17. Various martial arts.
18. Basic self-defense.
19. Using a hot-glue gun.
20. How to bathe a new baby.

21. Police equipment.
22. Firefighter's equipment.
23. Different types of home fire extinguishers.
24. How to use a casting rod.
25. Auto antitheft devices.
26. How an antilock braking system works.
27. How to shingle a roof.
28. How to wallpaper.
29. How to stencil.
30. How to set a table.
31. How to fold napkins creatively for a dinner party.
32. How to decorate a cake.
33. Fingerpainting.
34. How to transplant a plant.
35. Planting an indoor garden.
36. Wrapping presents and making bows.
37. How to lower a ceiling.
38. How to make candles.
39. Making ceramics.
40. How to create ornaments with stained glass.
41. How to make paper flowers.
42. Flower decorating.
43. How to make Christmas decorations.
44. How to make a Christmas wreath from pine cones.
45. How to make a collage.
46. Various types of collections (coins, stamps, sports cards, etc.).
47. How to manicure.
48. How to make animals from balloons.
49. How to decorate a candle.
50. How to make dolls from rags.
51. How to make a Caesar salad.
52. How to make an omelette.
53. Performing card tricks.
54. How to quilt.
55. How to solder.
56. How to identify counterfeit money.
57. How to wood-carve signs.
58. How to draw cartoons.
59. How to eat a lobster.
60. How to juggle.
61. Home security systems.
62. How to coordinate a wardrobe.
63. How to pack a suitcase.
64. How to pack a parachute.
65. How to shop and save with coupons.

MORE TOPIC SUGGESTIONS FOR AN INFORMATIVE TALK

1. Where have all the high-paying jobs gone?
2. Job prospects through the year 2050.
3. How valuable is a college degree?
4. How to select a grad school.
5. What is sexual harassment?
6. The early release of patients from hospitals.
7. How America's "Big Three" automakers recaptured their prominence.
8. Will there be a resurgence of the union movement?
9. Why are prayers prohibited in public schools, yet the distribution of condoms is not?
10. How to get Amtrak back on the right track.
11. How to cut vacation costs.
12. Planning an economical family vacation
13. Exercise might be a fast track to the grave.
14. How healthful is exercise?
15. What are natural foods?
16. Buying a computer.
17. How to avoid being ripped off by unscrupulous auto mechanics.
18. The high cost of supporting former presidents.
19. Are political pollsters getting out of hand?
20. Why do banks charge so much for basic services?
21. The impeachment process.
22. Psychic phenomena.
23. More crime and less punishment.
24. What is a financial planner?
25. How to buy a house.
26. Selecting a type of home mortgage.
27. Why so many national lawmakers have called it quits.
28. Is Congress for sale? (powerful lobbying groups).
29. The high cost of seeking and keeping public office.
30. The pros and cons of electronic banking.
31. What is a conservative?
32. What is a liberal?
33. The press has too much freedom.
34. Ethics in the media.
35. The dangers of secondhand smoke.
36. I'm dying for a cigarette.
37. The health dangers of the summer sun.
38. Child abuse.
39. Battered women.
40. What federal entitlement programs are citizens entitled to?

41. Defense fraud.
42. Lloyd's of London.
43. The functions of the World Bank.
44. Hang gliding.
45. Bungee jumping.
46. Paragliding.
47. Mountain biking.
48. A trip to Disney World.
49. Environmental concerns.
50. America's illiteracy problem.
51. Make your home more energy efficient.
52. How to deal for wheels (new or used).
53. Wearing seat belts can save lives.
54. The popularity of home equity loans.
55. College degree diploma mills.
56. How secure is Social Security?
57. The status of nursing home care.
58. A day in the life of a lobbyist.
59. Breathing can be dangerous to your health (air pollution).
60. Religion by television.
61. Who are the homeless?
62. Living at home.
63. Being a single parent.
64. Binge drinking on campus.
65. Selecting an alternative health-care provider.

More Topic Suggestions for a Persuasive Talk

1. To be eligible for government assistance, single mothers should be required to name the father.
2. Does society have an obligation to support more than one child of an unwed mother?
3. Sex education should (not) be taught in the public schools.
4. We should have a truth-in-sentencing law.
5. We should (not) eliminate all parole.
6. Plea-bargaining should (not) be eliminated.
7. There should (not) be a residency requirement to be eligible for government assistance.
8. The government should (not) spend more on public transportation.
9. Figure skating is not a sport and should be eliminated from Olympic competition.
10. We should do away with "Affirmative Action" and hire only the best qualified.

11. We should (not) stop sharing our nuclear secrets with other countries.
12. Many baseball players' salaries are out of the ballpark.
13. Taxpayers should (not) be forced to pay for a megaplex sports stadium.
14. America should (not) be playing policeman for the world.
15. What is our foreign policy?
16. Can there be lasting peace in Northern Ireland?
17. There is too much sex and violence on TV.
18. Juvenile offenders should (not) be sent to "reform" schools.
19. Students should (not) be forced, by law, to attend high school.
20. Public schools should (not) be permitted to distribute condoms or other types of birth control devices.
21. Curfews should (not) be imposed to curb juvenile crime.
22. We should (not) pay for illegal aliens' health care.
23. Alien felons should (not) be deported.
24. The U.S. should (not) stop paying for the security of Europe and Japan.
25. The difference between obscenity and pornography.
26. The case for or against SATs.
27. We should (not) continue to spend billions on our space program.
28. Gambling should (not) be legalized.
29. Prostitution should (not) be legalized.
30. Drugs should (not) be legalized.
31. Minors who commit adult crimes should (not) stand trial as adults.
32. Gays and lesbian couples should (not) be permitted to adopt children.
33. Prisons should be for punishment and not for rehabilitation.
34. Spouses of political candidates should (not) be required to make their financial statements and tax returns public.
35. The Miss America Pageant is (not) sexist.
36. Auto repair mechanics should (not) be licensed.
37. The incredible waste in the military.
38. Women should (not) have the right to decide on having an abortion.
39. A U.S. President should serve only one six-year term.
40. The presidential primaries should be shortened.
41. The electoral college should take a sabbatical.
42. Presidents should be elected by popular vote.
43. America is ready for a woman president.
44. Our fishing fleets are going down for the third time.
45. Women have yet to enjoy pay equity.
46. Why you should leave home without your credit and debit cards.
47. You should have a will.
48. We must prevent our maritime fleet from sinking.
49. Smokers should (not) have rights.
50. The government should (not) allow "double dipping."
51. Wearing seat belts should be the choice of the public and not the government.
52. More student discipline should be returned to the schools.
53. Tipping should (not) be allowed.
54. Why all students should study a foreign language.

55. Why teachers should (not) be able to strike.
56. A candidate's private life should (not) remain private.
57. Deregulation is (not) hurting our country.
58. Hostile business takeovers should not be legal.
59. America needs more daycare centers.
60. The government should (not) abolish all grants for student loans.
61. Why are members of Congress exempt from certain laws?
62. Every American should (not) have the right to own a gun.
63. We should have a VAT (value added tax) instead of an income tax.
64. A speech course should be mandatory for graduation.
65. Every American citizen should (not) have an identification card.

APPENDIX C

COMMON SEXIST WORDS AND PHRASES AND SUGGESTED NONSEXIST ALTERNATIVES

Instead of Using	Try Using
actress	actor
adultery	extramarital affair
adventuress	adventurer
airline stewardess	flight attendant
alumnae, alumni	graduate(s), alum(s) member(s) of the class of
anchorman	anchor
authoress	author
bag lady	homeless woman
barmaid	cocktail server
barren	infertility
baseman	base player
bellboy, bellman	bellhop
biological parent(s)	birth parent(s)
birth control methods	contraception

broken home	single-parent family
busboy, busgirl	waiter's helper, waiter's (or serving) assistant
businessmen	businesspeople
cameraman	camera operator or photographer
cavemen	cave dwellers, cave people
chairman, chairwoman	chair, head, presider, presiding officer, convener, leader, moderator
chambermaid	hotel worker
chorus boy/girl	chorus member/dancer/performer
cleaning girl/lady/woman	cleaner/domestic/office cleaner
clergymen	clergy, clerics, members of the clergy
coat-check girl	coat checker, coat attendant
co-ed	student
comedienne	comedian
congressman	representative, congressional representative
copy boy, copy girl	copy clerk, runner
corporate wives	corporate spouses
cowboy	ranch hand
cowgirl	ranch hand
craftsman	artisan or craftperson
deaconess	deacon
deliveryman	deliverer, delivery clerk, courier, delivery person
doorman	doorkeeper, doorkeep, door attendant
draftsman	drafter
drag	cross dressing
drum majorette	drum major, baton twirler
dual-worker families	two-income families
dykes	lesbians
employed mothers	mothers working outside the home
Englishman, Englishwoman	Englander, Briton
equestrienne	equestrian, rider, horseback rider
executrix	executor
ex-husbands	former husbands
ex-wives	former wives
family practice	family medicine
family violence	domestic violence
fatherhood	fathers, parenthood
female-dominated occupations	female-intensive occupations
female homosexuality	lesbianism
female homosexuals	lesbians
fireman	firefighter, stoker (ships, trains)
first lady	presidential or Governor's spouse
fisherman	fisher, angler
fishwives	fish seller
flagman	flagger
flexible hours	flexible work schedules
flextime	flexible work schedules
forefathers	ancestors, forebears, foremothers and forefathers

forelady, foreman	supervisor, boss, leader, head juror
frenchmen	the French
freshmen	first-year students, yearlings
gay woman	lesbian
gentleman's agreement	unwritten agreement, agreement based on trust
girl Friday, man Friday	administrative assistant, aide, key aide
handyman	fixer, jack-of-all-trades
hat-check girl	hat checker, hat-check attendant
headmaster or headmistress	principal
heiress	heir, inheritor
heroic woman	hero
heroine	hero
homosexual	gay
hooker	prostitute
horseman, horsewoman	rider, equestrian
hostess	host
househusband	homemaker
housewife	homemaker
household violence	domestic violence
joint custody	shared custody
key punch operator	data/computer operator
kinsmen	kin, kinfolk, relatives
lady	woman
ladies' auxiliaries	auxiliaries
laundress	launderer, laundry worker
laymen	laypeople, laity,
longshoreman	longshore worker
lumberman	lumber cutter
maiden name	birth name
maid	household worker
mailman	mail carrier, letter carrier, postal worker
male nurse	nurse
man, mankind (meaning the human species	the human species (*Homo sapiens*) humans, humanity, humankind, the human family, human beings, human societies, people
man (meaning person)	person, one, individual, you, I
man (as verb)	operate, work, staff, serve at (or *on* or *in*)
man-hours	work-hours, labor time
man-made	handmade, hand-built, human made, synthetic, manufacturered,
man of letters	literary person, writer, author, pundit
man of the Year	newsmaker of the Year
manpower	personnel, staff, human resources, labor, people power, muscle power, labor force
man-to-man	one-to-one, one-on-one, person-to-person
matron	married woman, supervisor, prison guard
mature student	adult student
meter maid	meter attendant, meter tender, meter reader

middleman	contact, go-between, intermediary, agent
mill girl	factory worker
minorities	ethnic groups, people of color
minority women	ethnic women
mistress	lover
mistress of ceremonies	master of ceremonies, host, emcee
motherhood	mothers or parenthood
murderess	murderer
newsman, newswoman	newsperson, reporter, journalist
nose job	cosmetic surgery
number one man	head, chief, number one
number two man	second in command, chief aide
office boy, office girl	office helper, office assistant, clerk
one man, one vote	one person, one vote
one-man show	one-person show, solo show, one-artist show
one-parent family	single-parent family
one-upsmanship	the art of one-upping
patroness	patron, benefactor, sponsor, mentor
pitchman	hawker, promoter
poetess	poet
policeman, policewoman	police officer
postmistress	postmaster
pressman	press operator
prophetess	prophet
proprietress	proprietor, owner, owner-manager
quadruplets, quintuplets, etc.	multiple births
repairman	repairer
returning women	reentry women
rewrite man	rewriter
right-hand man	chief assistant
rights of women	women's rights
salesman, saleswoman, saleslady, salesgirl	salesclerk, salespersons, sales agent, sales representative, (or rep)
Scotsman	Scot, Scotlander
sculptress	sculptor
seaman	sailor, mariner, seafarer
seamstress	tailor, needleworker
seductress	seducer
seeress	prophet, seer, clairvoyant
servant	household worker
sex role identification	sexual identity
sexual practices	sexual behavior
shepherdess	shepherd, pastor
signalman	signal operator, signaler
sorceress	sorcerer, enchanter
spaceman	astronaut, spacefarer, space traveler
spokesman, spokeswoman	spokesperson, representative
sportsmanlike	sporting
sportsman	sports enthusiast
sportsmanship	fair play, fairness,
spouse rape	domestic rape

starlet	young star, star in the making, aspiring actor
state policeman	state trooper, trooper
statesmanlike	diplomatic
statesmanship	diplomacy
statesmen	diplomats, political leaders
stewardess	steward, (ship, union shop) flight attendant (aircraft)
straw man	straw, straw person
street people	homeless
suffragette	suffragist
switchman	switch operator
temptress	tempter, enticer
test-tube babies	in vitro fertilization
the pill	oral contraceptives
trashman	trash collector
traveling salesman	traveling sales agent/rep sales woman
tribesman	tribe/tribal member, member of a tribe
triggerman	professional/armed killer, hired gun, assassin
tube tying	tubal ligation
two-career couples	dual-career couples
two-career families	dual-career families
unborn child	fetus
union man	union member, labor/trade unionist, member of a union
unman	unnerve, disarm, weaken, incapacitate, undermine
unmarried father	single father
unmarried man	single man
unmarried mother	single mother
unmarried women	single women
utility girl/utility man	utility worker/hand/cleaner
VD or venereal disease	sexually transmitted disease
villainess	villain, scoundrel
waitress	waiter, server
watchman	night guard, guard, security guard, caretaker, custodian
weathergirl/weatherman	Weathercaster, meteorologist (not all weather people are meteorologists), weather reporter, forecaster
weathermen	weather reporters
water boy	water carrier
welfare mother	welfare client/recipient
widow/widower	surviving spouse
women's lib	Feminism, women's movement
working girl/working man	worker, employee, wage earner job holder
working men/working women	workers, employees, wage earners, job holders
working mother	mothers working outside the home, wage earning/job holding/ salaried woman/mother

working wives	wives working outside the home.
workman	worker, wage earner
workmen's compensation	workers' compensation
yachtsman	yacht owner/captain, yachter
yardman	yard worker/laborer/supervisor railroad worker
young lady	young woman

More extensive listings of meanings of words and phrases with non-sexist alternatives can be found where these words were researched:

Mary Ellen S. Capek, editor, *A Women Thesaurus: An Index of Language Used to Describe and Locate Information By and About Women*, a project of the National Council for Research on Women and the Business and Professional Women's Foundation (New York: Harper & Rowe, 1988).

Rosalie Maggio, *The Bias-Free Word Finder, a Dictionary of Nondiscriminatory Language*, (Boston: Beacon Press, 1992).

APPENDIX D

SOME COMMONLY MISPRONOUNCED WORDS

For further practice in pronunciation, here is a list of some of the more commonly mispronounced words. The mispronunciations may be due from substituting one sound for another, an omission of one or more sounds, adding sounds, transposing sounds, or misplacing accents. The accented syllable(s) is underlined.

1. abdomen (<u>ab</u>-do-men)
2. absolve (ab-<u>solve</u>)
3. absorb (ab-<u>sorb</u>)
4. absurd (ab-<u>surd</u>)
5. accompaniment (ac-<u>com</u>-pa-ni-ment)
6. accompanist (ac-<u>com</u>-pa-nist)
7. accurate (<u>ac</u>-cu-rate)
8. admirable (<u>ad</u>-mi-ra-ble)
9. adult (a-<u>dult</u>)
10. almond (<u>al</u>-mond)
11. amicable (<u>am</u>-i-ca-ble)
12. analogous (a-<u>nal</u>-o-gous)
13. antidote (<u>an</u>-ti-<u>dote</u>)
14. antithesis (an-<u>tith</u>-e-sis)
15. applicable (<u>ap</u>-pli-ca-ble)
16. archipelago (<u>ar</u>-chi-<u>pel</u>-a-<u>go</u>)
17. arctic (<u>arc</u>-tic)
18. aria (<u>a</u>-ri-a)
19. auxiliary (aux-<u>il</u>-ia-ry)
20. aviator (<u>a</u>-vi-<u>a</u>-tor)
21. behemoth (be-<u>he</u>-moth)
22. beige (<u>bei</u>-ge)
23. beneficiary (<u>ben</u>-e-<u>fi</u>-ci-ar-y)
24. beserk (be-<u>serk</u>)
25. bilingual (bi-<u>lin</u>-gual)
26. blasé (<u>bla</u>-sé)
27. blatant (<u>bla</u>-tant)
28. bouquet (bou-<u>quet</u>)
29. bravado (bra-<u>va</u>-do)
30. buffet (buf-<u>fet</u>)
31. buoy (<u>bu</u>-oy)
32. cache (<u>cache</u>)
33. candidate (<u>can</u>-di-date)
34. cashmere (<u>cash</u>-mere)
35. casualty (<u>cas</u>-u-al-ty)
36. center (<u>cen</u>-ter)
37. cerebral (ce-<u>re</u>-bral)
38. chagrin (cha-<u>grin</u>)
39. chasm (<u>chasm</u>)
40. chimney (<u>chim</u>-ney)

431

41. coiffure (coif-_fure_)
42. comparable (_com_-pa-ra-ble)
43. corsage (cor-_sage_)
44. cuisine (cui-_sine_)
45. cumulus (_cum_-u-lus)
46. cupola (_cu_-po-la)
47. curriculum (cur-_ric_-u-lum)
48. debauched (de-_bauched_)
49. deluge (_de_-luge)
50. demise (de-_mise_)
51. despicable (des-_pi_-ca-ble)
52. diphthong (_diph_-thong)
53. dirigible (_di_-ri-gi-ble)
54. disparate (dis-_pa_-rate)
55. drama (_dra_-ma)
56. ecstatic (ec-_sta_-tic)
57. environment (en-_vir_-on-ment)
58. etiquette (_et_-i-quette)
59. exquisite (ex-_quis_-ite)
60. extraordinary (ex-_traor_-di-nar-y)
61. familiar (fa-_mi_-li-ar)
62. formidable (_for_-mi-da-ble)
63. genuine (_gen_-u-ine)
64. gondola (_gon_-do-la)
65. homage (_hom_-age)
66. human (_hu_-man)
67. hygienic (hi-gi-_en_-ic)
68. incomparable (in-_com_-pa-ra-ble)
69. interesting (_in_-ter-est-ing)
70. irreparable (ir-_rep_-a-ra-ble)
71. kindergarten (_kin_-der-_garten_)
72. laboratory (_lab_-o-ra-_tory_)
73. lamentable (la-_men_-ta-ble)
74. library (_li_-bra-ry)
75. massage (mas-_sage_)
76. medieval (_me_-di-_e_-val)
77. mischievous (_mis_-chie-vous)
78. ominpotent (om-_nip_-o-tent)
79. particular (par-_tic_-u-lar)
80. peculiarly (pe-_cu_-liar-ly)
81. plethora (_pleth_-o-ra)
82. poem (_po_-em)
83. poinsettia (poin-_set_-ti-a)
84. prerogative (pre-_rog_-a-tive)
85. pronunciation (pro-_nun_-ci-_a_-tion)
86. radiator (_ra_-di-a-tor)
87. reptile (_rep_-tile)
88. reputable (_re_-pu-ta-ble)
89. sandwich (_sand_-wich)
90. schism (_schism_)
91. secretary (_sec_-re-tar-y)
92. sentence (_sen_-tence)
93. similar (_sim_-i-lar)
94. statistics (sta-_tis_-tics)
95. strength (_strength_)
96. superfluous (su-_per_-flu-ous)
97. theater (_the_-a-ter)
98. tremendous (tre-_men_-dous)
99. Wednesday (_Wednes_-day)
100. zealous (_zeal_-ous)

While going over these words, it might be wise ... no, it _would_ be wise to have a dictionary handy.

GLOSSARY

Abstract words Words that derive their meaning from personal interpretation and opinion; the opposite of concrete words. (Ch. 6)

Actuate To convince people to take a form of action. (Ch. 11)

Agenda Matters to be discussed, acted or voted upon during a meeting. (Ch. 14)

Analogic reasoning Predicting that, because two things or situations are similar in several important respects, they will be similar in other respects and will therefore produce similar results. (Ch. 11)

Announcement A short statement of an event including all pertinent information. (Ch. 13)

Application letter A letter that usually accompanies a résumé telling the employer what you have to offer the company and why you should be hired. (Ch. 16)

Argument Persuading through evidence and reasoning. (Ch. 11)

Articulation Movements of lips, tongue, jaw, and soft palate that convert vocal sounds into speech. The most common faults among college students are running words together and omitting word endings. (Ch. 5)

Artifact Objects in our possession—clothes, jewelry, furniture, autos—that transmit messages about us, our education, status in the community, etc. (Ch. 3)

Assertive Able to express true feelings and opinions honestly and comfortably, and able to say no without feeling guilty. (Ch. 1)

Audience analysis Finding out as much as possible about the make-up of an audience. The more you know about the members of the audience, the more effectively you'll be able to communicate with them. (Ch. 6)

Audiovisual aids Material that helps a speaker clarify and reinforce his or her message; photographs, cartoons, objects, videotape, and so on. (Ch. 12)

Body language See *nonverbal communication.* (Ch. 2)

Bibliography A listing of authors and sources of information on a particular subject. (Ch. 7)

Body (of speech) The central part of a speech, which contains the key information, ideas, or emotions to be communicated by a speaker to the audience. (Ch. 8)

Brainstorming A stimulating exercise using the imagination for the purpose of generating as many ideas as possible. (Ch. 7, 14)

Browsers A client application that enables a user to view the markup language used for documents on the Web and then perform certain applications. (Ch. 7)

Buzz sessions Small groups of people who gather to try to solve a common problem. All of the participating groups collectively present their proposed solutions. (Ch. 14)

Card catalog A file of cards listing all books in a library by author's name, title, and subject and indicating where they may be found. (Ch. 7)

Causal reasoning Establishing a relationship between causes and effects. (Ch. 3, 11)

CD-ROM (Compact Disk-Read Only Memory) The term applied to a variety of storage formats by which audio, text, and graphics are retrieved from the disk by laser beam. (Ch. 7)

Chairperson or **chair** One who presides over a meeting, panel, forum, round-table discussion, or symposium; a moderator or discussion leader. (Ch. 14)

Chronemics The study of time as a mode of communication. (Ch. 3)

Cite To quote from a book, a speech, a magazine article or some other source. (Ch. 7)

Clichés Expressions that have been around and used for so long that they have become virtually meaningless. (Ch. 6)

Codes Messages or methods of communication. (Ch. 3)

Committee A small group of people delegated to investigate, consider, report, or act on a matter. (Ch. 14)

Communication In this book, the interpersonal exchange of ideas and feelings between speaker and listeners. (throughout text)

Communication cycle The activity in which a person speaks and another listens and responds to the speaker. (Ch. 16)

Conclusion (of speech) The ending of a speech, which often sums up the main points or stresses the major idea. A conclusion should contain no new material. (Ch. 8)

Concrete words Words that pertain to objects you can perceive through the senses; tangible things. (Ch. 6)

Consensus Unanimous agreement from all group members on a decision or solution. (Ch. 14)

Consonant A speech sound produced by a partial or total stoppage of the air stream—for example, the letters *t, k, f, b, p.* (Ch. 5)

Credibility The degree to which a speaker and/or his or her message is considered believable. (Ch. 3, 11)

Database A large collection of information stored in a well-organized format that can be retrieved by specific software. (Ch. 7)

Deductive reasoning Making deductions or drawing conclusions. It involves moving from a general principle to a specific principle. (Ch. 11)

Delivery The way a speech is given; it can be read, memorized, or spoken extemporaneously (with or without notes after preparation beforehand). Delivery may also refer to the use of the voice. (Ch. 9)

Demonstration talk A talk intended to show how to do or how to make something or to explain how something functions with the use of audiovisual aids. (Ch. 12)

Diction Pronunciation and enunciation of words: clarity, intelligibility, and distinctness are essential in public speaking. (Ch. 5)

Download To transmit data from a central to a remote computer, from a file server to a workstation, or from a computer to a floppy disk. (Ch. 7)

Duration Length of time that vowel sounds are held. (Ch. 5)

Easel An upright three-legged frame upon which to display something. (Ch. 12)

Editorialize To offer one's opinion as opposed to a factual account. (Ch. 13)

E-mail Electronic mail. Tool for sending messages over the Internet. (Ch. 7)

Empathy The ability to experience another person's feelings; "putting yourself in the other person's shoes." (Ch. 9)

Enthusiasm Interest, animation, emphasis, and excitement conveyed while speaking. (Ch. 9)

Enunciate To pronounce every syllable of a word clearly and distinctly; to articulate. (Ch. 5)

Ethics The branch of philosophy dealing with values relating to human conduct. Doing the right thing. (Ch. 1)

Ethos Speaker credibility. (Ch. 11)

Eulogy Also referred to as a speech of tribute. A speech given to honor the deceased. (Ch. 13)

Evaluative listening Questioning the validity of the speaker's message and credibility. (Ch. 4)

Evidence Facts and/or expert testimony to support a person's position or statements. (Ch. 11)

Expert opinion Testimony by a recognized authority in his or her field. Such testimony is admissible in a court of law. (Ch. 11)

Extemporaneous Researched, thought about, outlined, rehearsed, and then delivered with or without notes. (Ch. 9)

Eye contact A communicative two-way relationship in which a speaker constantly looks at the listeners and reacts to their feedback (cheers, boos, facial expressions, gestures). (Ch. 3)

Fact Any information which can be substantiated and is documented. (Ch. 11)

Feedback The audience's verbal or nonverbal reaction to your message. (Ch. 3)

Field One of many sections that come together to constitute an electronic record. (Ch. 7)

Forum A public speaking situation in which members of the audience are allowed to participate by asking questions or making comments. (Ch. 14)

General meeting A gathering of all active members of an organization. (Ch. 14)

Gestures Movements by hands, arms, head, shoulders, or body to emphasize or clarify spoken thoughts and emotions. (Ch. 2)

Gobbledygook Language that is hard to understand because of its wordy jargon. A master of this type of verbosity is the government. (Ch. 6)

Group discussion The verbal and nonverbal interaction among 5 to 20 people who are engaged in a discussion with a specific purpose and objective. (Ch. 14)

Handout Printed information distributed to members of the audience. (Ch. 10)

Haptics The study of touch as a mode of communication. (Ch. 3)

Hypertext A section of web-page text that responds to a user command by establishing a connection to a file of information. (Ch. 1)

Identification with audience Associating oneself with the ideas, opinions, and feelings of listeners, usually in an attempt to persuade them. (Ch. 11)

Impromptu talk A talk given on the spur of the moment, without prior notice or time for preparation. (Ch. 9)

Inductive reasoning The reverse of deductive reasoning; starts with specific examples or cases and ends with a general conclusion based on the examples or cases. (Ch. 11)

Inferences Drawing a conclusion or generalization based on observation, experience, and/or logic. (Ch. 11)

Inflection A change, up or down, in vocal tone or pitch. (Ch. 3)

Informative talks Communication in which the chief aim is to share knowledge and understanding with the audience. (Ch. 10)

Internet An electronic network linking computers together, originally called ARPANET, the Advanced Research projects Agency of the U.S. Department of Defense. (Ch. 7)

Interpersonal communication A verbal or nonverbal exchange of ideas, knowledge, and feelings between two or more people. (throughout text)

Interview Oral communication between two people or by a panel questioning an individual for the purpose of eliciting information. (Ch. 16)

Introduction (of speech) The part of a speech in which the speaker usually explains the purpose and scope of the speech and, at the same time, tries to win audience interest and goodwill. (Ch. 8)

ISP Internet Service Provider. Establishes connections between computers and the Internet. (Ch. 7)

Kinesics The study of body movements, such as posture, facial expressions, arm movement, and so on. (Ch. 3)

Laser pointer An instrument the size of a fountain pen that emits a beam that produces a small red dot on any surface. (Ch. 12)

LCD (liquid crystal display) panel Device positioned between a computer monitor and a projector to display a computer screen image on a screen or wall. (Ch. 12)

Lectern A speaker's stand with a slanted top that supports the notes (if any) of a speaker; a lectern may rest on a table or floor. See *podium*. (Ch. 2)

Lecture An exposition of a given subject to a group for the purpose of disseminating information. (Ch. 14)

Link A hypertext screen section, usually underlined words or a framed graphic, that responds to a user's command to move from one file of information to another on a web page or to another web site. (Ch. 7)

Listening Making an effort to hear and understand a speaker's statement. (Ch. 4)

Loaded words Words concerning race, religion, politics, or personal character that can produce overpowering, negative reactions. (Ch. 6)

Manuscript Copy that is written out word for word. (Ch. 9)

MC Master of ceremonies. (Ch. 8, 13)

Meeting A gathering of people to discuss topics of mutual concern and perhaps to make decisions on them. (Ch. 14)

Moderator A group leader whose basic responsibilities include introducing the members of a panel and its subject, presiding over a smooth and fair discussion, bringing the discussion to a close, and allowing questions from the audience. (Ch. 14)

Modes of communication Certain elements that communicate messages, often nonverbally—for example, facial expressions, eye contact, gestures, objects, space, time, touch, and paralanguage. (Ch. 3)

Monorate The tendency to speak each syllable, word, phrase, and sentence at the same rate of speed. (Ch. 5)

Monotone The tendency of a voice not to move up and down the tone scale, thus resulting in very little expression. The voice sounds flat, dull, and boring. (Ch. 5)

Motivation An inner drive, impulse, or incentive that causes a person to do something or to act in a certain way. (Ch. 11)

Nervousness An emotional state characterized by tension or fear. (Ch. 2)

Nonverbal communication The transmission and reception of messages, knowingly or unknowingly, other than by spoken words: through facial expressions; eye contact; posture; and gestures by hands, arms, head, shoulders, and body. Also known as body language, silent language, and soundless speech. (Ch. 2)

Note cards 3-by-5-inch or 5-by-7-inch cards on which key ideas are written or printed to aid a speaker's memory. (Ch. 7)

Online Connected to the Internet. (Ch. 7)

Opinion One's personal beliefs or thoughts, not necessarily based on facts. (Ch. 11)

Oral visualization Conveying a message by feeling, experiencing, or reliving the ideas and emotions one wishes to communicate. (Ch. 5)

Outline A plan of a talk that lists the topics and subtopics, plus their major and minor backup points. (Ch. 2, 8)

Pacing Creating an interesting rate and variety of delivery that will hold your listeners' interest. For example, you may slow down or speed up your delivery, or you may use pauses. (Ch. 5)

Panels Discussion groups of three to six or more people, led by a moderator or chair, who explore a subject. The purpose is to inquire, deliberate, and enlighten, not to argue and persuade. Audiences usually ask questions after the panelists have spoken. (Ch. 14)

Paralanguage How you say it as opposed to what you say. Some elements of paralanguage, or vocalics, are the quality of the voice, its pitch, rate of delivery, inflection, emphasis, and pauses. (Ch. 3)

Paraphrase Rewriting material in your own style and in about the same number of words as the original. (Ch. 7)

Parallel construction The repeated use of the same words, phrases, or clauses in a sentence or paragraph to achieve greater impact. (Ch. 6)

Parliamentary procedure A strict set of rules to follow during a meeting so as to maintain order and ensure fairness to to all participants. (Ch. 14)

Pauses Momentary silences in speaking. They can stress a point, separate ideas, and give a speaker time to organize his or her thoughts. (Ch. 3)

Persuasive speaking Speaking that tries, by logical reasoning and emotional appeals, to convince listeners to change their opinions, to hold fast to them, or to perform an action recommended by the speaker. (Ch. 11)

Pitch The highness or lowness of a voice. Normal pitch should allow a speaker to comfortably raise or lower his or her voice for varied expression. (Ch. 5)

Plagiarism The act of taking ideas and opinions, or actual wording, from another and passing them off as one's own. (Ch. 1)

Plosives Initial sounds produced by the sudden release of breath, such as k, p, and t. (Ch. 13)

Podium An elevated platform or stage, not to be confused with lectern or speaker's stand. (Ch. 2)

Prolongation Extension of the duration of a vowel sound. (Ch. 5)

Proxemics The study of space as a mode of communication. (Ch. 3)

Public address (PA) system An electronic amplification system used in halls or auditoriums so that speakers can be heard by a large audience. (Ch. 13)

Purpose What you want your audience to get from your speech. (Ch. 8)

Question-and-answer period A portion of time, after a talk, when the speaker answers questions from the audience. (Ch. 2)

Rate of speaking The average number of words spoken in one minute. The average person speaks between 130 and 160 words a minute. (Ch. 5)

Reasoning The forming of conclusions based on known or assumed facts; the use of reason. (Ch. 11)

Reflective Thinking Process A method of thinking involving five steps that was developed by educational philosopher John Dewey. (Ch. 14)

Résumé A written statement of a job applicant's work objective, employment experience, education, and other qualifications. (Ch. 16)

Round-table discussion A meeting in which several people sit at a table and, under a moderator or chair, discuss a given topic. See *forum, panel discussion,* and *symposia.* (Ch. 14)

Search engine A World Wide Web tool designed to look for and display information in response to a user's query. (Ch. 7)

Self-image What and how one thinks of oneself. (Ch. 3)

Silent language See *nonverbal communication.* (Ch. 2)

Slang Informal language that doesn't conform to standard usage. (Ch. 6)

Sloppy speech Careless speech habits such as poor pronunciation, diction, and articulation; not sounding all the syllables within words or word endings. (Ch. 5)

Small-group discussion A discussion in which as few as 5 or as many as 20 people may participate. There are many types of small-group discussion. (Ch. 14)

Soundless speech See *nonverbal communication.* (Ch. 2)

Space The distance between a speaker and listeners. Space may affect the quality of communication. (Ch. 3)

Speaker's stand See *lectern.* (Ch. 2)

Speaking apprehension See *nervousness.* (Ch. 2)

Special-occasion talks Speeches given under special circumstances and for a particular reason: presenting or accepting an award, nominating a candidate for office, making an announcement, and so on. (Ch. 13)

Speech tension See *nervousness.* (Ch. 2)

Stage fright Nervousness felt by the vast majority of speakers, both before and during speaking. (Ch. 2)

Summary The essence of a work, for example, the essence of an important paragraph in a few sentences. (Ch. 7)

Symposium A panel in which participants speak on specific phases of the same question. Then the participants answer questions from the audience. (Ch. 14)

Talk radio A radio program presided over by a host who encourages opinions and questions, by phone, from the general public. (Ch. 1)

Thesaurus A book of synonyms and antonyms. (Ch. 9)

Thesis statement A sentence that states the main purpose of a talk. (Ch. 7, 8)

Title A name, phrase, or sentence of a speech, book, chapter, poem, play, movie, etc., briefly depicting the content of the subject and/or to pique the audience's or reader's interest in the subject. (Ch. 8)

Touch In the context of this book, communication with a person with one's fingers or hands to express a meaning or emotion. (Ch. 3)

Transitions Words, phrases, or sentences that smoothly connect parts of a talk. (Ch. 8)

Transparency A positive film or slide with an image that is visible when light shines through it; usually projected onto a screen. (Ch. 12)

Videocassette recorder (VCR) A magnetic tape instrument that records audio and video signals; the recording can be played back any number of times. (Ch. 7)

Vocalics See *paralanguage.* (Ch. 3)

Vocalized pause A distracting hesitation filled with vocal "static" such as *ah, er, like, right, you know,* so on. It is caused by habit, nervousness, or both and can be cured by conscious effort. (Ch. 5, 6)

Vocal pitch The level of tone—low, medium, high—of a voice. (Ch. 3)

Vocal volume The loudness or softness of a speaker's voice. (Ch. 5)

Vowel The strongest sound in most syllables; the letters *a, e, i, o, u,* and occasionally *y.* (Ch. 5)

World Wide Web An international collection of information searchable using text or graphic browsers. (Ch. 7)

CREDITS

INDEX